Adult Corrections

Adult Corrections

International Systems and Perspectives

edited by
John A. Winterdyk

LYNNE
RIENNER
PUBLISHERS

BOULDER
LONDON

Published in the United States of America in 2010 by
Lynne Rienner Publishers, Inc.
1800 30th Street, Boulder, Colorado 80301
www.rienner.com

and in the United Kingdom by
Lynne Rienner Publishers, Inc.
3 Henrietta Street, Covent Garden, London WC2E 8LU

ISBN: 978-1-881798-50-7 (pb : alk. paper)
LC: 2004304985

First published in 2004 by Criminal Justice Press.
Reprinted here from the original edition.

Printed and bound in the United States of America

The paper used in this publication meets the requirements
of the American National Standard for Permanence of
Paper for Printed Library Materials Z39.48-1992.

CONTENTS

continued...

Contents

PREFACE

There is a rapidly growing body of literature on comparative and international criminal justice. And while there are a number of texts which focus on comparative criminal justice systems, there are far fewer books which have attempted to closely examine — in specific — the various elements of the criminal justice system (i.e., police, courts, and/or corrections). After having taught a course on juvenile offenders and eventually prepared a reader on comparative juvenile justice systems, and after experiencing first hand the keen interest of students, I found the same to be true when I started teaching a course on corrections at St. Thomas University in 2002 and attempted to integrate international perspectives and outcomes.

This anthology represents an effort to bring together a rich cross-section of correctional models and systems that, when combined with careful study of one's own system, will I hope provide a richer understanding of corrections and its issues and promises.

While there have been several other texts on comparative corrections, they tend to be narrower in focus (e.g., prison systems in Europe) rather than offering a true international overview.

This project would not have been possible without the support of Richard Allinson at Willow Tree Press, who warmly embraced the idea for the project. For without a publisher, the ideas and efforts of all those who participated would have been in vain. To all the contributors who pulled through in spite of language barriers and their other commitments, I am deeply indebted for all the time and effort they put into preparing their contributions. Thankfully, the contributors' willingness and cooperation have resulted in a collection that is not only original, but also provides insights from experts in their respective countries.

And while I acted as the editor for this project, I would be seriously remiss if I did not acknowledge the support and understanding of my dear partner, and best friend, Rose. Whatever claim to success I might make would not have been possible without her. I am also proud to acknowledge our two young boys Michael and Alex for their understanding. They must think their Dad is tied to a computer and must wonder if trying to be an academic is worth it. I can only hope that some of my enthusiasm for such work will rub off on them in a positive way. Yet, they are astute enough to know when to tell me "enough already Dad... let's go and...."

To my invaluable research associate and the co-author of the Indian contribution, Kiara Okita, THANK YOU! She is the dream of every educator and researcher — a person who not only rises to the task but embraces it in a manner that often served as an example for myself. Her template for the authors was a fabulous creation designed to assist everyone in not only addressing certain key pedagogical features, but also in providing succinct feedback to the author(s). The manner in which she helped out on the Indian contribution was simply "marvelous"!

Yet, in the end, any shortcomings in this collection of articles must lie with me. But, I am confident that readers will find the text both informative as well as prompt some to want to take the level of comparison to a higher level. I would welcome any constructive observations, comments, and/or suggestions.

Cheers,

John Winterdyk
jwinterdyk@mtroyal.ab.ca
April, 2004

GLOSSARY OF KEY TERMS

Auburn Model: An American-based system (circa 1816) that allowed prisoners to work and eat together during the day and to be housed in individual cells at night. A strict silent system, which forbade prisoners from communicating with or even gesturing to one another, was enforced at all times. It was also called the congregate system.

Case Management: The process by which identified needs and risks of inmates are matched with services and resources.

Classical School: An eighteenth-century perspective on crime and criminals set out in the writings of Cesare Beccaria and Jeremy Bentham. The theory assumes that criminal offenders exercise free will, are rational, and make informed decisions based on perceived risk/consequences. The perspective asserts that to be effective punishment must be certain and must fit the crime.

Classification: The process by which inmates are categorized through the use of various assessment instruments to determine their appropriate security level and program placement. Periodic reviews are usually conducted to determine if a more appropriate placement is possible.

Community Corrections: A term used to denote various forms of correctional programs, usually involving some degree of supervision, that are delivered in community settings (e.g., house arrest, halfway houses, and work release programs).

Conditional Release: A generic term for the various means of leaving an institution before the prescribed sentences have been fully served. Typical examples include parole and supervised work furloughs.

Corrections: The structures, policies, and programs that are delivered by local, state, and federal governments, non-profit agencies and organizations to sanction, treat, and supervise, in the community and in correctional institutions, persons convicted of criminal offences. Corrections represents the official response by the criminal justice system agencies to the punishment of convicted offenders.

continued...

Day Fines: First developed in Scandinavian countries, and based on the Classical School of thought (i.e., equitable punishment), day fines are imposed by judges as a penalty stated in units. Each unit represents the offender's daily disposable income. For example, you might be fined 30 units for going 20 kilometers over the speed limit, and the amount you paid would be determined by your income.

Detention: Involves the legally authorized confinement of an offenders, usually subject to a court decision.

Deterrence: A principle derived from the Classical School (see above), which asserts that the risk or consequence of the punishment is sufficient to discourage future criminality.

Earned Remission: Represents an incentive for good conduct and industriousness while serving one's sentence. Based on the good conduct, a portion of the sentence imposed by the courts may be remitted on the basis of established formulae.

Justice Model: One of a number (e.g., medical model, crime control, rehabilitative, etc.) of models of corrections. The justice model minimizes the goal of crime control and lays greater emphasis upon ensuring that justice is administered in a "fair" manner. To limit discretion and variation in punishment, there is greater reliance on fixed sentences, abolishing parole, and making participation in rehabilitation programs strictly voluntary.

Medical Model: A corrections perspective that emerged in the 1960s and held that the offender was ill — physically, mentally, and/or socially — and criminal behaviour was a symptom of this illness. As in medicine, diagnosis and treatment would ensure the effective rehabilitation of the offender.

Net Widening: A potential, unanticipated consequence of diversion programs in which persons who would otherwise have been released outright by the police or not charged by prosecutors become more involved in the justice system than they would have been if no diversion program had been available. The net-widening effect may also occur with other alternatives to confinement, such as electronic monitoring.

NIMBY (Not in My Back Yard): A term used to describe the resistance of community residents and neighbourhoods to efforts by corrections to locate programming and residences for offenders in the community.

Parole: A type of conditional release that allows qualified inmates to serve a portion of their sentence (sometimes as much as five-sixths) outside of prison in a halfway house, treatment facility, or private residence.

Penal Populism: A term used to describe those corrections-related policies which are electorally attractive but are usually unfair and ineffective. Such views are not consistent with the true extent of public opinion.

Pennsylvania Model: Conceived in the 1820s in the United States, it represents a "separate and silent" system in which prisoners were completely isolated from one another, including being kept out of eyesight of one another. Hence, also known as the "separate system." Inmates ate, worked, and slept in separate cells. The Pennsylvania system became the model for prisons in Europe, South America and Asia.

Positivist School: A perspective on crime and criminals set out in the writings of Cesare Lombroso, Enrico Ferri, and Raffaelo Garofalo in the 1800s. A basic tenet of this perspective is that criminal behaviour is determined by biological, psychological, physiological, and/or sociological factors that can be studied and understood by application of the scientific method.

Probation: A formal sentence imposed on an offender by a judge in the criminal court which provides for supervision (up to a fixed period of time) of the offender in the community by a probation officer. Probation orders usually contain compulsory conditions to which the offender must adhere. The conditions tend to pertain to the specific needs and requirements of the individual probationer.

Recidivism: The traditional method used to determine success in correctional intervention/treatment. The rate includes the number of offenders who, once released from confinement, are returned to some form of detention either for a technical violation of a condition of their release or for the commission of a new offence.

Reductionist Policy: Supported by the Council of Europe and many academics, the policy recognizes the detrimental effects of imprisonment and advocates the use of more humane and less punitive means of dealing with offenders (e.g., use of non-custody options and reducing the detention of offenders involved in non-serious offences).

Rehabilitation: A broad concept that is based on a utilitarian objective of sentencing in which a variety of services and programs may be available to assist the offender. The offender is assumed to be treatable and the services/programs used are designed to positively reinforce pro-social behaviour.

Reintegration: The process whereby an inmate is prepared through graduated release programs to be released into the community after serving time in prison. The objective is to facilitate the re-entry of the offender back into the community.

Restorative Justice: Based on the assertion that crimes involve the violation of a person(s) by another person(s). The orientation of restorative justice model is to "make things right" between the parties involved in a crime. This can involve restitution and healing for the victim(s) as well as some formal mediation and reconciliation among the offender and the victim and, if appropriate, the community. The model gained widespread acceptance as a viable justice option in the early 1990s.

Risk Assessment/Needs Assessment: Drawing on the medical model, it assumes that offenders exhibit certain risk behavior (e.g., anti-social cognition, substance abuse, low verbal intelligence, etc.). By understanding these risks (usually through administering some type of psychological instrument), steps can be taken to address the needs of the offenders so as to assist them in dealing with their issues (e.g., reducing chemical dependencies, increasing self-control, etc.). Risk and needs assessments are used to develop various treatment programs for offenders.

Social Control: A sociological term that refers to the control exercised by the regulatory institutions of society, which include law enforcement, the judiciary and the correctional system and their operations.

Social Defence: A correctional philosophy that is premised on nonviolent responses to aggressions. It occurs when a community chooses to intervene in a nonviolent manner to actively to prevent crime problems. These responses can take several forms such as crisis intervention and alternative dispute resolution.

INTRODUCTION.
ADULT CORRECTIONS:
INTERNATIONAL SYSTEMS AND
PERSPECTIVES

by

John A. Winterdyk

"We share a noble mission. We experience many of the same influences and we share many of the same problems and to some extent, some of the basic ideas in the area of solutions. We can learn from each other and can help one another."

~ Ole Ingstrup (former Commissioner of
the Correctional Service of Canada), 1998

The opening quote is an excerpt from the introductory remarks made by Mr. Ingstrup, the current President of the International Corrections and Prison Association (see Web-links at end of this chapter), to an international group of experts on corrections. The conference was the first to focus exclusively on exploring alternatives to incarceration within an international context. Even though corrections, as most of us know it today, has been with us for several centuries, there are few places in the world today that are not confronted with a number of pressing issues, such as growing prison populations and overcrowding, the lack of appropriate health and education services for offenders, the special requirements of certain offender groups such as women and the elderly, and the need to establish viable alternatives to incarceration, among others. Recently, Dan Beto (2004:15) noted that at the 1870 National Congress on Penitentiary and Reformatory Discipline, held in Cincinnati, Ohio, the resolutions passed — relating to issues ranging from prison discipline to pardons — "are still being discussed today." Beto went on to quote his father, George Beto, who in 1987 wrote: "a review of the literature on corrections reveals little that is new today... Apparent innovations are hailed in this hour and rejected in the next" (p.15). Yet, few would likely disagree that all societies prefer "social order" — however that may be defined across cultures and different political structures.

In light of this somewhat pessimistic outlook, it would appear timely, if not overdue, for corrections to join the related fields of criminology and criminal justice in their growing use of comparative and international research (see page 8 below). Moreover, it is generally accepted that in order to examine anything related to criminal justice in a comparative context, a historical perspective is also required since the phenomena being studied (in this case adult corrections) have developed and evolved under unique economic, political, and social structures. Accordingly, the method employed by the authors in this book is referred to as the "historical-comparative method" (HCM). The power of this perspective is grounded on its ability to make comparisons either across time (i.e., historical) or, as is the case with this anthology, across places, and thereby to improve our understanding of the social world (in this case corrections). And the HCM allows one to expand the generalizability of criminological theory and dispel "persistent myths about the way things were" (Taylor, 1994 cited in Neuman et al., 2004). Although the HCM method of inquiry has not been as commonly used among criminologists as, say, quantitative or qualitative methods, many of the early ideas about criminology were based on the HCM as found in the works of Durkheim (1858-1917), Weber (1864-1920), and Marx (1818-1883).

The study of comparative issues within criminal justice is barely 30-odd years old, although its rise has built upon the more established field of comparative criminology. This anthology focuses on the topic of comparative corrections. Limited to some extent by history, and to varying extents by politics, economy, social, and cultural structures, most countries suffer, to varying degrees, from ethnocentrism, which is the view that our own ideas are the best and should apply to other parts of the world — the "we are the best" mentality. For example, while many

Third World, or developing countries (e.g., Namibia) look to the Western world for guidance based on the success of some of our systems, we would be foolish to think that any one nation's system represents the model that should be universally imitated or emulated. Similarly, one could not reasonably expect that the "criminology of liberation" popular in some Latin American countries — an outdated Marxist perspective purported to benefit the masses and free them from exploitation and suppression by the state — would be well received by many Western countries.

Fortunately, with the advent of growing international awareness and exchanges (and in some cases a return to honoring some of the early work in criminology), we are increasingly recognizing that our own nations do not necessarily possess the best correctional (i.e., social control) practices, and that other countries might have practices/ideas from which we can learn and/or adapt or hybridize to our own system.

Hence, this anthology relies on a collaborative approach — drawing upon the expertise and shared experiences from many countries — in order to provide an overview of adult correctional practices and issues from around the world.[1] The need for such a work has become very keen as most countries today strive to control and address the needs of those who are sentenced to custody or non-custody sanctions. And as reflected in the chapters in this collection, while there are certain commonalities in the range of correctional options that are used by diverse nations, there are few, if any, consistent international standards being adhered to. (See, for example, the wide range of national incarceration rates illustrated in Figure 0.1.) This is in spite of various standards and regulations established by the United Nations and the European Union Commission, as well as by various special interests groups such as Amnesty International, The Human Security Net, and Human Rights Watch, which are all intended to bring a sense of uniformity and conformity to correctional practices among member states or signatory members.

Figure 0.1: International Comparisons of the Rate of Prisoners in Europe and North America per 100,000 General Population in the Year 2000

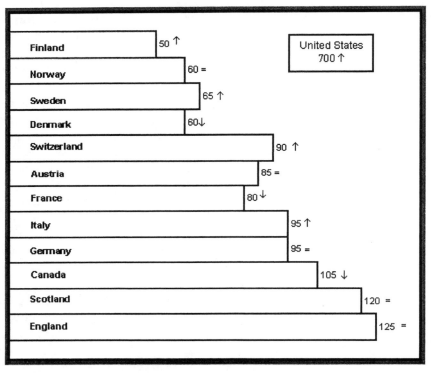

Source: *World Prison Population List, Research Findings No. 166*, Home Office Research, Development and Statistics Directorate, United Kingdom. Note: Arrows indicate an increase or decrease over the previous year.
Source: http://www.csc-scc.gc.ca/text/faits/facts08-02_e.shtml.

For the purpose of this anthology, adult corrections is examined as a bureaucratic, political, and social enterprise, rather than strictly at the theoretical level. Specifically, corrections can be understood in reference to four general areas: (1) *Corrections as a social concept:* How do the respective countries actualize/rationalize the concept of corrections (i.e., social control)? As will be evidenced, there is considerable diversity in how different countries approach and operate their correctional systems (see next section). (2) *Corrections as a legal entity*: This perspective can be divided into two levels: "corrections as an activity of government provided by law" or as an "activity subject to the general rules of law." In other words, how does a country's correctional ideology affect the administration and management of its offenders? (3) *Corrections as a range of programs*: Within the scope of the law and sentencing options, the court has three broad categories of disposition: incarceration, non-custody (e.g., probation), and alternative sanctions (e.g., community-based programs, restorative initiatives, etc.). How do countries differ with respect to the use of different correctional based services? And (4) *Corrections as a subsystem within the criminal justice system*: As the criminal justice system also comprises law enforcement and the courts, how do these sister agencies work with corrections towards supporting and enforcing social order as defined by the state? (see Ekstedt and Griffiths [1988] for further detail). In other words, how well does a country's correctional system work within the context of its criminal justice system?

THE VARIABLE FACE OF CORRECTIONAL IDEOLOGIES

An ideology is a frame of reference that we can use to explain and understand some aspect of our culture — past or present. Within corrections there are three broad ideologies that apply to correctional practices: punishment, treatment, and prevention.

Punishment

Punishment is the oldest form of societal response to a wrongdoer. In the past it was divided mainly into two categories: death or a wide range of corporal punishments (e.g., flogging, mutilation, branding, etc.) — with the intent of inflicting physical pain. Traditionally, many forms of punishment were conducted in public so as to serve as a deterrent for other possible offenders, and in the case of corporal punishment the intent was often to add humiliation (similar to "reintegrative shaming" today) to the penalty itself. While today the severity of such punishments may have abated in most parts of the world, punishment has been couched in specialized terminology and rationalized on the grounds of various theoretical models.

The three main rationales used to justify punishment include: *retribution, deterrence,* and *incapacitation.* Retribution has a long history dating back to the practice "an eye for an eye": that is, when harm is done to someone, he or she deserves compensation for having been wronged. A modern variation of this is the notion of "just deserts," in which the offender is given a punishment he or she "deserves" because it is proportionate to the gravity of the offence. For example, taking another person's life may equate to the loss of the offender's life in some countries or to life imprisonment in others.

Deterrence is premised on the notion that people have free will, and that a threat of punishment, if proportionate to the crime, should be sufficient to deter a potential offender from offending. Thus, invoking the criminal law, the risk of going to prison, and the risk of having to pay a hefty fine etc., are all intended to serve as forms of deterrence.

The primary objective of incapacitation is to prevent the offender from committing any further offences by some form of imprisonment that removes him or her from society and temptation.

And while these various forms of maintaining social order are the oldest means of trying to maintain social control, and while they are used to varying extent around the world, they have met with marginal to minimal success.

Treatment

Emerging out of the Age of Enlightenment, the treatment approach is thought to be more humane and responds to the individual rather than the offence per se. Criminals are consider to be "dis-eased" in some manner, and thus in need of corrective intervention — analogous to the approach used in medicine. That is, criminals are assumed to be treatable.

The treatment ideology can be divided into three subcategories. They include: (1) The *medical or treatment model,* which assumes that offenders can be diagnosed for their needs and risks, after which appropriate programs are selected to assist them (see, for example, the chapter on Canada). Under this model, correctional officials embrace the notion that the problem of criminality is somehow associated with the constitutional make-up of the offender. The response or solution is first to diagnose the "ailment" and then treat the "patient." Based on the medical analogy, most correctional systems offer programs such as anger management, educational and vocational training, life skills workshops, family intervention initiatives, and the like with the intent of helping the offender "fix" his or her problem. (2) The *reformatory model* dates back to the Calvinistic doctrine that ignorance sometimes leads to poor choices. Therefore, through the use of education, and provision of vocational and/or occupational skills within a strict regime, one can convert offenders into engaging in acceptable behavior (see, for example, the chapter on Japan). (3) The *reintegration model* also has a long history, but it has been popularized as a correctional option since the 1960s. The basic idea is to find ways by which to resolve the conflict between the offender and the victim by providing an opportunity to allow the two parties to understand each other's situation and make amends in a reasonable manner. The concept has also been referred to as transformative justice, reintegrative shaming, and restorative justice (see Glossary). Several of the countries in this anthology practice the reintegrative model in different ways. As with punishment, the jury is still out as to which approaches in the treatment ideology work and/or how well. Some critics have questioned the underlying premise that an offender can be *re*habilitated, wondering how someone can return to a former state that has never been experienced previously.

Prevention

Both punishment and treatment are reactive correctional ideologies: they address the problem after it has already manifested itself. The prevention ideology is proactive. It attempts to identify potential risks (i.e., environmental, social, and economic conditions) and to take steps to reduce the likelihood that an offence will occur. As the 18th century Italian criminologist Cesare Beccaria once said: "it is better to prevent crimes than to punish them." Within the correctional arena there are a number of prevention-based approaches, including programs to strengthen the ties between prisons and their surrounding communities so as to facilitate inmates' post-release reintegration, and to repeal those criminal laws that have no deterrent effect (e.g., certain drug offence laws, the death penalty, indeterminate sentences, torture, etc.).

As will be seen throughout this book, no one country subscribes entirely to one model or ideology. Rather, one tends to see a blending of ideologies as countries struggle to find the best approach for maintaining social order and social control (see Winterdyk, 2001:13-19).

WHY COMPARE CORRECTIONAL SYSTEMS AND PRACTICES?

"In addition to being characterized by overcrowding and underfunded, the state of Tajikistan has provisions allowing women to serve the sentence for their husband or son." ~ Access, Nov. 19, 2002

As will be seen throughout this book, no one approach to social order or social control is considered better or superior to another, yet we will see that different countries emphasize some approaches over others. Japan, for example, tends to emphasize a community and re-educational approach, while Namibia is endeavoring to follow a restorative approach. Meanwhile, the United States essentially subscribes to a punishment and confinement approach.

In recent years there has been a proliferation of textbooks and anthologies examining criminal justice systems as a whole (see, for example, Terrill, 2002; Fields and Moore, 1996; Fairchild and Dammer, 2001; Reichel, 2002). In addition, many introductory level textbooks on criminology and/or criminal justice are increasingly speaking to the importance of comparative research on such issues. This movement has been given further support through the formation of special international interest groups at most major criminology/criminal justice and correctional conferences. As seems to be the case with any new discipline, it eventually evolves into a more complex set of sub-disciplines. Even more recently, criminology/criminal justice has seen the emergence of comparative material on youth/juvenile justice (see, Winterdyk, 2002; Bala et al., 2002), policing (see, Barak, 2000; Sheptycki, 2000), prisons (e.g., Ruggiero et al., 1995; Weiss and South, 1998), and legal systems (e.g., Glendon et al., 1982; Glenn, 2000). However, in spite of being one of the oldest forms of formal social control, very little has been done on comparative evaluation of correctional systems. Ruggiero, Ryan and Sim (1995), for example, note that while we may have "quite detailed knowledge of other Western European penal systems there was no readily available introductory text in English for undergraduates or interested professionals on these neighboring systems" (p.ix). This is not only true for Europe, but for the world at large.

Yet, the history of corrections (as has been the case with all areas of the criminal justice system) has been marked by constant change. These changes have, in part, been influenced by the evolving economic, political, and social institutions that characterize respective cultures. Historically, and internationally, correctional practices have undergone numerous dramatic shifts, and often with little fanfare. Being the final formal link in the criminal justice system, corrections is sometimes euphemistically referred to as the "hidden element" of the system because it is the least understood sub-system (Winterdyk, 2001). Yet, it represents a unique element of the criminal justice system that deserves better understanding. For example, how effective is the use of day fines[2] (first developed in Scandinavian countries), as compared to the varying forms of restorative justice programs (first developed in New Zealand and Australia)? Or, how are other countries dealing with the "NIMBY" (Not-In-My-Back-Yard) syndrome (i.e., the term used to describe the resistance of community residents to efforts by corrections to locate programming and residences for offenders in the community)? Or, what are the effects of (extreme) overcrowding in prisons? Or, can Finland's success in reducing the use of incarceration (as described in this text) be replicated elsewhere? And how can that "success" be replicated under different social, economic, and political conditions?

As will be seen throughout this anthology, most of the countries have adapted correctional practices from other countries and/or made varying attempts to comply with a growing number of international agreements that identify "basic principles," "standard minimum rules," and "protocols" (see the OHCHR listing in the Web-links section at the end of this chapter). This process of adaptation is often carried out with only modest planning and evaluation. For example, while there is sufficient literature to illustrate that chain gangs have, at best, marginal corrective potential, this did not discourage certain parts of Canada from considering the use of this approach. This is in spite of the fact that it could be argued that such practices contravene the UN *Basic Principles for the Treatment of Prisoners* — adopted in 1990. The consideration of chain gangs stopped only after the initial pilot stage project demonstrated what was already known about their defects. Similarly, while the concept of restorative justice or family group conferencing (see Glossary), originally developed in New Zealand, has become a hot topic and an alternative to traditional correctional practices, the concept has been adapted into a wide range of ideologically-related programs around the world bearing such descriptors as: victim offender reconciliation programs, victim offender mediation programs and reintegrative shaming. For example, when in 1996 Canada introduced new legislation that opened the door for the use of alternative sentencing measures that included restorative justice options, it was met with considerable enthusiasm. However, a number of practical and pragmatic concerns were raised; ranging from "how will the legal system avoid 'widening the net' of social control?" — i.e., keeping persons who would otherwise have been released outright from become involved in the justice system — to "will restorative justice as administered by the legal system promote a better quality of justice?" (Winterdyk, 1998:22).

The rationale for studying and comparing issues and/or aspects of the criminal justice system has become well established and generally widely accepted. Therefore, I will only briefly summarize the main points.

- The process of comparing is essential to facilitating our understanding of how we view our society and that of the rest of the world.

- More specifically, by learning about different nations' correctional systems, we are able to discern common problems and themes as well as learn from the experience and practices of others.

- Comparing common and dissimilar social, cultural, economic, and political approaches to corrections provides us with an opportunity to broaden our understanding of different approaches, programs, administration etc., thereby contributing to better correctional policies across the diverse span of what constitutes corrections.

- Since many countries share similar problems and challenges in administering corrections, comparisons on points of interest can help to refine solutions that might transcend cultural and political boundaries (see Fairchild and Dammer [2001:6-9], and Reichel [2002:3-10] for more detailed discussions).

Yet, in spite of the advances being made in comparative studies, such efforts are not without their pragmatic and methodological challenges (see Tuene, 1992). Newman (1977) has identified several key obstacles, some of which include:

- *Language barriers* — If you do not have access to an interpreter this can pose a major challenge.

- *Definition/ideological barriers* — The practice of corrections is largely defined by a country's sentencing policies. For example, in the United States the sentencing policy tends to emphasize crime control and to embody an ideology premised on "just deserts" as reflected in the unprecedented rise in the prison population in the past 20 years. By contrast, sentencing practices in New Zealand tend to subscribe more to a prevention ideology, as the restorative justice model is heavily practiced within corrections. As explained above, there are three broad ideologies that apply to correctional practices: punishment, treatment, and prevention. Since no one ideology is adhered to exclusively by any one country, it is important to discern the relationship between the ideologies before engaging in comparisons.

- *Cultural barriers* — Different cultural values and norms can play a key role in whether a country embraces certain correctional practices or not. A case in point is that in November of 2002 Lithuania held the world's first prison beauty pageant — to select a Miss Captivity! A 24-year-old inmate won. Why and for what purpose the pageant was held was not made clear ("Prisoners Vie for...," 2002). In the chapter on Namibia, we see how some of the cultural differences within the country have presented several unique challenges for the administration of certain correctional practices. Similarly, the chapter on Iran serves to illustrate how different cultural, political, religious, and social barriers can raise concerns about some of that country's correctional practices.

- *Reporting and recording practices* — In the United States, for example, it was not until 1983 that the National Prisoner Statistics program and the Uniform Parole Reports were combined into one reporting system — the National Corrections Reporting Program (NCRP). This step was taken both to improve and to consolidate data on corrections at the national level. By contrast, many developing countries have no formal collection and reporting system.

- **Administrative variations** — Aside from disparate methods that are used to record and report correctional practices, diverse laws and variations in the efficiency of enforcement of these laws can impact the ability to obtain valid and reliable impression of correctional practices with different countries. This is illustrated in some of the contributions in this book (adapted from Winterdyk, 2002). For example, parole is widely used in most Western countries, but is less prevalent in non-Western countries. Similarly, restorative justice initiatives have become popular throughout North America, but are a relatively recent correctional alternative being explored in Germany (see chapter 4).

Nevertheless, in spite of these apparent challenges, academics, practitioners, and policymakers have increasingly made significant strides in establishing templates so as to allow for informative comparisons and exchanges. As the world becomes euphemistically smaller and our provincial concerns become international issues, it is imperative that we make every effort to engage in objective study that may provide new insights and better understanding into complex issues.

UN STANDARD MINIMUM RULES FOR THE TREATMENT OF PRISONERS

"Prisons have few friends; dissatisfaction with them is widespread."
~ Morris, 1974:ix

The United Nations (UN), formed in 1945, has 191 member countries. Its mandate "is to bring all nations of the world together to work for peace and development, based on the principles of justice, human dignity and the well being of all people" (see "Office of the High Commissioner" in Web-links).

While there are six principal organs of the UN, under the Office of the High Commissioner for Human Rights (OHCHR) there are some 22 agreements that address issues in the administration of justice, ranging from the independence of the judiciary to the protection of prisoners against torture. (See the OHCHR Web-link at the end of this chapter to access the agreements.)

Given the large number of conventions and/or covenants, this section will simply focus on the UN *Standard Minimum Rules for the Treatment of Prisoners.*

In 1955, at the First United Nations Congress on the Prevention of Crime and the Treatment of Offenders, held in Geneva (Switzerland), the standard minimum rules for the treatment of prisoners were adopted and subsequently approved. The rules were revised in 1957 and again in 1977.

The guidelines are not intended to "describe in detail a model system of penal institutions," but to offer "the general consensus of contemporary thought and the essential elements of the most adequate systems today" (p.1). Appreciating the social, economic, legal, and geographic conditions of the world, the UN recognizes that not all states can implement all the standards and rules equally. Since the entire document can be found at the on-line site listed below under Web-links, we will only highlight some of the key standard minimum rules for the treatment of offenders. In so doing, the reader can then reflect on the extent to which countries represented in this reader comply with the standards:

- There shall be no discrimination on grounds of race, color, gender, language, religion, political or other opinion, national or social origin, property, birth or other status.

- In every place where persons are imprisoned there shall be kept a bound registration book with all incarceral relevant material.

- The different types or classifications of prisoners shall be kept in separate institutions or parts of institutions.

- Each prisoner shall occupy by night a cell or room by him/herself. If not possible, prisoners should be carefully selected as being suitable to associate with one another.

- Every prisoner shall be provided by the administration with... food of nutritional value adequate for health and strength...(and) drinking water shall be available to every prisoner whenever they need it.

- Every prisoner shall have at least one hour of suitable exercise in the open air daily.

- Discipline shall be no more restrictive than what is necessary... cruel, inhuman and/or degrading punishments... shall be prohibited.

ORGANIZATION OF THIS ANTHOLOGY

This anthology is composed of 10 chapters written by individuals who have academic and/or practical/professional knowledge of their respective correctional systems. This approach helps to ensure that the readers of this book are not only are presented with a sound overview of each country's correctional system, but also will benefit from the most current and relevant information in regards to policy and administrative issues (rather than rely on sometimes dated secondary sources). Furthermore, the contributors are able to provide concrete and practical insights into their respective correctional practices. In addition to offering an overview of the pragmatic elements of corrections across different countries and approaches, each chapter provides provocative questions about the various aspects of corrections, questions that are intended to encourage critical and comparative analysis in a way that might prompt a deeper and richer understanding of corrections practices and philosophy. As with my own Canadian corrections textbook, the overriding intention is to "stimulate discussion and encourage the reader to explore issues beyond the scope of what the book" could possibly offer, and thereby enrich its contribution to the literature on comparative correctional perspectives (Winterdyk, 2001:p.xvi).

In an effort to facilitate comparisons without implying any prejudices towards any one correctional system or country, the contributions are presented in alphabetical order in accordance with the country's name.

This anthology examines the 10 countries' respective correctional practices without any overarching assumptions as to what should be compared. The format is intended to provide sufficient descriptive detail for analysis either of an individual national approach (e.g., how does the Belgian correctional system work?) or a comparison of two or more countries (e.g., gauging the extent to which different correctional options, or administrative/managerial styles, are used in different countries). In addition, it is possible to engage in a transnational analysis in which a number (if not all) countries are examined in light of the larger international issues such as prison overcrowding or finding effective alternatives to incarceration Each of the contributing authors has been asked to address a series of elements that reflect some of the primary issues surrounding correctional practices and philosophy. The primary areas covered by each of the contributors include:

- A descriptive overview of their country;

- A historical synopsis of the development of the country's correctional practices and philosophy;

- Current corrections practices;

- A profile or description of the offending population;

- Social, economic, and/or political issues confronting corrections today;

- Future issues and considerations; and,

- Where appropriate, the conformity of their nation's practices and standards to the standards and guidelines set out in various UN conventions and/or covenants.

This approach ensures that the same topics/issues are covered in each chapter for each country. This then allows for in-depth analysis within a social and political context as Reichel (2002) and Terrill (2002) have done in their examinations of international criminal justice systems. The contributors were not asked to make any direct comparisons of their country's corrections system with any one particular system or ideology. Rather, the point is to enable the reader to examine correctional practices, philosophy, and related pragmatic issues within a somewhat neutral context.

While it could be argued that corrections is an "issue"-based topic (e.g., issues such as correctional philosophy, sexual offender programs, emerging correctional practices, administrative programs by type and objective, etc.), given the goal of this anthology and the diversity of countries represented, these issues are better examined within a more holistic (i.e., social, cultural, and political) context. For example, while treatment and prevention practices might work well in Finland because of that nation's homogeneous population, they might not work as well in a legalistic and crime control-oriented country such as Germany.

Special Features of This Book

In addition to the original contributions from scholars in their respective fields, this textbook offers the following elements that are intended to help the reader:

- *Glossary* — offering definitions of specialized terms used throughout the book.

- *Box Inserts* — expounding points of interest regarding that particular country.

- *Web-links* — for further inquiry or to allow follow-up on key points of interest.

- *Study and Discussion Questions* — to draw attention to the key aspects of the chapter and stimulate comparative analysis.

- *Key Terms and Concepts* — to draw the reader's attention to significant terms or concepts.

SUMMARY

This collection brings together both original and informed accounts of correctional systems and practices from around the world. The objective is to provide an up-to-date account of corrections as a whole (i.e., beyond a discussion of prison systems) from an international and comparative perspective. The anthology is intended for upper-level undergraduate level courses and/or graduate level seminars on comparative corrections. The text should also be of interest to professionals, administrators, and policymakers within the criminal justice arena.

To enrich the content of the material presented, all contributing authors include a host of special features that will enable the reader to not only keep abreast with current events and issues within the correctional arena, but also assist the reader in focusing on key issues and concepts so as to enrich the comparative study of correctional practices.

Discussion/Study Questions

(1) Why should we study different correctional systems and practices?

(2) Identify and discuss one transnational correctional problem that can also be found in your country. What are some of its major concerns?

(3) Using any media source, find two or more examples of correctional practices in your country that can trace their origins to other countries.

(4) Visit the OHCHR web site and review some of the links related to the administration of justice. Note the terminology used by the various conventions and covenants (e.g., rules vs. principles, encourage vs. demand, etc.). How important is it to have such agreements? What problems/issues might they present for member nations who have signed the agreements?

Helpful Web-links

Amnesty International:
http://www.amnesty.org/.

Human Security Network:
www.humansecuritynetwork.org.

The International Corrections and Prison Association:
http://www.icpa.ca/.

Prison rates for private facilities in the U.S.:
http://www.doc.state.ok.us/DOCS/Priv%20Prison%20Rate%20Study%20Master.pdf.

John Walker's webpage on prison rates:
http://members.ozemail.com.au/~born1820/prisfor.htm.

Office of the High Commissioner for Human Rights:
http://www.unhchr.ch/html/inlinst.htm.

The United Nations Minimum Standard Rules for the Treatment of Prisoners and Offenders:
http://www.hri.ca/uninfo/treaties/34.shtml.

World Prison Brief: International Centre for Prison Studies:
http://www.kcl.ac.uk/depsta/rel/icps/worldbrief/world_brief.html.

REFERENCES

Access (2002). "A Woman's Place." Access TV Edmonton. Nov. 19.

Bala, N., J. Hornick, H. Snyder and J.J. Paetsh (eds.), (2002). *Juvenile Justice Systems: An International Comparison of Problems and Solutions.* Toronto, CAN: Thompson Books.

Barak, G. (ed.), (2000). *Crime and Crime Control: A Global View.* Westport, CT: Greenwood Press.

Beto, D.R. (2004). "Random Thoughts on the Future of Corrections." *Crime and Justice International* Jan/Feb:15-21.

Burns, J.F. (2002). "Hussein and Mobs Virtually Empty Iraq's Prisons." *New York Times,* Oct. 21 (online).

Carcach, C. and A. Grant (1999). *Trends and Issues in Crime and Criminal Justice.* Canberra, AUS: Australian Institute of Criminology.

Ekstedt, J.W. and C.T. Griffths (1998). *Corrections in Canada: Policy and Practice* (2nd ed.). Toronto, CAN: Butterworth.

Fairchild, E. and H. Dammer (2001). *Comparative Criminal Justice Systems* (2nd ed.). Belmont, CA: Wadsworth.

Field, E. and R.H. Moore, Jr. (1996). *Comparative Criminal Justice Systems* (2nd ed.). Prospect Heights, IL: Waveland.

Glendon, M.A., M.W. Gordon and C. Osakwe (1982). *Comparative Legal Traditions in a Nutshell.* St. Paul, MN: West Publishing Co.

Glenn, H.P. (2000). *Legal Tradition of the World.* Oxford, UK: Oxford University Press.

Human Security Network (1999). (Available online at: http://www.human securitynetwork.org/.)

Ingstrup, O. (1998). "Introductory Remarks." Presented at the "Beyond Prisons International Symposium," Kingston, ON.

Morris, N. (1974). *The Future of Imprisonment.* Chicago, IL: University of Chicago Press.

Neuman, W.L., B. Weigand and J.A. Winterdyk (2004). *Criminal Justice Research Methods: Qualitative and Quantitative Approaches* (Canadian ed.). Toronto, CAN: Pearson Education.

Newman, G.R. (1977). "Problems of Method in Comparative Criminology." *International Journal of Comparative and Applied Criminal Justice* 1(1):17-31.

"Prisoners Vie for Beauty-queen Title" (2002). *Toronto Sun* (online), November 15.

Reichel, P. (2002). *Comparative Criminal Justice* (3rd ed.). Englewood Cliffs, NJ: Prentice-Hall.

Ruggeiero, V., M. Ryan and J. Sim (eds.), (1995). *Western European Penal Systems.* Thousand Oaks, CA: Sage.

Sheptycki, J. (ed.), (2000). *Issues in Transnational Policing.* New York: Routledge.

Terrill, R.J. (2002). *World Criminal Justice Survey* (4th ed.). Cincinnati, OH: Anderson.

Teune, H. (1992). "Comparing Countries: Lessons Learned." In: E. Oyen (ed.), *Comparative Methodology.* Newbury Park, CA: Sage.

Walker, J. (2000). "Modelling Global Money Laundering Flows." (Online at: http://members.ozemail.com.au/~born1820/mlmethod.htm.)

Weiss, R.P. and N. South (eds.), (1998). *Comparing Prison Systems: Towards a Comparative and International Penology.* Amsterdam, NETH: Gordon and Breach.

Winterdyk, J.A. (ed.), (2002). *Juvenile Justice Systems: International Perspectives* (2nd ed.). Toronto, CAN: Canadian Scholars' Press.

—— (ed.), (2001). *Corrections in Canada.* Toronto, CAN: Pearson Education.

— (1998). "It's Time, It's Time... Is It Time for Restorative Justice?" *Law Now* April/May:20-22.

NOTES

1. An alternative approach would be the "safari" method in which the author visits a host of other countries (or gathers extensive literature from these countries) and then attempts to draw comparisons. This method is considered somewhat more limiting as it requires considerable resources to travel, meet the appropriate people, and gain access to the necessary information. If one relies on the work produced by others, it is already (usually) dated and at times more difficult to check for accuracy.

2. Judges impose a penalty stated in units. Each unit represents the offender's daily disposable income. For example, you might be fined 20 units for shoplifting, and the amount you would pay is determined by your income.

CHAPTER 1.
ADULT CORRECTIONS IN BELGIUM

by

Sonja Snacken

Kristel Beyens

and

Hilde Tubex[1]

Department of Criminology
Vrije Universiteit Brussel
Brussels, Belgium

"The mood and temper of the public in regard to the treatment of crime and criminals is one of the most unfailing tests of the civilisation of any country."
~ Winston Churchill, 1910

BASIC FACTS ON BELGIUM

Area: At 32,545 square kilometres, Belgium is one of the smaller European countries, sandwiched between The Netherlands to the north and France to the south, and with the North Sea as its western border and Germany and Luxembourg to the east.

Population: As of January 2003, there were approximately 10.3 million inhabitants, of whom some 846,734 were of non-Belgian origin. The overall *density ratio* is 339.2 residents per square kilometres. The *birth rate* is 10.45 births/1,000 population (2003 estimate) and *death rate* is 10.07

deaths/1,000 population (2003 estimate). The major cities include: Brussels (population 992,041), the capital of Belgium and also headquarters of the European Union; Antwerp (population 452,474); Gent (population 228,016); Charleroi (population 200,460); Liege (population 184,303); and Namur (population 105,705).

Climate: Belgium is characterized as having rainy, humid and cloudy conditions, with average temperature of 11.2° Celsius. Winters are rather mild and summers cool.

Economy: The labour force is divided into: services 73%, industry 25%, and agriculture 2% (1999 estimate). The unemployment rate in 2002 was 7.6%. The crime rate is 8,195 offences per 100,000 population, and the detention rate is 90 per 100,000.

Government and politics: Belgium is a member state of the European Union (EU). Belgium, together with 11 of its EU partners, began circulating Euro currency in January 2002. Belgium has a federal parliamentary democracy under a constitutional monarch. There are three official languages: Dutch — spoken by 60%, French — 40%, and German — less than 1%. The ethnic/language division question led to a federal state. The Dutch-speaking Flemings of the north opposed the exclusive use of the French language in government and cultural affairs and demanded cultural self-determination. The French-speaking industrial working classes of the south (Walloons) resisted the majority of the north and demanded regional socio-economic autonomy. Constitutional amendments led to an increased cultural and regional self-government. Following the institutional reforms of 1980 and 1988, all aspects relating to social welfare (e.g., social aid to offenders, victims and their families) became the exclusive responsibility of the regional authorities. Penal policy and corrections remain under the competence of the federal state. Since May 2003, the federal government has been led by a coalition between the Liberal and Social-democratic parties, with Guy Verhofstadt (Liberal party) as Prime Minister. It is important to note that since the beginning of the 1990s, the extreme right *"Vlaams Blok"* has achieved an ongoing electoral success in Flanders, becoming the first or second party in all major cities.

★   ★   ★

GENERAL HISTORY OF CORRECTIONS IN BELGIUM

"Mission of the Directorate General of Prisons: To implement the penalties, measures and judicial decisions on the persons put in its trust, with due regard to their maximal personal development in view of their reintegration, insofar as in accordance with security. This is pursued in circumstances guaranteeing the safety of society, staff and prisoners."

~ Directorate General of Prisons, Annual Report, 1997

When Belgium became an independent country in 1830, the correctional system was highly fragmented, consisting of 182 detention facilities (compared to the current 33). Only four of the institutions were administered by the central authority, while the remainder came either under provincial (9), urban (20) or local (149) authorities.

Among the central prisons was the central **prison of Gent**, which was internationally known at that time for having been described by John Howard (1726-1790) as the best place of correction (*"maison de force"*) he had encountered during his extensive travels (Howard, 1788). Opened in 1773 in line with the ideas of Vilain XIIII, burggraaf of Gent, to combat vagrancy, mendacity (i.e., begging) and other crimes, it offered a combination of individual segregation at night and meaningful, productive communal work during daytime as a means of rehabilitation, and would eventually form the European model for the *Auburn system* (see Glossary). During the subsequent French and Dutch rule, this "model prison" would, however, offer no exception to the general state of serious overcrowding, promiscuity between all different categories of detainees, and emphasis on economic profit-seeking found in the other places of detention.

Edouard Ducpétiaux (1804-1868) was appointed in 1832 as the first Inspector General of Prisons for the new Belgian kingdom, and he would determine its future for more than a century. Having himself experienced imprisonment as a political opponent during Dutch rule, he was horrified by the promiscuity in those institutions, which he attributed to lack of any segregation between sexes, ages, penal or civil offences. Convinced that criminality was the consequence of immorality and lack of religious commitment, he believed that the *Pennsylvania model* of corrections, based on total individual segregation, education and religion, was conducive to real moral penitence and improvement. Work in one's cell could only be allowed for long-term prisoners. The political establishment was relatively indifferent and gave him "carte blanche" to implement his ideas. No legislation on cellulary confinement was passed until 1870 — two years after his death. Following Ducpétiaux's ideas, 29 institutions were built throughout Belgium from 1844 until 1919. All of these prisons are still in operation today. The typical star-shaped institutions with three to five wings, also known internationally as the **Belgian model,** offered individual cells of about 10 square metres and a chapel where mass and education were offered, but no communal rooms or workplaces. All contact between prisoners was strictly forbidden, prisoners had to wear a hood whenever taken out of their cells and the chapel was built with individual compartments. The moral improvement of the prisoner was monitored by the prison guards, who were supposed to keep a moral account of each individual prisoner.

After release from prison, the offenders' moral education and control were supposed to be taken over by the *patronage*, a group of middle-class volunteers of "high moral value." Although well intended, the volunteers exerted limited influence over the former detainees. This led to the introduction in 1888 of the first law on *conditional release*. Prisoners were eligible for conditional release after having served one-third of their sentence and at least three months; recidivists had to serve two-thirds and at least six months. Only prisoners who had shown moral repentance were eligible. This system gave the members of the *patronage* real power on the released prisoners, as noncompliance with the conditions and guidance by the *patronage* could result in re-incarceration.

In 1907, Belgium was, with Argentina, the first country in the world to introduce an anthropological laboratory in prison designed to apply the biometric studies of prisoners prescribed by Lombroso. The introduction of *positivist* (see Glossary) ideas and policies was, however, fiercely resisted in practice. In penal theory, the conflict between the *classical* (see Glossary) penal theory of retribution and deterrence versus the *modern positivist* theory based on protection of society by scientific analysis and treatment of the causes of crime, led to the eclectic **Belgian penal school of thought.**[2] The classical theory remained valid for all offenders considered to be responsible for their actions (i.e., the majority of offenders). The *social defence* positivist theories and legislation were limited to special categories of offenders such as vagrants (Act 1891), juveniles (Act 1912), and the mentally ill and habitual offenders (Act

1930). The latter led to *preventive measures* of detention, either in special institutions or in normal prisons (Tubex, 2002).

Individual segregation of prisoners hence remained the predominant prison regime until after the Second World War, albeit in a gradually less restricted form (e.g., abolition of the hood and of enforced silence, etc.). The typical Ducpétiaux-architecture of the Belgian prison system, with a capacity of around 6,000 prisoners, created problems after the Second World War when 60,000 political collaborators were sentenced to imprisonment. Special detention camps were created, with communal regimes and reconstruction work in the community (e.g., roads and mining). The success of these regimes in guaranteeing good order in the camps finally convinced policymakers and practitioners to shift the emphasis in prisons from individual segregation to a communal regime and employment. The incarceration during wartime of some leading penalists (e.g., Léon Cornil) also helped to foster reforms.

Throughout the 1960s and 1970s, official penal and prison rhetoric followed the new **social defence** theory of the Frenchman Marc Ancel, emphasizing resocialization and responsibility of the offender/prisoner (Ancel, 1966 [1981]). In practice, however, the *treatment ideology* never became predominant. The Royal Decree of 1965 regulating the prison management, which is still in force today, makes passing reference in its Introduction to the social reintegration of the prisoner and to normalisation of prison regimes as a general aim. A high quality multi-disciplinary centre for scientific diagnosis, prognosis and treatment was established in 1963 (the Penitentiary Orientation Centre, directed by Prof. J-P. De Waele). It received international attention, but with a total capacity of some 20-odd places (compared to the 20,000 incarcerations per year) it had to limit its actions to the most serious cases. It led to innovative scientific typologies of murderers (De Waele, 1990), but its impact on the general prison population and regime remained marginal. Major reforms during this period included the gradual liberalization of some regime aspects, especially the opening-up of prisons to the outside world by allowing prisoners more contacts with free citizens (e.g., visits, correspondence, prison leave, and semi-detention), and allowing more outside services into the prisons (e.g., education and preparation for release). Currently, despite the international trend towards fostering prisoners' rights, and a period of turmoil and riots inside the prisons, prison regimes in Belgium remain based on privileges and sanctions decided by the Prison Administration without much judicial oversight (Tubex, 2001).

In the 1980s, *prison overcrowding* became a major issue. The over-crowding resulted from a growing number of detainees in remand custody and long-term prisoners (more than five years), including an increasing number of foreign prisoners, violent, sexual and drug offenders. The expansion of prison capacity, coupled to a "back door" policy of not carrying out short-term prison sentences (less than four months) and relying on more systematic early releases of sentences up to 18 months (later expanded to three years), failed to stem the tide.

In June 1996, the *White Paper on Penal and Prison Policy* (Ministre de la Justice, 1996) was presented by the then-Minister of Justice S. De Clerck. It was the first attempt in many years to develop a coherent penal and prison policy. The report analysed several problems faced by the penal and prison systems in Belgium. They included issues of: prison overcrowding, lack of prisoners' rights, and ineffective treatment of different categories of prisoners (e.g., drug addicts, sexual offenders, mentally ill offenders). The *White Paper* proposed a coherent policy based on a "reductionist" approach that envisions the use of imprisonment as a last resort only. This fostered the promotion of community sanctions and measures as well as the reform of prison regimes and parole.

Prof. Lieven Dupont, a leading penologist from the University of Leuven, was charged with drafting the first Belgian Prison Act ever. In August 1996 however, the **Dutroux case** exploded (see Box 1.1), leaving Belgian society in shock. As Dutroux allegedly committed his crimes of abduction, sexual abuse and murder of young girls while on parole, the topics of parole and treatment of sexual offenders received immediate political priority, while the promotion of the reductionist approach virtually vanished from the political agenda. Victim policies become a priority and parole legislation was reformed in 1998. The draft first Prison Act, dealing with the internal legal position of prisoners, was presented to Parliament in 2000 (Commission "Loi de Principes concernant l'Administration Pénitentiaire et le Statut Juridique des Détenus," 2000), but still has not been fully discussed yet. At the request of the Minister of Justice, other drafts of the Prison Act have been prepared, one on the external legal position of prisoners and the creation of a multidisciplinary supervision court (Commission "Tribunaux de l'Application des Peines Statut Juridique Extreme des Détenus et Fixation de la Peine," 2003), and one on the reform of legislation and practice concerning mentally ill offenders (Commission "Internment," 1999).[3] At the time of preparing this chapter, none of the commission reports had yet been discussed in Parliament.

Box 1.1: The Dutroux Case

"The 'Dutroux-case,' uncovered in August 1996, shocked Belgian society, discredited the Belgian political, penal and prison systems and even received international coverage. Not only did the heinous nature of the offences — abduction, sexual abuse and murder of young girls — shake Belgium's fundamental moral values. But the way in which the case had been previously investigated raised questions about the efficiency — and even possible corruption — of the police services and magistrates involved. M. Dutroux having allegedly committed his crimes while on parole for a previous sentence for sexual abuse of minors, the treatment of sexual offenders in prison and under parole was severely criticised. A Parliamentary Commission was instituted to analyse all these failures, to point to (individual) responsibilities and to propose reforms. The hearings of this commission were broadcast live (a novelty in Belgium) and attracted wide public attention. It was a sad spectacle and an illustration of the ongoing "police-war" (the three major police forces in Belgium had, for historical reasons, overlapping competences), and of distrust between police and judiciary and between judiciary and media. The testimonies by the parents of some of the victims on the way they had been treated by police and judiciary added fundamental questions about the position and rights of the victims in our inquisitorial criminal procedure. When the investigating judge in charge of the case was subsequently discharged by the Supreme Court (*Cour de Cassation*) for breach of impartiality,[4] a huge public demonstration took place in support of the victims and the magistrate ("White march," September 1996).

"In short, the whole criminal justice system fell into disrepute" (Snacken, 2001:32-33)

Several initiatives were taken as a result: parole legislation was reformed, increasing the counter-indications and strengthening control and revocation; the position of the victims was enhanced during trial (better access to judicial files) and in the parole system; restorative justice was advocated at all levels of the criminal justice system, including within corrections; and sexual offenders were subjected to different kinds of restrictions.

With the trial taking place in Spring 2004, Belgium has not yet recovered from this trauma.

Conclusion: Corrections Today

"The standards of a nation's civilization can be judged by opening the doors of its prisons."

~ Dostojewski, *The House of the Dead*

As a result of this evolution, the major issues confronting adult corrections in Belgium today are: prison overcrowding and electronic monitoring, a changing prison population, dealing with special categories (e.g., foreigners, drug offenders, mentally ill and sex offenders), the effects of the new parole legislation, the lack of a coherent prison policy model and the growing emphasis on victim issues and staff issues.

We will deal with these issues in more detail after some explanation about the organisation structure of the prison administration and the profile of the prison population.

Organization Structure

Administration

In the federal state of Belgium, the Prison Administration is a department of the Ministry of Justice, which is a federal ministry (see Appendix 1.1). The Prison Administration consists of a central administration, 33 prisons and one institution for "social defence" (i.e., mentally ill offenders). There are two separate institutions for psychiatric patients and mentally ill offenders. These institutions fall under the joint administration of the federal Ministry of Justice and the regional Ministry of Public Health.

Each prison is directed by a prison governor and one or several deputies. A majority of these have a university degree in criminology.[5] The majority (85%) of the prison staff consists of prison guards. However, after the Dutroux case financial efforts were made to ensure that each prison now has a "psycho-social team" — at least one full-time social worker, a part-time psychologist and a part-time psychiatrist. Due to the reform of the parole system in 1998, these teams are increasingly pressed into a predominantly diagnostic function, leaving prisoners with few opportunities for voluntary guidance and care. Custodial staff was traditionally gender-based (men for male prisoners, women for female prisoners), but the introduction of mixed staff (with a minimum and maximum of 20% "other sex") was decided in 1997 and is now implemented in all prisons.

Following the institutional reforms of 1980 and 1988, all aspects relating to "forensic welfare" (i.e., social aid to offenders, victims and their families) are the exclusive responsibility of the regional authorities, which are distinguished according to their language base. Many regime aspects in prisons can, however, be seen as part of both the serving of a prison sentence and the preparation for the social reintegration of prisoners (e.g., prison labour, education, vocational training, health care, sports). The political debate concerning their respective competences — and hence, budgets— in 1994 led to "Cooperation agreements" between the Ministry of Justice and the regional authorities, and to the introduction of mixed "welfare teams" in prisons, in which inside social workers and external services delimit their respective tasks (Snacken, 2001).

Participation of the community at large in prisons, however, remains modest and has developed unequally between regions. The Flemish Community has recently developed a "Strategic Plan" aiming at the implementation of the idea that a prisoner continues to be a citizen and thus has a right of access to all services available outside prison as long as they are compatible with the imprisonment. This means that individuals who are not under the authority of the Ministry of Justice, or the prison governor, are employed inside prisons to ensure that help and social services are available. Cooperation between prison staff and such external groups is not easy and problems may arise concerning, for example, the transfer of information and professional secrecy.

With the psychosocial services of the prison pressed into a mainly diagnostic function, and the uneasy and unequal introduction of welfare services by the communities, it is clear that the development of a complete package of help and social services to detainees is a serious challenge for the future.

Levels of Institutions

Prisons in Belgium are formally divided into remand prisons (in each major city), and open, half-open and closed prisons for the carrying out of sentences.

Remand prisons have a closed, cellular regime, and are used for pretrial detention. All major remand prisons have a psychiatric annex and a unit for female prisoners. Most remand prisons are also used for serving sentences, either by design (subdivisions) or due to prison overcrowding (sentenced prisoners waiting for their transfer).

The division between open, half-open and closed prisons is based on the level of security inside the prison. Open prisons have a dormitory system and prisoners are expected to voluntarily accept prison discipline, while half-open prisons have an open regime during the day and a closed regime at night. Open and half-open prisons are located in remote areas, where prisoners deemed unlikely to escape can work on the surrounding land or receive educational or vocational training.[6] Since the 1990s, part of the open capacity has been transformed into closed capacity (now totalling 80.3% of the total prison capacity), due to a changing prison population and the overcrowding in remand and closed prisons, which have increased the need for closed capacity.

A classification of prisoners was designed by the Prison Administration in 1971, based on legal and administrative criteria such as length of sentence, criminal history, gender, age, and language. In the '80s, attempts to foster the detention of prisoners as close as possible to their homes and social relations (the principle of "regionalization") were hampered by the increasing overcrowding. Since then, the quantitative increase in some categories of prisoners, such as drug addicts and sexual offenders, has led some prisons to offer special programmes, thus also influencing classification.

Profile of the Correctional Population[7]

Belgium has been confronted with an increasing prison population since the '80s. This evolution can best be illustrated by the detention ratio, which shows the average daily number of prisoners per 100,000 of the general population. While during the '80s the ratio fluctuated around 65/100,000, it has risen to 90/100,000 in 2003. In the same period, the prison capacity was also increased, but is still limited to about 8,000 places for about 9,300 prisoners, resulting in serious overcrowding. Moreover, as noted earlier, most Belgian prisons date from the 19th or first half of the 20th century and lack adequate facilities for even the most basic hygienic or health needs (e.g., no toilets or running water in the cells, no communal areas for employment or sports). Extensive, but often slow renovation work has been undertaken since the '70s, but this in itself causes additional, if temporary, loss of capacity. The over-crowding itself renders renovation more difficult and slow.

While the average daily prison population has steadily increased since the 1980s, the number of incarcerations sharply decreased in the '90s and has remained stable throughout the first part of the new millennium (see Table 1.1). This shows, therefore, that the average length of deten-tion has increased, a situation which is true for both remand and sen-tenced prisoners.

Sentencing Trends

In principle, and according to legislation, remand custody should only be used in exceptional circumstances. Under law, the suspect still enjoys the presumption of innocence, and only serious reasons of public safety may lead the investigating judge to curtail the fundamental right to freedom of a citizen not yet proven guilty. Research has shown, how-ever, that in practice the application of remand custody is increasingly ruled by risk-thinking and deterrence: an immediate reaction which protects society against the potential risk of recidivism and feelings of impunity (Snacken et al., 1997). For example, in the course of the '90s, approximately 33% of the prison population was awaiting trial; in 2003 this number increased to 40% (N=3,680) (see Table 1.2).

The largest increase of detention has been among the long-term pris-oners[8] — those sentenced to five years or more (see Table 1.3). While their proportion of the total prison population was only 8% (N=448) in 1980, their number increased continuously throughout the '90s, reaching the threshold of 20% in 1996, and further rising to 27% (N=2,531 at the beginning of 2003).

The number of life-sentenced prisoners quadrupled over the same period with, however, a slight decrease since the last three years.[9] The number of long-term sentences for felonies has increased by 100 in just one year (2002-2003) (see Table 1.4). A consequence of this trend has been the added pressure on the prison capacity problem in the future.

Table 1.1: Average Daily Prison Population[a] and Annual Number of Incarcerations,[a] 1980 – 2003

Year	Average daily population	Index	Incarcerations	Index
1980	5677	100	19719	100
1981	5784	102	20153	102
1982	6112	108	20802	105
1983	6450	114	22274	113
1984	6728	119	22166	112
1985	6454	114	19879	101
1986	6695	115	20102	102
1987	6497	118	18437	93
1988	6688	114	17308	88
1989	6549	118	18202	92
1990	6549	115	17406	88
1991	6194	109	18221	92
1992	6869	121	19058	97
1993	7489	132	18261	93
1994	7489	132	16976	86
1995	7693	136	15853	80
1996	7935	140	15660	79
1997	8522	150	14688	74
1998	8707	153	14127	72
1999	8143	143	14434	73
2000	8543	150	14960	76
2001	8536	150	14443	73
2002	8804	155	15695	80
1/3/2003	9308	164	-	-

Source: Prison Administration (FOD Justitite), data adapted by the authors.

a. Totalling sentenced and remand prisoners.

Table 1.2: Remand Prisoners and Sentenced Prisoners, 1980 – 2003[10]

Year	Remand			Sentenced prisoners		
	Average daily population* –	Index	Proportion of the total population	Average daily population –	Index	Proportion of the total population
1980	1458	100	26%	2377	100	42%
1985	2004	137	31%	2726	115	42%
1990	1821	125	28%	3236	136	49%
1991	1722	118	28%	2910	122	47%
1992	2191	150	32%	3080	130	45%
1993	2431	167	32%	3723	157	50%
1994	2614	179	35%	3616	152	48%
1995	2546	175	33%	3953	166	51%
1996	2497	171	31%	4344	183	55%
1997	2469	169	29%	4922	207	58%
1/03/98	2773*	190	32%	4615*	194	53%
1/03/99	2554*	175	31%	4580*	193	56%
1/03/00	3023*	207	35%	4900*	206	57%
1/03/01	2951*	202	35%	4776*	201	56%
1/03/02	3238*	222	37%	4497*	189	51%
1/03/03	3680*	252	40%	4807*	202	52%

Source: Prison Administration (FOD Justitie), data adapted by the authors.

*Population on March 1st.

Comment: Adding the proportion of remand and sentenced prisoners and pre-trial detainees accounts for only about 90% of the population. The remaining 10% of the population consists of mentally ill offenders in prison (cf. internment).

Table 1.3: Average Daily Population of Sentenced Prisoners, 1980 - 2003

Year	Sentence of 5 or more years		Sentence of less than 5 years	
	Average daily population*—	Proportion	Average daily population* —	Proportion
1980	448	8%	1929	34%
1985	739	11%	1987	31%
1990	1238	19%	1998	31%
1991	1185	19%	1725	28%
1992	1100	16%	1980	29%
1993	1279	17%	2444	33%
1994	1308	17%	2308	31%
1995	1447	19%	2506	33%
1996	1646	21%	2698	34%
1997	1857	22%	3065	36%
1/3/1998	1913	22%	2702	31%
1/3/1999	2082	26%	2498	31%
1/3/2000	2341	27%	2559	30%
1/3/2001	2402	28%	2374	28%
1/3/2002	2308	26%	2189	25%
1/3/2003	2531	27%	2276	24%

Source: Prison Administration (FOD Justitie), data adapted by the authors.

*Population on March 1st.

Table 1.4: Different Categories of Long-term Sentences, 1999 - 2003

Category	1/03/99	1/03/00	1/03/01	1/03/02	1/03/03
Death penalty	2	1	1	1	0
Life sentence	278	271	266	243	237
Sentence of more than 5 years (felony)	306	301	273	268	374
Sentence of more than 5 years (misdemeanours)	1496	1768	1862	1796	1920
Long-term prisoners	**2082**	**2341**	**2402**	**2308**	**2531**

Source: Prison Administration (FOD Justitie), data adapted by the authors.

Demographic Trends

In addition to changes in sentencing practices, there has been a significant shift in the profile of the population. The number of detained persons not having Belgian nationality is steadily increasing. Since the 1980s their numbers have increased threefold rising from 21% of the total prison population in 1980 to 42% in 2003. Since non-Belgian nationals constitute only 9% to 10% of the total population, it would seem they are strongly overrepresented in the prison population. However, one has to take into account that other categories also fall within the definition of "foreign prisoners," including illegal aliens detained for administrative reasons or for having committed an offence, and offenders involved in cross-border or organized crime. It also should be noticed that non-Belgians are disproportionately represented in the population of remand prisoners: e.g., on March 1st 2003, 48% of all prisoners with a non-Belgian nationality were remand prisoners, compared to only 32% of the Belgian prisoners.

Over the last decade, Moroccans have represented the largest group within the population of non-Belgians in prison. Scientific research has shown that ethnic minorities, especially Moroccans, are at greater risk of being imprisoned than Belgian suspects or convicts (De Pauw, 2002).

The opening-up of the borders between Western and Eastern Europe has, however, altered the mix of foreign nationalities in prison. Since the beginning of the '90s, the number of prisoners with a former Soviet nationality (i.e., Central and Eastern Europe, Russia and Community of Independent States) has steadily increased. In March 2003, their numbers were virtually the same (N=1,030), as the population (N=1,043) of Moroccans. Meanwhile, the number of prisoners with a Western European nationality stabilised around 830 prisoners.

Another dramatic increase in the 1990s has been in the number of sexual offenders. The Dutroux case in 1996 triggered a number of initiatives with respect to sex offenders at all levels of the criminal justice system: e.g., the number of punishable offences was broadened (criminalization), sentences became more severe, and early release was made more difficult since more conditions had to be satisfied (see Tubex, 2001). The cumulative effect of these measures has been that the number and proportion of sex offenders in Belgian prisons has greatly increased. On 1st March 2003, there were 1,612 sexual offenders being detained in custody. This represented 17.5% of the prison population. In contrast, in March 1996, just before the discovery of the above-mentioned case, this figure was only 11%. In the '80s, sexual offenders only represented 6% to 7% of the prison population.

Non-custodial Sentences

Non-custodial sanctions can be applied at different levels of the criminal justice system. In 1990, an alternative to remand custody was introduced, the so-called "freedom under conditions." In view of the still increasing remand population, this alternative has not been very successful in reaching its aim. At the prosecution stage, mediation was introduced in 1994; at the sentencing stage, probation has been applied since 1964 in combination with a conditional prison sentence or a suspended sentence. In 1994, community service orders and training orders were introduced as probation measures. However, in 2002 community service became an autonomous sanction and is now called a "working penalty," expressing the more punitive character of this community punishment. Table 1.5 shows the increasing use of these community sanctions since 1999. However, this has not reduced the use of imprisonment and shows rather the extension of punishment at all levels of the criminal justice system.

Table 1.5: Community Sanctions — Yearly Number of Assignments, 1999 - 2002

Community Sanction	1999	2000	2001	2002
Freedom under conditions	812	769	877	1170
Mediation	6583	6686	6217	6110
Probation	7414	7858	8199	8470
Community service or training order	2295	3544	5037	6572
Working penalty				528

Source: Director General Judicial Organisation, FOD Justitie, *Justitie in Cijfers* (Justice in Numbers). Http://www.juridat.be/img publi/pdf/318-NL.pdf.

ISSUES CONFRONTING CORRECTIONS TODAY

Prison Overcrowding

Prison overcrowding is the result of a quantitative imbalance between prison population and prison capacity, but it also creates many qualitative drawbacks both for prisoners and prison staff. Material living conditions for prisoners deteriorate, and hence do also the working conditions for staff. For example, prisoners in the overcrowded remand prisons have to live 23 hours a day with two or three persons in 10 square metre cells designed to hold only one inmate, raising fear for their physical integrity. Aside from the impact on inmates, staff also experienced greater difficulties in getting to know the prisoners, to prevent conflicts, or to sense pending trouble. Prison regimes fail to take into account different individual needs and security requirements, and develop into a common denominator.

During its first visit to Belgium in 1993, the European Committee for the Prevention of Torture and Inhuman and Degrading Treatment or Punishment (CPT) found the combination of overcrowding, lack of sanitation and lack of activities in one of the remand prisons to amount to inhuman and degrading treatment (European Committee for the Prevention of Torture and Inhuman or Degrading Treatment or Punishment, 1994). Overcrowding and lack of activities continued to be found in other remand prisons during its later visits in 1997 and 2001 (European Committee for the Prevention of Torture and Inhuman or Degrading Treatment or Punishment, 1998, 2002).

The expansion of prison capacity and the **back door strategy** of early releases of short-term prisoners do not tackle the origins of the overcrowding and hence cannot bring a solution. The early releases are even thought to have increased the level of severity of sentencing, some judges thus attempting to ensure a minimum period of detention. Despite official rhetoric and legislation to foster alternative, non-custodial sanctions and measures (1990 — alternative to remand custody; 1994 — extension of probation, introduction of mediation and community service; and 2002 — community service as an autonomous sanction), Belgium does not follow a coherent reductionist penal policy (Rutherford, 1984). Several laws have indeed at the same time increased the scope and the severity of the penalties, especially towards drug, violent and sexual offenders. The comparison of different European countries shows that only a coherent reductionist policy can effectively reduce the detention rate in the long run (Snacken, Beyens and Tubex, 1995).

Electronic Monitoring[11]

In Belgium, electronic monitoring (EM) has been introduced as a modality of administering a prison sentence, in a preparatory stage for early release (cf. "back door strategy"). Electronic monitoring was mentioned in the *White Paper on Penal and Prison Policy* (June, 1996) as an important instrument in the struggle against the rising prison population. EM was first introduced at St. Gillis–Brussels prison in November 1997,[12] and implemented in April of 1998. By the time the program commenced operation, a second Ministerial circular letter[13] had already expanded the eligibility for entering the programme: all convicted prisoners with a prison sentence up to three years and eligible for early release can apply for electronic monitoring. Candidates must have a fixed abode in the judicial district of Brussels, must possess a fixed telephone line and be able to pay 124 euros per month to share costs. Although in the beginning the experiment included the technique of voice verification as well as bracelets (i.e., active system),[14] only the latter are now used. In Belgium, electronic monitoring is always coupled with a program of individual guidance. An offender under electronic monitoring gets an individual schedule, defining the number of hours per week for work, training, education and/or treatment. The rest of the time, the offender is supposed to stay at home and to be available for phone calls from the prison service.

The option of EM as a mode of detention shows that it is not presented as a "soft alternative," which should be a guarantee against net-widening (see Glossary). However, Kaminski rightly points out that this does not preclude its use for low-risk offenders or short-term prisoners, who otherwise would have been released without EM (Kaminski, 1999).

To date, the administration of electronic monitoring has been regulated by 14 successive Ministerial circular letters, all redefining and mainly expanding the scope of EM. By the end of 1998,[15] convicted prisoners who were six months from their possible early release were eligible for EM, without limit as to their sentence length. On the other hand, certain types of offenders were excluded (e.g., sex offenders with victims of minor age, offenders involved in trafficking of human beings, and offenders without legal residence permit). Also some contra-indications with regard to the possibility of social reintegration, the personality of the prisoner, conduct in prison and the risk of reoffending are grounds for exclusion from EM.[16] Another interesting point is that the offender's contribution to the costs of EM was first considerably reduced[17] and later on even completely abolished.[18]

In 2000, the Belgian government decided to implement EM nationwide, and established a "National Centre for Electronic Monitoring" which will be responsible for the coordination of electronic monitoring all over Belgium. This geographical expansion and structural reorganization[19] ushers in a new episode in the use and administration of electronic monitoring in Belgium. Indeed, the balance between support and control has become a major issue with the professionals involved. Until the establishment of the "National Centre for Electronic Monitoring" the social support and guidance of those under EM was provided by the national Probation Service. However, discussions and tensions gradually increased between the probation officers and the organizers of the EM from the prison service over issues of the just and desired balance between care and guidance on the one hand, and the responsibility for following up violations, control and surveillance on the other. Probation officers operate in a professional culture dominated by an equal emphasis on support and control, and find it difficult to cooperate in the much stricter control of EM participants and to report on any violation to the prison service. In other words, they refused to be integrated in a more controlling and public security oriented framework. This eventually led to the establishment of a separate social service for electronic monitoring in 2000, operating independently from the probation service and belonging hierarchically to the National Centre for Electronic Monitoring (Prison Service). A private company is responsible for the delivery and installation of the technical equipment.

At that time, the number of prisoners serving their sentence under EM was still very low (up to 30 on a daily basis). In 2001, fostering the use of EM as a means to reduce prison overcrowding became a major political goal: a "target number" of 300 prisoners was set. As a result, another far-reaching measure of expansion was introduced in April 2001 allowing all offenders with a prison sentence up to three years (with the continued exception of sexual offenders) to be immediately put under electronic monitoring,[20] without having any prison time. Since April 2001, there has been a steady rise in the daily rate; up to 124 persons in July 2001 and to 204 by May 2002. Since then, the number of persons under EM has fluctuated between 200 and 250 (October 1st 2003: N=265) (see Figure 1.1).

It should also be noted that the average period of supervision time under electronic monitoring is also rising, from a mean daily period of 53 days in January 2003 to 90 days in September 2003.

Figure 1.1: Mean Daily Population on Electronic Monitoring between October 2000 and September 2003

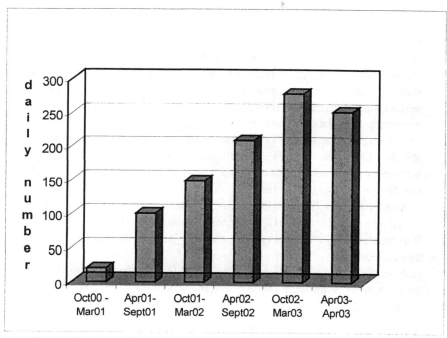

Source : National Centre for Electronic Monitoring (FOD Justitie).

The "target number" of the government has recently been increased to 450 people on EM on a daily basis. This target figure again illustrates the current policy, especially in periods of crisis,[21] of presenting and encouraging the use of electronic monitoring as a means of controlling the size of the prison population and the resulting overcrowding problem. However, to date the Belgian electronic monitoring program has had no significant impact on the size of the prison population. On the contrary, since its introduction the prison population has been constantly on the rise. This does not prevent the government from continuing to present EM as *the* solution for overcrowding problems.

Electronic monitoring is also increasingly promoted as a cost-effective means to manage the soaring prison population. And indeed, at first sight, EM has the advantage of a lower daily cost per person (41 euros), compared to a daily cost of a prisoner (approximately 90 to 100 euros, which means twice as high). However, if electronic monitoring is liable to result in net-widening, the net effect will disappear.

So far, a very cautious selection and screening of the candidates has been carried out by the actors involved. However, further problems of understaffing (28% less staff than foreseen in October 2003), combined with a rising daily population on electronic monitoring, may lead to a less careful selection policy and lower quality of guidance by the social assistants and thus to more violations in the future.

To conclude, we can state that EM will certainly gain importance in Belgian punishment and the administration of prison sentences. Regularly the question of introducing EM as an autonomous sanction, imposed by the courts or as an alternative to remand custody turns up. These proposals have, however, not been realized to date. Both national (Snacken and Raes, 2001) and international research (Byrne, Lurigio and Petersilia, 1992) has shown that the risk of net-widening is even greater at these levels.

Prison Policy Model

Since the demise of the cellular segregation model of Ducpétiaux, Belgium has had no clear prison policy model. Political interest in this issue tends to be low and there is still no overarching prison legislation. The Royal Decree of 1965 only very generally refers to social reintegration of prisoners and normalisation of prison regimes, leaving an enormous leeway to ministerial circular letters. Daily prison policy is hence decided on the basis of these circular letters, which may change overnight, and by local initiatives by the prison governors. This has resulted in large differences between the prisons, even of the same category, depending on the particular interests, efforts or views of the governors. Since many of these governors are criminologists, this may have stimulated penological creativity in practice. However, it also results in a lack of coherent central policy on other issues (see section below on "International Standards of Human Rights").

In general, the main feature of the prison policy of the last 20 years has been an attempt at opening up the prisons and some normalization of prison regimes. These initiatives, however, have been seriously hampered by overcrowding and the increasing number of foreign prisoners. These increasing efforts at some normalization, coupled to the lack of legal rights of prisoners, have, however, resulted in even more discretionary power for prison staff. Hence, the demand for increased administrative and judicial supervision on decisions taken by the local or central prison administration. Administrative supervision has recently been reinforced by the reorganization of "Boards of visitors" and a "Central council for the execution of sentences" in 2003. Judicial supervision has recently increased through civil and administrative suits by prisoners and human rights lawyers, and is further the object of the Draft on the introduction of "supervision courts" (Commission "Tribunaux de l'Application des Peines Statut Juridique Externe des Détenus et Fixation de la Peine," 2003).

We mentioned earlier that Belgium never really implemented the "*treatment ideology*" of the '60s and '70s, found in the Anglo-Saxon and Scandinavian prison systems. With the increasing proportion of drug offenders and sexual offenders in the prison population, the question of treatment has however reemerged.

It is certainly admitted that punishment alone is not sufficient for these kinds of offenders and that treatment is essential in the prevention of further recidivism. The question is, however, whether prison is a suitable environment for such treatment programmes, taking into account the artificial surroundings, the involuntary character of programmes in a prison context, etc. As far as drug or sexual offenders are concerned, Belgium has chosen to organize the treatment outside prison and to restrict initiatives during detention to diagnosis, medical treatment and preparation for therapy after (conditional) release. Hence no treatment programs are provided during detention. This raises two major problems. First, there is the concern about how to deal with the long-term prisoners who may spend many years incarcerated before actually having an opportunity to deal effectively with the causes of their imprisonment. Secondly, there is concern for the insufficient number of competent treatment centres in society, resulting in long waiting lists for prisoners willing to enroll in such a program. By the time they gain entry to treatment, they may have already served such a large proportion of their sentence that they lose interest in a conditional release coupled to treatment (with a minimum period of two years!). Consequently, an increasing number of sex offenders serve their complete sentence and are subsequently released into society without having received any treatment or guidance.

Mentally ill offenders were always supposed to form an exception to this dearth of treatment. They are imprisoned for an indeterminate period because their mental disorder renders them criminally irresponsible. Their release is decided by a special "commission of social defense" on the basis of their mental improvement. This indeterminate period of detention is hence supposed to be used for treatment of the offender. This treatment can take place in a psychiatric institution outside the prison or in special departments of the prisons. Unfortunately, transfer to outside institutions is not always easy (some categories, such as arsonists, are often refused) and resources inside the prisons have been terribly lacking, resulting in an unacceptable level of care (see International Standards below).

Victims' Rights Issues

Early Release and Victims

In Belgium, a discretionary and mandatory release system work in unison. Thus, some 80% of prisoners are released under provisional release schemes applicable when the actual length of sentence does not exceed three years. The system was introduced in 1972 for prisoners serving sentences of up to one year to whom the long and complicated conditional release procedure could not be applied. Originally, it was an individual decision, but it has been constantly made more flexible because of prison overcrowding and is increasingly applied in a more automatic way. The most important condition which must be fulfilled is a time condition: the director of the prison can decide about a provisional release after a stipulated period of the sentence has been served, provided there is no indication that the inmate is unfit for release and provided s/he has sufficient prospects for social reintegration. Their release may be conditional on their receiving social counselling, if the director considers it necessary.

As a result of this evolution, the system of conditional release (CR) is only applicable in practice to those prisoners who have received a sentence longer than three years. CR has existed since 1888, but the law was thoroughly revised after the Dutroux case in 1998. Since then the final decision has been taken by a multidisciplinary board composed of full-time professionals. There are six parole boards, each covering the judicial district of one of the appeal courts. Each board is chaired by a judge who is assisted by an expert in sentence enforcement and an expert in social reintegration. A member of the public prosecution is attached to each board. The advantage of a multidisciplinary board is that the chances of a successful CR can be gauged from several angles.

In both systems of early release there are special rules for sex offenders. Prisoners who have been convicted of sexual abuse of minors and serve sentences of more than one year are, since 1996, subject to special rules. They must satisfy two extra conditions:

- a service specialized in the treatment or guidance of sex offenders must give its reasoned opinion on the advisability of early release; and,

- the involved offenders must declare themselves willing to undergo treatment or guidance at a specialized institution after release.

In the new law on CR, explicit attention is given to the victims. This recognition is applied at several levels (Snacken and Tubex, 1999).

The victim's interests are first taken into account as one of the possible counter-indications that must be checked when proposing CR, whatever the sentence. One possible counter-indication is the prisoner's attitude towards the victims of his/her offence. Subsequently, in the course of a CR procedure, there are other possibilities for taking into account the interests of the victim, provided certain conditions are met. A distinction has to be drawn here between two kinds of victims: for some offences the victim is contacted automatically unless s/he has previously made it known that s/he does not wish to be personally involved. This requirement applies mainly for sex offences and violent crimes with a permanent effect on the victim. For other offences, the victim must have previously expressed a wish to be informed throughout the release procedure, which is possible only if the offender has been sentenced to at least one year's actual imprisonment. The possibilities open to the victim are as follows:

- To be informed of any release.

- To suggest any particular conditions that might be imposed in the victim's interest.

- Before deciding whether parole should be granted, the board interviews the prisoner and his/her legal counsel, the state prosecution service and the prison governor. In cases provided for by Royal Decree, the victims (if the victim is a natural person) — or, if the victim is deceased, his/her descendants or ascendants — may request the opportunity to state what conditions should be imposed in their interest (provided they can prove that they have a direct, legitimate interest in the matter.) Victims may be assisted by their legal counsel or a representative of a public body or an association authorised to perform this function, but may not be represented by them. The board may also decide to hear other people. The board meets in the prison and the hearing is adversarial, which implies that the victim must go to the prison and confront the prisoner.

- If parole is granted, the board informs the victims at their own request and sends them a registered letter setting out the conditions ensuring the protection of their interests, provided they have a legitimate, direct interest in the matter.

Restorative Justice in Prison

Since the early '90s, there has been a strong academic lobby in favor of **restorative justice** (see Glossary) in Belgium.[22] The ideas of restorative justice were officially introduced by the *White Paper on Penal and Prison Policy* (June, 1996). The already increased attention for victims in the administration of criminal justice, with the Dutroux case as catalyst, also resulted in an attempt to sensitize the prison system towards a more victim-oriented policy. As a result, in October 1997 an action-research project was started in six Belgian prisons (three Walloon and three Flemish prisons) to explore how a more balanced correctional system for offender, victim, and society could be introduced (Robert and Peters,

2003). In the fall of 2000, the Minister of Justice decided to recruit a "restorative justice consultant" for each prison and two coordinators.[23] The mission of the consultants is to develop a "restorative prison culture" in which restorative justice is supported by all aspects of prison life. The task of the restorative justice consultants is a structural one. Rather than being involved in mediation practices in individual cases, they have to encourage direct and indirect processes of communication between victims and offenders. Therefore, they have to develop initiatives with respect to prison staff, prisoners, victims, and social services from outside the prison so as to establish a professional culture with respect for victims and offenders. The process includes the provision of information and sensitising prison staff on victimization and restorative justice. However, unilateral introduction of more victim-sensitivity among prison personnel might result in a more repressive attitude towards the prisoners. Therefore, the focus of an educational program on "victims and restorative justice" has been changed to "offender-victim-restorative justice." This approach allows for a better understanding of the interrelationship dynamics between being a victim and becoming an offender.

In addition, the consultants have to provide prisoners with information on the redress fund, civil action and "mediation for redress" (*herstelbemiddeling*). Prisoners are encouraged to pay civil action settlements if they are convicted by the criminal judge. However, the debts and insolvency of many prisoners, combined with a high rate of unemployment and a very low salary level in the prisons, complicate the feasibility of compensation arrangements.

Restorative justice consultants organize office hours for inmates where juridical advice and procedural assistance are provided by lawyers and organizations from the field. Also training sessions where the prisoners are given the opportunity to become acquainted, in a non-confrontational way, with the experiences of victims are arranged in the prison.

Finally, restorative justice consultants have to inform victims, social workers and volunteers on the administration of punishment and restorative detention. Initiatives taken include: information leaflets on financial compensation of victims and the position of victims in the parole procedure; the establishment of a "compensation fund" through which prisoners can start paying compensation; and contacts with external social services and victim organisations.

To conclude, restorative justice is still in its infancy in Belgium. Restorative justice consultants have encountered enormous structural problems in carrying out their tasks (e.g., lack of space to organize communal activities). And in spite of the best intentions of its proponents, in practice, restorative justice ideals come up against a wall of scepticism. In addition, prison staff has to cope with the daily problems of prison overcrowding and, working in a prison culture that is still heavily dominated by expectations of control and public safety, remain very reluctant to cooperate in restorative initiatives.

International Standards of Human Rights

Belgian prisons have been severely criticized by European Human Rights supervision bodies. As already mentioned, the "European Committee for the Prevention of Torture and Inhuman or Degrading Treatment or Punishment" (CPT) visited Belgium three times (in 1993, 1997, 2001). Although situations varied among prisons, similar shortcomings were noted with each visit: overcrowding and lack of activities in remand prisons, a lack of adequate regimes for long-term prisoners and drug offenders, the absence of prisoners' rights and an effective complaint system resulting in great legal insecurity and tensions, insufficient guarantees against inter-prisoner violence, a lack of central policy to prevent suicides, and an unacceptably low level of psychiatric help for prisoners, including mentally ill offenders (see Appendix 1.2).

In one remand prison visited in 1993, the combination of overcrowding, lack of sanitation and lack of activities was even described as amounting to inhuman and degrading treatment. In another prison the lack of psychiatric help for mentally ill offenders was described as "beneath the acceptable minimum from an ethical and humane point of view" (CPT/Inf (94) 15, par. 85 and 191).

This lack of psychiatric treatment for mentally ill prisoners even led to a case before the European Court of Human Rights (Aerts v Belgium, 30 July 1998). It concerned a seriously mentally ill offender who was kept for nine months in a remand prison without adequate psychiatric help or treatment. Although the court accepted the CPT findings concerning the unacceptably low level of psychiatric care in that particular unit, confirmed by the psychiatrist in charge (who was responsible for 800 prisoners), it did not find[24] that Mr. Aerts had sufficiently proven that his mental health had further deteriorated as a result. Hence the court rejected the alleged violation of article 3 of the European Convention of Human Rights on inhuman and degrading treatment. However, the internment of a mentally ill offender for several months without providing psychiatric treatment was considered an illegitimate form of detention and hence in breach of article 5 of the Convention (i.e., legitimate exceptions on the right to freedom and security). Taking into account that the situation of Mr. Aerts is by no means an exception in Belgium, this case can be considered as entailing serious criticisms on the system of internment in Belgium.

On most of these critical issues research has been carried out, reforms have been proposed, and draft legislation has been prepared between 2000 and 2003 by the three different commissions. The main question is whether in a period of increasing attention to the public's feelings of insecurity and social and economic instability there will be sufficient political will to vote the laws and to implement them, including the financial costs they will entail. Although building new prisons seems popular, spending money on prisoners is not.

CURRENT AND FUTURE ISSUES

The problems of the past 20 years are at the same time the current and the future challenges for the Belgian penal and prison system.

Priorities are without doubt:

Prison overcrowding. Ways must be found to effectively counter the penal population growth through a coherent reductionist policy. This entails developing a convincing "front door strategy" by enhancing the credibility of community sanctions with the penal actors. More financial investment in the preparation and follow-up of community sanctions is necessary for them to become real and realistic alternatives to imprisonment. This is not yet the case. Both the prison population and the number of offenders under community sanctions are increasing, resulting in a general increase in the "level of punishment" in Belgium. Both legislators and actors involved in imposing punishment should be convinced that prison sentences have many counterproductive effects and that offenders, as well as victims and the society are better served with more constructive sanctions.

A coherent prison policy model: It is now up to Parliament to discuss, vote and implement a first Prison Act for Belgium. The draft by the *"Commission Loi de Principes"* (2000) states clear aims for the application of prison sentences: limiting the detrimental effects of imprisonment, preparing offenders for social reintegration, and reparation to victims. This text should form the basis for the discussions (see Appendix 1.3).

Staff issues: A coherent prison policy model will also provide a better framework for the reorganisation, selection and training of staff, improving their working conditions, and allowing also higher expectations from them in return.

International standards: Belgium must urgently reinforce the internal and external legal position of prisoners, improve the material living conditions and prison regimes, and thoroughly reform the system of indeterminate internment of mentally ill offenders. Better cooperation with outside services will be necessary to achieve this aim.

The political will: Such will is required in order to achieve these reforms. Some of the proposed reforms require legislative changes and budgetary efforts which must be decided by Parliament. The Minister of Justice in 2003 seems personally convinced of the importance of prison reform. This is an important starting point.

CONCLUSION

The history of corrections in Belgium has been marked by large periods of political indifference, leaving prison policy to leading practitioners. The majority of the Belgian prisons were built in the 19th and beginning of the 20th century, based on the ideas of cellular segregation and religious reform. This architecture often limits the implementation of more communal regimes.

Reforms in Belgian prisons have been the result of three movements: the imprisonment of leading penologists in periods of turmoil (e.g., Ducpétiaux and Cornil); violent incidents in prison or in society (e.g., leading to restorative justice in detention and parole reform after the Dutroux case); and the growing presence of criminology-trained practitioners within the local and central prison administration.

At the political level, major legislative work has been prepared over the last few years, which could shape future policy: the first draft Prison

Act (see Appendix 1.3) regulating the internal legal position of prisoners, a reform of the external legal position of prisoners, and a comprehensive reform of the internment legislation. The future will show whether there is sufficient political will in the federal Government and Parliament to vote these drafts. At regional level, the most important development to watch will be the involvement of the regional communities in the preparation of the social reintegration of prisoners (see Appendix 1.4). Again, this will mainly depend on the political will of the regional Governments and Parliaments, but also on the coordination and integration of these initiatives into a coherent prison policy.

Key Terms and Concepts

Belgian model	Back door strategy	Belgian School of Thought
E. Ducpétiaux	Dutroux Case	Prison of Gent
Social defence	Restorative justice	

Discussion/Study Questions

(1) How did and still does prison overcrowding influence Belgian penal policy and prison practice?

(2) How did the *White Paper on Penal and Prison Policy* of 1996 influence prison policy in Belgium?

(3) Is, or can, electronic monitoring be a solution for prison over-crowding?

(4) Explain: there has been a rising attention to victims in Belgian penal policy.

(5) How does Belgium's adult correctional system compare to the system in your country?

Helpful Web-links

Belgium Government:
   http://www.fgov.be/.

Belgian Ministry of Justice:
    http://www.just.fgov.be/index_fr.htm.

National Institute of Statistics:
    http://www.statbel.fgov.be/home_en.htm.

Belgian Police:
    http://www.poldoc.be/.

REFERENCES

Ancel, M. (1966 [3rd ed., 1981]). *La Défence Sociale nouvelle. Un mouvement de politique criminelle humaniste.* Paris, FR: Ed. Cujas.

Beyens, K. and H. Tubex (2002). "Gedetineerden Geteld." (Prisoners counted.) In: S. Snacken (ed.), *Strafrechtelijk Beleid in Beweging.* (Penal policy on the move.) Brussels: VUBPress.

―― S. Snacken and C. Eliaerts (1993). *Barstende Muren. Overbevolkte Gevangenissen: Omvang, Oorzaken en Mogelijke Oplossingen.* (Bursting walls. Overcrowded prisons: size, causes and possible solutions.) (Vol. 26.) Antwerpen, Arnhem: Kluwer, Gouda Quint.

Byrne, J.M., A. Lurigio and J. Petersilia (eds.), (1992). *Smart Sentencing: The Emergence of Intermediate Sanctions.* London, UK: Sage Publications.

Commission "Loi de Principes Concernant l'Administration Pénitentiaire et le Statut Juridique des Détenus" (2000). *Avant-Projet de Loi de Principes concernant l'Administration Pénitentiaire et le Statut Juridique des Détenus.* Bruxelles: Ministère de la Justice.

Commission "Tribunaux de l'Application des Peines Statut Juridique Externe des Détenus et Fixation de la Peine," (2003). *Rapport Final.* Bruxelles: Ministère de la Justice.

De Pauw, W. (2002). "Justitie onder invloed." (Justice under influence.) In: S. Snacken (ed.), *Strafrechtelijk Beleid in Beweging.* (Penal policy on the move.) Brussels: VUBPress.

De Waele, J.-P. (1990). *Daders van dodingen. Vergelijkende analyses.* (Killers. A comparative analysis.) (Vol.. 20.) Antwerpen: Kluwer Rechtswetenschappen.

European Committee for the Prevention of Torture and Inhuman or Degrading Treatment or Punishment (CPT), (2002). *Rapport au Gouvernement de la Belgique, CPT/inf (2002) 25.* Strasbourg, FR: Council of Europe.

—— (1998). *Rapport au Gouvernement de la Belgique CPT/inf. (98) 11*. Strasbourg, FR: Council of Europe.

—— (1994). *Rapport au Gouvernement de la Belgique, CPT/ Inf (94) 15*. Strasbourg, FR: Council of Europe.

FOD Justitie (2003). *Justitie in Cijfers 2003*. (Justice in numbers 2003). (http://www.juridat.be/img publi.pdf/318-NL.pdf.)

Howard, J. (1788). *Etat des Prisons, des Hôpitaux et des Maisons de Force, II Vol*. Paris.

Kaminski, D. (1999). "L'assignation à Domicile sous Surveillance Électronique: de Deux Expériences, l'autre. " *Revue de Droit Pénal et de Criminologie*, 5:626-653.

Ministre de la Justice (1996). *Politique pénale Exécution des peines: Note d'orientation*. (White Paper on Penal and Prison Policy.) Bruxelles, BEL: Ministère de la Justice.

Robert, L. and T. Peters (2003). "How Restorative Justice is Able to Transcend Prison Walls: A Discussion of the 'Restorative Detention' Project." In: E. Weitekamp and H.-J. Kerner (eds.), *Restorative Justice in Context: International Practice and Directions*. Devon, UK: Willan Publishing.

Rutherford, A. (1984). *Prisons and the Process of Justice*. London, UK: Heinemann.

Snacken, S. (2001). "Belgium." In: D. van Zyl Smit and F. Dünkel (eds.), *Imprisonment Today and Tomorrow. International Perspectives on Prisoners' Rights and Prison Conditions* (2nd ed.). Den Haag, London, and Boston: Kluwer Law International.

—— K. Beyens and H. Tubex (1995). "Changing Prison Populations in Western Countries: Fate or Policy." *European Journal of Crime, Criminal Law and Criminal Justice* 3(1):18-53.

—— and A. Raes (2001). *Onderzoek naar de Toepassing van de Voorlopige Hechtenis en de Vrijheid Onder Voorwaarden*. (Research on the application of remand detention and freedom under conditions.) Brussels: Vrije Universiteit Brussel, Ministerie van Justitie.

—— A. Raes, P. Verhaeghe, K. De Buck and K. D'Haenens (1997). *Kwantitatief onderzoek naar de Toepassing van de Voorlopige Hechtenis en de Vrijheid onder Voorwaarden*. (Quantitative research on the application of remand detention and freedom under conditions.) Brussels: Vrije Universiteit Brussel - Nationaal Instituut voor Criminalistiek en Criminologie.

—— and H. Tubex (1999). "Libération Conditionnelle et Opinion Publique." *Revue de Droit Pénal et de Criminologie* 52(5):33-52.

Tubex, H. (2002). "Dangerousness and Risk. From Belgian Positivism to New Penology." In: N. Hutton and C. Tata (eds.), *Sentencing and Society: International Perspectives*. Ashgate: Aldershot.

—— (2001). "Politique pénale en Belgique, répression sélective: 'sexe, drogue et violence.'" In: P. Mary and T. Papatheodorou (eds.), *Délinquance et Insécurité en Europe. Vers une Pénalisation du Social ou une Nouvelle Modèle de Justice? Actes des 2° et 3° Séminaires du Groupe Européen de Recherches sur la Justice Pénale Tenus à Corfou du 5 au 7 Octobre 1998 et du 3 au 5 Juin 1999*. Bruxelles: Bruylant.

—— and S. Snacken (1995). "L'évolution des Longues Peines, Aperçu International et Analyses des Causes." *Déviance et Société* 19(2):103-126.

Appendix 1.1: Prison Administration in Belgium

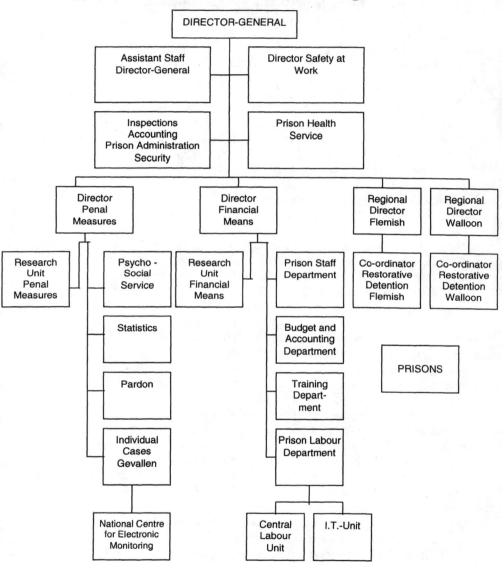

Appendix 1.2: Third Report of the European Committee on the Prevention of Torture in Belgian Prisons (2001)
(CPT/Inf [2002] 25)

Three prisons were visited during the third visit by CPT to Belgium: a follow-up visit to the psychiatric unit of the prison of Lantin, a first visit to the prisons of Antwerp (remand prison) and Andenne (sentenced long-term prisoners). In the psychiatric unit of Lantin, no improvements were found compared to the earlier visit in 1997: the situation concerning the infrastructure, staff, level of care and situation of the patients was described as unacceptable. As similar problems were encountered in the prisons of Antwerp and Andenne, CPT resorted to the "immediate observations" allowed under art.8§5 of the European Convention on the Prevention of Torture, requiring a solution by the Belgian Government within three months. The Government has since closed the unit in Lantin and plans to regroup mentally ill offenders in selected prisons, where staff levels and quality should reach the norms of outside society. In its answer to CPT, the Government states that this will require more financial means and additional training of staff, without however giving any formal promises in this regard.

In the remand prison of Antwerp, 546 prisoners were held at the time of the CPT visit in facilities with a rated capacity of 390 places; 60% of the prisoners were foreigners, representing 40 different nationalities. In Andenne, 377 prisoners were held in a rated capacity of 400 places, with 40% foreigners, a majority of whom were Moroccans. Very few complaints of violence by staff were heard by CPT in Antwerp — despite the serious overcrowding — relations between inmates and staff were even rather good. However, there were many allegations of violence between prisoners of different nationalities in both prisons. In Antwerp the governors and prison guards were actively involved in attempts at reducing conflicts and violence, but this was only true for the governors and a minority of prison guards in Andenne. As a result, racketeering, extortion and blackmail between prisoners seemed to rule the prison.

Material conditions were acceptable in both prisons, except for the overcrowding in Antwerp (a renovated Ducpétiaux prison, while Andenne was built recently). The level of activities offered to the prisoners was however totally insufficient. In Antwerp, this was mainly due to the 19th century infrastructure and high level of overcrowding. In Andenne however, 60% of these long-term prisoners had no activities or prison labour, and hence no income.

The level of health care was unacceptable in Antwerp, where 32 prisoners were seen by the medical doctor in exactly 40 minutes! There was one psychiatrist for six hours a week (including travel time) for 69 mentally ill offenders. In Andenne, there was no psychiatrist at all.

As in both earlier visits, CPT found quantitative staffing levels and training of staff grossly insufficient. It also repeated its earlier criticisms on the lack of legal protection for prisoners in Belgium. As the Draft Prison Act has integrated all criticisms of CPT in its reforms, its swift discussion and adoption in parliament is recommended. Finally, the delays and uncertainties relating to the new parole procedure were found to be the source of high levels of stress and anxieties among the long term prisoners in Andenne, resulting in individual forms of auto- and hetero-aggression, and one serious riot in 2001. A review of this parole procedure is recommended. This has recently been finalised by the "Commission on the External Legal Position of Prisoners" (Commission "Tribunaux de l'Application des Peines, Statut Juridique Externe des Détenus et Fixation de la Peine," 2003).

Appendix 1.3: First Draft Prison Act
(Commission "Loi de Principes concernant l'Administration Pénitentiaire et le Statut Juridique des Détenus," 2000)

The basic principles underlying the Draft are of a legal and a penological nature.

Legal principles:

(1) the content of the administration of a measure or sentence of detention should be laid down in legislation and is hence of the competence of Parliament;

(2) such legislation should recognize the continued legal citizenship of prisoners: the recognition of fundamental rights is the rule, limits to such rights are the exception and must be explicitly enumerated in legislation, justified by a legitimate purpose and proportionate to that purpose;

(3) hence a code of subjective rights for prisoners during their detention should be elaborated.

Penological principles:

(1) the aims of the imprisonment must be made explicit: they must form the guidelines for decision making in practice, not only concerning individual prisoners, but also for the reorganisation of the Prison Service, policies concerning prison staff, infrastructure etc.;

(2) the execution of sentences must be allowed a relative autonomy from sentencing: the aims of the criminal law correspond with different priorities at different levels of the criminal justice system. Whatever the aims of imprisonment may have been at the level of sentencing (retribution, general prevention, incapacitation), these cannot be regarded as having automatically determined the manner in which the sentence of imprisonment must be executed;

(3) the aims of the execution of imprisonment are prevention of harm by the detention, reparation towards the victim and social reintegration. The first is seen as an absolute prerequisite for any other aim and refers to the detrimental effects of imprisonment following from the modifications suffered in total institutions, the development of prison subcultures and the loss of identity and autonomy. They must be countered as much as possible by fostering the legal position of the prisoner, by maximal normalisation of daily prison life, by opening prisons to outside society and by developing individual detention plans that aim at an early release. Reparation and social reintegration refer to activities and services which are offered to the prisoner to meet his needs as much as possible, but are not imposed on him

The basic principles in this Draft are hence the principles of respect for the prisoner, of participation by the prisoner (in his detention plan, in consultative bodies) and of normalisation of prison regimes.

✦

Appendix 1.4: Disappearing Categories of Prisoners

Since the 1990s, some specific categories of prisoners, such as vagrants, illegal immigrants, youngsters and Jehovah's witnesses, have been gradually disappearing from prison. However, for a long time, these categories supplied a considerable amount of prisoners in the total Belgian prison population.

Vagrancy has only been decriminalized since 1993. Following the Social Defence philosophy (Act 1891), vagrants were perceived as dangerous because they were assumed to commit crimes in order to survive. In practice, these people found a refuge in prison which was not available elsewhere. In more recent times, they usually lived under a relatively free regime and tried to work in prison in order save some money to be released. Now considered to be amongst the least dangerous prisoners, they often got jobs which required some confidence, such as distributing the meals into the cells in closed prisons or working outside the walls in open prisons. Until the 1980s, vagrants made up around 15% of the total prison population (1981: N=865). Since 1981 their number has decreased steadily, and in 1991 they only made up 7% of the total prison population (N=435). Now only a few vagrants still remain in prison, mainly because they cannot adapt to the special homes in outside society.

Illegal immigrants, who have not committed a crime but do not have valid residence permits, previously also landed in prison. Throughout the 1980s there were on average 60 illegal immigrants in prison on a daily basis. At the end of the '80s and the first half of the '90s, their number increased considerably (daily prison population between 200 and 250 prisoners; number of incarcerations between 2,500 and 4,500). In the mid-1990s, they were transferred to special closed centres for illegal immigrants, where they must stay until a decision concerning their expulsion is made. However, if they cause trouble in these closed centres, they still can be — and are — transferred to prison.

Until 1994, *delinquent juveniles or juveniles in danger* (under 18 years old) could by means of an exceptional measure be placed for up to 15 days in prison, if the youth judge could not find a suitable youth institution to hold them. This emergency imprisonment of minors in adult prisons was greatly contested. In 1988, Belgium was even reprimanded by the European Court for Human Rights for this emergency measure, which was applied 11 times in one year towards one juvenile, obviously without the intent to bring him before the competent authority or to provide specific education (Arrest Bouamar, EHRM 29 February 1988). As a result, the abolition of this provisional custody was promulgated in 1994, but temporarily postponed due to lack of sufficient closed capacity in juvenile educational institutions. Restricted in 1994 to juveniles over 14 years of age suspected of having committed an offence, this possibility to imprison juveniles in adult prisons was finally abolished on 1 January 2002. As the lack of sufficient closed capacity in juvenile institutions had not been resolved since 1994, a special federal closed institution for minors was opened (the so-called "Everberg-prison") on March 1, 2002. This prison has been established in an unprecedented speed and is generally considered to be a symbolic political measure, to hush up popular emotions on youth crime.

Finally, another category that has disappeared from Belgian prisons are the *Jehovah's Witnesses,* who refused to do military service. Consequently, they were sent to prison for what would have been the period of their military service. In most cases they were treated as trustee inmates and did jobs around the prison. Since the abolishment of military service in the 1990s, they have also disappeared from the prisons.

NOTES

1. All three authors are professors at the Department of Criminology, Vrije Universiteit Brussels. Contact address: Pleinlaan 2, 1050 Brussels, Belgium. E-mail: <Sonja.Snacken@vub.ac.be>, <Kristel.Beyens@vub.ac.be>, <Hilde.Tubex@vub.ac.be>.

2. As expressed by Léon Cornil (1882-1962), professor of criminal law at the Université Libre de Bruxelles and General Prosecutor at the Supreme Court (*Cour de Cassation*).

3. The work of this commission resulted in a preliminary draft of legislation: *"Projet de loi relatif à l'internement des délinquants atteints d'un trouble mental. Projet de loi modifiant les lois relatives à la libération conditionnelle et modifiant la loi du 26 juin 1990 relative à la protection de la personne des malades mentaux"* (2003).

4. He went to a spaghetti-dinner organized for the surviving victims who had been discovered in M. Dutroux's cellar.

5. Until recently, only criminologists (which is a separate degree in Belgian universities) or professionals already working in a prison could participate in selection exams for prison governor.

6. The term "open" therefore does not refer — as in some other countries — to the fact that prisoners are allowed to leave the prison to work in outside society: this possibility exists in Belgium as "semi-detention," but is organized from closed prisons.

7. More details on the evolution of the prison population can be found in Beyens, Snacken and Eliaerts (1993) and Beyens and Tubex (2002).

8. For more details on the evolution of long-term prisoners from an international point of view, see Tubex and Snacken (1995).

9. We note in passing that Belgium was one of the last Western European countries to legally abolish the death penalty, in 1996. Apart for crimes during the Second World War, the death penalty had, however, not been carried out for more than 100 years.

10. We prefer to use average daily data, but these are not available for the last six years. The use of data on a certain date can give a misleading picture since they only refer to the situation on that moment. Calculations are based on the average daily prison population.

11. We thank Ralf Bas, Director of the National Center for Electronic Monitoring, for providing us with the most recent information on electronic monitoring in Belgium.

12. Ministerial circular letter nr. 1670.IX, November 26, 1997.

13. Ministerial circular letter nr. 1683/IX, March 27, 1998.

14. In the near future, experiments with continuous tracking (cf. Global Positioning Systems (GPS)) will be started.

15. Ministerial circular letter nr. 1692/IX, November 28, 1998.

16. These are the same contra-indications as defined in the law on conditional release.

17. Entire or partial exemption from contributing to the costs has, however, always been provided.

18. Except from a guarantee of 124 euros.

19. Until that time, everything was organized from the prison of St. Gillis (Brussels).

20. Ministerial circular letter nr. 1727, April 12, 2001.

21. Cf. the long-lasting strike of the prison guards as a protest against overcrowding in May 2003.

22. Academics such as Lode Walgrave, Tony Peters, and Ivo Aertsen, all from the Catholic University of Leuven, have been actively involved in promoting the ideals of restorative justice in penal theory and practice.

23. Cf. Ministerial Circular Letter, no. 1719 of October 4th, 2000. Most of these consultants are criminologists.

24. Contrary to the provisional finding of the European Commission of Human Rights.

CHAPTER 2.
CANADIAN ADULT CORRECTIONS: THE (RE)EVOLVING PROCESS

by

John A. Winterdyk

Department of Justice Studies
Mount Royal College, Calgary

BASIC FACTS ON CANADA

Area: 9,984,670 square kilometers of which 891,163 square kilometers is fresh water.

Population: 31.414 million in 2002. One of the lowest density ratios of any nation at 3.1 residents per square kilometer. Birth rate in 2000, 10.8/1,000 and death rate 7.2. The capital is Ottawa (population: 1.06 million in 2001), which is the fourth largest urban area. Other major cities include Montreal (3.4 million), Toronto (4.6 million), and Vancouver (1.9 million).

Demographics: Originally inhabited by indigenous peoples, Canada was then settled by Europeans, and it has grown recently into a multi-cultural and multi-ethnic nation. Canadians have an average of 12.7 years of education. The crime rate dropped from 9,309.9 offenses per 100,000 population in 1996 to 8,572.5 per 100,000 in 2001.

Climate: Given the expansiveness of Canada, it is no surprise that the country's climate varies widely by region and latitude. Winters range from cool to cold (average: 0° to -15°C) with summers ranging from mild to warm (average: 18° to 26°C).

Economy: Rich in natural resources such as: fishing, pulp and paper, gas and oil, farming, and mining (e.g., gold, silver, diamonds, coal, asbestos, uranium, hydroelectricity, etc). Unemployment rate was 7.5% in November, 2002; and gross domestic product grew a modest 0.3% over 2001.

Government: A federal parliamentary model and 10 provincial legislatures and three territories. Since November 2000, and for the third consecutive term, the Liberal Party has been the leading party. Other major parties include: The Canadian Alliance, New Democrats, and Bloc Quebecois. The ruling party can hold office for up to five years before calling an election.

★   ★   ★

"It is a lot safer to talk about the weather than it is to talk about criminal justice policy."

~ Ole Ingstrup, 1999

BRIEF HISTORY OF CANADIAN CORRECTIONS

Ever since the original four provinces (i.e., Ontario, Quebec, Nova Scotia, and New Brunswick) formed the Dominion of Canada in 1867, Canada has had a formal adult correctional system. But, not unlike many of the countries represented in this anthology, the system has evolved, or at least in principle, over the past 140-odd years. Canada's early correctional system was influenced by its primary European settlers, the English and the French. For example, based on England's **Bloody Code** (circa 1870s), the death penalty existed for some 350 offences; and in New France, now known as Quebec, there were some 11 legal methods of execution, of which hanging was the most common (Carrigan, 1991). While appearing extremely draconian, such practices were the norm in Europe.

Coinciding with the efforts of **John Howard** (1726-1790), the Sheriff of Bedford, and his historic book *The State of the Prisons in England and Wales* in 1777, penal reformers began to apply scientific methods to the administration of corrections. **Elizabeth Fry** (1780-1845), a wealthy Quaker matron, was also instrumental in forging correctional reforms —

especially for women. In fact, the *British Prison Act* of 1823 incorporated a number of her recommendations, such as the separation of male and female offenders, which also became part of Canadian correctional practices (Griffiths and Cunningham, 2000).

Until Confederation under the **British North America Act** (BNA Act) in 1867, there was little interest in social reform or rehabilitation — punishment was the norm (see Cayley, 1998). The BNA decreed that the legal system would be based on England's common law system and that the correctional system would be divided — parole and penitentiaries to the federal government and the rest to the provinces (Erdhal, 2001). The passage of the first *Penitentiary Act* (1868) brought the prisons in Kingston (Ontario), St. John (New Brunswick) and Halifax (Nova Scotia) under federal jurisdiction, hence formalizing the federal-provincial distinction (see Box 2.1).

Box 2.1: Upper Fort Garry — The First Correctional Facility, and Kingston Penitentiary — The First Federal Prison

Although the last of five forts to have been built in the area around what is now the city of Winnipeg, Manitoba, the fort (initially called Fort Garry) was rebuilt in 1835 by Governor George Simpson after the first version was demolished. The "new" fort was called Upper Fort Garry after Nicholas Garry, an important director of the Hudson's Bay Company. Initially used as a fur trading post, it was later converted to a correctional facility, but it has also been used as an insane asylum.

In 1831, J.C. Thomson was appointed to help design a new federal prison. After visiting several different countries, he decided upon the Auburn system — or "silent associated system," in New York, which he considered embodied his ideas of order and morality. Kingston penitentiary became Canada's first federal prison. It opened on June 1, 1835 (and was the largest building in North America at the time) and is still operating today. The first warden of Kingston, Henry Smith, was renowned for his "reign of terror" in the prison in spite of the prison being modeled on "order and morality."

During its formative years, Canadian correctional philosophy was based on punishment for wrongdoings and on a philosophy of deterrence. However, there was also general support for reform, which was based on the theory of **social determinism** — i.e., that people broke the law because of their compromised social, economical, and/or personal circumstances. This perspective has become the backbone of the John Howard Society and the Elizabeth Fry Society (see Helpful Weblinks below).

With the passage of the BNA and under the influence of the humanitarian efforts of social reformers, corrections in Canada began to move (in principle) towards a system known as moral reformation which was premised on the philosophy of spiritual change through penitence — later known as the **reform model.** Unfortunately, there was a lack of political and economic support to fully implement the ideals of the model. Nevertheless, corrections in Canada continued to evolve.

The evolution of Canada's correctional system has been marked by a series of inquiries and/or commissions. These commissions have served to forge the direction that correctional practices, administration, and operations have taken over the years. Following is a brief summary of some of the major commissions and their recommendations.

- The **Brown Commission** emerged in the aftermath of complaints about Kingston penitentiary. George Brown, who founded the *Globe* newspaper and was an active social reformer, was asked to chair a commission charged with investigating the operation of prisons. In his first report, in 1848, Brown condemned the prison's use of corporal punishment, but not the structure of hard labour and a strict regime. In the second report, released in 1849, the commission recommended that: offender reform should be the major objective of incarceration; moral suasion should replace physical force; and government-run facilities should be subject to regular inspections (Beattie, 1977). While some have debated the impact of the Brown Commission, several years later the *Penitentiary Act* of 1851 and the *Prison Act* of 1857 contained many of its recommendations.

- In 1924, the Superintendent of Penitentiaries, W.S. Hughes, noted in his *Report on Prison Affairs* that prison reform still had no clear direction in Canada. Yet, while still subscribing to the reform model, Canada saw the emergence of an inmate classification system (i.e., a process by which inmates are subdivided into

groups based on a variety of social, personal, and behavioral related characteristics), special facilities for young offenders, the
creation of industrial prison farms, and legislation for earned remission (i.e., based on "good" behavior an inmate could reduce
his or her sentence by up to one-third), and parole (Erdhal, 2001).

- The **Archambault Commission** (1936-1938) report was prepared in the aftermath of growing violence and unrest within
Canada's federal prisons. The commission is commonly acknowledged as marking the turning point in modern Canadian correctional reform. Under the direction of Justice Joseph Archambault,
the commission came up with 88 recommendations which left
virtually no aspect of the system unaddressed. Perhaps one of the
most striking conclusions of the report was that change could not
be effected through punishment. The commission recommended
that corrections should emphasize crime prevention, focus on rehabilitation, and deter prospective habitual offenders. The report
condemned existing correctional facilities for their lack of effective programming; a skewed emphasis on punishment; terrible
prison conditions; and a general lack of regard for inmate rights
and privileges. The report noted that with a recidivism rate of
70% of the offending population, this hardly spoke to any form
of success under the prevailing practices. While the report drew
considerable attention, the advent of World War II postponed any
constructive reforms. Yet, history would be witness to the enduring impact of Archambault Commission. For example, the report played a key role in Canada's decision to become an official
United Nations member on November 9, 1945, and many of the
recommendations were eventually embodied in the *Corrections and
Conditional Release Act* (CCRA) in 1992.

- The **Fauteux Report,** in 1953, brought a new series of recommendations under the direction of Justice Joseph Fauteux. In
many respects the Commission reinforced most of the ideas of
the Archambault Commission, concluding that the primary objective of corrections should be the rehabilitation of the offender.
This was to be accomplished through *retraining* and *reeducating* offenders. As Carrigan (1991) observed, this is the first time the notion of "corrections" became part of the ideology in Canada. The

report spawned the development of specialized aftercare programs for addicts, sex offenders and inmates suffering from various psychological disorders. In addition, other initiatives that emerged in the aftermath of the report included: the construction of new medium-security institutions; mandatory review of parole in which every inmate serving a sentence of imprisonment of two years or more automatically has his or her case reviewed after a fixed period of time; increased use of pre-sentence reports; and the creation of a new national federal parole board. The report marked the arrival of the **medical model** of corrections in Canada, which embraced the notion that the problem of criminality was somehow associated with the constitutional make-up of the individual; the *Penitentiary Act* was amended in 1961 to establish new procedures for the operation of federal prisons. In addition, in 1963 a plan to construct 10 new penitentiaries across Canada also reflected the Fauteax Committee's vision. This was followed by the **Ouimet Report** in 1965 which, among other recommendations, called for "community corrections." It stated that unless "there are reasons to the contrary, the correction of the offender should take place in the community, where the acceptance of a treatment relationship is more natural, where family and social relationships can be maintained" (p.277).

- The **Carson Report,** in 1984, was the result of an initiative by the Solicitor General of Canada to review the management of Correctional Service Canada (CSC) in the aftermath of a high incidence of suicide and violence within the system. The report found that due to excessive centralization of control at the federal level, correctional facilities lacked autonomy, and most facilities were being poorly run — at least in accordance with the mandate of CSC. For example, the report found that wardens tended to be assessed on the degree to which they followed the directives from their regional or national headquarters, rather than on the performance of their institutions. Today, nearly 20 years later, wardens continued to report difficulty in balancing the demands of the public, the inmates, their staff, and CSC. All this in spite of a 1996 initiative in which, responding to a major prison incident, the Arbour Commission (see below) called for the improvement of inmate treatment and training programs. The report also addressed special needs offenders (e.g., mentally disturbed and Native offenders, but made no mention of female offenders) as requiring increased support. The creation of **CORCAN** Corporation was the first time inmates were allowed to make products that were sold outside prisons. (Their motto is "in the business of employability.") Ironically, many of the concerns voiced in 1984 still persist today. But, the **Daubney Report**, in 1988, was instrumental in the expansion of treatment programs for sexual offenders, dangerous offenders, and substance abuse programming. This action was in response to one of the Report's recommendations which called for the need to reduce reliance on imprisonment as a sanction. Yet, despite the increased allocation of resources to such treatment programs, the risk for reoffending among the special needs populations remained relatively unchanged!

- In partial response to the "failure" of specialized programming, the 1980s was witness to another shift in correctional ideology. The **opportunistic model** was the brainchild of the Subcommittee on the Penitentiary System of Canada in the late 1970s, which argued that the offender is ultimately responsible for his/her behaviour. With this ideological shift, corrections placed the responsibility for reform onto the shoulders of the offender. Corrections would provide the programs but the inmates were responsible for choosing whether they wanted to participate or not. By the early 1990s, as Duguid (2000) observes, Canada experienced yet another ideological shift in its correctional mandate. The shift came as a result of the new *Mission of the Correctional Service of Canada* in 1991. It essentially called for a blending of the opportunistic model with the old rehabilitation model.

- The **Arbour Commission,** in 1996, marked another melancholy event in Canadian corrections. The commission, chaired by Justice Louise Arbour, was in response to a series of tragic events involving the mistreatment of female offenders that occurred in the Prison for Women (P4W) in Kingston. Though the commission found that corrections officers had violated prison regulations and Canadian law, the CSC took no overt action to address the misconduct of the officers. Rather, the CSC blamed the inmates for the event! P4W was closed in 1997.

It is perhaps clear from the above synopsis that corrections in Canada has not been static. It has evolved largely in response to social, economic, and situational circumstances, and even dominant theoretical perspectives. And more recently, policy has evolved in response to what Anthony Bottoms (1995) termed **penal populism** (i.e., generally defined as "the promotion of policies which are electorally attractive" [Roberts et al., 2003:5]). For example, as late as 1930 many Canadians still believed that crime was hereditary, and that habitual offenders should be sterilized. These circumstances follow closely the conventional theoretical ebb and flow of criminal justice ideology, but they give no concrete direction as to what critical criminology[1] and/or more recent postmodern[2] ideas have focused on. The basic value of these perspectives is that our past correctional practices have failed to realistically assess and/or address the true causes of crime. So while Canada has moved towards a more humane approach and one that attempts to embrace principles of reform, rehabilitation, and reintegration, it can hardly be argued that the evolution of corrections in Canada has been based on sound reasoning (see Future Direction below). In fact, it has been argued that Canada has evolved a correctional system that is analogous to "penal saturation" (see Brodeur, 1996) — we continue to find new ways within a non-critical framework to expand and reinforce the dominant class interests or follow popular opinion, which is commonly recognized as being ill informed (see, generally, Gamberg and Thomson, 1984; Roberts, 2001; Roberts et al., 2003). These interests and views are, as Brodeur (1996:343) suggests, organically linked to the past, which hinders us from identifying "the signs of a possible transformation in penology." Hence, the various commissions and scholarly reports over the years have been largely reactive, and the agreements to coordinate and facilitate the delivery of correctional services have continued to be plagued by the problems that positivist and classical ideologies have long been criticized for. That is, the solution to Canada's correctional woes lies neither solely with the individual nor with the law and society. The end result is that Canadian corrections continues to be subject to various challenges (see below), and its ongoing inability to positively affect the convicted offender has led to periodic attempts to reform and revise its correctional strategies. Nevertheless, today corrections in Canada has been heralded, by traditionalists, as a model worthy of replicating (see Box 2.2).

Box 2.2: Namibia and Others Look to CSC for Guidance

In 2002, four Correctional Service Canada staff spent three-months on a teaching assignment in the African nation of Namibia. The staff members delivered four training programs — two each for correctional officers and parole officers, so as to provide them with the skills to address the administration and handling of their correctional facilities. For example, although this small nation only has 5,000 inmates, most of whom have only committed minor crimes, there are high AIDS and tuberculosis rates among the prison population. The Canadian staff, as part of an agreement between CSC and Namibian correction authorities, will provide assistance in shifting from traditional methods of prison management to a case management approach. The Namibian Commissioner was quoted as saying: "we have a vision of becoming one of the best correctional services in Africa, and CSC is helping us to reach our goal" (Rankin, 2002:20). At the time of preparing this chapter, CSC had just finished participating in the Central Europe Justice Cooperation Project which included providing presentations on conditional release, restorative justice, parole, Aboriginal issues, and institutional reintegration programs. See Chapter 8 for further discussion of the Namibian correctional system.

CORRECTIONS TODAY

"'It's chaos,' he said of provincial jails, 'it's a zoo.'"
~ Quebec prison lawyer commenting of the idea of allowing civilians to pay to spend a day in jail (Peritz, 2003)

The plight of the correctional practices in the past might, in part, be explained by a widely accepted observation that public knowledge of today's correctional system continues to be "poor and biased towards a negative view of the system" (Roberts, 2001:61). This in spite of the fact that there is widespread support for the concept of rehabilitation among the public. For example, a recent report noted how judges in Nova Scotia, who sentence criminals to house arrest, convey a "misperception that the sentence is imposed and (the offender) can just walk away and forget about it and just carry on as before" (Fraser, 2002:4). This apparent incongruity is attributable to the fact that corrections remains the least understood element of the criminal justice system and is sometimes even referred to as the "hidden element" of the justice system (Schmalleger et al., 2000).

Since the late 1970s, there have been concerns about the effectiveness of the rehabilitative model (see Gamberg and Thomson, 1984). The ideological pendulum began to swing towards *community-based treatment* for offenders and a "deinstitutionalization" trend. As indicated below, the use of parole, probation, and community-based alternatives has increased. In addition, there has been a dramatic growth in the use of a case management approach (i.e., a process by which the needs and risk of inmates are matched with available services and resources) in what Ekstedt and Jackson (1996:6) refer to as "clinical criminology." The result has been a concerted effort to develop more effective assessment and treatment programs and increased attention to victims of crime. Yet, the actuality of such an approach being effectively employed remains debatable (see below).

Administrative Process

In accordance with the BNA, all three levels of government (i.e., federal, provincial, and territorial) share responsibility for the administration of custodial and non-custodial dispositions. Offenders who are remanded into custody pending trial or sentencing, and inmates serving custodial sentences of less than two years, are the responsibility of the provincial and territorial governments. The facilities at this level are typically referred to as "prisons."

Meanwhile, the federal government of Canada is responsible for administering sentences which involve two or more years of imprisonment. The federal government also manages the institutions (referred to as "penitentiaries") for such offenders, as well as being responsible for the supervision of offenders who are either on some form of statutory release or have been conditionally released on parole (Motiuk, 2001).

The *Report of the Auditor General of Canada to the House of Commons* (1997) articulates the importance of **public sector administration and**

its relation to politics. As Mitchell and Sutherland (1999) note, the federal government's role is to provide services and apply policy that reflects the social and political climate. Hence, political forces can, and do, shape the management environment of senior administrators. In fact, a number of scholars argue that all correctional organizations are public service organizations and operate in accordance with the principles of public administration (e.g., see Roberts et al., 2003).

Table 2.1: Sample of Missions, Mandates and Visions of Canadian Correctional Agencies

Jurisdiction	Statement
Federal	The Correctional Service of Canada, as part of the criminal justice system (CJS) and respecting the rule of law, contributes to the protection of society by actively encouraging and assisting offenders to become law-abiding citizens, while exercising reasonable, safe, and humane control.
Provincial (representative examples)	Alberta Correctional Services is committed to managing with openness and integrity while being accountable to the people of Alberta; constructive change through initiative and innovation; a climate that promotes professionalism; respect in the workplace and excellence in correctional practices...providing offenders with assistance and opportunities to become law-abiding citizens; and the right of victims and the community to participate in the justice process.
	The Ontario Correctional Services Division contributes to the protection of the public safety through effective supervision of the adult and youth offenders in community and institutional settings.
Territorial	The North West Territories Corrections Division, as part of the criminal justice system, manages offenders in the least restrictive manner required to protect society and assists offenders through restorative justice and culturally relevant programs to become healthy, law-abiding members of the community.
	Both the Yukon's and Nunavut's correctional agendas are under development.

Source: Adapted from Motiuk 2001:70-71.

Correctional agencies across Canada, whether federal, provincial, or territorial, share one common purpose: to "contribute to public protection." As Motiuk (2001) illustrates, this aim is well entrenched in the daily activities of the various jurisdictional organizations. Table 2.1 shows a cross-section of how the aim is articulated across the three levels of correctional agencies in Canada.

Since it is beyond the scope of this chapter to address the manner in which all levels of corrections in Canada are organized and structured, we will focus primarily on corrections at the federal level. This limitation is largely due to the fact that in Canada the provinces are responsible for providing their own information and data, which are not always readily accessible or comparable due to different provincial/territorial standards and management styles. However, under "Helpful Web-links" the reader will find a series of links to various provincial level correctional websites.

Policy and planning at the federal level reflect a close relationship between the law (i.e., Criminal Code of Canada) and the *Corrections and Correctional Release Act* (1992), which constitutes the primary force behind the planning and policy framework of CSC. Other key factors include the mission statement which reports on plans and priorities; core values (see Box 2.3) which represent the key results of commitment within CSC; guiding principles which are reflected as business plans; strategic objectives which are derived from a policy framework; the planning, reporting, and accountability structure which is based on directives from Ottawa; and corporate objectives, which are defined through annual departmental performance reports.

In terms of its organizational structure, CSC is a federal agency within the department of the Solicitor General of Canada. The Solicitor General Department is also responsible for overseeing several other criminal justice agencies and organizations. At the head, the senior executive officer of CSC is a Commissioner (in 2003 it was Lucie McClung — the first female Commissioner of Corrections in Canadian history). This individual is also a deputy minister in the Public Service of Canada and is directly accountable to the Solicitor General. Under the commissioner there are five Regional Deputy Commissioners, a Senior Deputy Commissioner at the National headquarters in Ottawa, various Assistant Commissioners ranging from communications to personnel and training, a Deputy Commissioner for female offenders, and a Director General, counsel who oversees legal services for CSC (see Figure 2.1). These administrators collectively oversee the operation of some 50-odd penitentiaries in the five major Regions (i.e., Atlantic, Quebec, Ontario, Prairies, and Pacific — see Table 2.2), 17 community correctional centres, 70-odd parole offices, and some 20 district offices (CSC, 2002). In addition, there are legal arrangements by which the three levels of corrections can exchange services between institutions and for the exchange of supervision services.

Box 2.3: Correctional Service of Canada Mission Statement, Role, and Core Values

Mission Statement: The CSC, as part of the criminal justice system and respecting the rule of law, contributes to the protection of society by actively encouraging and assisting offenders to become law-abiding citizens, while exercising reasonable, safe, secure and humane control.

Role: The Correctional Service of Canada (CSC) is the federal government agency responsible for administering sentences of a term of two years or more, as imposed by the court. CSC is responsible for managing institutions of various security levels and supervising offenders under conditional release in the community.

Core Values:

Core Value 1: We respect the dignity of individuals, the rights of all members of society, and the potential for human growth and development.

Core Value 2: We recognize that the offender has the potential to live as a law-abiding citizen.

Core Value 3: We believe that our strength and our major resource in achieving our objectives is our staff and that human relationships are the cornerstone of our endeavor.

Core Value 4: We believe that the sharing of ideas, knowledge, values and experience, nationally and internationally, is essential to the achievement of our mission.

Core Value 5: We believe in managing the Service with openness and integrity and we are accountable to the Solicitor General.

Note: These values are reasonably consistent with several of the key UN agreements that pertain to treatment and detention of offenders.

Source: CSC, 2002 (see for further details: http://www.csc-scc.gc.ca/text/ organize_e.shtml).

Figure 2.1: An Overview of Events in the Adult Correctional System

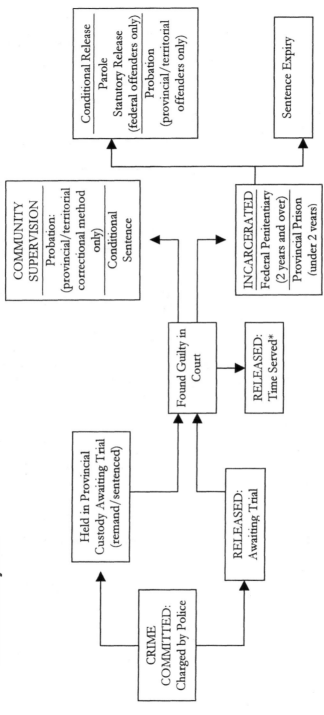

* An individual whose sentence approximates time already served in custody (i.e., while awaiting trial) is generally released by virtue of having already served his or her sentence.

Source: Canadian Centre for Justice Statistics "Adult Correctional Services in Canada 1996/1997," p.3 (figure reproduced).

Table 2.2: Inmate Classification, According to Security Level, April 2001*

Security	Men	%	Women	%	Aboriginals	%
Maximum	1709	14	32	9	360	16
Medium	7426	59	144	40	1348	62
Minimum	2580	21	160	44	375	17
Unclassified	715	6	24	7	111	5
TOTAL	12430	100	360	100	2194	100

Source: CSC, 2002.
Note: This table does not include 25 federal women offenders serving sentences in provincial institutions, who are classified according to provincial policies and procedures.
*Federal offenders represent 5% of the total number of persons placed into custody and approximately 8% of offenders supervised in the community.

In 2000/01, nearly $2.5 billion was spent on operating adult correctional services in Canada — a 1% increase over the previous year. The federal portion of corrections (i.e., salaries and benefits for custody and non-custody) and community supervision was (C)$1.3 billion (52% of total spending), while the territorial/provincial portion was $1.2 billion (48% of total spending). For all levels of adult corrections, the cost associated with operating corrections throughout Canada absorbed the second largest share of justice dollars, at 22%. (Police activities represented 61% of the total spending budget, with courts at 9%, legal aid plans at 5%, and criminal prosecution at 3%.) Consistently, the largest proportion of corrections expenditures over the years has been for custodial services (approximately 73%), followed by community supervision services (13%) and headquarters and central services (12%). Between 1990 and 2000, the total spending in constant dollars at the federal level decreased some 3%, while provincial/territorial spending rose 6%.

As can be seen from this brief description, the administration of corrections in Canada is three-tiered (i.e., federal, provincial, and territorial), with each level being responsible for a different aspect of corrections. Yet, in accordance with the Criminal Code and correctional legislation, the system is somewhat fluid, allowing offenders to be transferred (i.e., *cascaded*) from one jurisdictional level to another.

Aside from the formal levels of corrections in Canada, there are a number of private, non-profit sector organizations that play a significant role in the management and administration of corrections at all levels of formal jurisdiction. In fact, Canada has a rich history of involvement of private, nonprofit organizations in the delivery of correctional programs and services.

There are a wide range of private, non-profit organizations but some of the more active agencies include the John Howard Society, the Elizabeth Fry Society, the Salvation Army, the St. Leonard's Society, and a host of Aboriginal organizations such as the Native Clan Organization in Regina, Saskatchewan and Mi'kmaq Justice Institute in Sidney, Nova Scotia (Griffiths and Cunningham, 2000).

In essence, these programs/organizations tend to cater to the needs and rights of the offender, and attempt to provide reintegrative and support services such as vocational employment programs for offenders, supervision, court workers' programs, and other relevant services. These efforts are consistent with principle number 60 of the 1977 UN *Standard*

Minimum Rules for the Treatment of Prisoners, which calls for the participation of community and social institutions in the treatment of offenders.

In many cases, the *Standard Minimum Rules* have become the voice for correctional reforms. So while the three levels of corrections are firmly established as bureaucracies, the public and non-government organizations play a significant role in forging correctional policies and practices. Yet, the relationship between the government and non-government correctional operations is strained as the public remains relatively naïve about corrections. Fortunately, CSC personnel have become more proactive in informing the public through the media and public forums about the scope, mandate, and success of corrections. Nevertheless, corrections in Canada remains something of a *decoupled organization,* which Stojkovic et al. (1998:64) define as: organizations which "face multiple environments and interests with each environment at different organizational levels." While there are broad overriding principles of administration, the decentralization of corrections continually results in friction between federal, provincial, territorial and public interests (see section above on "Administration" and below on "Issues Confronting Corrections Today").

Profile of the Correctional Population

Beginning in the early 1990s, the adult correctional population (i.e., custody and non-custody) began to increase as a result of Canada's somewhat conservative "get-tough" stance on serious offenders and the expansion of alternative options for less serious offenders. This is reflective of a "net-widening" effect. In accordance with most of the other articles presented in this anthology, this does not appear to be a unique trend. However, what is disconcerting is the fact that in spite of the various initiatives that have been undertaken, the correctional population has not declined. We appear to have come to accept the rates of incarceration and the expanding scope of correctional practices as normal. This trend is slowly coming to define what kind of nation and what kind of people we have/are becoming.

In federal institutions during the year 2000-2001, it cost about $66,381 to incarcerate a male versus $110,473 to incarcerate a female offender. The daily cost to incarcerate one inmate in a provincial institution in 2000/01 was (C)$137.44 versus $189.21 to incarcerate a federal inmate. This compares to approximately $16,800 for supervising a federal and provincial/territorial offender on parole or statutory release during 2000-2001 (CSC, 2002). The 2002-2003 CSC budget totaled $1.468 billion — almost a 6% increase over 2000-2001.

At the federal level, some 47% of the men incarcerated in 2000-2001 were between the ages 20-34, versus 56% of women between the same ages. Some 62% of the male offenders were serving their first penitentiary sentence, versus 82% of women offender serving their first penitentiary sentence. Also at the federal level, Aboriginal people represented approximately 15% of the federal offender population but only about 3% of the general Canadian population. Proportionately, female Aboriginal offenders were more commonly represented in federal facilities than male Aboriginal offenders (i.e., 23 vs. 18%) (CSC, 2002). Some 25% of federal inmates in custody were homicide offenders, another 19% were sex offenders, some 36% had a robbery conviction, and 21% were drug offenders.[3] In 2001-2002, the recidivism rate for those on supervised conditional release was 9% and the majority of their offences were non-violent in nature.

Tables 2.3 to 2.5 provide some descriptive details on admissions and length of time served at the three levels. The data are aggregated and do not reflect geographical variations or variation in sentencing practices. For example, in Quebec 59% of sentences came under provincial or municipal statutes while in Nova Scotia 38% of the sentences were for failure to comply with an order (Carriere, 2003).

Although there are exceptions to the general rule, Canada attempts to house one offender in a cell. This is consistent with principle 9(1) of the UN's *Standard Minimum Rules of the Treatment of Prisoners*. Yet, in 2001-02 double bunking accounted between 20% to 25% of the total number of inmates. In the 27th Annual Report of the Correctional Investigation (2003) it was noted CSC was making progress in eliminating double-bunking, but that it will likely be unrealistic to entirely eliminate the problem.

Table 2.3: Length of Time Served, Provincial and Territorial Releases from Sentenced Custody and Remand, 2001/02

	Sentenced custody	Remand
31 days or less	50	80
>1-3 months	22	11
>6-12 months	8	3
> 12 months	5	0

Source: adapted from Carriere (2003).

Table 2.4: Length of Aggregate Sentences on Admission of Federal Custody, 1990/00 and 2001/02

	1999/00	2001/02
2 years to < 3 years	43	47
3 years to <4 years	22	22
4 years to <5 years	12	11
5 years to 10 years	16	14
10 years or longer – excl. life	3	2
life	4	4

Source: adapted from Carriere (2003).

Table 2.5: Total Daily Counts of Offenders in the Correctional System vs. Admission to Correctional Services in 2001/02*

	Number	Percent of total count
Probation	101,915/84,852	66/24
Provincial parole	1,388/2,309	1/1
Conditional sentence	11,941/18,578	8/5
Community release (National Parole Board)	7,627/7,324	5/2
Prov./terr. sentenced	10,931/82,875	7/23
Remand	7,980/126,060	5/35
Other temporary detention	351/3,395	<1/9
Federal custody	12,811/7,611	8/2

* From 1994/95 to 2001/02 the overall incarceration rate declined from 153 per 100,000 to 133 per 100,000 (-13%).

Source: Adapted from Carriere (2003).

ISSUES CONFRONTING CORRECTIONS TODAY

While CSC and its provincial and territorial counterparts work hard at trying to provide correctional services that are reflective of their mandate as well as international standards, correctional services in Canada share many of the challenges that the other elements of the criminal justice system encounter. Common concerns include: policies and programs (e.g., to fight drugs, eliminate double bunking, training initiatives, sexual harassment, use of force, strip search policy, inmate grievance procedures, etc.) that are of undetermined effectiveness (see Annual Report of the Correctional Investigators, 2003). The irony is that many of these issues were identified some 20 years ago by Gamberg and Thomson (1984) in their book *The Illusion of Prison Reform: Corrections in Canada.* As they conclude: reform cannot take place when it is "disconnected from reform of the larger society" (p.142). That is to say, since correctional practices are reflective of social attitudes, significant reforms need to be made within the context of social acceptability in order to gain acceptance. For example, various community-based programs and halfway houses have met with public resistance because of general misunderstanding on the part of the public and most government legislators of criminal justice/correctional matters.

Corrections operates in an environment that is financially cumbersome (see above). In addition, as with virtually every other component of the criminal justice system, correctional services operate in a reactive rather than proactive manner. Therefore, they also tend to be subject to the effects of national social, economic, public, and political events and pressures more so than pressures emanating from any international agreement.

Aside from the challenges that Canadian corrections shares with its criminal justice counterparts, correctional services have their own unique challenges. The following represent an overview of some of the more pressing demands on corrections in Canada.

- *Protecting the rights of victims.* It seems almost ironic, but yet reflective of Canada's ideological approach to corrections, that until the early 1990s only limited attention had been paid to the perspective of victims in international human rights and humanitarian law. However, in signing the Rome Statute of the International Criminal Court (located in The Hague in the Netherlands) on July 17, 1998, Canada has in principle committed itself to embracing the rights of the victim in a broader social context. In recent years, a growing number of correctional agencies, in particular in the Province of New Brunswick, have begun informing victims about inmate passes from their institutions (e.g., "temporary absences"), and assisting in preventing the harassment of victims. Victim statements are also sometimes used to provide helpful details on the background and social history of an offender. These ideas are expressed, to varying degrees, in the UN's *Declaration of Basic Principles of Justice for Victims of Crime and Abuse of Power,* adopted Nov. 1985.

- *Identifying effective alternatives to incarceration.* In 2002, the Correctional Service of Canada and the Church Council on Justice and Corrections joined forced to start producing the publication *Satisfying*

Justice. It is a booklet that promotes credible alternatives to incarceration and is intended to mobilize more effective strategies for changes to justice and sentencing in Canada and elsewhere. They claim to want to "get tough" on crime by listening to the victims and focus on community-based responses. The impact of the publication remains to be seen, but it is representative of corrections moving towards a restorative justice model and a more community-based system. Programs that have been developed for offenders range from: teaching living skills, providing cognitive skills training and literacy programs, and family violence prevention programs, among others. Most of these programs share a common theme — that is, they offer offenders an opportunity to address what are considered primary risk areas. For example, "while 5-10% of the general population have learning disabilities, the figure among inmates in federal institutions is 25%" (cited in Ostiguy, 2000). While some of these measures compliment the standards set out in the UN's *Standard Minimum Rules for the Treatment of Prisoners,* there is no direct reference made to these standards.

- *Increasing community awareness and involvement.* A 1999 public survey revealed that some 82% of Canadians believed that a key priority of the government is to protect them from crime and abuse. But, as noted earlier, the public's knowledge about corrections is limited. Efforts are being made to understand how the public perceives the causes of crime and how to better inform citizens as to the realities of corrections. In recent a number of public awareness initiatives have been created to ensure that CSC efforts are understood. They include such programs as: Restorative Justice Week, Speakers' Kit, and National Crime Prevention Week, among others.

- *Improving offender risk/ need assessment and management.* In 1997, CSC held a major conference from which emerged a number of recommendations that addressed offender reintegration and risk management. The objective of the conference mirrored the Core Values of CSC. Again, it is too early to note whether or not the recommendations have been (effectively) implemented. Whether Canada has the resources, support, or inclination to fully actualize such an initiative remain suspect. However, CSC is optimistic that utilizing such an approach will facilitate the reintegration potential of offenders in a fruitful manner.

In the late 1990s, CSC undertook a major initiative to determine "what works" in corrections. Based on the resulting meta-analysis of the efficiency of correctional rehabilitation programs, Gendreau et al. (2000:13) concluded that "when it comes to reducing individual offender recidivism, the 'only game in town' are appropriate cognitive-behavioural treatments[4] which embody known principles of effective intervention." Somewhat ironically, an area that has shown promise but which has received considerably less attention has been the "personal-interpersonal-community-reinforcement perspective" (PIC-R), developed by Don Andrews to evaluate the employability of released offenders. Yet, Gillis (2002) found that employment interventions have been superseded by cognitive skills programming although there is a history of data supporting the merits of using employment intervention as an effective indicator of risk assessment. For example, CSC has a number of instruments it uses to determine reintegration potential (e.g., the Custody Rating Scale, the Statistical Information on Recidivism, etc.) but these instruments are at best only moderately effective. A recent study reveals that approximately 60% of the offending population between the ages of 18-25 have at least one or more prior convictions (Thomas et al., 2003).

Again, while these initiatives are not directly driven or influenced by international agreements, Canada's efforts in this area are consistent with the guidelines set out in the *Convention of the Committee against Torture and other Cruel Inhuman or Degrading Treatment of Prisoners.*

- *Improving the services to and for female offenders.* At the "10th UN National Congress on the Prevention of Crime and the Treatment of Offenders," in 2000 in Vienna, a special workshop on the treatment of female offenders and women as victims was held. At the workshop it was noted that aside from the growing number of female offenders around the world, that major steps needed to be taken to address the needs and protect the rights of female offenders.

The issues and concerns identified during the workshop apply to Canada, where only about 2% of federal inmates are female and over half of them were housed in Kingston Penitentiary's P4W unit. In the aftermath of Louis Arbour's condemnatory report in the late 1990s on the plight of female offenders there are now a growing number of programs oriented toward the female offender. They include, among others: mother-child residential programs, a modified cognitive skill program, and programs for survivors of abuse and trauma. Again, as with the programs designed for male offenders, these programs relate to the needs of most of the female offenders as they reflect the needs and challenges many female offenders must overcome while being incarcerated. For example, a majority of the female inmates are victims of abuse and typically are socially and educationally challenged. The female offender, however, is not the only type of offender in need of special consideration or attention. While CSC boasts of its efforts to honour the UN requirements directed at offenders, there are no comparable standards for staff. Nevertheless, that the tone is more positive than it has been is reflected in the comments of a female deputy warden, Danielle Boisvert, at a national workshop in 1999: "Canada can be proud of the advances made in the field of women's corrections." This is in spite of a recent report from the front-line workers, who caution that the maximum-security facilities for women are ill equipped to handle the more dangerous offenders ("Women's Perceptions...," 2003). A similar cautionary tone is expressed in the 2003 Annual Report of the Correctional Investigators.

- *Finding the balance with the private sector.* The high cost of crime has compelled CSC to seek out alternatives to traditional and conventional approaches that attempt to find a balance between protecting members of society while still holding offenders responsible. To this end, there has been a softening towards allowing the private sector to take over some of the correctional practices as well as alternative programs such as *restorative justice* initiatives.

In 2001, Ottawa agreed to host a UN experts' meeting to review country comments on draft elements of *Basic Principles of the Use of Restorative Justice Programmes* in an effort to stimulate international awareness (see restorative justice link under Web-Links). However, David Daubney (2001:3), General Counsel of the Sentencing Reform Team, suggested that Canada will "never have strong public support for restorative justice unless the public sees that there is widespread victims' support for this approach."

FUTURE DIRECTIONS

If the past 140-odd years is any indication, then it is inevitable that corrections in Canada will continue to evolve, largely under its own directives and indirectly through its participation in international agreements. Since the early 1960s, many correctional changes have taken place. For example, we abolished flogging and the death penalty in 1967 and 1976 respectively; we also established the first inmate committees in 1978; expanded alternative programs and initiatives (e.g., restorative justice); and developed programs for women and Aboriginals (e.g., International Indigenous Symposium on Corrections in 1999). Finally officials have created special needs groups throughout the 1990s, and Operation Bypass was established in 1999. The later program was designed to streamline the case management process.

While Canadian corrections currently emphasizes an effective case management approach (defined above), official recidivism data to date have yet to provide compelling evidence as to its success. This approach focuses on effective treatment programs rather than the medical or rehabilitative models of the past. Yet, there is no certainty as to what corrections will look like 10 or 20 years from now. For example, after the dramatic increase of prison admissions across all levels of government in the early 1990s (approximate increase of 22%), by the late 1990s the Federal/Provincial/Territorial Ministers Responsible for Justice called upon the heads of corrections at all jurisdictional levels to identify viable options. What ensued was a steady decline in the sentenced admissions, from 223,383 admissions for all three levels of corrections in 1996/97 to 215,639 in 2000/01. The year 2001/02 saw a slight increase in admission to 226,688 — the increase occurred entirely in the provincial and territorial correctional systems — which was largely motivated more by pragmatics rather than the effectiveness of existing options. Nevertheless, it serves as a clear example of how corrections has and will continue to evolve — whether due to social, political, economic, or other factors —

corrections is dynamic. In addition, Canada's "population is aging, becoming increasingly diverse culturally, ethnically, racially, and religiously, and the Aboriginal birthrate is growing rapidly" (CSC, 2002). These challenges are reflective of interesting times for CSC as it tries to meet these new demands. Notwithstanding some of the immediate concerns, it could be suggested that with increasing support for globalization of efforts and through the cooperative efforts of "best practices," Canada can effectively move "beyond prisons" and closer towards a correctional model and practice that is representative of the UN standards and guidelines or even along the lines of the more detailed standards and rules set out by the Council of Europe on Human Rights. For example, Canada's rehabilitation programs have received international acclaim, as countries like Finland recently introduced our approach on a trial basis (Gardner, 2002). Yet, such optimism needs to remain guarded, for as a senior Finnish observer noted, Canada's correctional philosophy of "tough on crime" is mimicking the American approach. This being the case we'll end up with their problems, too (see chapter 10 for further discussion)!

For Canadian corrections to operate in a political and social vacuum is impossible. Yet, with increased internationalization and cooperation among different countries, Canada seems, in principle, receptive to the creation of inter- or supranational correctional institutions/initiatives — as are being attempted by the European Union and the United Nations and as reflected, to a large extent, in the restorative justice movement — that might well enable it to bear the mantle of a "model system."

CONCLUSION

In 1910, Sir Winston Churchill observed that the mood and temper of the public towards crime and criminals is "one of the unfailing tests of the civilization of any country" (cited in Menninger, 1968:250). Judged by this standard, since the mid to late 1990s Canada's correctional system has been continuing to strive for a balance between political will, public sentiment, and international guidelines and agreements, while moving towards a community-based model that effectively uses alternatives to incarceration. For example, community supervisions and conditional sentences in 2001/02 were up some 8% from the previous year and 26% since 1997/98. As a former Commissioner of CSC noted a few years ago, CSC is making every effort to move beyond its reliance on prisons without compromising public safety. However, although significant strides have been made, CSC continues to be plagued by poor quality program evaluation, lack of support from the public, and addressing its conflicting goals — how to best protect society as well as achieving CSC objectives. And on a broader scale, various CSC officials recognize and have called for greater communication and sharing of information and ideas within the international community.

Key Terms and Concepts

Fauteaux Report	Arbour Commission	Penal populism
Ouimet Report	Public sector administration	
Brown Commission	Bloody Code	John Howard
British North America Act	CORCAN	Daubney Report
Elizabeth Fry Society	Reform model	Medical model
Archambault Commission	Carson Report	Opportunistic model

Discussion/Study Questions

(1) How does the correctional system of Canada differ/compare with that of other countries presented in this anthology?

(2) How effective have the various reports and commissions been at reforming the philosophy and orientation of Canadian corrections?

(3) How well does Canada's correctional system comply with the various UN guidelines and standards.

(4) To what extent are correctional practices the outcome of informed and reasoned debate in Canada?

Helpful Web-links

Correctional Service of Canada:
www.csc-scc.gc.ca.

CORCAN:
http://www.csc-scc.gc.ca/text/prgrm/corcan/home_e.shtml.

National Parole Board:
www.npb-cnlc.gc.ca.

Statistics Canada:
www.statcan.ca.

The restorative justice directory of Canada:
http://www.restorativejustice.ca/canada.asp?target=Adult.

The Canadian Family and Corrections network — an extensive list of restorative justice and related links:
http://www3.sympatico.ca/cfcn/research.html.

Edmonton Institution for Women:
http://www.csc-scc.gc.ca/text/facilit/institutprofiles/edforwomen
_e.shtml.

The following site provides links to all federal, provincial and territorial, and non-profit organizations within the correctional arena:
http://www.csc-scc.gc.ca/text/links_e.shtml.

John Howard Society of Canada:
http://www.johnhoward.ca.

Elizabeth Fry Society of Canada:
http://www.elizabethfry.ca/caefs_e.htm.

REFERENCES

Annual Report of the Correctional Investigation: 2002-2003 (2003). Ottawa, ON: Ministry of Public Works and Government and Services Canada.

Beattie, J.M. (1997). *Attitudes Towards Crime and Punishment in Upper Canada, 1830-1850.* Toronto, CAN: Centre of Criminology, University of Toronto.

Bottoms, A.E. (1995). "The Philosophy and Politics of Punishment and Sentencing." In: C. Clarkson and R. Morgan (eds.), *The Politics of Sentencing Reform.* Oxford, UK: Clarendon Press.

Brodeaur, J-P. (1996). "Penal Saturation." In: T. O'Reilley-Felming (ed.), *Postcritical Criminology.* Scarborough, ON: Prentice-Hall.

Carrigan, O. (1991). *Crime and Punishment in Canada: A History.* Toronto, ON: McClelland and Stewart.

Carriere, D. (2003). "Adult Correctional Services in Canada, 2001-02." *Juristat* 23(11).

Cayley, D. (1998). *The Expanding Prison.* Toronto, CAN: Anansi.

Correctional Service Canada (CSC), (2002). Correctional Service Canada main website: http://www.csc-scc.gc.ca/text/organize_e.shtml.

Daubney, D. (2001, March 28-31). "1000 Word Summary of Papers." Paper presented at the conference on "Restorative and Community Justice: Inspiring the Future." Winchester, UK.

Duguid, S. (2000). *Can Prisons Work?* Toronto, ON: Toronto University Press.

Ekstedt, J.W. and M.A. Jackson (1996). *The Keeper and the Kept.* Scarborough, ON: Nelson.

Erdhal, A. (2001). "History of Corrections in Canada." In: J.A. Winterdyk (ed.), *Corrections in Canada: Social Reactions to Crime.* Toronto, CAN: Pearson.

Fraser, A.P. (2002). "House Arrest Not Just Slap on Wrist, Judges Say." Halifax, NS: *The Chronicle-Herald,* Dec. 3, p.A4.

Gamberg, H. and A. Thomson (1984). *The Illusion of Prison Reform: Corrections in Canada.* NY: Peter Lang.

Gardner, D. (2002). "Why Finland is Soft on Crime." *The Ottawa Citizen,* March 18, p.A1.

Gendreau, P., C. Goggin, F. Cullen and D.A. Andrews (2000). "The Effects of Community Sanctions and Incarceration on Recidivism." *Forum on Corrections Research* 12(2):10-13.

Gillis, C.A. (2002). "Understanding Employment: A Prospective Exploration of Factors Linked to Community-based Employment among Federal Offenders." *Forum on Correctional Research* 14(1):3-6.

Griffiths, C.T. and A. Cunningham (2000). *Canadian Corrections.* Scarborough, ON: Nelson.

Menninger, K. (1968). *The Crime of Punishment.* NY: Viking Press.

Mitchell, J.R., and S.L. Sutherland (1999). "Ministerial Responsibility: The Submission of Politics and Administration to the Electorate." In: M.W.

Mestmacott and H.P. Mellon (eds.), *Public Administration and Policy*. Scarborough, ON: Prentice-Hall.

Motiuk, L. (2001). "Public Administration and Management." In: J.A. Winterdyk (ed.), *Corrections in Canada: Social Reactions to Crime*. Toronto, CAN: Pearson.

Ostiguy, J. (2000). "The Cognitive Skills-building and Reintegration Program." *Let's Talk* 2(23). (Available on-line: www.csc-scc.ca/pblct/l;etstalk /vol2/23_e.shtml.)

Peritz, I. (2003). "You're in the Jailhouse Now, But Will You Pay to Stay?" *Globe and Mail*, Feb. 11, p.A3.

Rankin, B. (2002). "CSC in Namibia." *Let's Talk* 27(3):20.

Roberts, J. (2001). "Corrections in Canada: Public Knowledge and Public Opinion." In: J.A. Winterdyk (ed.), *Corrections in Canada: Social Reactions to Crime*. Toronto, CAN: Pearson.

—— L.J. Stalans, D. Indermaur and M. Hough (2003). *Penal Populism and Public Opinion: Lessons from Five Countries*. New York: Oxford University Press.

Schmalleger, F., D. MacAlister, P. McKenna and J. Winterdyk (2000). *Canadian Criminal Justice Today*. Toronto, CAN: Prentice-Hall.

Stojkovic, S., D. Kalinich and J. Klofas (1998). *Criminal Justice Organizations* (2nd ed.). Boston, MA: West/Wadsworth.

Thomas, M, H. Hurley and C. Grimes (2003). "Pilot Analysis of Recidivism among Convicted Youth and Young Adults – 1999-00." *Juristat* 22(9).

Westmacott, M.W. and H.P. Mellon (eds.), (1999). *Public Administration and Policy*. Scarborough, ON: Prentice-Hall.

Williams, F.P., III and M.D. McShane (1999). *Criminological Theory* (3rd ed.). Upper Saddle River, NJ: Prentice-Hall.

"Women's Perceptions regarding Maximum Security" (2003). Ottawa: Correctional Service of Canada. (Available online http://www.csc-scc.gc.ca/ text/prgrm/fsw/mcdonagh/mcdonagh_e-06_e.shtml)

NOTES

1. This approach critically examines how the normative content of the law and corrections is internalized by different segments of society.

2. This perspective includes ideas that range from a total deconstruction of corrections as we know it to a host of novel practical and ideological changes.

3. Offenders overlap as some have more than one offence category.

4. This strategy attempts to restructure antisocial cognitions of an individual and the person in learning new adaptive cognitive and life skills.

CHAPTER 3.
ADULT CORRECTIONS IN FINLAND

by

Ulla Mohell
Tapio Lappi-Seppälä
Jouko Laitinen

and

Aarne Kinnunen
Ministry of Justice, Helsinki, Finland

BASIC FACTS ON FINLAND

Area: Finland has a total landmass of 337,030 square kilometers, of which 31,560 are water and 305,470 are land. It is the sixth largest country in area in Europe. It is the furthermost eastern country of the northern Scandinavia region, bordering the Baltic Sea, Gulf of Bothnia, and Gulf of Finland, and lies between Sweden to the west and Russia to the east. Much of the country is lowland, but high rounded fells form the landscape in the most northern part of the country, known as Lapland. Other outstanding features of Finland's scenery are its myriad lakes and islands.

Population: As of July 2002, the population was estimated at around 5.2 million inhabitants (i.e., 17 persons per square kilometer). The age group 15-64 makes up about 67% of the population, with very even balance between men and women. The population is quite homogeneous both ethnically and linguistically: 93% have Finnish and 6% Swedish as mother tongues. The Sami people comprise less than 1%. Yet the number of foreign citizens has more than tripled since 1990.

Demographics: The literacy rate, for those 15 years and older is 100%. One distinguishing feature of the Finnish school system is the large number of languages taught. English is the most popular non-domestic language. The average lifespan of a Finn is nearly 78 years. Most Finns, some 67%, now live in urban areas, while 33% remain in a rural environment. The three cities of Helsinki, the capital, population 560,000, Espoo, 216,900, and Vantaa, 179,900, form the fast growing Helsinki metropolitan region, which is now home to roughly one-sixth of the country's total population.

Climate: Finland's climate ranges from cold temperate maritime to potentially sub-arctic in the north. But given its northern latitude, the overall temperatures are comparatively mild because of the moderating influence of the North Atlantic Current.

Economy: Finland has an advanced industrial economy: the metal, engineering and electronics industries account for 50% of export revenues, the forest products industry for 30%. Finland is one of the leading countries in Internet and mobile phone use. Finland's road to industrialisation started in the 19th century with the harnessing of forest resources. Forests are still Finland's most crucial raw material resource, although the engineering and high technology industries have long been the leading branches of manufacturing. Electronics is a success story in Finnish exports. In 2001, Finland was named the world's most technically advanced and also the least corrupt country. The net wealth of Finnish households is on a par with most member states of the European Union. It was the only Nordic state to join the Euro currency system at its initiation in January 1999. In 2000, Finland's Gross National Product per capita was around 25,500 euros (ca. 22,600 U.S. dollars). In the early 1990s, Finland experienced a severe economic crisis, when the unemployment rate rose from 3.5% to 18%. Among the long lasting consequences of the economic crisis were increased long-term unemployment, poverty and social exclusion as well as larger income differentials. Because of the high fiscal costs of unemployment the Finnish version of the Nordic welfare model came under significant financial strain. By the end of the 1990s the public economy stabilized with the help of vigorous economic growth and expenditure cuts. The public sector deficit has shrunk rapidly, although interest on government liabilities still remains at quite a high level.

Government: Finland is a Scandinavian welfare state and the public sector produces the bulk of educational and health services, and provides a wide range of services for children and the elderly as well as the statutory retirement insurance. The public sector makes wide-ranging policy decisions regarding business life and strives to manage regional development and income distribution. Finnish society desires to take care of the poor, the disabled and others displaced from active life. The consequences are high public expenditures and heavy taxation. The amount of income one is ready to devote to such activities depends on the level of solidarity towards fellow citizens. Compared to other nations, Finland has proved true to the idea of solidarity as a society; thus, Finland's income differences are the smallest in the OECD. The country became a member of the European Union in 1995. The head of state is the President of the Republic, who is elected for a period of six years and may serve a maximum of two consecutive terms. The President is chosen by direct popular vote, with a run-off between the two leading candidates to emerge after the first round of voting. The government consists of the prime minister and the appropriate number (no more than 17) of other ministers. Most of them are also members of parliament, although this is not a formal requirement. The government must enjoy the confidence of parliament, which has 200 members elected every four years. The best guarantee for enjoying parliament's confidence is to have a government coalition consisting of political parties that together have a majority in parliament.

A BRIEF HISTORY OF FINLAND

"Swedes we are not; Russians we do not want to become; so let us be Finns."
~ A.I. Arwidsson (1791-1858)

For 700 years, from about 1150 to 1809, Finland was a province of the Kingdom of Sweden, equal in status to any other Swedish province. This common history is the basis of the similarities between the Finnish and Swedish societies and it is also reflected in their respective political and legal structures. The distinctive Nordic traditions have always been prevalent in the evolution of Finnish law and legal culture. Feudalism was not part of this system and the Finnish peasants were never serfs; they always retained their personal freedom. Even the Russian hegemony in 1809-1917, when Finland had an autonomous status as a Grand Duchy under Russian Tsar, allowed Finland to maintain its fundamental laws from the time of Swedish rule. Matters pertaining to Finland were presented to the Tsar in St. Petersburg by the Finnish Minister Secretary of State. This meant that the administration of Finland was handled directly by the Tsar, and the lesser Russian authorities were therefore unable to interfere.

The obliteration of "Finnish separatism," under a policy known as **Russification**[1] started during the "first era of oppression" (1899-1905) and continued during the second era (1909-1917). After gaining independence from Russia in 1917, Finland shared a 1566-kilometer long border with the then-communist Soviet Union. A bitter War of Liberation was still fought from January to May 1918, in which rebellious "Red" socialist forces were defeated by "White" forces of the government. This didn't prevent Finland from developing a free-market economy, and the life of Finnish citizens was firmly based on Western traditions, a democratic political system, and full respect for human rights.

During the Second World War, the Soviet Union attacked Finland and the Winter War was fought in 1939-40. Fighting between Finnish and Soviet forces resumed in the Continuation War of 1941-44. Some territory was ceded to the Soviet Union, but Finland was never occupied and preserved its independence, sovereignty and democracy throughout the wars.

THE HISTORY OF CORRECTIONAL TREATMENT IN FINLAND

The application of prison sentences became common in Western Europe at the beginning of the 19th century, and in Finland from the 1870s on. As prison sentences became prevalent, they were increasingly used as a punishment for offences that previously had led to capital or corporal punishment. And though prisons existed before the 1870s, they were mostly used to house persons waiting for trial or the determination of their punishment.

The 1734 Criminal Code from the times of Swedish rule remained in force in Finland to the end of the 19th century. According to that code, there were two forms of deprivation of liberty. The more severe form was penal labour, in practice implying compulsory labour. The more lenient, and less used, form was custody. It could imply either custody on bread and water or normal custody. Fines could be expiated with prison labour.

The preparation of a new criminal code was started when parliament was convened in 1863 after a break of 50 years. This parliament adopted the general outlines for the development of the penal system. When the preparation of the new Criminal Code was still going on, a new Decree of Prison Sentence Enforcement was enacted in 1866. The basis of criminal policy was grounded in the *classical school* of penal law (see Glossary).

According to the Decree, the purpose of punishment was based on the philosophy of *retribution*. It was considered that punishment should have a sufficient deterrent effect and that it also should serve as a general deterrent measure. To this extent, imprisonment entailed the deprivation of liberty in three main forms: confinement, provision of only bread and water, and a general loss of liberty. According to the Decree, prisoners were also expected to perform hard labour. However, soon after the adoption of the criminal code in 1894, the principles of *reform* (i.e., rehabilitation) began to impact legislation and correctional practices.[2]

The legal changes were accompanied by new legislation which required that new prisons be built and old ones renovated. And so, by the beginning of the 1890s, prisons and aftercare in Finland already had become modern on a European scale due to a comprehensive programme of construction. In the new prisons inmates were housed in cells that replaced the previous big common rooms, which were considered detrimental to the goals of correctional treatment. However, even after the reforms it was still considered necessary that sentences should be sufficiently severe. In a regulation on prison labour, for example, from the beginning of the 1890s, it was stated that:

since compulsory labor constitutes one of the most important elements in penal servitude, the work given to the inmates should by its very nature not give them too much satisfaction (Arvelo, 1935:7).

Prison labour started to be purposefully developed right at the end of the 19th century while Mr. Alexis Gripenberg was the General Director of Prison Administration. Various jobs in carpentry, shoemaking, tailoring, spinning and weaving were considered best suitable for the conditions in prison workshops and cells, in addition to housekeeping and maintenance jobs in the institutions. The products were in large part made for military purposes.

The number of prisoners started to grow in the first years of the 20th century. This was partly due to the growth of crime, which the courts tried to prevent by observing severe sentencing practices. Growing crime was caused by several changes in society, such as rapid population growth, industrialisation, urbanization and the problems of the landless population in the provinces. Penitentiaries and provincial prisons soon became overcrowded. Attempts were made to control the overcrowding problem by releasing inmates through extensive acts of clemency, which was granted, for example, in honour of various festival days of the Russian Tsar's family. The effective relocation of prisoners in profitable work was considered the main goal of the Prison Service in the 1920s.

The wars of 1939-1944 required tremendous resources and significantly impacted the work of the Prison Service. Some prison premises were transformed into prisoner-of-war camps, initially maintained by the Prison Administration, later on by the armed forces. The socio-political circumstances profoundly changed after the wars, and the new political situation was reflected in all parts of society. Prison Service policies were also changed, and a Correctional Treatment Reform Committee was established to prepare the reforms.

In spite of these initiatives a number of practical problems persisted. There was, for example, a desperate lack of prison equipment immediately after the war. The prison population was growing due to increasing theft offences, and by 1946 there were on an average 9,000 inmates in Finnish prisons. In an effort to help reestablish the Finnish economy, many labour colonies were founded around 1950. Most of these camps were used to complete work for the National Board of Roads and Waterways. At the peak of this development there were some 30 labour colonies. Most of the labour colonies were working only for a short time, their activities ceasing when they had accomplished their particular task. Subsequent projects have lasted considerably longer.

As in many other Western countries, political and subsequently correctional ideology in Finland underwent profound changes in the late '60s and '70s. The situation in the Nordic countries was in the 1960s marked by a heated social debate on the effects and justification of involuntary treatment (e.g., in mental health care and alcohol treatment) (Eriksson, 1967). The same argument moved inevitably over to concern prisoners. In Finland, the criticism of the *treatment ideology* was accompanied by questions about the overly punitive approach towards sentencing in the Criminal Code. The resulting crime policy ideology was labelled as "humane neo-classicism." It stressed both legal safeguards against coercive powers and a general use of less repressive measures. The ultimate goal of the criminal policy came be minimising the harms that crime as well as crime control causes to society. This means preventing crime with different criminal and social policy measures, among which the deterrent effects of punishment are only one part of the entire policy (see Patrik Törnudd [1996] for further details).

The Finnish Prison Service did not escape the effect of the social, political, and ideological unrest in the 1960s. Several legislative reforms relating to correctional treatment were carried out by the end of the decade. At the same time, changes were made in the management of prison institutions. For example, the characteristic features of the military-type hierarchy were reduced in the prisons and their administration. Correctional operations were in the '60s made more professional by hiring correctional and administrative experts, and by introducing psychological services in the prisons.

The systematic legislative reforms in the 1960s and 1970s included a considerable number of amendments related to correctional treatment. Several improvements to the rights of inmates were made as well. The most severe form of imprisonment, the penitentiary, was abolished. Correctional facilities were transformed into open institutions in accordance with the new legislation. However, the share of open institutions and labour colonies remained much smaller than the plans had indicated. The closed institutions were still remarkably overcrowded throughout the 1970s, particularly in the wintertime.

The content of correctional treatment, traditionally stressing prison labour, also underwent an ideological shift. Embracing a *resocialisation* perspective,[3] basic and vocational training of inmates was made more extensive and comprehensive. Various activity programs designed to reduce the risk of reoffending were introduced in the middle of the 1990s. Many of these programs (see "Activities in Penal Institutions" below) were based on experiences from other countries. However, unlike many other countries, the new emphasis on the principles of *proportionality*, and the values of justice did not result in a more severe system of sanctions.[4] The most significant reform in Finnish criminal policy between the late 1960s and the early 1990s was clearly a purposeful movement towards a more lenient system of sanctions, and especially towards a reduction in the use of custodial sentences. The tangible results of this policy change can be seen in the consistent fall in prisoner rates in Finland.

The Fall of the Finnish Prison Rate: 1950-2000

> *"Regardless of what happens in the future one important lesson has been learned. It proved possible to significantly reduce the use of imprisonment without repercussions in other parts of the system."*
> ~ Patrik Törnudd (1993:30)

In the early 1950s, the prisoner rate in Finland was almost 200 per 100,000 population — four times higher than in other Nordic countries. Even during the 1970s, Finland's prisoner rate continued to be among the highest in Western Europe. However, during the early 1990s, as prison rates continued to increase in most European countries, the rates in Finland began to decline dramatically. By 2001, the Finnish rate had dropped to 57 per 100,000. At the time, this represented the lowest incarceration rate among all European Union countries.

This long-term development cannot be explained with reference to just one or two simple factors. The change has been affected both by macro-level structural factors and an ideological shift in penal theory. The long-term rise in productivity and rapidly growing economy enabled Finland to grow wealthier and to achieve social reforms. One of the major aims was the development of a welfare state (Pesonen and Rihinen, 2002). This had its effects also in the way the aims of criminal policy were conceived and conceptualised. The aims of criminal policy were defined so that they were in accordance with the aims of the new welfarist social policy. The traditional main goals (such as deterrence, the elimination of criminality or the protection of society) were replaced by more sophisticated formulas. From the 1970s onward the aims of criminal policy in Finland were usually expressed with a twofold formula: (1) the minimisation of the costs and harmful effects of crime and crime control (the aim of minimisation); and (2) the fair distribution of these costs among the offender, society and the victim (the aim of fair distribution). In criminal policy the role of punishment was seen to be relative. Also the aims and justification of punishment were subjected to re-evaluation. The failures of penal treatment moved the attention in the early 1970s from special prevention, once again, towards general prevention. However, this concept was now understood in a different manner. It was assumed that this effect could be reached not through fear (deterrence), but through the morality-creating and value-shaping effect of punishment (indirect general prevention). According to this idea, the disapproval expressed in punishment is assumed to influence values and moral views of individuals. As a result of this process, the norms of criminal law and the values they reflect are internalised; people refrain from illegal behaviour not because such behaviour itself is regarded as morally blameworthy. According to this theory, principles of proportionality and perceived procedural fairness are key factors that influence the willingness of the people to obey law (Lappi-Seppälä, 2001; Törnudd, 1993).

In addition, there were a number of significant legal reforms as well and changes to sentencing practices and prison enforcement. And while these changes did not all occur at once, their collective inertia helps to explain the drop in Finland's incarceration rate. This was seen to be a reaction against overly repressive policies instigated by the legislature during the exceptional post-war conditions. Systematic legislative reforms, in turn, started during the mid-1960s, and continued up until the mid-1990s. Penalties for both traditional property offences and drunken driving were heavily reduced. At the same time, the role of non-custodial sanctions (e.g., petty and day-fines, and community services) was strengthened. A long-term analysis of Finnish sentencing practices reveals a steep downward trend in sentencing levels starting from the 1950s until the 1990s (Lappi-Seppälä 2001).

Coinciding with these sentencing reforms there were also amendments made to the general penalty structure. In order to replace short-term prison sentences with other sanctions, the scope of suspended sentences and fines was extended in the mid-1970s. In the 1980s, the use of imprisonment for younger age-groups was further restricted. Also enforcement practices have contributed in this change. A series of legislative acts were carried out in the 1960s in order to restrict the use of imprisonment as a default penalty for unpaid fines. In the early 1970s, the use of **preventive detention** was heavily limited. The system of parole and early release has also proven to be a very powerful tool in controlling prisoner rates.

During the 1990s the penalties remained fairly constant. The only major amendment (Act of 14 December 1990 [1990/1105]) in the correction system was the introduction of *community service*. The legislators' idea was that community service should be used only in cases where the accused would otherwise have received a non-conditional sentence of imprisonment. After an initial trial period in 12 rural districts and six cities, the program was widely accepted and in 1996 was established as a standard part of the Finnish penal system.

Along with the increase in the number of community service orders, the number of unconditional sentences of imprisonment decreased in the years 1992-1998. By 1998, the average daily number of offenders serving a community service order was about 1,200 and the corresponding prison population was about 2,800. It is therefore reasonable to argue that, within a short period of time, community service has proven to be an important alternative to imprisonment in Finland. At the time of preparing this chapter, the use of this sanction appears to have peaked. In fact, between 1999 and 2003, the number of community service orders has been slightly falling while the number of prison sentences has been increasing (see "Profile of the Correctional Population" below).[5] This supports the assertion that for one section of repeat offenders this option has now been "consumed out." If offending continues, the courts might well move from community service to unconditional prison sentence (see Box 3.1).

Box 3.1: Community Service Orders in Finland

Community service can be assessed to be a sanction, that incorporates several unpleasant elements, as — by definition — a punishment should hold. At the same time it is a punishment that makes it possible to begin and maintain a new style of life...It is necessary to build in the field of criminal justice different possibilities that do not force prisoners into one and only life-world.

Henrik Linderborg in *Haaste-magazine* 1/2001.

THE SYSTEM OF SANCTIONS IN FINLAND

"Finland's criminal justice system is, in short, a liberal's dream and a conservative's nightmare."

~ Dan Gardner, March 18, 2002, *Ottawa Citizen*

The Finnish constitution forbids the use of death penalty — as well as any other sort of degrading and inhumane punishments. The last execution in Finland took place in 1826. After that capital punishment has been imposed only when Finland has been at war. Capital punishment even during war time was abolished in 1972. As noted above, the sanctions currently available to the courts include: fines, conditional imprisonment, community service and unconditional imprisonment.

Fines

In Finland, a fine is imposed as a *day-fine* (see Glossary). This system was adopted in Finland in 1921. The main objective of the day-fine system is to ensure "equal severity" of the fine for offenders of different income and wealth. In this system the number of day-fines is determined on the basis of the seriousness of the offence, while the amount of the day-fine depends on the financial situation of the offender. The amount of the day-fine equals roughly half of the offender's daily income after taxes. The number of day-fines for a single offence varies between one and 120 (usually between 10 to 40 day-fines). Failure to make these payments can be converted into one day of imprisonment for every two day-fines.

An example: The typical number of day-fines for drunken driving with a BAC of 1.0 would be around 40 day-fines. The monetary value of one day-fine for a person who earns 1,500 euros per month would be 20 euros. For someone with a monthly income of 6,000 euros, the amount of one day-fine would be 95. Thus, the total fine for the same offence would be 800 euros for the former person, and 3,800 for the latter.

Imprisonment

A sentence of imprisonment may be imposed either for a determinate period (at least 14 days and at most 12 years for a single offence and a total of 15 years for several offences) or for life. Prisoners serving a sentence not exceeding two years are placed in an institution with an appropriate residential setting.[6] A life sentence may be imposed for a relatively restricted number of offences, such as murder, treason and genocide. A life term is a mandatory sentence for murder, which also is the only offence in practice punishable by a life sentence. At the moment there are about 90 persons serving a life sentence. Those serving such a sentence actually spend approximately 11 to 12 years in prison. After this they are normally released on the basis of a pardon by the President of the Republic.

Imprisonment may be either *conditional* or *unconditional*. Prison sentences of up to two years may be imposed conditionally (i.e., a "suspended sentence"), provided that the seriousness of the offence, the culpability of the offender, or previous convictions of the offender do not require an unconditional imprisonment. In the younger age-groups, the presumption in favour of a conditional imprisonment has been strengthened by a special provision which allows the use of an unconditional imprisonment for offenders up to the age of 18 only if certain extraordinary reasons call for this. In practice this means either that the offence is especially serious or that the offender had several prior convictions.

An offender who is sentenced conditionally is placed on probation for a period of one to three years. For adults, such probation does not involve supervision. However, a young offender who is sentenced conditionally may be placed under supervision for the period of probation.

A conditional imprisonment sentence may be ordered enforced if, during the probation period, the offender commits a new offence for which s/he is sentenced to imprisonment. Since being introduced in 1976, the law no longer contains any other behavioural restrictions or conditions for the offender.

Community Service

Community service was introduced on an experimental basis in 1991 in four judicial districts. In 1994 the system was extended to cover the entire country, and community service became a standard part of the Finnish system of sanctions. Community service is imposed instead of unconditional imprisonment. The prerequisites for sentencing the offender to community service are: (a) that the convicted person consents, (b) that the sentence imposed on the offender does not exceed eight months, (c) that the offender is deemed capable of carrying out the community service order, and (d) that prior convictions do not prevent the use of this option. The offender's ability to carry out the work is evaluated on the basis of a specific suitability report. This report may be requested by any one of the parties, the prosecutor or the court. The suitability report is prepared by the Probation Service.

In order to ensure that community service will really be used in lieu of unconditional sentences of imprisonment, a two-step procedure was adopted. First the court is supposed to make its sentencing decision by applying the normal principles and criteria of sentencing, without even thinking about the possibility of community service. If the result is unconditional imprisonment (and certain requirements are fulfilled), then the court may commute the sentence into community service. In principle, community service may, therefore, be used only in cases where the accused would otherwise receive an unconditional sentence of imprisonment. In commuting imprisonment into community service, one day in prison equals one hour of community service. Thus, two months of custodial sentence should be commuted into approximately 60 hours of community service. If the conditions of the community service order are violated, the court normally imposes a new unconditional sentence of imprisonment (for details, see Takala, 1993).

Community service involves unpaid work for the good of the community, for at least 20 hours and at most 200 hours during the offender's leisure time. Only work for a non-profit organisation is allowed. The Probation Service is responsible for enforcing and supervising the offender. Unlike the other Nordic countries, community service does not include any extra supervision aimed, for example, at controlling the offender's other behaviour. The supervision is strictly confined to his or her working obligations.

In 2001, approximately 35% of the unconditional prison sentences not exceeding eight months were converted to a community service order. During each of the past five years, on average 3,750 community service orders have been issued, of which an average of 2,800 have been completed. The most common offence (e.g., 55% in 2001) for which community service has been sentenced has been aggravated drunken driving.

Waiving of Measures

The Finnish law recognizes a specific legal institution called the **"waiving of measures."** The provisions in question give the police, the prosecutor or the judge the power to waive further measures under certain circumstances that are defined in greater detail in law. Accordingly, the law speaks of non-reporting (in respect of the police), non-prosecution (in respect of the prosecutor) and waiving the sentence (in respect of the court). In all of these cases, the guilt of the suspect should be ascertained. The waiving of measures does not relieve the offender of liability for any damage caused by the offence.

The "Ladder Model of Penal Sanctions"

Sentencing in Finland is relatively uniform, in accordance with the principle of **predictability**.[7] The leading principle in sentencing is: "the **proportionality** between the seriousness of the crime and the severity of the sanctions" (Criminal Code, Chapter 6, section 1). The type and the amount of punishment are determined by the perceived blameworthiness of the act and the culpability of the offender.[8] Accordingly, penalties can be graded according to their severity in what is in effect a ladder model, where different types of penalties represent different levels of severity. As the blameworthiness of the offence and the culpability of the offender increase, one moves step by step up the ladder. At the top is unconditional imprisonment. The other alternatives can be arranged roughly as follows:

Figure 3.1: The Ladder Model of Penal Sanctions

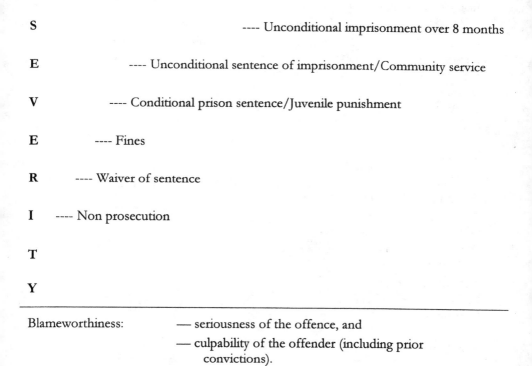

S   ---- Unconditional imprisonment over 8 months

E   ---- Unconditional sentence of imprisonment/Community service

V   ---- Conditional prison sentence/Juvenile punishment

E   ---- Fines

R   ---- Waiver of sentence

I   ---- Non prosecution

T

Y

Blameworthiness: — seriousness of the offence, and
                  — culpability of the offender (including prior convictions).

PRISON AND PROBATION SERVICES

As illustrated in Figure 3.2, in Finland prison and probation services are the administrative responsibility of the Ministry of Justice. The strategic guidelines for the field are drawn by the Department of Criminal Policy. The Criminal Sanctions Agency is in charge of the direction and development of the enforcement of community sanctions and prison sentences. This is a national administrative board which came into force in 2001. The Criminal Sanctions Agency is divided into four units, which are responsible for the direction of the activities of the Prison Service, the direction of the activities of the Probation Service, the enforcement of prison sentences and community sanctions, and the joint administration of the Prison and Probation Services.

Figure 3.2: The Organizational Structure of the Criminal Sanctions Agency

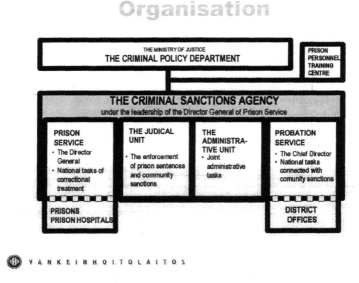

The personnel overseeing the enforcement of sentences consist of the staffs of the Prison Service, the Probation Service and the Criminal Sanctions Agency. At the end of the year 2002, there were a total of 3,203 persons employed full-time, 98% of whom had the status of a civil servant. Over half (57%) of the Prison Service personnel are performing tasks of guarding and supervision, the majority of whom perform continuous three-shift duty. Of the Probation Service personnel, 68% are client workers: social workers or instructors, who take care of the duties of the implementation of community sanctions (*Annual Report...* 2002:8-9). In the Prison Service the majority of the personnel are male (69%), while in the Probation Service and in the Criminal Sanctions Agency females are the majority (76% and 67%, respectively).

The Prison Service

The Prison Service enforces the prison sentences and fine conversion sentences determined by the courts of justice and detentions and apprehensions connected to trials. The Prison Service has altogether over 30 prisons located in various parts of Finland: 17 *closed institutions,* 18 *open institutions* or *units* and 2 *hospital units* (see Table 3.1). The institutions have been divided into three separate prison service regions (i.e., western, eastern and northern, and southern). Beside penal institutions, the Prison Service operates the Prison Mental Hospital and the Prison Hospital connected to the Hämeenlinna prison.

Prisoners serving a sentence longer than two years are placed in *the assessment and placement unit* that is closest to their home municipality. In a prison functioning as an assessment and placement unit, a risk and need assessment and a preliminary plan for the term of sentence are made for the prisoner. The factors that sustain the prisoner's criminal behaviour and which should be dealt with during the imprisonment are registered in the plan. The goal of the plan is to increase the prisoner's capability to cope in the society after release from the prison.

The Prison Service decides on the placements in the different prisons. Unlike prisons in many other countries, Finnish prisons are not formally classified according to their security status, nor are the prisoners classified according to any security grading. However, the intensity of supervision varies to some extent among the closed prisons.

Table 3.1: Closed Prisons in Finland: Places in Use and Number of Prisoners as of 1.10.2003

Closed Institutions	Average Number of Places		Number of Prisoners		
	M	F	M	F	Total
Helsinki prison	250	0	307	0	307
Hämeenlinna prison	69	96	90	98	188
Hämeenlinna prison hospital	65	5	21	4	25
Jokela prison	122	0	141	0	141
Kerava prison	155	0	166	0	166
Konnunsuo prison	195	0	210	0	210
Kuopio prison	53	0	67	0	67
Kylmäkoski prison	102	0	134	0	134
Lounais-Suomi prison	321	9	388	13	401
Mikkeli prison	74	0	102	1	103
Oulu prison	81	8	100	8	108
Pelso prison	183	6	206	7	213
Pyhäselkä prison	70	15	71	20	91
Riihimäki prison	212	0	188	0	188
Sukeva prison	172	0	188	0	188
Vaasa prison	61	4	78	3	81
Vantaa prison	139	19	175	18	193
Total	2,324	162	2,632	172	2,804
Open institutions	640	34	532	36	568
Labor colonies	260	0	190	0	190
Total	**3,224**	**196**	**3,354**	**208**	**3,562**

Source: Statistics of the prison administration and probation administration in 2002, updated by prison administration.

If the sentence of imprisonment is no longer than two years, the sentence may be ordered enforced in an open institution. A further requirement of assignment to an open prison is that the offender is capable of working or of participating in other activities offered in the institution and that he or she presumably will not leave without permission. The regime in open institutions is more relaxed. Prisoners in an open institution receive wages which are comparable with wages outside the prison. Out of these wages, they pay normal taxes. One-quarter of their wages goes for their maintenance. Open institutions are in practice prisons without walls: the prisoner is obliged to stay in the prison area, but there are no guards or fences. In open institutions inmates always wear their own clothes. All open institutions are intoxicant-free environments. Prisoners are obliged to work or to take part in vocational training or other activities unless they are relieved from that duty on the grounds of health or for other reasons. Prisoners may also receive permission to pursue other studies either within or outside the institution. For those serving sentences in excess of two months, a prison furlough may be granted. A prisoner may be furloughed from prison for a maximum of six days over a four-month period.

Box 3.2: Labour Colonies After the 1950s

> The conditions in labour colonies are as far as possible made normal. The inmates are paid current wages according to collective agreements. Inmates pay normal taxes on their wages, and also pay the labour colony for food and housing. Surveillance is less strict than in normal prisons. The inmates, however, are not allowed to leave the colony territory without permission. The use of alcohol and other intoxicating substances is prohibited. Inmates violating the regulations are transferred to closed institutions, except for cases of slight infractions. Previously, many offenders who served their sentence in labour colonies were convicted for drunken driving. Nowadays many other inmates, convicted to shorter sentences for other offences, and convicts serving the latter part of a long-term sentence, can be located there, too. Still, many other inmates, convicted to shorter sentences for other offences, and convicts serving the latter part of a long-term sentence, serve their sentences there, too.

Four labour colonies have been established where inmates participate in certain projects (see Box 3.2). These include, for instance, the restoration of cultural-historically valuable sites — where work is carried out together with the National Board of Antiquities — and other important building and repair work (e.g., building a third runway at the Helsinki-Vantaa Airport).

The testing of the "prisoner positioning system" started in 2001 in the Vanaja **open prison** section located in Hämeenlinna. In the prisoner positioning system prisoners have, with specific preconditions, the opportunity to work or study outside the prison. If a prisoner is allowed to leave the institution they are required to carry a GSM mobile phone which enables surveillance of the prisoner to be carried out from the prison. The prisoner may only use the mobile phone for contacting the prison and the alarm centre. Preliminary studies indicate that the prisoners expressed a positive attitude towards the use of the phone and there were no incidents of improper use of the phone. On the basis of the positive experiences, the testing of the positioning system is being expanded to all prison service districts. The objective is to expand the use of the positioning system to cover almost every prison. The system will also be tested during longer prison furloughs and, for example, in monitoring the restraining orders imposed on the prisoners, according to information from the Department of Criminal Policy.

The prison population increased by some 10% in 2002 and the fiscal budget increased about 5% to 150 million euros. In 2002, the cost to maintain a prisoner per day was some 112 euros, while revenues generated from the work activity of all inmates was worth around 10 million euros. The annual average prison population was 3,433 while two years earlier it was 2,855. In 2002, the average prison population in open institutions was 794. In open prisons and open prison units there were on the average 583 inmates, and in work colonies 211 prisoners.

The Probation Service

Community sanctions are a significant part of the enforcement of sentences system in Finland. The Probation Service is in charge of administering community sanctions and other activities connected to community sanctions and other **non-custodial punishments.** The overall goal of the Probation Service is to contribute to safety in society and prevent recidivism. Community sanctions are enforced in the sphere of everyday life and assisted by cooperative networks. The Probation Service has 21 district offices and 11 local offices. At the end of the year

2002, there were a total of 300 probation staff working full-time. The roots of the Probation Service are in the work of the Prisoner's Association, which was founded in 1870 and which focused exclusively on a helping mission. The work of the Prisoner's Association broadened when the registered Probation Association was founded in 1966. After the reorganisation of the Ministry of Justice in 2001, the probation services were placed in the framework of the Criminal Sanctions Agency (see Figure 3.2).

An offender who has committed his/her crime when he/she was been under 21 years of age, can be ordered to *supervision* to enhance the conditional imprisonment passed by the district court. Supervision is ordered if it is considered to improve the offender's social coping and prevent recidivism. The Probation Service is in charge of organising supervision in the whole country. During the year 2002, there were 2,551 young offenders under supervision.

In *community service* the convict carries out non-profit work on his/her leisure time. For the implementation of each community service sentence, a service plan is made and it is confirmed by the Probation Service. The service plan includes information on the service place, the schedule of the service and conditions of the service which the convict has to comply with. The Probation Service supervises the carrying out of the community service.

The community service is scheduled to occur during the term of the original prison sentence. The Probation Service determines the service place and makes an agreement with it. In arranging the service place, suitable tasks for the convict are sought. During the year 2002, the enforcement of 3,378 community service sentences was started.

Parole (conditional liberty) and possibly supervision of the parolee, are a part of prison sentence passed by a court. A fixed portion is served of the prison sentence, after which the convict is conditionally released (see below). A prisoner to be released is ordered to supervision if the remaining prison sentence is 1½ years or longer. The Probation Service is in charge of organising the supervision and an official of the Probation Service functions as a supervisor. In some cases a private person chosen for the task may act as a supervisor. During the year 2002, there were 2,134 parolees under supervision.

FINLAND AND INTERNATIONAL AGREEMENTS

Finland has ratified all the main human rights documents that influence sentence enforcement and the treatment of those who are deprived of their liberty. All the international agreements that Finland has bound itself to observe are part of the Finnish judicial system, once incorporated by the decision of the parliament. However, the human rights conventions do not have a general or absolute precedence over other statutory law in Finland. Still, in cases where the provisions of the agreement and the contents of national law are in contradiction, a doctrine of interpretation, "favourably disposed to human rights" was adopted in Finland (by the Constitutional Committee of the parliament). According to this doctrine, the interpretation and application of laws shall endeavour to obtain a result that corresponds to the international obligations of Finland in the field of human rights. The same principle is also declared in the new Finnish Constitution, which entered into force in 2000. For example, according to section 22, the public authorities shall guarantee the observance of basic and human rights. As a result, the Finnish courts have increasingly referred to the articles of the convention in their decisions.

Finland became a member of the UN, and a party to the UN Charter in 1955. The International Covenant on Civil and Political Rights entered into force in Finland in 1976. Finland originally made seven reservations about the Covenant, and three of them still remain in force. One is related to the separation of juvenile and adult offenders. Finland also ratified the UN Convention on Economic, Social and Educational Rights. Finland has approved the possibility for individuals to make appeals under both conventions.

The UN Convention against Torture and Other Cruel, Inhuman or Degrading Treatment or Punishment entered into force in Finland in 1989, and the Convention on the Rights of the Child in 1990. Both conventions are important to the treatment of those who are deprived of their liberty.

The agreements and recommendations prepared within the Council of Europe are particularly important from the point of view of the guaranteeing of human rights of prisoners and other persons deprived of their liberty. The most important of these documents are the European Convention for the Protection of Human Rights and Fundamental

Freedoms (ECHR) and the supplementary protocols. The European Human Rights Convention entered into force in Finland in 1990, and the provisions of the convention can be applied by national courts. The convention has had a considerable influence on national legislation. The system of individual appeals to the European Court for Human Rights is exceptional in the sense that it may lead to judgments that are legally binding on states.

A convention which is of practical importance to prisoners is the European Convention for the Prevention of Torture and Inhuman or Degrading Treatment or Punishment. It entered into force in Finland in 1991. A European committee with the task of protecting persons deprived of their liberty against inhuman or degrading treatment (the CPT) was formed through the convention. For this purpose the CPT makes visits of inspection to institutions and places where persons deprived of their liberty are being kept in the contracting states. Such institutions include prisons and police premises. The CPT has made three visits to Finland, in 1992, 1998 and 2003.

The Council of Europe has also prepared a considerable number of recommendations. Although these recommendations are not legally binding on the member states, they play an important part in the treatment of prisoners and in the preparation of new legislation. (See Helpful Web-links for further details on the council.)

CORRECTIONS TODAY

The Objectives and the Institutions

Up till 1975 prison sentences were enforced and carried out following the "principle of progression": When arriving at prison and starting to serve the sentence, lack of trust from prison staff left the inmate with a minimum amount of rights and personal freedom. Then, as time passed, an inmate's position improved in accordance with the "progression" the prisoner might have demonstrated. As a part of the political shift on crime of the early 1970s, the aims and objectives of the enforcement were redefined by adopting the *principle of normalization* (rehabilitation) as the basis for corrections. According to this principle, the conditions of prisoners serving a sentence should be arranged so that they correspond as much as possible to the living conditions in society in general. According to chapter 1 of the Penal Custody Decree, "the sentence should be carried out so that the punishment only entails the loss of liberty." The sentence should be enforced so that it does not needlessly hinder, but instead promotes, the placement of the prisoner in society (see in more detail Lahti, 1977).

Activities in Penal Institutions

Activities arranged for the prisoners during the working hours include work, studies or some other activity organised or approved by the institution. The goal of the activities is to promote a prisoner's potential to cope in society after release. In order to find the best suited, targeted form of activity, the prisoner's work and functioning capability is assessed. The aim is to influence problems of life control, educational background and work and functional effectiveness shown by the assessment by placing the prisoner in an appropriate activity.

During recent years, the prisoners' options for participating in activities intended to decrease their use of intoxicants or their re-offending have been greatly increased. In order to guarantee a continuum after release, prisons cooperate with authorities of the prisoner's home municipality. About two-thirds of prisoners participate daily in work, education or other activity (see Box 3.3). Under certain conditions a prisoner has the possibility of going to work or study outside prison. A prisoner may also be placed in rehabilitation for a short period outside prison. About half of the prisoners work daily. Their products are marketed to state and municipal institutions, to businesses or directly to consumers through shops.

Classes are organised in prison together with nearby educational institutions. Prisoners receive their certificates from institutes so that it is not apparent that their studies have been carried out in prison. By far the most popular form of studies are vocational studies. In 2002, 104 vocational or preparatory courses of study were arranged in institutions, in 15 different vocational branches. Under certain conditions prisoners may study outside the institution with permission. In 2002, 116 prisoners were studying outside the institution.

Box 3.3: Targeted Activity Programs

Targeted activity programs or other activities sustaining functioning ability in Finnish prisons and the share (%) of prisoners participating in them in 2002 (N=5,182):

Informing and motivating intoxicant programs	49%
Intoxicant rehabilitation programs	29%

The rehabilitation programs are based on cognitive-behaviourist therapy, various group therapy forms and community treatment models.

Activity sustaining functioning ability: (arranged for the less able prisoners)	10%
Programs for violent offenders	4%

There are two activity programs: a longer Cognitive Self Change, which is intensive and meant for prisoners with difficult history of violent behaviour, and a shorter anger management course which aims at controlling feelings of anger and aggression.

Cognitive Skills programs	1%
Teaching e.g., problem solving and social skills, Programs for sexual criminals (STOP)*	< 1%

*Elaborates thinking models connected to sexual offences, practises means necessary to avoid recidivism and strives to be aware of the victims' experiences.

Source: The Finnish Prison and Probation Services.

The need for studies varies greatly. The proportion of guidance and preparatory education has increased somewhat at the same time as vocational studies have decreased. The change is connected to the weakening of study capabilities due to increased intoxicant problems. Most prisoners have a poor educational background: many have interrupted their comprehensive school. Some prisoners, however, also need higher education.

The various rehabilitative activities may involve different courses, day programs of rehabilitative units or short camps. Most of all, various types of substance abuse rehabilitation are offered, which are available in nearly all institutions. The Prison Service also arranges programs that aim to reduce commitment of certain crimes (sexual and violent).

Preventive Detention

The Finnish sentencing provisions generally rule out predictive sentencing on the basis of dangerousness. Still, there are some specific arrangements reserved for extreme cases. A small group of dangerous recidivists are still kept in preventive detention. This system is reserved for those violent offenders who have previously been sentenced for a serious violent offence and who are deemed to present a particular danger to the life or health of another. A dangerous recidivist may be placed in preventive detention in case all of the following three requirements are met: (1) The offender is sentenced to prison for a determinate period of at least two years for an offence that involves serious violence or particular danger to the life or health of another (for example murder, manslaughter, aggravated assault or rape). (2) During 10 years preceding the offence, the offender had been guilty of similar offences. (3) On the basis of the evidence, he or she is manifestly deemed to present a particular danger to the life or health of another.

The sentences are enforced in normal prisons. In principle, the sentence is enforced like any other longer sentence, with some restrictions concerning prisoner furloughs. The principal difference between preventive detention and normal sentences of imprisonment is that prisoners ordered to preventive detention are normally not allowed to obtain release on parole (conditional release).

The actual practice of preventive detention is quite restricted. Recently, there have been about 23 prisoners held at any one time in preventive detention. In recent years, no one has been kept in custody longer than the term of his/her original sentence. The significance of the security system is therefore restricted to the fact that a small number of prisoners will not receive the benefit of early release on parole. Even in its limited use, preventive detention contradicts the prevailing Finnish sentencing ideology, which is very reluctant to accept assessments of dangerousness as a basis for criminal sanctions.

At the time of preparing this chapter, the entire existence of this system is uncertain. According to a recent proposal, the entire system of preventive detention should be abolished. The dangerousness of the offender could be taken into account through normal rules of release on parole.

Release from Prison

All offenders sentenced to a determinate sentence of imprisonment are released on parole by the decision of the director of the prison in question (in accordance with instructions issued by the Ministry of Justice). In general, recidivists are always released after they have served two-thirds of their sentence, and first-time prisoners are released after they have served one-half of their sentence (see Sentencing Act, chapter 2, section 14). In all cases, a further condition is that the prisoner has served at least 14 days.[9] An offender who is serving a sentence of life imprisonment may be released only if pardoned by the President of the Republic.

Release may be postponed beyond these minimum periods in general by one month or, at times, by even more if the grounds for discretion noted in the law are deemed to exist. In practice, release on parole is postponed only for two reasons: either the offender had committed a new offence within a very short time of his/her previous releases, or s/he has violated the conditions of the furloughs granted during the sentence. Postponement of release on the grounds of the type of offence and a prognosis of dangerousness is very rare. In all, parole is postponed in about 6% of the cases. Earlier release may be possible for various reasons related to after-care (e.g., education, employment, and housing) or general social reasons (e.g., illness, family-related reasons). In practice, few offenders are released on parole earlier than usual.

The law requires that the period of parole should not exceed the length of the original sentence, but it should be at least three months and no more than three years. About one-third of those released on parole are placed under supervision. The supervision is arranged by the Probation Service and in most of the cases the supervisor is a Probation Service Officer. In some cases it can be decided that a private person fulfils the task. In principle, the supervision involves both control and support. The court decides on revocation of parole if the offender commits an offence during the period of parole and on the grounds of a behavioural infraction. In practice, all parole revocations are based on new offences.

The Reform of Sentencing Enforcement Legislation

The new Finnish Constitution which entered into force in 2000 created needs for amendments in prison enforcement legislation. Therefore a total reform, including proposals for a new Prison Act, a new Pre-trial Detention Act and a new Criminal Code chapter on release on parole, was prepared in the Ministry of Justice.

The basic idea of the reform of sentence enforcement legislation is to enact regulations on prisoners' rights and obligations and on restrictions of their basic rights in an accurate and comprehensive way on the level of law, in accordance with the requirements of the Constitution and the obligations prescribed by human rights conventions. The reform also tries to observe the changes taking place in the composition of the prison population, in prison service and criminal-policy thinking.

The aim is to give the governmental proposal to Parliament in spring 2004.

Profile of the Correctional Population

The average daily prison population was 2,974 in 1997. It then declined to 2,743 in 1999. After that it steadily increased to 3,433 in 2002.

Today, many of the inmates have serious drinking and drug problems. The number of foreign prisoners is considerably smaller in Finland than in most other European countries. Their numbers, however, have started to increase. The largest category of prisoners has been convicted of aggravated violent offences (approximately one-third of the prison population). The number of prisoners sentenced for narcotics offence as a principal offence has grown six-fold since the end of late 1980s. Now they make-up nearly 20% of the prison population (*Annual Report...*, 2002).

A new Finnish Constitution entered into force at the end of the 1990s and affected the activities of the Prison Service. Legal provisions on the rights and duties of the inmates and the powers of the staff shall now be more precisely indicated than previously. The Prison Service is at the same time expected to contribute to the reduction of reoffending more efficiently than before.

The fundamentally changed situation made it necessary to specify the goals and guidelines of Prison Service activities. A Basic Programme and an Intoxicant Prevention Strategy were confirmed by the Prison Service at the end of the 1990s. At the same time, a Building Stock Development Programme, covering the period until 2010, was drawn up. An investment programme was agreed upon in this context, as the ownership and possession of Prison Service real estate was being reorganised.

CONCLUSION AND FUTURE DIRECTIONS

The history of the Finnish correction system is full of dramatic changes during the past 50-odd years. The prisoner rate in Finland was four times higher than in other Nordic countries in the early 1950s. The rates in Finland began to decline dramatically during the early 1990s at the same time as prisoner rates continued to increase in most European countries. In 2001, Finland's incarceration rate was one of the lowest among all EU-countries.

Several legislative reforms relating to correctional treatment were carried out during 1960's. Furthermore, changes were made in the management of prison institutions. Features of the military-type hierarchy were reduced in the prisons and their administration. Correctional and administrative experts were hired and psychological services were introduced in the prisons.

At the same time, several improvements of the rights of inmates were made. The more severe form of imprisonment, the penitentiary, was abolished. Several correctional facilities were transformed into open institutions. Finland ratified all the main human rights documents that influence sentence enforcement and the treatment of those who were deprived of their liberty.

The Finnish crime policy of the past decades may be characterised as both rational and humane. The reform ideology, which guided the law reforms from the early 1970s onwards, represented a pragmatic, non-moralistic approach to the crime problem. In this framework, the role of criminal law as a means of policy was reserved a much less prominent place than before. This pragmatic-rational approach had also a strong social policy orientation ("good social policy is the best criminal policy"). This view reflected also the values of the Nordic welfare-state ideal, and it was widely shared by penological experts, as well as the leading officials in the Ministry of Justice and prison administration. Humanisation of the sanction system and the decline in incarceration rates were the tangible effects of this reform movement.

However, for some time now, the international trends in criminal policy have moved to the opposite direction. Criminal policy has become increasingly "a tool of general politics." The measures adopted through this type of discourse are often influenced by motives other than rational criminal policy, to say nothing of considered analysis of goals, means and values. In the hands of politicians, criminal policy is often a way to transmit "symbolic messages," a way to "take a stand," a way to "make strategic choices" and so on. Argumentation in matters of penal law remains far from the detached and evidence-based criminal political analyses where criminal law should be treated as *ultima ratio* — to be used only in cases where other means do not apply, and only when it produces more good than harm. Instead, criminal justice interventions are often determined by a political need just to "do something." The rule of thumb seems to be that the higher the level of political authority, the more simplistic the approaches advocated. The results can be seen in programs and slogans that are compressed into two or three words, along the lines of "three strikes," "prison works," "truth in sentencing," "war on drugs," and so on. (The social and political forces behind these changes in English-speaking countries are well analysed in Garland, 2001.)

Unfortunately, also at the EU-level, criminal policy is now characterised by excessive trust in the effectiveness of the penal system and custodial sentences. This is one reason why a large segment of Nordic scholars in criminal law remain less enthusiastic towards political attempts to harmonise criminal law. It seems evident that the growing international aspect of crime and crime control, the increased pressure on the harmonisation of criminal law within the European Union, as well as the general tendency to politicise criminal policy, all include greater risks of increased repression also in Finland. Increasing signs of such populist punitive approach can already be seen also in the Finnish debate. The number of prison sentences, as well as the number of prisoners, have again started to increase. Behind these changes are the increased number of foreign prisoners (mainly from Russia and Estonia), and especially sentences for drug trafficking. Sentences for violent offences have become somewhat stiffer and the number of default prisoners and the use of remand has increased as well.

However, there is still room for optimism. The path taken by many other European penal systems is not an inevitable one. Very few of the social, political, economic and cultural background conditions that explain the rise of mass imprisonment in the U.S and U.K. apply to Finland, as such. For example, welfare state was never openly discredited in Finland. The social and economic security granted by the Nordic Welfare State model may still function as a social backup system for a tolerant crime policy. The social equality and demographic homogeneity of Finnish society produces fewer racial and class tensions/distinctions, fewer fears and fewer frustrations to be exploited by marginal political groups, with their demands for increased control and exclusion. And the political culture still discourages politicians to use tough crime policies as general political strategies.

But for how long, the sceptic might ask? Crime is a problem and politicians are responsible to offer solutions for this problem. If nothing else is offered, criminal law and the prison system may become the primary shield against crime. But this can be counteracted: Expanding the scope of non-custodial sanctions and enhancing the application of these alternatives, explaining the cost-ineffectiveness and social destructiveness of the large scale use of imprisonment, and informing public opinion, the politicians and the media of the potentials of other crime prevention strategies outside the domain of criminal law; these are all becoming tasks of increased importance for those working in field of criminal justice.

As noted, the profile of the correctional population has become more "hard core" and serious since the mid-1990s. Today many of the prisoners have drinking and drug problems. The end result is that in 2003 Finland has more "difficult" and "dangerous" people in prisons than before. At the same time the relative resources of the correctional system are getting smaller. This dilemma that concerns the whole society still waits to be solved.

Key Terms and Concepts

Closed vs. open prisons

Non-conditional punishments

Preventive detention

Waiving of measure

Humane Neo-classicism

Penal rehabilitation   Predictability

Proportionality   Russification

Discussion/Study Questions

(1) How has being a Nordic country influenced the evolution of corrections in Finland?

(2) What might be some of the pros and cons of using the principle of *proportionality*?

(3) Finland was one of the few countries able to drastically reduce its prison populations throughout the 1950s and 1990s. Does its approach offer any constructive insights for the international community?

(4) Relative to other countries presented in this text, to what extent does Finland adhere to the various key international standards and conventions?

Helpful Web-links

The Council of Europe:
http://www.coe.int.

The European Convention on Human Rights:
http://www.pfc.org.uk/legal/echrtext.htm.

Finnish Ministry of Justice http:
//www.om.fi/333.htm.

Prison Service in Finland http:
//www.vankeinhoito.fi/5141.htm.

REFERENCES

Annual Report (2002). Helsinki, FIN: The Finnish Prison and Probation Services.

Arvelo A.P. (1935). *Vankilatyön suuntaviivoista.* Helsinki, FIN.

Eriksson L.D. (1967). *Pakkoauttajat.* Helsinki, FIN.

Garland D. (2001). *The Culture of Control. Crime and Social Order in Contemporary Society.* Oxford University Press.

Gardner, D. (March 18, 2002). "Why Finland is Soft on Crime." *Ottawa Citizen.* (Online: http://www.canada.com/ottawa/ottawacitizen/archives/story. asp?id=2F2065F5-826B-4056-94DD-725BA21E45D6 retrieved July 18.03.)

Joutsen, M., R. Lahti and P. Pölönen (2001). *Finland: Criminal Justice Systems in Europe and North America.* Helsinki, FIN: HEUNI.

―――― and R. Lahti (1997). *Finland: Criminal Justice Systems in Europe and North America.* Helsinki, FIN: HEUNI.

Komiteanmietintö (1946). *Vankeinhoidon Uudistuskomitean Mietintö.* (A Report of the Committee for Prison Reformation. Committee Report.)

Lahti, R. (1977). "Criminal Sanctions in Finland. A System in Transition." *Scandinavian Studies in Law* 21:119-57.

Lappi-Seppälä, T. (2001). "Sentencing and Punishment in Finland: The Decline of the Repressive Ideal." In: M. Tonry and S.R. Frase (eds.), *Sentencing and Sanctions in Western Countries.* Oxford, UK: Oxford University Press.

―――― (2000). *Rikosten Seuraamukset.* Helsinki, FIN: Werner Söderström Lakitieto Oy.

―――― (1998). *Regulating the Prison Population. Experiences from a Long-Term Policy in Finland.* Helsinki, FIN: National Research Institute of Legal Policy.

Linderborg, H. (2001). "Yhdyskuntapalvelu Rangaistuksena." (Community Service as a Punishment.) *Haaste* 1/2001.

Pesonen, P. and O. Riihinen (2002). *Dynamic Finland. The Political System and the Welfare State.* (Studia Fennica. Historica 3.) Helsinki, FIN: Finnish Literature Society.

Takala, J-P. (1993). *Rangaistus ja Siihen Soveltuminen. Yhdyskuntapalvelukokeilun Alkuvaiheita ja Ongelmia.* (English Summary: Punishment and suitability for punishment: Initial phases and problems of Finland's community service experiment.) Helsinki: National Research Institute of Legal Policy. Publication no. 120.

Törnudd, P. (1996). *Facts, Values and Visions. Essays in Criminology and Crime Policy.* Helsinki, FIN: National Research Institute of Legal Policy. Publication no. 138.

―――― (1993). *Fifteen Years of Decreasing Prisoner Rates in Finland.* (A report presented to a Study Group from Western Australia in 1991 with a Postscript 5 November 1993.) Helsinki, FIN: National Research Institute of Legal Policy. Research Communications 8.

NOTES

1. For an interesting overview of the era of Russification see: http://www.1upinfo.com/country-guide-study/finland/finland22.html.

2. The new Criminal Code was, after a protracted preparation, finally adopted by Parliament in 1894.

3. The resocialization perspective is an ideology that the time in prison should — as far as possible — be used to educate and train the person so that life in the civil society would be as easy as possible after the sentence. We noted above that the treatment ideology was criticized in the late 1960s; the resocialization perspective, mainly in the mid-1990s, was, in a way, a revival of the idea that inmates could be helped.

4. In the 1960s, when treatment ideology was being criticised, the principles of proportionality became stronger, emphasizing human rights. In Finland, this led to more humane and more rational criminal policy.

5. As reflected in other contributions in this book, there appears to be a return towards greater punitiveness (editor's note).

6. Female offenders are placed in institutions which have a women's ward.

7. Joutsen and Lahti (1997:22) define *predictability* as: "this principle holds that it must be possible for a knowledgeable person to state, within reasonable limits, what the probable sentence would be for a specific offence." This notion is somewhat analogous to Jeremy Bentham's classical doctrine of "moral calculus."

8. According to the general provision of the criminal code (RL 6:1), the type and the amount of punishment must be determined by the perceived blameworthiness of the act and the culpability of the offender. The starting points of the concept blameworthiness are "harmfulness" and "dangerousness" of the act. When harmfulness and dangerousness are measured, this is always done keeping in mind what is the object and intention of the protection of the provision in question. When measuring the culpability of the offender, the starting point is the *act*, not the *offender*: e.g., lifestyle of the offender does not influence the culpability. However, prior convictions do have an effect. An important distinction is made between intention and negligence when culpability is measured. Also offenders' subjective ability and possibilities to perceive risks must be taken in account (Lappi-Seppälä, 2000:329-340).

9. Supervision of youth under the age of 18 is the responsibility of social service authorities.

CHAPTER 4.
THE CORRECTIONAL SYSTEM IN THE FEDERAL REPUBLIC OF GERMANY

by

Kai Bammann

and

Johannes Feest
Faculty of Law, Universität Bremen
Bremen, Germany

BASIC FACTS ON GERMANY

A unified German nation state (without Austria) was formed in 1871. After the end of the Nazi regime and the Second World War (1945), the Federal Republic of Germany was founded on May 23, 1949 with the declaration of a Constitution. For about 40 years, two German states coexisted, separated by the Iron curtain. In 1989, the demise of the German Democratic Republic led to (re-)unification.

Area: 357,023 square kilometers of which 808,550 consist of fresh water. The country is bordered by France, Belgium and the Netherlands in the West, by Switzerland in the southwest, by Austria in the south, by the Czech Republic and Poland in the east and by Denmark as well as the North Sea in the north.

Population: 82.44 million in April 2003. A density ratio at 231 residents per square kilometer. Birth rate in 2001 was 734 per 1,000 population and death rate was 829 per 1,000. The capital city is Berlin (population:

3.4 million). Other major cities include Frankfurt/Main (population 646,000), Hamburg (population 1.7 million), and München (population 1.2 million).

Demographics: Relatively strict citizenship laws, dating back to the early years of the German nation state, are still in place, making it difficult for non-Germans to acquire citizenship. In recent years, Germany has made some efforts to accommodate and naturalize a growing non-German population. Despite these efforts, the rate of non-citizens is still around 9%. Most of them are from former *Gastarbeiterländer* (e.g., Turkey, former Yugoslavia, Greece, and Italy) countries who contributed labour that helped to rebuild the German economy after the Second World War. German has remained the only official language, with exceptions extended only to the tiny minority of slavic Sorbs in their areas of residence. On the basis of the recent European Language Charter, some cultural privileges are extended to a few other traditional minorities (the Danes, the Frisians, the Low-Germans and the Sinti/Roma). The crime rate dropped from 8,125 offenses per 100,000 population in 1996 to 7,736 per 100,000 in 2001.

Climate: Mid-European climate with cool winters and warm summers.

Economy: Germany is a highly industrialized county, with a variety of industries. Natural resources include: fishing, wood-production, farming, coals and — mostly in the northern sea — gas and oil. Unemployment rate was 10.8% in April 2003.

Government: The country follows the model of a representative democracy. It is a federal republic with 16 *Länder* (states) including three city-states (Berlin, Hamburg and Bremen). Its federal legislature consists of two chambers: a parliament with elected members (*Bundestag*) and a representation of all *Länder*/states (*Bundesrat*). Each *Land*/state has its own state-parliament, elected independently from the Federal parliament. There are numerous political parties and alliances in German politics. Since October 2002 the "red/green" coalition of the Social Democrats (SPD) and the Greens has been in its second legislative majority, after a coalition of the Conservative Christian Democrats (CDU/CSU) and the National Liberals had formed the government for more than 20 years. In most *Länder*/states, the CDU is part of the government, while it is in opposition in the federal parliament. This means that in some legislative matters an overarching consensus is necessary.

This is also true for laws like the Penal Code, the Code of Criminal Procedures and the Prison Act.

BRIEF HISTORY OF GERMAN CORRECTIONS

"While serving the sentence, the prisoner shall be enabled to lead, in social responsibility, a life without criminal offences (goal of corrections)."

~ Art. 2 German Prison Act

As is the case in other European countries, German prisons, as we know them today, are a modern invention. The reason is that until the 19th century, corporal (including capital) punishment accounted for most of the sentences meted out by criminal courts. People were usually held in custody only until trial or for reasons other than punishment (e.g., debt, ransom, etc.). And until the establishment of the German Empire in 1871, each German state had its own penal code and was responsible for administering its correctional practices. Quantitatively, imprisonment became the leading form of punishment in the course of the 19th century (while capital punishment remained the qualitatively most important sanction). During the 1920s, fines replaced imprisonment as the most frequent sanction, with imprisonment serving as the back-up sanction and later becoming the official measuring stick for fines in the fine system.

The idea of making prisoners work spread from the Netherlands to Germany, where Bremen established its first **Zuchthaus** (workhouse prison) in 1609. It was based on the Amsterdam model. Soon other cities in the German territories followed (Lübeck 1613, Kassel 1617, Hamburg 1622, Danzig 1629, and so on). This contributed to a shift in sentencing away from the death penalty towards prison sentences. But the model of the "modern" workhouse prison was the exception rather than the rule. Until the 19th century, in most German territories imprisonment was typically carried out in old monasteries, castles, and towers. Their regimes had nothing to do with the progressive Dutch ideas: there was no work, prisoners lived in squalid holes, often chained to the walls, with hardly any food.

Prison reform, pioneered by John Howard and Sir Walter Crofton in England (see the Introduction), came late to the German territories. In 1804, the Prussian Ministry of Justice published a "general plan" for the improvement of prisons and penitentiaries. But, because of the Napoleonic Wars (1796-1815) and economic problems, its implementation never came about. Hence, the Penal Code of 1871 was influenced by the French Penal Code of 1810 as well as the Bavarian Penal Code of 1813, and the Prussian Penal Code of 1831. *Retribution* was the dominant philosophy of the code, but this orientation was short-lived (see below).

Later, reformers like Theodor Fliedner and Nikolaus-Heinrich Julius were instrumental for importing the Pennsylvania penitentiary system (see Glossary) to Germany. The new British prison in Pentonville became the model for similar panoptic prison buildings in Germany: Berlin-Moabit prison (1848) and Bruchsal prison (1848). But during the second part of the 19th century, the religious reform ideas of the Pennsylvania system lost their influence in German prison practice.[1] General and special deterrence became the leading ideologies of German criminal law far into the 20th century. These developments owe a lot to **F. v. Liszt** and the "Marburg Programme" (see Box 4.1).

Box 4.1: Franz von Liszt (1851-1919)

The most influential German criminal law theorist and ideologist of the 19th century, von Liszt was also elected to the parliament of Prussia (in 1909) and to the German Reichstag (1912). His systematic book on criminal law, first published in 1871, reached 26 editions. In his numerous publications, v. Liszt criticized the "classical" idealist retributive conceptions of criminal law derived from Kant and Hegel. The starting point of his own "modern" or "sociological" school was the contention that criminal law should have a socially constructive purpose. According to one of his many famous dictums, occasional offenders should be restrained by individual deterrence, and offenders capable of being reformed should be dealt with by a reformative punishment, but those who cannot be reformed should be incapacitated. He was also one of the founders (in 1889) of the Internationale Kriminalistische Vereinigung, the successor of which is today's International Association of Criminal Law (for details see Radzinowicz, 1991).

The Weimar republic in the 1920s saw a brief interlude of liberal educationists in some the German states, before the Nazis took over to practice an explicitly authoritarian criminal law and brought in harsh and sweeping changes.[2] While prisons in the past had been administered by the individual states that formed the German *Reich*, they now came under direct control of the central government.[3] The concept of *deterrence* was based on extreme severity of punishment (e.g., death penalty).

After the Second World War and the end of the Nazi regime, the death penalty was abolished by Art. 102 of the new German constitution. Legislation in criminal matters remained the responsibility of the central government, but the administration of criminal justice (including prisons) went back to the states (*Länder*), as a consequence of the Federal structure of the new German state mandated by the wartime allies. In 1971, a federal German Penal Code was enacted, followed by a federal Code of Criminal Procedure, but no prison code was thought necessary. According to the then-dominant theory in German public law, prisoners had no rights vis-a-vis the State, since they were supposed to be in a "special relation of subjugation" (*besonderes Gewaltverhältnis*), which means that they were seen as an internal matter of the state.

This theory came under critical scrutiny, after the German Constitution was passed in 1949. But it took almost another 30 years for the German Constitutional Court to rule (BVerfGE 33, 1) that prisoners, just like other citizens, have fundamental rights, protected by the constitution, and that these rights can only be infringed upon on the basis of formal laws duly passed by the legislature.

After long deliberations in commissions outside and inside the German legislature, the Prison Act *(Strafvollzugsgesetz)* was finally passed in 1976 and came into force of law on January 1, 1977.

Correctional Norms

The **Strafvollzugsgesetz** (Prison Act) is the only legal basis for prisoners rights and duties. As are all aspects of the German criminal justice system, correctional practices are based on *civil* law rather than the common law that forms the basis for the systems in Canada, the United States, and several other countries represented in this book. The Act pertains only to adult corrections. There is no equivalent legal regulation for juvenile corrections (see Box 4.2), nor for pre-trial imprisonment (see Box 4.3).[4]

Box 4.2: Youth Corrections

Youth Corrections (*Jugendstrafvollzug*) was separated from adult corrections in Germany in 1923. But apart from two very general articles in the Youth Court Law (*Jugendgerichtsgesetz*), no legal regulation of the rights and duties of juvenile prisoners exists. Most rules of the 1976 Prison Act for adults have, however, been copied into administrative regulations for Youth Prisons (*Verwaltungsvorschriften für den Jugendstrafvollzug*). According to German law, however, these administrative regulations cannot replace a law. Therefore, a broad discussion has been started, both in academia and in practice, about the un-constitutionality of the current situation of Youth Prisons. Almost all experts demand a special Act on Youth Corrections. Respective cases are pending before the Federal Constitutional Court. The Federal Ministry of Justice is already working on a draft for such an Act.

Box 4.3: Pre-trial Detention

Detention before trial (*Untersuchungshaft*) is not seen as punishment, but as a way to ensure the presence of the accused at the trial or to prevent the accused from tampering with the evidence. In Germany, pre-trial detention shall be served in institutions *(Untersuchungsgefängnisse)*, separate from those for sentenced prisoners. Under German law, pre-trial prisoners have special privileges on the basis of the presumption of innocence. But, *de facto*, the incarceration regime is known to be tougher in pre-trial detention. Apart from one article in the German Code of Criminal Procedure (art. 119 StPO), there is no legal regulation that details the prisoners' rights and duties in pre-trial detention. The only existing body of rules is an administrative regulation *(Untersuchungshaftvollzugsordnung)*.

Also in 1977, the East German Democratic Republic passed its own Prison Act. It included some rather progressive features[5] (e.g., giving inmates a right to paid work with all the normal social security benefits and a right to gainful employment after release from prison). The East

German prison law was, however, primarily a propaganda measure directed towards the West, as can be also seen from the fact that the text of the Act was never made available to inmates.

The (West) German Prison Act includes a few general principles as well as some 200 individual provisions. The most important principle relates to what in Germany is usually referred to as the resocialization or rehabilitation goal (*Resozialisierungsziel*):

> "While serving the sentence, the prisoner shall be enabled to lead, in social responsibility, a life without criminal offences (goal of corrections)" (Art. 2, Prison Act).

Other important general principles, partly modelled on the UN Standard Minimum Rules for the Treatment of Prisoners, are included in Art. 3 of the Prison Act:

- *Angleichungsgrundsatz* (principle of normalization): life in corrections shall as much as possible resemble general living conditions outside prison; and

- *Gegenwirkungsgrundsatz* (principle of damage reduction): correctional authorities shall counteract the damaging consequences of imprisonment.

More specific regulations encompass cell accommodation, food, health, religion, work, leisure activities, security and discipline. Of central importance for the implementation of the rehabilitation goal are the norms about individual correctional planning (arts. 6 and 7, Prison Act). They stipulate that, as a rule, the prison administration is obliged to investigate the prisoner's background and needs in order to develop specific measures for his reintegration into society. In practice, the most important of these measures seem to be the so-called relaxations (*Lockerungen*), which include home leaves, work furloughs, open prisons and other ways to give the prisoner a chance to be outside the prison while still serving the sentence. This was started in some parts of Germany (e.g., Hamburg and Bavaria) some years before, and this successful practice was then generalized in the Prison Act. The only prerequisites for such measures are that there is neither a risk of absconding nor of committing new offences.

German law differentiates only between "open prisons" and "closed prisons": the latter imply the presence of effective measures against absconding, while the former make do with few or no such measures. In practice, however, special high-security units (*Hochsicherheitstrakte*) were introduced without much legal basis in the 1970s in order to effectively separate politically motivated offenders, especially those of the so-called Red Army faction (see Box 4.4).

Box 4.4: Red Army Faction (RAF)

Formed in 1970, this self-styled revolutionary organization was active until the early 1990s and formally dissolved in 1998. Through kidnappings and assassinations of leading members of German industry and the German state, the group aimed at destabilizing the capitalist system. The arrest, pre-trial detention and the death under mysterious conditions of its leading members (Andreas Baader, Ulrike Meinhof and Gudrun Ensslin) led to strong national and international interest in German prison conditions. The isolation of some of the prisoners was especially criticized as "isolation torture." The demand of RAF prisoners to officially grant them the status of "political prisoners" was never met. But they were, on their own request, kept in small groups, separate from the rest of the prison population. For this purpose specially designed high-security units (*Hochsicherheitstrakte*) were constructed. Today, almost all RAF prisoners have been released, usually by way of executive clemency.

Of particular importance are also the norms about prisoners' access to the courts. Special judges for the supervision of corrections (*Strafvollstreckungsrichter*) are appointed at the court nearest to a particular prison. They are competent to decide about all complaints prisoners may have against the prison administration, as well as about questions of early release (parole). Many prisoners make frequent use of this possibility. But research shows that they are only in rare cases successful.[6]

The Prison Act also stipulates that working prisoners are to be included in the general system of health insurance and old age pensions. Yet, at the time of preparing this chapter (2003), these provisions had not yet been brought into effect, because the finance ministers of the *Länder* asked for a delay. The idea to adjust prison wages as much as possible to outside standards has been met with a similar fate. The original plans called for a gradual increase of the prisoners' wages; but this legislative promise has never been honoured. As a result, inmate wages have remained at a level of 5% of the average outsider wages. Only recently, a decision of the Federal Constitutional Court[7] forced the legislature to agree on a moderate increase (from 5% to 9% of the average outside wages).

Major changes were made in the 1999 Act To Change the Prison Act (*Strafvollzugsgesetz-Änderungsgesetz*). Most important are the new norms for data protection and data exchange in art. 178 ff. Worth mentioning are also other changes such as the newly introduced right of prisoners to buy and use private TV sets for their prison cells (art. 69 StVollzG). These changes are largely attributable to prisoners' court actions.

As can be seen from the above review, correctional practices in Germany have come a long way since the German Constitutional Court forced the legislature to pass a Prison Act. But, the Prison Act remains partly unimplemented and falls short of the goals of its makers. In recent years, however, opposition to these very goals has been forming (see below: Future Directions).

Administrative Process

While the Prison Act (*Strafvollzugsgesetz*) is a federal law, its implementation and administration rests with the hands of the individual states. The Prison Act is supplemented by a great many administrative regulations on the level of individual states as well as on the level of particular prisons. With regard to important matters, the states have agreed among themselves on country-wide administrative regulations *(bundeseinheitliche Verwaltungsvorschriften)*. These administrative regulations are not regarded as legal rules, but only as internal guidelines for the interpretation of the federal law and the use of discretion. These administrative rules are also not binding for the courts. But since they are binding for the members of the administration, they have considerable impact on the administrative process and therefore on prison reality. For example, home leaves are regulated in great detail by (changing) administrative rules, while the relevant clause of the Prison Act has remained unchanged.

German prisons follow the hierarchical administrative model. The highest echelon in this hierarchy is the Minister of Justice of the respective state, responsible for the supervision of the prisons of his territory (see Figure 4.1).

Figure 4.1: Organigram of the German Prison Administration

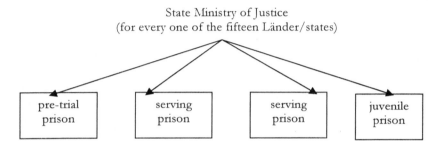

Federal Ministry of Justice
(no competency for the administration of prisons; there are no Federal prisons)

State Ministry of Justice
(for every one of the fifteen Länder/states)

| pre-trial prison | serving prison | serving prison | juvenile prison |

The state-level Justice Ministries are authorized to promulgate general administrative guidelines *(Verwaltungsvorschriften)*, binding for the staff of all their prisons. Such guidelines also specify conditions under which the Ministry of Justice reserves decisions for itself or makes them subject to their approval.[8] Such direct interventions of the Ministries into prison affairs continue despite of misgivings among prison directors and despite academic questioning of their legality.

Each prison is governed by a prison director, who, according to the Prison Act (art. 156) has complete responsibility for the operation of the institution. S/he may, however, delegate certain tasks to other staff members. During the 20th century, the position of director was usually filled by someone with a legal background. However, in recent years, jurists have begun to lose their monopoly on the position as psychologists and social workers are making important inroads. The director, like the rest of the staff, is of course bound by the Prison Act, which includes numerous provisions whereby the director has considerable discretion in how to administer the institution. This is particularly true for decisions to grant "relaxations" *(Lockerungen)*.

Home Leaves and Relaxation

In practice, **home leaves** (*Urlaub*) and other **relaxations** (*Lockerungen*) have become the most important single feature of the contemporary German prison system.[9] Since 1977, every prisoner can get up to 21 days of home leave per year, plus an unlimited number of day leaves (*Ausgang*). "Between 1977 and 1996 the number of periods of home leave granted increased from 243 to 649 per 100,000 prisoners and the number of periods of short prison leave increased from 219 to 1,069 per 100,000 prisoners of the daily sentenced population."[10] The states making up the former German Democratic Republic started to practice home leaves only after reunification. Since the reunification, these states have largely caught up with the national average.

The rate of prisoners' abusing relaxations is low. Less than 1% of all prisoners granted home leaves do not return on their own. Also (known) criminal offences committed during home leaves are relatively few and usually minor. Research covering all home leaves (over 90,000) granted to prisoners in Lower Saxony during two years shows that 246 known criminal offences were committed by prisoners on home leaves. Most of these offences were minor property offences; only one was a sexual offence.[11] This success of relaxations arguably reduces some of the typical negative consequences and side effects of imprisonment (e.g., forced sexual abstinence; loss of contact with relatives, friends and societal developments, etc.). Relaxations are also responsible for the virtual extinction of the traditional practice of swallowing objects (from forks to razor blades) in order to be temporarily removed from prison to a hospital. On the other hand, the denial of home leaves (and other relaxations) has become the most important and effective disciplinary measure, even though not foreseen as such in the Prison Act.

Prison Staff

Prison staff are largely composed of full-time guards. Hiring prison staff is, like all administrative matters, in the competency of each individual state; there are no known national criteria. Until the 1970s, female staff worked only in women's prisons, but now they are also hired to work in male prisons (with the idea to "civilize" the prison culture). Prison staff receives mainly on-the-job training. In addition, there is a long tradition of staff members with an agricultural or artisanal background (*Werkbeamte*) running the prison industries. The hiring of academically trained personnel began to become more common after the Prison Act (1977) specifically provided for medical clerics, medical doctors, educators, psychologists and social workers. These full-time services are supplemented by visits from some of the regular social services of the community or the state (e.g., drug counsellors, labour counsellors, etc.) and private non-governmental organizations offering aftercare services. Legal services for prisoners are mostly lacking since legal advice may only be offered by practicing lawyers.[12]

Privatization

Wholesale privatization of prisons is not seen, by most legal experts, as an option under German law. But some of the services originally performed by prison staff are being increasingly farmed out to semi-private or private organisations. This is true for much of the sphere of prisoners' work. Major private companies (e.g., Siemens, Lufthansa, etc.) run production lines in prisons. About 10% of all working prisoners do so outside prison, on work furlough, for regular wages. The experience with this policy is rather good, except that high unemployment outside prisons has a negative impact on such programs.

PROFILE OF THE CORRECTIONAL POPULATION

In German adult sentencing there are only two major alternatives to imprisonment: the suspended prison sentence (*Strafaussetzung zur Bewährung*), and the day fine (*Geldstrafe nach Tagessätzen*). Fines make up about 80% of all criminal sentences (but about 5% lead to imprisonment for fine default). The remaining 20% are prison sentences, of which two-thirds are suspended. Specifically, the option of community work does not exist in Germany as a sentencing alternative for adults, but only as a way to avoid imprisonment in cases of fine default. In about half of the suspended prison sentences, a "probation helper" (*Bewährungshelfer*) is appointed, usually a full-time professional probation officer. Despite such help, many suspended sentences have to be revoked because of new offences or because of some violation of the conditions of the suspension. In what follows, we will concentrate on unconditional imprisonment, which is quantitatively the least important sanction in Germany, but still represents the backbone of the German correctional system.

As has been the case with a number of other countries represented in this text, the imprisonment rate in Germany decreased in the 1980s[13] and reached its lowest point in 1991. Interestingly, in the first few years after reunification, the East German prison population fell from 24,000 to 5,000. This is largely attributable to the fact that many political prisoners were released and that the West German Criminal Code became applicable.[14]

Since 1991, however, the rate of imprisonment has gone back to its previous level of about 90 per 100,000 of the general population.[15] But there are signs that the increase may not have reached its highest point yet (see Table 4.1). This increase is not due to a similar increase in major crime, but rather to more and longer prison sentences and to a reduction in the use of parole. Since the 1980s, drug offenders have contributed most heavily to the increase in longer sentences (by now, they make-up at least one-third of the prison population). Furthermore, since 1990 the number of life sentences has more than doubled (while the number of paroled lifers has remained the same). In the late 1990s, a "moral panic" about sexual crimes (especially crimes involving children) led to major changes in the German Penal Code[16] and contributed again to longer sentences.

Table 4.1: Development of Sentences for Adult Offenders in Germany*

Year	Total sentenced offenders	Imprisonment	Suspended sentence	Fine
1980	599,832	35,972	68,878	494,114
1990	615,089	32,749	69,705	512,343
2000	638,893	40,735	84,552	513,336

*Source: Federal Statistical Office (data for the states of the Federal Republic are available only for the period before unification).

Germany has been host to foreign workers since the end of World War II. They were instrumental in helping to rebuild the country. However, given national laws, it used to be difficult to obtain German nationality status. This situation has been changing lately; since the year 2000 half a million foreigners have obtained German citizenship. In 2003, foreign workers and refugees made up 8.9% of the general prison population. This figure rises to approximately 10% when the estimated number of illegal foreigners is added, even though Germany has a system which requires all foreigners working, studying, or visiting for six weeks or more to register with the local town/city administration office.

Another important shift in the correctional population occurred with respect to "aliens." The number of imprisoned persons without German citizenship in the adult prisons has increased from 7% (in 1980) to almost 25% (1999). In some juvenile prisons (e.g., Adelsheim and Baden-Württemberg) the number of imprisoned foreigners is even higher. Table 4.2 shows the number of correctional inmates (adults only), with and without German citizenship from 1971 to 2002. It also shows that the trend to ever higher percentages of foreigners in German prisons seems to have come to a stop.

Women form only a small part (about 4%) of the prison population. As a rule, they have to be kept separate from male prisoners. There are eight prisons just for women in Germany; the rest of female prisoners are housed in separate wings of men's prisons (see Figure 4.2). Exceptions from this "principle of separation" (*Trennungsgebot*) are legally possible in favour of joint treatment measures. Among the few examples of such practices are:

- The small socio-therapeutic institution in Hamburg-Altengamme (see Box 4.5), which is run on a completely co-correctional basis; and,

- The training kitchen of the women's institution in Vechta (Lower Saxony), which accepts also male trainees.

Table 4.2: Development of the Prison Population in Germany

Year	Serving prisoners total	German nationality	Non-German nationality	Non-German in %
1971	27,614	26,589	1,025	3.7
1972*				
1973	29,894	28,406	1,488	5.0
1974*				
1975*				
1976	37,860	35,672	2,188	5.8
1977	33,559	31,501	2,058	6.1
1978	34,868	32,653	2,215	6.4
1979	35,594	33,269	2,325	6.6
1980	35,537	32,982	2,555	7.1
1981*				
1982	38,620	34,897	3,723	9.6
1983	40,819	36,845	3,974	9.7
1984	42,140	37,997	4,143	9.8
1985	41,852	37,785	4,067	9.7
1986	39,407	35,667	3,740	9.5
1987	36,978	33,325	3,662	9.9
1988	36,076	32,344	3,732	10.3
1989	36,101	32,000	4,101	11.4
1990	34,799	30,432	4,367	12.5
1991	33,392	28,757	4,367	13.9
1992	35,401	30,076	5,325	15.0
1993	37,128	30,739	6,389	17.2
1994	39,327	31,447	7,880	20.0
1995	41,353	32,428	8,925	21.6
1996	43,475	33,686	9,789	22.5
1997	45,718	34,720	10,998	24.0
1998	50,021	37,788	12,233	24.5
1999	52,351	39,597	12,754	24.4
2000	53,183	40,555	12,626	23.7
2001	52,939	40,810	12,129	22.9
2002	52,988	40,823	12,165	22.9

Source: Statistisches Bundesamt, Rechtspflege, Reihe Strafvollzug, different years.
* = missing data.

Figure 4.2: Prisoners in Germany
Imprisonment Rates as of March 31, 2001
© InfoKrim / CimInfo [H.J.Kerner et al., Tuebingen / Germany 2002]

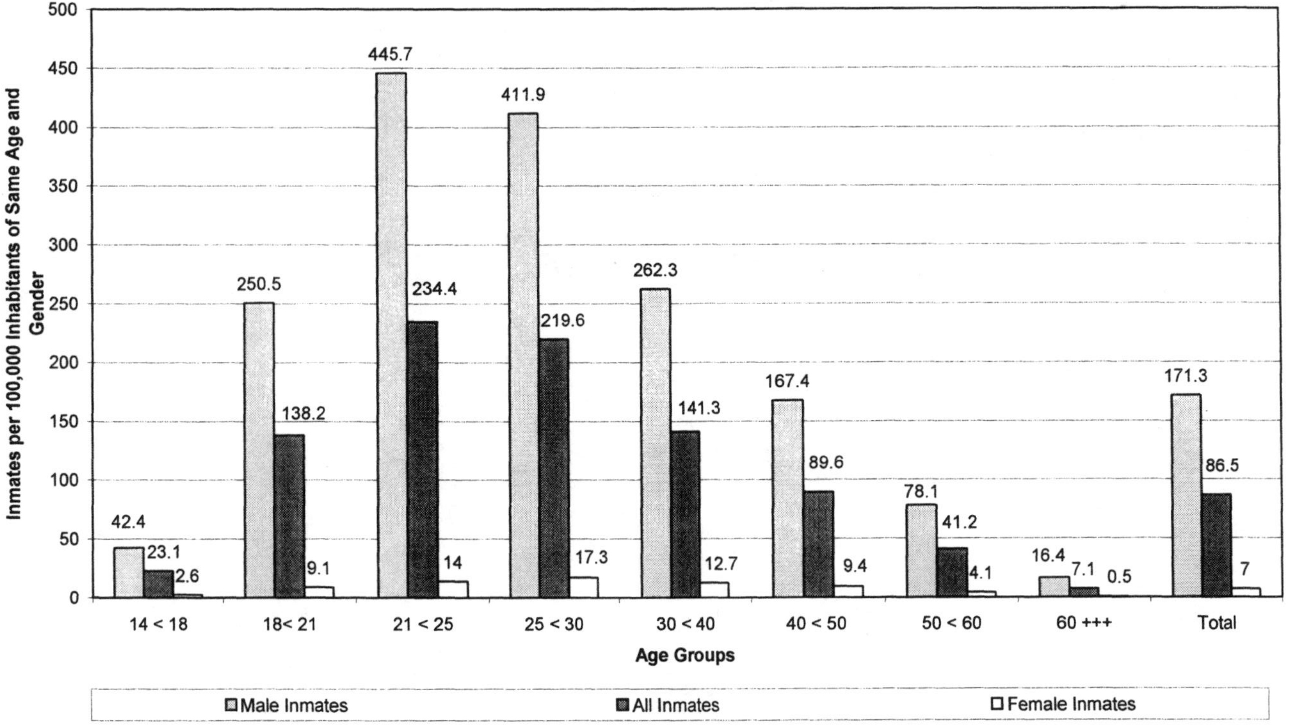

Inmates per 100,000 Inhabitants of Same Age and Gender

Age Groups

□ Male Inmates   ■ All Inmates   □ Female Inmates

Age Group	Male	All	Female
14 < 18	42.4	23.1	2.6
18 < 21	250.5	138.2	9.1
21 < 25	445.7	234.4	14
25 < 30	411.9	219.6	17.3
30 < 40	262.3	141.3	12.7
40 < 50	167.4	89.6	9.4
50 < 60	78.1	41.2	4.1
60 +++	16.4	7.1	0.5
Total	171.3	86.5	7

Box 4.5: Hamburg-Altengamme

"This socio-therapeutic institution was founded in 1984. It was planned and is run on a co-correctional basis. Among its 60 inmates are usually up to ten women. Between 6:00 and 22:00 all inmates can move freely on the premises. Together they can participate in training, leisure and work. They also may visit with each other in their one-person cell rooms. This realistic and down-to-earth program has proved successful, since it tends to mirror those conflicts and communication problems commonly found between men and women (e.g., in the forms suppression/submission) that also in liberty foster violence and unhappiness. As promising as these programs are, they can only be conducted when the conditions of detention are intensively normalized" (Gerhard Rehn, founder and first director of the institution, in: Feest [2000], page 760).

ISSUES CONFRONTING CORRECTIONS TODAY

There are many issues confronting the German correctional system today. We have chosen to concentrate on only three of them: the health issues raised (e.g., HIV and HCV) by imprisoning large numbers of drug addicts,[17] the human dignity issues raised by overcrowding, and the debate about privatizing prisons.

Drug Addicts and Infection Prophylaxis

Drug abuse was not a big problem in Germany until the 1970s. Since then, there has been a continual increase of drug arrests, of sentences for drug-related offences and of drug users in prison. The number of drug users in prison cannot be gleaned from official statistics, since these refer only to persons sentenced for possession and trafficking (while drug-related offences like robbery, theft, etc. are not counted as drug offences). But it has been suggested that over 50% of the prison population are drug users.[18] Research is largely lacking and it is methodologically difficult because of the reluctance of many drug addicts to be treated while in prison. Estimates indicate that at least one-third of the prison population is dependent on illegal drugs (the number of alcohol addicts may be even larger). Needle-sharing and ensuing HIV-infections have become a major concern for prison medical services. But, unlike many of its European counterparts, German prisons do not provide hepatitis B vaccinations to prisoners. To reduce this risk, methadone programs in prison were introduced in the 1990s. A few prisons have successfully experimented with supplying sterile hypodermic needles to addicts. For example, the women's prison in Vechta and the Lingen I men's prison have been using prevention measures including sterile syringes since 1996 (Jutta and Stoever, 1997).

Germany is among the few European countries that provide this service to inmates. But these programs have suffered political setbacks recently and their future is uncertain.[19] A related concern is that in German prisons, doctors are paid by the institution, thereby limiting the opportunity to develop a patient-and-physician relationship. Some research reveals that inmates have a tendency to mistrust doctors and "meet them with reservation and prejudice," thereby compromising the effectiveness and attraction of maintenance programs (see Keppler and Stoever, 2003). According to a European Union report, in 2000, there were some 350 drug counsellors who were providing services in German prisons. Currently, the maintenance treatment program has not been implemented throughout all prisons. In fact, there is a noticeable difference in the acceptance of such programs throughout the country. While the various states continue to explore the use of such psychosocial programs, the five new states in former East German do not have the same drug addiction problem as the western states.

Overcrowding and Human Dignity

Until the late 1980s, prison overcrowding seemed a thing of the past, and some of the old prisons were even closed, or converted into such settings as offices for prosecutors. As reflected in Table 4.1 above, increasing prison populations have led to renewed overcrowding, claims of inhuman living conditions and to prison building programs. Recent decisions by the Federal Constitutional Court (see Box 4.3) have underlined that certain living conditions may indeed violate the human dignity of prisoners. As a consequence, in 2003 a court in Hannover awarded monetary damages to a prisoner for having been placed in such conditions by the state of Lower Saxonia.[20]

Privatization

As in many other Western countries, in recent years privatization has been impacting correctional practices. The Federal constitution includes, however, a provision that explicitly prohibits wholesale privatisation of sovereign competencies (*hoheitsrechtliche Aufgaben*).[21] On this basis, legal experts in Germany[22] are largely in agreement that key aspects of the prison operations, especially those pertaining to the deprivation of liberty, the use of physical force and disciplinary matters have to remain a monopoly of the state. Other areas are seen as legally valid candidates for outsourcing (e.g. medical services, providing food and work for prisoners, etc.). The area of treatment is in dispute. A first partly privatized prison is presently being planned in Northrhine-Westfalia (see Box 4.6).

Box 4.6: Prison Partly Privatized

In Northrhine–Westfalia, the first partly private prison in Germany is going to be built. This was announced yesterday by justice minister Wolfgang Gerhards (SPD). The prison in the area of Düsseldorf/Duisburg will have a capacity of 850... The Justice Department wants to test with this pilot project, whether the partly privatized construction and running of a prison is indeed more economic. In a 25-year time-span of this cooperation, savings of 54 million euros have been calculated. "This will not be a private prison" says Gerhards. The sovereignty-related parts will stay in the hands of the state. But more than one-fifth of the regular tasks — like kitchen or storage — can be handled by private contractors.

(Newspaper report: *Kölner Stadtanzeiger*, 05.06.2003)

Available German experience with outsourcing indicates, however, that the attempt to separate these areas causes considerable organizational problems that reduce the advantages hoped for. No published German research studies exist, but the state of Bremen is, after only a few years, reconsidering its outsourcing of medical, educational, and labour services.

FUTURE DIRECTIONS

Changes in German prison and correctional practices are being impacted on two levels: national and within the greater European community.

As we have indicated, current German prison law treats resocialization/rehabilitiation as the only goal to be sought through imprisonment. Ideally, the whole apparatus (i.e., planning, relaxations, early release, etc.) is supposed to be geared towards this goal. Relaxations of the prison regime, especially home leaves, have been the outstanding feature of the German prison practice since the mid-1970s. But change seems to be imminent. Since 1998, leading politicians have started to question and dismantle the resocialization goal enshrined in the German Prison Act. This move has, in part, been driven by *"penal populism"* (i.e., the idea that the population demands more emphasis on security from imprisoned offenders than on their eventual resocialization — also see the Introduction to this anthology). The very concept of resocialization is increasingly regarded as belonging to the 1960s and 1970s and as now obsolete. Since this contradicts the clear language of the Prison Act, legislation to change this language is currently under construction. But while the outcome of legislative action is still unclear, many States have already started to implement the new policy. Starting in 1999, statistics of home leaves and other relaxations have taken a nosedive in many German states, with Hessen and Brandenburg taking the lead (see Table 4.3).

Meanwhile, most other German states seem to be following this trend. In the long run, this is bound to lead to longer times spent in prison. Only one state — the biggest of them all, Nordrhein-Westfalen — is still resisting this trend, showing a consistent increase in home leaves year after year. It remains to be seen which side will eventually give in.

Europeanization of Corrections

Criminal law in general and prisons in particular have not been among the agenda and competencies of the European Community. Therefore, genuine European legal regulations do not yet exist in these areas. Even in the new European Union Treaty prisons are still relegated to the "third pillar" of matters that need to be negotiated between governments. Over the years, these same governments have, however, co-operated with respect to criminal justice in the context of the Council of Europe (a regional organization based in Strasbourg). There are two noteworthy instruments that have resulted from this cooperation: the European Prison Rules and the European Committee for the Prevention of Torture and Inhuman or Degrading Treatment and Punishment (CPT).

Table 4.3: Home Leaves Granted to Prisoners in German States

	Home leaves (peak year)	Home leaves (2002)	Percent change from peak year to 2002
Hessen	32,301 (1998)	17,096	minus 47%
Brandenburg	7,230 (1999)	4,100	minus 43%
Bremen	7,072 (1999)	4,310	minus 39%
Sachsen	7,090 (1999)	4,990	minus 30%
Schleswig-Holstein	9,202 (2000)	6,915	minus 25%
Rheinland-Pfalz	18,744 (1999)	15,142	minus 19%
Saarland	7,855 (1999)	6,566	minus 16%
Bayern	28,845 (1996)	24,518	minus 14%
Sachsen-Anhalt	2,829 (2001)	2,496	minus 12%
Baden-Württemberg	25,254 (2000)	23,199	minus 09%
Hamburg	17,066 (2001)	15,725	minus 08%
Berlin	34,232 (2000)	32,244	minus 06%
Thüringen	3,464 (2001)	3,252	minus 06%
Mecklenburg-Vorpommern	6,354 (2001)	6,206	minus 02%
Niedersachsen	no data available	no data available	no data available
Total Germany (without Nordrhein-Westfalen)	195,159 (1999)	166,749	minus 15%

	home leaves (1999)	home leaves (2002)	percent change
Nordrhein-Westfalen	107,142	127,399	plus 16%
Total Germany	302,301	294,148	minus 03%

Source: Calculated on the basis of unpublished statistics collected by the German Federal Ministry of Justice.

The Council of Europe's **European Prison Rules**[23] are a European version of the United Nations Standard Minimum Rules. Rather than binding law, they represent a recommendation to governments to "be guided in their internal legislation and practice by the principles set out in the text of the European Prison Rules" (Recommendation No. R (87) 3 of the Committee of Ministers to member States) (see Box 4.7). They can be seen as an expression of international legal consciousness. In practice they have gained importance through the work of the CPT's prison inspectors who regularly visit prisons of Council of Europe members. In their reports to the respective governments, these inspectors, frequently refer to the European Prison Rules as an accepted minimum standard for "good prison practice." This in turn can lead to a modicum of harmonization with respect to national practice and, sometimes, prison legislation in Europe. So far, the CPT has made three regular visits and one ad hoc visit to Germany. This has led to a number of changes on the level of individual prisons, but it has also led to a change in the German Prison Act.[24]

Box 4.7: The Purpose of the European Prison Rules

As found under the section Preamble, the following four points represent the general purpose of the European Prison Rules:

(a) to establish a range of minimum standards for all those aspects of prison administration that are essential to human conditions and positive treatment in modern and progressive systems;

(b) to serve as a stimulus to prison and administrations to develop policies and management style and practice based on good contemporary principles of purpose and equity;

(c) to encourage in prison staffs professional attitudes that reflect the important social and moral qualities of their work and to create conditions in which they can optimise their own performance to the benefit of society in general, the prisoners in their care and their own vocational satisfaction; and,

(d) to provide realistic basic criteria against which prison administrations and those responsible for inspecting the conditions and management of prisons can make valid judgements of performance and measure progress towards higher standards.

Source: http://www.uncjin.org/Laws/prisrul.htm.

The cooperation in the context of the Council of Europe cannot fail to have some effect on future European Union directives with respect to prisons, once the European Union has expanded its jurisdiction to criminal law matters.

CONCLUSION

German corrections has come a long way from an authoritarian, quasi-military system to a system where the rule of law and the goal of rehabilitation are officially acknowledged. German prisons have by and large remained total institutions,[25] which makes it more difficult for the rule of law to be implemented into the day-to-day operations. Total institutions are also not a very congenial setting for rehabilitating/resocializing people. In addition, rehabilitation/resocialization, enshrined in the German Prison Act as the only goal of corrections, is being challenged from politicians, who demand that "security" be given at least the same importance. The future of the German correctional system is, however, not in the hands of the German alone. It is likely to be more and more influenced by regulations and court decisions emanating from the European Union.

Key Terms and Concepts

European Prison Rules	Home leaves	F. v. Liszt
Relaxations	Strafvollzugsgesetz	
Zuchthaus		

Discussion/Study Questions

(1) Is there an official goal established for corrections in Germany?

(2) Do prisoners have rights in Germany? How do these rights compare with others countries covered in this text?

(3) In France, Great Britain, Italy and Spain, the prisons are managed by a centralized prison administration. Is this also true for Germany? Explore the implications.

(4) What is the importance of home leaves and other relaxations in Germany?

(5) Mother-child units in prison have spread from Germany to other countries. Discuss advantages and disadvantages.

(6) Why do no private prisons exist in Germany? Based on the experience with private prisons in several of the other contributions, are there issues that the German Ministry of Justice might want to consider?

(7) Does European Union policy influence German prison conditions?

Helpful Web-links

Attached to the University of Bremen, the following Web Page includes mainly legal information (including the text of the Prison Act) for prisoners, their relatives and their legal advisors (in German language):
Strafvollzugsarchiv (www.strafvollzugsarchiv.de).

This Web page includes a wealth of information on German prisons (in German language):
Knastnet (www.knast.net).

This Web Page is organized by prisoners from inside the JVA Tegel, the main Berlin prison (in German language):
Planet Tegel (www.planettegel.de).

This site includes the CPT's reports on several visits to German places of detention, including police stations and psychiatric wards (in English and French):
Committee for the Prevention of Torture (www.cpt.coe.int).

This site provides an English version of the Council of Europe's Prison Rules:
European Prison Rules (http://www.uncjin.org/Laws/prisrul.htm).

REFERENCES

Albrecht, H-J. (2002). "Juvenile Crime and Juvenile Law in the Federal Republic of Germany." In: J. Winterdyk (ed.), *Juvenile Justice Systems: International Perspectives* (2nd ed.). Toronto, CAN: Canadian Scholars' Press.

Arnold, J. (1995). "Corrections in the German Democratic Republic: A Field for Research." *British Journal of Criminology* 35(1):81-94.

Council of Europe (1987). *European Prison Rules* (rev. ed.). Strasbourg, FR.

Dünkel, F. and D. Rössner (2001). "Germany." In: D. van Zyl Smit and F. Dünkel (eds.), *Imprisonment Today and Tomorrow. International Perspectives on Prisoners' Rights and Prison Conditions* (2nd ed.). The Hague, NETH: Kluwer Law International.

Feest, J. (ed.). (2000). *Kommentar zum Strafvollzugsgesetz* (4th ed.). Neuwied: Luchterhand.

—— (1999). "Imprisonment and Prisoners' Work." *Punishment & Society* 1(1):99-107.

—— (1991). "Reducing the Prison Population: Lessons from the West German Experience." In: J. Muncie and R. Sparks (eds.), *Imprisonment: European Perspectives.* Hemel Hempstead, UK: Harvester Wheatsheaf.

—— W. Lesting and P. Selling (1997). *Totale Institution und Rechtsschutz. Eine Untersuchung zum Rechtsschutz im Strafvollzug,* Opladen: Westdeutscher Verlag.

—— and H-M. Weber (1998). "Germany: Ups and Downs in the Resort to Imprisonment – Strategic or Unplanned Outcomes?" In: R.P. Weis and N. South (eds.), *Comparing Prison Systems. Toward a Comparative and International Penology.* Amsterdam, NETH: Gordon and Breach Publishers.

Harling, A. von (1997). *Der Mißbrauch von Vollzugslockerungen zu Straftaten. Eine empirische Untersuchung zur Bewährung der Lockerungspraxis am Beispiel Niedersachsens in den Jahren 1990 und 1991.* München, GER: Fink.

Jutta, J. and H. Stoever (1997). "Germany – Needle Exchange in Prisons in Lower Saxony: A Preliminary Review." *Canadian HIV/AIDS Policy and Law Newsletter* 3(2-3).

Kamann, U. (2002). *Handbuch für die Strafvollstreckung und den Strafvollzug, Recklinghausen.* Recklinghausen, GER: ZAP.

Keppler, K. and H. Stoever (2003). "Methadone Maintenance in German Prisons." Online (retrieved August 22/03) at: www.q4q.nl/network/newsletter14/prison.htm.

Lines, R., R. Jürgens, H. Stöever, D. Laticevschi and J. Nelles (2003). "Prison Needle Exchange: A Review of International Evidence and Experience." *Canadian HIV/AIDS Policy & Law Newsletter* 2(4).

Müller-Dietz, H. (2000). *Recht und Nationalsozialismus. Gesammelte Beiträge.* Baden-Baden: Nomos.

Radzinowicz, L. (1991). *The Roots of the International Association of Criminal Law and their Significance. A Tribute and a Re-assessment on the Centenary of the IKV.* Freiburg, GER: Max Planck Institute for Foreign and International Penal Law.

Walter, M. (1991). *Strafvollzug* (2nd ed.). Stuttgart, GER.

NOTES

1. The influence of religious ideas decreased in the national-liberal climate of German politics in the late 19th century. While clerics had played a major role in organizing and running prisons before, they were now relegated to the status of mere priests.

2. In addition to prison changes, the Nazis introduced concentration and extermination camps.

3. Müller-Dietz (2000), pp. 89-131.

4. For an overview of the juvenile justice system in Germany see Albrecht (2002).

5. For details cf. Arnold (1995).

6. See Feest, Lesting, and Selling (1997).

7. See Feest (1999).

8. For example, in all states lifers can get home leaves only with the approval of the Justice Ministry; in some states, this requirement is extended to other categories of prisoners (sexual offenders; crimes of violence, etc.).

9. For details cf. Dünkel and Rössner (2001), pp. 327-332.

10. See Dünkel and Rössner (2001), p. 327.

11. See Harling (1997).

12. For background and implications see Kamann (2002), p. 673.

13. See Feest (1991).

14. Even prior to the unification in 1990, East Germany had begun to modify its criminal justice and correctional procedures and practices.

15. On the background of these contractions and expansions cf. Feest and Weber (1998).

16. See: Ulrich Eisenberg/Achim Hackethal (1998). "Gesetz zur Bekämpfung von Sexualdelikten und anderen gefährlichen Straftaten vom 26.1.1998." *Zeitschrift für Strafvollzug und Straffälligenhilfe* 196-202.

17. According to reports from the Council of Europe, drugs are seen as one of the major social problems of the current prison system not only in Germany but throughout Europe.

18. Research shows that about 30% of all male prisoners and about 70% of all female prisoners are "addicted to illegal drugs or at least strongly endangered" (Walter, 1999, p. 282).

19. See Limes et al. (2003).

20. LG Hannover *Strafverteidiger,* October 2003.

21. "The exercise of sovereign powers as a continuing task has to handled as a rule by civil servants, who are duty-bound within a public-law relationship of loyalty and trust" (Art. 33, para 4, GG).

22. cf. Christoph Gusy/Olivia Lührmann, "Rechtliche Grenzen des Einsatzes privater Sicherheitsdienste im Strafvollzug" *Strafverteidiger* 2001, pp. 46-54; S. Braum/M. Varwig,/Ch. Bader "Die 'Privatisierung des Strafvollzugs' zwischen fiskalischen Interessen und verfassungsrechtlichen Prinzipien" *Zeitschrift für Strafvollzug und Streaffälligenhilfe* 1999, pp. 67-73.

23. Council of Europe (1987).

24. For details cf. the CPT's web page *(www.cpt.coe.int).*

25. "Total institution" is used in Goffman's sense: i.e., everything under one roof, highly centralized command, fundamental distinction (and distrust) between inmates and guards (see Feest et al., 1997).

CHAPTER 5.
ADULT CORRECTIONS IN INDIA

by

Tapan Chakraborty
Bureau of Police Research and Development
New Delhi, India

and

Kiara Okita
Research Associate
Edmonton, Canada

BASIC FACTS ON INDIA

Area: The Indian Union is 135.79 million square kilometers. India is bordered by Pakistan to the northwest; China to the north; Tibet, Nepal and Bhutan in the East; and to the southeast, south and west by the Indian Ocean. The capital of India is New Delhi, with a population of 13,782,976 in 2001 (1.34% of India's total population) (India Census, 2001).

Population: As of 2001, India's total population was 1.027 billion, or 324 persons per square kilometer. India is therefore one of the most populated countries in the world, with a gender ratio of 933 females per 1,000 males. In 2000, India's birth rate was 25.8 per 1,000, and the death rate was 8.5 per 1,000 persons. Major cities include Bangalore (4.3 million), Ahmedabad (3.5 million) and Lucknow (2.2 million).

Demographics: India is composed of Hindus (82.41%), Muslims (11.67%), Christians (2.32%), Sikhs (1.99%), Buddhists (0.77%), Jains (0.41%) and other (0.43%) religious affiliates, as per the 1991 census.

Provided by the Constitution, India's official language is Hindi, however English can also be used for official purposes. India's overall literacy rate is 65.38%. India's crime rate in 2000 was 176.7 offenses per 100,000 population, which represents a decrease from 1996 when the crime rate was recorded at 183.4 per 100,000.

Climate: India's climate is characterized by four seasons, winter (December-March), summer (April-May), rainy (June-September) and post monsoon (October-November). Because of India's great climatic diversity, it is more practical to view the climate in terms of average local temperatures, rather than in terms of national averages.

Economy: Rich in natural resources, India's primary industries include farming, forestry, fishing, mining, quarrying, textiles, and the manufacturing of teas, sugar, cement, pharmaceuticals, chemicals, steel, machine tools and automobiles. India's unemployment rate was 7.32% in 1999-2000. The per capita income was rupees (Rs.) 16,487 at current rates (roughly 45 Rs = 1 US dollar).

Government: India is a secular state. The bulk of the population is theist, with the majority (80%+) observing Hinduism. India is also the largest democratic country in the world and became a sovereign federal democratic republic on January 26, 1950. As of August 2003, the National Democratic Alliance led by Bharatiya Janata Party (BJP) is governing the country.

★ ★ ★

"Hate the sin and not the sinner."
~ Mahatma Gandhi (1869-1948)

GENERAL HISTORY OF INDIAN CORRECTIONS

India's criminal justice system consists of four primary components: the police, prosecutions, the courts, and corrections. India's prison system (and other correctional services) has existed from time immemorial, although its purpose and use has varied. For example, in ancient India (i.e., during the Hindu Kingdom from 1000 B.C. to 1205 A.D.), prisons were erected in provincial capitals primarily for detaining individuals awaiting trial and for housing convicts. During this time, prison administration was based on the Hindu ideology (see *Arthashastra*)[1] and incarceration was used as the chief form of punishment. Towards the end of the 11th century however, Muslim rulers replaced the Hindu reign, and commenced the **Muslim Period** (1206-1756) of Indian correctional history. The Muslim administration was based on Islamic law, which reduced the use of imprisonment as punishment for an offence. Instead, justice was based on the retributive dictum of "an eye for an eye." This dictum was used literally, and laws of this period prescribed that life and/or limb was to be taken for life and/or limb. The basis of this philosophy was *deterrence* (see Glossary).

Box 5.1: Bloodmoney (*Diya*)

A form of punishment employed in lieu of *kisa* during the Muslim reign in India involved that of *diya* or *bloodmoney*. This form of punishment applied to kisa offences such as murder and maiming private individuals. In these cases, bloodmoney was awarded to the victim or the heirs of a victim according to a fixed scale.

In cases of *kisa* offences, the recipient could forego his or her right to accepting the bloodmoney and instead pardon the offender. However, in a case of multiple heirs, if one of the beneficiaries accepted *diya* or gave the offender a pardon, the other heirs had no other alternative but to instead accept their share of the bloodmoney awarded. According to a *fatwa* (a judicial decision) delivered in March of 1791, a man named Mongol Das murdered his wife and one of her heirs pardoned him. Therefore, the death sentence could not be imposed despite the remaining heirs' insistence that it be carried out. The victim's other remaining family had no choice but to accept the *diya* as a result of her murder.

Another notable feature of Muslim criminal law was the requirement that death sentences be executed by the heirs of the deceased victim.

The additional deterrent effects of **exclusion** and **expiation** guided other penal orientations employed during this time. Imprisonment, death and transportation were types of punishments derived from the principle of *exclusionism*, which generally meant to exclude a criminal from society so that s/he would be prevented from contaminating it.

Fines and compensation were forms of punishment originating from the goals of *expiation,* which intended for offenders to make reparation or atonement for the crimes they committed.

Another alternative to incarceration (*kisa*) used during the Muslim period involved that of **bloodmoney**, or a requirement that the offender pay money to the victim of his or her crime, or to the victim's family (see Box 5.1). Under Islamic law, prisons were used principally for persons awaiting trial or for persons who delayed or defaulted in their payment of *bloodmoney* (also see the Iran contribution in this text).

During the Muslim period, the use of **Quaranic Law** (based on the Islamic holy book, also spelled Koran) gained ascendancy. This form of law also minimized the use of imprisonment, and instead prescribed comparatively brutal punishments for criminal activity. The law was composed of four classes: (I) *Hadd,* (II) *Tazir,* (III) *Quisas,* and (IV) *Taskhir* law. (*Quatl* law is sometimes considered the fifth branch of *Quaranic Law.*)

(1) **Hadd** law is considered *"the right of God,"* and provided specific punishments for certain offences that no human judge could alter. The primary purpose of this level of punishment was general deterrence. Some of the forms of punishment and crimes within this category include: stoning one to death for the commission of adultery; scourging one for drinking wine and other intoxicating liquors; cutting off the right hand of a thief; and, death either by sword or impaling for crimes such as robbery or murder. Sound evidence was required to prove commission of these offences and to execute *hadd* punishments.

(2) **Tazir** law involved types of punishment intended to reform criminals and included offences not covered under *Hadd* laws and *kisa*. Examples of crimes punishable by *Tazir* law include thefts and highway robberies. These were considered crimes against the sovereign as distinguished from offences against God and offences against private persons. The punishments for these offences were left entirely to the discretion of the judges. Punishment could therefore fall within any one of the following categories:

(a) *Tadib,* or public reprimand;

(b) *Jir*, or dragging the offender to the door of the courthouse and exposing the individual to public scorn (akin to putting a man on the pillar);

(c) Imprisonment or exile; or,

(d) Humiliating the offender by boxing on the ear, scourging.

Since the punishments for *tazir* offences were entirely in the discretion of magistrates, in many cases punishments were whimsical and subjective.

(3) **Quisas** or *retaliation*, rested on the personal right of the victim or the next of kin to choose how the offender would be punished. Examples of offences punishable under *Quisas* law include maiming and murder. The victim or the victim's next of kin could demand legal punishment of the offender, which might include punishment according to the dictum "an eye for an eye"; accept *bloodmoney*; or, pardon the offender unconditionally, if the victim or the victim's family so wished. For minor offences, forms of retaliation were similar to Mosaic Law (and to the above) — "a tooth for a tooth, an eye for an eye" — with certain exceptions.

(4) **Taskhir** or *public degradation* was a popular form of punishment during the Muslim Period (as well as in Hindu India and medieval Europe). An example of a crime punishable by *Taskhir* law is the use of abusive language. An example of such punishment included shaving the offender's head, covering him or her in dust with a garland of old shoes placed around his or her neck, and making the offender ride backwards on a donkey paraded through the streets while loud music played. Another example involved simply turning the individual out of the city.

(5) **Quatl** or *capital punishment* was inflicted in certain cases of immorality such as illicit intercourse/rape, highway robbery, and apostasy from Islam, among other crimes. Prevalent forms of execution included trampling offenders with infuriated elephants, burying them alive, stinging them to death by cobras, or pressing them to death.

The **British Period** (1757-1947) commenced when British rulers succeeded the Muslims. Subsequently, they enacted the *Indian Penal Code* (IPC) in 1860 as well as other laws that altered the purpose and use of prisons in India's correctional system. Contrary to the Muslim rulers, the British provided imprisonment as punishment for most offences, which then necessitated a prison system established on a more regular and permanent footing. The prison conditions established previously were horrid and in dire need of change. ***Lord Macaulay*** (1800-1859), a British legal expert employed to assist in the reorientation of Indian penal law, was of the view that imprisonment should be a terror to wrongdoers, however that prison conditions should not be shocking to humanity. It was at his insistence that in 1836 the Prison Discipline Committee was set up, and important steps were taken to unify the laws governing prisons. For example, the administrative approach toward prisons was systematized, with particular reference to the security, health and hygiene of prisoners. The subsequent enactment of the *Prisons Act,* 1894 and the *Reformatory Schools Act,* 1897 heralded an era of serious thought given to the problems faced by prisoners (both juveniles and adults), with the ultimate aim of establishing a clear purpose for punishment.

It was only at the beginning of the 19th century that the *reformation* and *rehabilitation* (see Glossary) of offenders was accepted as the overall philosophy of the correctional system. Since these early times, India's approach has changed, albeit haltingly, from deterrence and retribution to correction and rehabilitation. These gradual changes have humanized and profoundly influenced the way in which India has consequently handled its correctional policies and practices. In fact, in 1919 and 1920, during the existence of the Indian Jail Administration Committee, for the first time in India's prison administration history, reformation and rehabilitation of offenders was accepted as the overall philosophy of the correctional system. This was a landmark orientation in the field of correctional management in India. Ironically, while formal steps were taken to alter the existing correctional practices, most of the recommendations made by the committee could not be implemented for two primary reasons. First, the provincial governments considered restructuring of the prison administration to be a low priority. Second, widespread political agitation during the decades following the submission of reports to the committee, and government's preoccupation with these agitations, overshadowed the goal of prison reforms.

It was only after India's independence (in 1947) that the government of India began to make concerted efforts to implement changes to improve the existing conditions of prisons and other correctional services in the country. In the years 1951 and 1952, support and direction for these changes emerged through the efforts and assistance of criminologist Walter C. Reckless (most well known for his association with containment theory) and UN experts invited by the Indian Government to study and improve India's correctional system. Reckless's 1952 report entitled "Jail Administration in India" is considered a landmark document in India's prison reform history. After its submission to the Indian Government in 1952, a national conference was held to examine and respond to the recommendations contained in the report. In essence, all involved parties embraced the suggestions made in Reckless's report, some of which included:

- the revision of outdated jail manuals;

- the development of full-time probation, parole, and revision boards for the aftercare services of prisoners;

- the creation of an integrated department of correctional administration to oversee prisons, Borstals (a type of training school), children's institutions, and parole, probation and aftercare services;

- the establishment of a central government correctional administration advisory board to assist the state government in developing correctional programmes;

- the creation of a national forum to provide for the exchange of professional expertise and experience; and,

- provisions for periodic and regular conferencing of senior correctional department staff.

After a careful review of the recommendations in 1957, the Indian Government established an "All India" Jail Manual Committee. The committee was given the responsibility of reconstructing the correctional framework of both prisons and prisoners in accordance with the minimum level of international standards. Despite such efforts, actual practical undertakings have seriously lagged behind these cherished goals. The condition in most Indian prisons, therefore, continues to leave much to be desired.

CORRECTIONS TODAY[2]

The motto of India's prison administration today is to rehabilitate the offender in such a way that he or she can again become a productive member of Indian society. Hence, state governments are allocating funds to provide adequate facilities to prisoners for their comfortable living and to impart training in certain vocations that are felt will be useful in their rehabilitation. Aside from funds provided by the respective states, the central government also allocates grants toward the betterment of prisons and prisoners. Recognizing the need to improve the conditions of Indian prisons, the central government has instituted a scheme of prison reforms to be implemented during the years of 2002-2003 to 2006-2007, on a 75:25 cost sharing basis between the central government's contribution and the state governments' share. The scheme visualizes the investment of Rs. 1796.55 crores (Rs. 10 million = Rs. 1 crore) in the construction of new prisons, the renovation of existing prisons, the construction of staff quarters and provisions for improved sanitation and sanitary water supplies in prisons.

Prison Structure and Jailing Facilities in India

In the 28 states and seven union territories (UTs) there are several tiers of prisons or jails. The most common and standard types of jails that are found in these states/UTs are known as central jails, district jails and sub-jails. Other facility categories include women's jails, borstal schools, open jails, special jails, lock-ups and temporary jails (see Table 5.1).

It should be noted that state or union territory government administrations oversee the operation of all prisons. No prison in India is operated by the central government.

Table 5.1: Number of Jails, Capacity, Population and Occupancy Rates, 2000

Type of Facility	Number of Facilities	Capacity of Facilities	Inmate Population	Occupancy Rate
Central Jails	90	96,037	111,215	115.8
District Jails	256	62,080	111,621	154.9
Sub Jails	635	30,831	40,890	132.6
Women's Jails	14	2,010	1,889	94.0
Borstal Schools	12	2,150	1,158	53.9
Open Jails	21	2,041	1,153	56.5
Special Jails	20	4,654	3,359	72.2
Other	10	1,917	794	41.4
TOTAL	1,058	211,720	272,079	128.5

Source: *Prison Statistics 2000,* National Crime Records Bureau, Government of India. (Also, see section on "Overcrowding" below.)

Although the term differs from state to state, a common feature to most *central jails* is that they typically house offenders serving long sentences. With proper rehabilitation facilities, central jails have larger capacities than most other jails — although not every state contains a central jail. In states/UTs lacking central jails, *district jails* often play a lead role. For example, in the state of Assam which lacks a central jail, there are 23 district jails. In states having central and district jails, the former are meant for convicts sentenced to death or long-term imprisonment and the latter for other categories of convicts. Where both do not coexist, a central jail also serves as a district jail for the district in which it is situated; bail detainees are kept in both of these types of jails (see Appendix 5.1).

Sub Jails are situated at sub-divisional headquarters in different states. They also have smaller capacities than do central or district jails. A sub-jail is meant for offenders sentenced to a short term of imprisonment, approximately up to three months. A sub-jail is affiliated with and subordinate to district or central jails.

Most young offenders in the age group of 12-18 years are kept in **Borstal Schools** so that they do not come into contact with adult offenders, to prevent exploitation by and/or the influence of adults. The main emphasis of these schools is to impart education to the juveniles, in order to prevent future recidivism. There are 12 states in India containing Borstal Schools. The highest capacity of a single school is found in the state of Madhya Pradesh which has provisions for lodging 408 young persons. Typically only males are kept in each state's/UT's Borstal Schools, with the exception of the states of Haryana, Himachal Pradesh and Orissa, where co-ed provisions have been established. In states/UTs where Borstal Schools only oversee young male offenders, young female offenders are kept in children's homes established under the *Juvenile Justice (Care and Protection of Children) Act*, 2000. Young offenders in States/UTs that lack Borstal institutions are kept instead in children's homes.

Open Jails exist for inmates who have displayed sufficiently good behavior, and satisfy certain norms prescribed by prison rules, such as the following: (a) The inmate is fit for manual labor; (b) He or she has not more than one previous conviction; and, (c) He or she has served a minimum of one-fifth of his or her substantive sentence if sentenced for a period of not more than seven years; or, (d) He or she has served one-fourth of the sentence if sentenced to more than seven years imprisonment.

Such facilities are typically of minimum security, and the inmates are trained in agriculture, which continues to be the principal avocation of India's rural population. Agriculture also serves as a viable industry within such jails. Open jails function in 11 states, and the state of Rajasthan has seven open jails in operation, the highest number of all other states/UTs.

Special Jails operate to confine particular classes of prisoners, such as: (i) prisoners with disciplinary issues who have seriously violated prison regulations, (ii) prisoners demonstrating violent and/or aggressive tendencies, (iii) habitual offenders who pose disciplinary problems, and (iv) other difficult discipline cases such as offenders involved with organized crime and/or professional criminals.

Lock-ups are cells provided on police station premises to temporarily detain individuals required to be held during the investigation of offences. These cells are also provided on court premises for the detention of prisoners pending their appearance before magistrates or judges.

Temporary Jails are established on an ad hoc basis as required, usually for dealing with mass crowds. For example, on November 26 of 2002, the state government of Punjab established 70 temporary jails in different state districts to receive agitators who were planning on participating in a massive *jail bharo andolan* (pack the jail agitation) which was to take place the following day. These uprisings are resorted to in order to highlight the vastness of public support behind various demands. These jails are usually set up in educational institutions, state government guesthouses, and so forth.

Aside from the above jails, some states and UTs also contain other jails. For example, the union territory of Chandigargh has another jail type, termed a "Model Jail," which has a 1,000-inmate capacity. This is deemed to be a model jail in view of its amenities, congenial environment, training facilities, and for its inmates. Goa state has three, the UTs of Andaman and Nicober Island have two each, and the states of Assam, Karnataka, Maharastra and Uttar Pradesh each have one "other jail."

Correctional Services

Traditional Indian approaches toward crime control guided by the concepts of deterrence, retribution and offender incapacitation have gradually been replaced by a diversified framework of *reintegrative* correctional strategies intended to assist released offenders in their transition back into mainstream society. It has long been established that the protection of society against recidivist crime is best achieved by reshaping the behaviors of convicted offenders. Moreover, it has been suggested that reintegrative services aid in reducing inmate "prison subculture contamination," which is manifested in numerous undesirable activities that are associated with prison life. It is within this context that the importance of inmate care and welfare, vocational programs, inmate-family contact and self-discipline incentives (such as remissions, leaves, transfers to open institutions, parole, etc.) cannot be overemphasized. For example, Temples, Gurudwaras (shrines of Sikhs) and Mosques have been established in all central and district jails to inspire prisoners with religion; prisoners are given newspapers at government expense; and libraries in various prisons have been augmented with the goal of offering inmates a form of wholesome recreation and self-education.

Box 5.2: Diets and Amenities in Indian Prisons

Through meal preparation, prisoners are able to maintain some sense of autonomy and productivity while incarcerated. Subject to appropriate times and the permission of jailing authorities, designated inmates are permitted to cook their own meals. Because receiving food or drink from external sources is prohibited, thereby preventing inmates from possessing goods of their choice, they are expected to sustain themselves on the meals and food provided by the official kitchens.

Despite the fact that the jail manual requires that, with due regard to the budget, the prisoners' food should be varied to include different vegetables and dishes, the food supplied by the official kitchens is often unappetizing and dull. This has resulted in the occurrence of several negative incidents related to prisoners' resentment over the quality and quantity of food supplied to them in many of the jails throughout the country.

Prisoners' *panchayats* are also associated with the preparation and distribution of meals. For example, during festivals, special dishes are often served to prisoners. Additionally, many jails have farms and gardens which supply green vegetables and food grains for the prisoners' kitchen.

Medical officers and superintendents have a special responsibility to ensure the adequacy, wholesomeness and hygiene of the food and water supplied to prisoners; therefore meal ingredients often include vitamins and antiscorbutics. For health reasons, medical officers may vary the diets supplied to prisoners, and/or may also sanction a larger meal plan for ailing and convalescent prisoners.

Additional amenities provided to prisoners include: morning and evening tea; electric fans; the inclusion of an additional 500ml of milk per head in juvenile facilities; where possible, incarceration in a jail nearest the inmate's home district; and, flour (*atta*) kneading machines for food preparation. Furthermore, activities and entertainment are provided in some jails and prisons, such as gaming and sports activities; entertainment facilities such as radios, TVs and VCRs; music and other cultural activities; celebration of festivals with guests; and the teaching of yoga and meditation.

Non-governmental organizations are credited for their substantial contributions to the above amenities.

For the aforementioned reasons, a host of in-house correctional services such as general education, vocational training, and self-discipline programs are available to inmates of Indian prisons, as well as provisions for various aftercare services. (See Box 5.2 and Appendix 5.2.)

Education

There are regular teachers posted in all central and district jails to assist in promoting literacy among the inmates. The main purpose behind educating prisoners is to encourage post-release, non-criminal autonomy, and to improve inmates' subsequent employability. For example, some institutions offer opportunities such as participation in bagpipe bands wherein band members are released for paid work at marriages, festivals and other functions.

Borstal institutions include high schools and trade training in handicrafts and various agricultural operations. Schooling in agriculture is offered by the prison department in various institutions for two primary reasons: (1) offering employable skills to inmates, and, (2) reducing prison maintenance costs through profits earned from produce (see below for further details). An additional aim of offering an agricultural education has been to impart a sense of self-sufficiency among prisoners in relation to the production and home-based growth of vegetables.

Finally, the value India places on schooling can be seen in jails that incorporate nurseries for the children of inmates wherein their older children are given a primary education.

Vocational Training and Inmate Employment Opportunities

Most Indian prisons are equipped with vocational training programs to furnish inmates with the skills necessary to pursue various post-release employment opportunities. Such training was provided to 88,011 inmates in 1999 and another 31,718 inmates in the year 2000.

Paid work, however, is not limited to opportunities outside of the prison. According to a prison "earning scheme" which is used in all Borstal schools and district jails, all incarcerated individuals who have served at least three months of their sentences, civil prisoners,[3] and *undertrials* (pre-trial detainees) who volunteer to work are paid wages at prescribed rates. In some states if a prisoner completes his daily work quota satisfactorily, the individual is entitled (by way of incentive) to a wage at double the rate. The regular rates for skilled, semi-skilled and unskilled prisoners in Punjab states are Rs.12, Rs.10 and Rs.8 respectively per head, per full day of working in jail farms or jail factories. From their wages prisoners may pay outstanding fines, purchase authorized goods from the prison's canteen, and/or remit money to their family members. In the *Prison Reforms Enhancement of Wages Case* (AIR, 1983 Kerala 261), the high court held that a prisoner under sentence can claim wages for his work, the wages must be reasonable and the court is competent to compel the requisite funds. The wages are over and above the average per capita cost of food and clothing of an inmate.

Prisoners' Councils (Panchayats) and Prisoners' Standing Committees

Prisoners' *panchayats* (councils) are a regular feature of jail administration in many states. They continue to show satisfactory results and immensely contribute towards maintaining jail discipline and sanitation, as well as improving arrangements for the cooking and distribution of food among prisoners. The *panchayats* have created an atmosphere of cordiality between staff and prisoners, and many involved problems are solved through their intervention.

The prison department in Punjab provides for the existence of five standing committees. These committees are elected from and by the prisoners periodically and assist prisoners in matters relating to food, medical care, drug control and discipline inside the jails and for parole/premature release cases. These committees have been instituted by way of follow-up action on prisoner grievances brought to the notice of the national human rights commission (see Box 5.3).

Health Care Services

Indian law requires that for every prison a hospital shall be provided. For example, in the state of Punjab the rules provide that there shall be at least one medical officer for every jail which is populated by 500 inmates. Where the population exceeds 500, supplementary medical staff is to be provided. In addition to medical treatment of the sick, a medical officer:

- is in charge of the medical and sanitation administration of the prison;

- has to visit the jail at least once a day;

- for sanitation reasons, has to ensure that the jail premises (cells and surrounding areas) are kept clean and that the prisoners are in sound health;

- can refer a prisoner to a specialist from a governmental hospital;

- is expected to inspect the stores, kitchens and cooking utensils to make certain they are clean;

- has to make daily inspections of prisoners' food to verify that the food is of good quality and has been properly cooked;

- has to periodically examine the water supplied to the prisoners so as to ensure that it is adequate and free from defects; and,

- has to make daily visits to all latrines and urinals to confirm that they are sanitary.

Non-Institutional Correctional Services

Aftercare of Released Prisoners

The aftercare of released prisoners is one of India's most effective methods of curbing recidivism and forms an integral part of Indian corrections. Because a released offender faces several personal and social obstacles such as unemployment and societal stigmas, aftercare programs have been instituted to mitigate these problems. Among the physical properties given to released offenders, aftercare programs typically offer free or subsidized rail/bus fares, free supplies of tool kits for tradesmen, assistance in acquiring employment, financial support for those who seek self-employment, and housing in various halfway houses and aftercare centers.

Non-governmental organizations offer immense assistance in the continuation and provisions of aftercare programs. Social activists, affluent people and the Indian government have also come together to create a comprehensive set of these programs for released offenders.

Aftercare programs have been instituted because it has been seen that imprisonment causes shock, fragmentation and demoralization to an offender's family; the programs therefore facilitate reintegration between offenders and society, as well as between offenders and their families.

Probation

Among the non-institutional correctional services in India, probation is viewed as the most important. Dealing with offenders as individuals rather than as groups provides a more therapeutic approach than does incarceration. Probation also allows the offender to remain in familiar surroundings while concomitantly under the supervision of a probation officer, therefore protecting the offender from the negative effects of prison life. Moreover, probation minimizes the social stigma associated with a conviction, and is more economic than imprisonment. One of the perceived quandaries associated with probation, however, is that the victims of offenders released on probation often feel that they have been deprived of proper justice.

Some of the legislation governing probation is contained in *The Probation of Offenders Act,* 1958, which has further liberalized the provisions surrounding probation. Section 360 of the subsequently enacted *Criminal Procedure Code,* 1973 also relates to probation and contains similar provisions to those contained in the *Probation of Offenders Act.* When the *Act* came into force, section 360 of the *Code* became wholly inapplicable. The Act is now in force in all states of the country.

Under the *Act,* probation officers are required to submit pre-sentence enquiry reports (i.e., Social Investigation Reports) to the courts regarding offenders convicted of specified offences. The *Act* also requires the supervision of probated offenders by probation officers, with the goal of changing any existing negative, criminalistic attitudes offenders might have so as to assist in their readjustment and reintegration into the community. Recent indications reveal that the police and the judiciary have started gradually appreciating the utility of this act.

Parole, Furloughs and Remissions

Systems relating to parole, early release and remissions have been integral parts of India's prison administration for many years. These systems are seen to function as a positive incentive to prisoners for their good behavior and work. The systems evolved by way of transitional steps from custodial confinement, to the reformative treatment of offenders in which good behavior and constructive work are considered essential prerequisites for reducing individual terms of imprisonment. These systems encourage industrious habits and promote good conduct among prisoners. However, on the negative side they also constitute an area highly prone to corruptive maneuvering by criminally crafty prisoners. For example, the Punjab Human Rights Commission (PHRC) has registered a complaint case wherein the Patiala central jail authorities in conspiracy with the Rajindra government hospital authorities allowed rich and influential inmates to escape portions of their prison term by securing emergency medical parole on the basis of forged records. The case recently came before the commission on February 3, 2003. For the most part, however, these systems are viewed more as a benefit to offenders than a detriment to the correctional system.

Parole

The *Good Conduct of Prisoners (Temporary Release) Act,* and the *Good Conduct of Prisoners (Temporary Release) Rule,* provide for the procedures involved in the release of convicts on parole and furlough (see below). The journey expenses of indigent persons granted parole or furlough are borne by the state exchequer. Parole is granted (subject to certain safeguards and conditions) to a prisoner for a specified period if: (a) a member of his or her family has died or is seriously ill, or; (b) the marriage of the prisoner's son or daughter is to be celebrated, or; (c) his or her temporary release is necessary for agricultural operations on his or her land if no relative or friend of the prisoner is prepared to undertake these operations during the absence; or, (d) it is desirable to do so for any other sufficient cause. (See Box 5.3.)

Furlough

A prisoner who has been sentenced to a term of imprisonment, (for example, exceeding five years) may be released temporarily on furlough, subject to certain conditions and safeguards, if: (a) he or she has been imprisoned for a specified period (such as three years); (b) he or she has not, during this time, committed any offences while in jail; and, (c) he or she has earned a prescribed number (such as three) annual good conduct remissions.

Box 5.3: Parole and Parenting Rights

A male resident of the city of Ludhiana was incarcerated subsequent to his conviction in a criminal case. The man's wife has recently given birth, and in November of 2002 she appealed to the Punjab State Human Rights Commission on the basis that her basic human right — the right to motherhood — has been violated. Her claim was founded in the argument that the right to motherhood includes cohabitation with her husband, whom she argues should be released on parole.

While the Punjab Jail Manual allows for prisoner release on parole on various grounds, there is no specific provision in the manual allowing parole on the grounds claimed by the new mother. Ultimately the question has become whether or not parole is permissible under Punjab law on the grounds that the right to motherhood is violated when an inmate is unable to care for his wife and child.

The commission has since directed Punjab prison authorities to study the matter from various viewpoints and submit a report for further consideration of the woman's claims.

Furloughs are not available to a habitual offender or to a person who has been convicted of certain specified offences. The furlough period is generally three weeks during the first year of eligibility, and two weeks during each successive year. The period of furlough generally counts toward the total period of the sentence. Furlough is akin to a leave given to employees. It facilitates a reintegrative process for prisoner and reduces hardships apart from serving as a good conduct incentive for prisoners.

Remissions

In Indian corrections, remissions (shortening of sentences) take three forms: ordinary remissions, special remissions, and state government remissions. Ordinary remissions are granted according to a prescribed scale to prisoners who are well behaved and duly perform assigned tasks. Special remissions are granted to prisoners who render commendable services such as protecting a prison officer from attack, and state government remissions are granted to categories or prisoners decided upon from time to time by the state government. No ordinary or special remission can be granted to a prisoner who has served in excess (for example, two-fifths) of his or her prescribed minimum sentence (Jindal, 1998).

ADMINISTRATIVE PROCESS

As the Indian Constitution is federal in nature, there is a division of powers between the federal center and the states/UTs. All correctional institutions fall within the sphere of the states/UTs (Article 246 of the Indian Constitution). The management of prisons and the confinement, treatment and discipline of prisoners (as well as other matters relating to prisoners) are governed by various Acts and committees. These Acts and committees are enacted either due to shortcomings in previously existing acts, or to cope with changing social circumstances. The principal central (National) Acts include:

- The *Prisons Act,* 1894

- The *Prisoners Acts,* 1900

- The *Identification of Prisoners Act,* 1920
- The *Transfer of Prisoners Acts,* 1950
- The *Prisoners (Attendance in Courts) Acts,* 1955

- The *Probation of Offenders Acts,* 1958
- The *Mental Health Act,* 1987

- The *Protection of Human Rights Acts,* 1993
- The *Juvenile Justice (Care and Protection of Children) Act,* 2000

The chief committees appointed for prison reform include:

- The Indian Prison Committee, 1919-1920
- The All India Prison Manual, 1960
- The Model Prison Manual, 1960

- The Working Group on Prisons, 1972

- The National Expert Committee on Women's Prisoners, 1987
- The All India Model Prison Manual Committee, 2000
- The Parliamentary Committee on Empowerment of Women, 2001-2002

National commissions for protection of human rights and other civil rights include:

- The National Human Rights Commission (NHRC)
- The National Commission for Women (NCW)

- The National Commission for Minorities (NCM)
- The National Commission for Scheduled Caste and Tribes (NCSST)

State commissions include:

- The States Human Rights Commissions (SHRC)

- The States Commissions for Women (SCW)

Macro-level Correctional Administration

Prison Staff Profile

The primary objectives of the prison administration are to:

(1) Ensure that prisons are a safe place by maintaining the security and discipline of prisoners according to objective terms;

(2) Make optimal use of prisons for reformative and rehabilitative purposes; and,

(3) Provide facilities to inmates that preserve and maintain their basic human dignity.

Hence, to fulfill such objectives, basic requirements for the efficient management of prisons (i.e., appropriately staffed facilities) are essential. Accordingly, proper training of personnel is paramount.

Indian prisons are staffed by three categories of personnel: jail officials, correctional staff and medical staff. A numerical representation of Indian prison staff in the year 2000 is depicted below in Table 5.2.

Table 5.2: Indian Prison Staff Profile/Strength in the Year 2000

Sanctioned Strength of Prison Staff	47,378	
Present Strength of Prison Staff	41,067	**(86.68%)**
Senior administrative officers	374	(.91%)
Middle level supervisory officers	2,984	(7.27%)
Head wardens/wardens	35,776	(87.12%)
Medical officers	368	(0.90%)
Para-medical workers	1,102	(2.68%)
Other correctional staff	463	(1.13%)
Teeth to tail ratio	1:12	
Staff to inmates ratio	1:7	
Present strength of female staff	1,742	
Percentage of female staff	4.24	
Staff to inmates ratio (female institutions)	**1:5**	

Source: Crime in India 2000, National Crime Records Bureau, Government of India, (compilation of tables).

The Indian government views prison personnel training as a crucial part of promoting and sustaining the efficiency of its prisons. Until recently, however, training of prison staff was an area neglected within the correctional sphere. As of late, the importance of proper instruction and staff guidance has been realized, and efforts are being made to implement more appropriate and suitable training programs for new and existing personnel. Diploma courses, junior certificate courses, refresher courses in prison management and courses in criminal justice represent merely a few areas in which various categories of Indian prison personnel are currently being trained or reeducated. Among others, the Institute of Correctional Administration, the National Institute of Social Defence, and the National Institute of Criminology and Forensic Science are primary institutions in which the training of jail personnel in various aspects of correctional administration is undertaken. The bulk of these courses are filled by senior and middle level police and prison officers, and are taught chiefly by staff of both educational and professional institutions and serving and/or retired officers. Available statistics indicate that 4,985 corrections-related employees underwent such training in the year 2000.

Profile of the Indian Correctional Population

Prison Population Demographics

As of the year 2000, India's correctional facilities held a total of 272,079 individuals. The majority of offenders were between the ages of 30 and 50 (48.1%), though inmates aged 18 to 30 also represented a large segment of the correctional population (45.4%). Offenders over the age of 50 represented 5.6% of the total prison population, while 0.9% of this population was represented by offenders under the age of 18. The vast majority of offenders (96.65%) in Indian correctional facilities are male.

Most convicted offenders did not have a high school education (41.4%) or were illiterate altogether (35.8%), while inmates who were graduates, post graduates or those who had technical diplomas/degrees represented a minority of offenders in Indian prisons (4.7%, 1.5% and 0.5%, respectively).

Of all offenders held in Indian correctional facilities in the year 2000, most identified themselves as believers in either the Hindu (74%) or Muslim (16.7%) faith; the remainder identified themselves as Sikh, or Christian (*Prison Statistics,* 2000).

Convicted offenders represented a minority of the total prison population, (23.5% and 19.2% of males and females, respectively); most of the population was made up of *undertrials* (pre-trial detainees), who accounted for 71.2% of male and 68% of female inmates (*Prison Statistics,* 2000).

Finally, first-time offenders represented the majority of India's inmates (83.4%). The statistics indicate that only a small percentage of the prison population are multiple recidivists (see Table 5.3).

Table 5.3: Prison Demographics Relating to Number of Convictions, 1999-2000

Number of Convictions	2000 Statistics	1999 Statistics
First time offenders	83.4%	78.8%
Offenders convicted once	13.9%	18.2%
Offenders convicted twice	1.9%	2.3%
Offenders with 3+ convictions	0.8%	0.9%
TOTAL	**100.0%**	**100.0%**

Source: Prison Statistics 2000, National Crime Records Bureau, Government of India.

ISSUES CONFRONTING INDIAN CORRECTIONS TODAY

India's correctional system also faces large-scale issues requiring rectification, including: prison overcrowding, neglect of proper prison conditions, and poor staffing accommodations.

Overcrowding

Like other countries, India struggles with issues of inmate overcrowding. In Table 5.4, Prison Statistics India indicates India's prison overcrowding rates for the year 2000.

The principal reason for overcrowding in Indian prisons, according to the Third Report (1980) of the National Police Commission (NPC), was that a major portion of the arrests were connected with very minor offenses, and hence may be regarded as unnecessary from the viewpoint of crime prevention (p.31). Consequently, overcrowding accounts for 43.2% of jail expenditures.

Overcrowding problems also result in a strained prison infrastructure, hampered inmate correctional services, and an increased spread of contagious and/or infectious diseases. Moreover, overcrowding negatively affects the prison administration through amplified prisoner discipline and violence matters, and the diversion of prison staff to oversee more routine duties such as the distribution of food, security and guarding. According to Lord Wolf, "Owing to overcrowding, very often [prisoners are] more embittered and hostile than when they arrived" (Sen, 2000).

Table 5.4: Occupancy and Overcrowding Rates in India, 2000

Inmate Category	Population in 2000	Percentage Increase from 1999
Convicted inmates	63,975	23.51
Undertrials	193,627	71.17
Detenus,[a] mentally ill, etc.	14,477	5.32
Total Population	272,079	100.00
Authorized capacity	211,720	
Actual occupancy rate	128.51 %	
Percentage of overcrowding	28.51 %	

Source: Prison Statistics 2000, National Crime Records Bureau, Government of India.

a. *Detenu* is neither a convict nor an undertrial. He/she is a person convicted to prison custody to prevent him from creating disorder. Such detenues can be ordered, in appropriate cases, by executive authorities empowered to do so by law. Such detenue status is temporary and subject to review by judicial/quasi-judicial authorities.

Part of the overcrowding issue in India is furthered by the increase in female offenders in Indian correctional institutions. Overcrowding of female offenders in Indian prisons was extremely high in 2000, particularly as reflected in the occupancy rates seen in the state of Harayana (486.4%), Punjab (200.6%), Manipur (160%), Bihar (141.3%), Maharastra (135.6%), Uttar Pradesh (135.4%), Delhi (115.5%) and Tamil Nadu (103.8%). (In the remaining states/UTs, female inmates did not exceed the prisons' maximums.) Speculated reasons for this dramatic rise in the number of females in Indian prisons include widespread unemployment and an increased awareness and involvement of women in mainstream society. It is speculated that because women in general need

no longer necessarily concentrate only on gender-based household endeavors, they have become more active participants in other daily activities, some of which involve criminal activity.

Employing sanctions other than incarceration for first-time offenders
may in part, rectify the overcrowding issue. Though existing legislation
such as the *Probation of Offenders Act* authorizes officials to divert these
offenders from institutional confinement and treatment in the open
community, first-time offenders are still regularly detained in prisons
(see Table 5.3).

Furthermore, there is evidence to suggest that overcrowding may, in
part, also be attributable to socially disadvantaged inmates who lack the
resources that may enable them to avoid incarceration-based punishments (e.g., lack of finances for qualified legal representation, lack of
information concerning rights, etc.). The All India Committee on Jail
Reforms (also called the *Mulla Committee,* 1980-1983) remarked during its
visit to Indian prisons that many prisoners were from underprivileged
segments of society, leaving the committee with the impression that
those with influence and financial means generally manage to remain
beyond the law's reach, even when they are in violation of it. These observations appear valid today in most state/UT jails in the country.

Indian prisons are crowded by inmates serving relatively short terms
for petty offences such as snatching, being a "ticketless traveler," and
burglary, etc. Studies have indicated that short-term imprisonment
serves little purpose and has little positive effect. Such (often avoidable)
terms often needlessly stigmatize the incarcerated individual, which in
many ways reflects the ineffectiveness of India's system of probation.
For example, only 8-10% offenders eligible for release on probation are
actually granted it. This is in stark contrast with the United States and
the United Kingdom, wherein 60-65% and 50-60% (respectively) of offenders are granted probation (Rajan, 1983). It appears counterproductive for Indian officials to continually incarcerate individuals convicted
of technical crimes and crimes of necessity when other, more favorable
options are available. More regular use of these alternatives would likely
prove advantageous and help minimize India's overcrowding problems.

Prison Neglect, Poor Staff Accommodations and Lowered Staff Morale

Chronic neglect has become the fate of Indian prisons, which are often housed in old and dilapidated buildings. In spite of casual repairs and an occasional whitewashing from time to time, cracks, crevices, crusting and an overall dinginess generally characterize Indian prisons. In order for these buildings to be in a livable standard and condition, they require extensive repairs and renovations. For example, the lavatories for prisoners in these buildings are poorly made, and the drains within them typically overflow, resulting in problems such as open sewage and water logging.

Staff quarters are constructed no better, thereby effectively reducing staff morale. Because of a lack of sufficient and properly maintained residential accommodations, low paid prison guards often resort to living in undesirable areas of a city. These areas are commonly infested with antisocial elements and in general proximity to the "underworld of crime," and thus have been found through association to heighten the chances that guards will develop vested interests in the prison's inmates. Whether to benefit themselves through small material advantages or to avert physical threats directed at themselves or their families, guards have been known to breach general codes of conduct, a problem attributed in part to lodging concerns.

It is hypothesized that this problem could be effectively managed by providing adequate residential accommodations to all prison personnel. An additional benefit of this solution would be that a ready availability of forces around the clock would be ensured by the residential facility's proximity to the prison campus, thereby ensuring backup support in an emergency situation.

FUTURE DIRECTIONS

To further improve India's correctional system, future goals and directions noted and discussed by scholars and administrators include: a general improvement of existing facilities, the establishment of a model prison manual, and potentially privatizing some correctional institutions.

Improvement of Existing Correctional Facilities

Recognizing the need for improving existing Indian prison conditions, prison staff and prisoners alike, the Ministry of Home Affairs (MHA) and the government of India have analyzed the available prison infrastructure in assessment of the requirements needed to bring Indian prisons to certain minimum standards yet unmet. As a result, a scheme has been orchestrated which will be implemented over a period of five years commencing in 2002-2003. Among other items, the scheme includes the following components: (a) construction of additional jails to reduce overcrowding; (b) repairs and renovations to existing jails; (c) improvement in the sanitation and water supply of existing jails; and, (d) providing living accommodations for prison staff.

Among others, some of the more notable guidelines for the preparation and implementation of the scheme include the following:

- The state-empowered committee will meet quarterly to review the progress of the implementation including the disbursement and utilization of funds.

- In the first year, the allocated funds will be released to the state governments as per the plan, however the funds in subsequent years will be released in proportion to the utilization of funds released in the previous year(s).

- The central government will monitor the implementation of the scheme, among other methods, by sending teams of officers to the states for its monitoring on a micro-level scale.

- The scheme will be reviewed every two years during the period of implementation.

- The parliamentary committee on the empowerment of women has undertaken a study on the condition of female prisoners. Among other items, it has highlighted the need to provide facilities such as crèches[4] for the children of female inmates (who are kept in jails with their inmate mothers), and promotes more hygienic living conditions and provisions for separate kitchens maintained for female inmates. The Supreme Court has also shown concern with regard to the plight of children who are housed in jails with their mothers, and has taken this into account in preparation of the five-year prospective plan and the annual action plan for the funds earmarked under the scheme.

Model Prison Manual

In order to unify a state-based prison administration, the Bureau of Police Research and Development, an organ of the central government, has recently prepared a draft model prison manual for adoption by all the states. The goals of the Model Prison Manual are to:

- Bring basic uniformity in the legal framework of prison administration throughout the country;

- Lay down a common framework for the custody and treatment of offenders;

- Ensure uniformity and standardization of prison practices;

- Set out minimum standards for the care, protection, treatment, education, training and resocialization of prisoners;

- Help develop procedures for human rights initiatives in prisons;

- Individualize the institutional treatment of prisoners;

- Objectively delineate the duties and functions of various levels of prison staff;

- Provide a scientific basis for the treatment of women, adolescents and high-security prisoners;

- Develop coordination and communication systems between prisons and other components of the criminal justice system;

- Forge constructive links between prison programs and community-based welfare institutions;

- Make prisons safer places by maintaining security and disciplinary measures;

- Ensure that prisons are used effectively for the reformation and rehabilitation of offenders; and,

- Provide basic minimum facilities to prisoners in order to maintain their sense of human dignity. This is partially indicative of India's perception that prisoners are *made*, not *born*; that they are sent to prison not *for* punishment but *as* punishment; and, that imprisonment does not transform an individual into a non-person. Rather it is the *crime* and not the *criminal* that is to be hated.

The draft model incorporates the recommendations made by the committees on prison reforms, conforms to statutory provisions and laws laid down by the Supreme Court and other lower courts, and takes into account the welfare of prison staff and the development of human resources for the prison administration. State representatives and the National Commission for Women were also consulted in drafting the manual.

Additionally, along similar lines as the awarding of various police medals, an *Institution of Recognition for Correctional Personnel* has been considered to reward, motivate and provide incentives for prison personnel and other correctional staff in providing exceptional services. Some of the intended awards would include: The President's Correctional Service Medal for Distinguished Services; The President's Correctional Service Medal for Gallantry; The Correctional Service Medal for Meritorious Services; and, The Correctional Service Medal for Gallantry.

Prison Privatization

There is a recent school of thought that strongly advocates for privatization of Indian prisons. Based on the arguments that private corporations can build, finance and operate correctional services more inexpensively and effectively than can government bodies, promoters of privatized prisons assert that private operators can also manage prison facilities more efficiently and economically than can the government. These arguments are furthered by the proven success of private prisons in countries such as England and the United States.

Opponents of privatizing prisons argue that prisons should remain the exclusive responsibility of the state. They contend that private companies are of benefit to corrections when performing services such as catering etc., but that it is completely improper to allow private agencies — whose motivation is commercial — to have coercive authority over inmates, which the management of prisons entails.

Support for privatization has been mixed. To improve the conditions within jails, the Indian National Human Rights Commission supports the use of private agencies insofar as they are used for purposes such as catering and escorting prisoners to and from jails, courthouses, hospitals, etc. The West Bengal Human Rights Commission, on the other hand, has remarked that the government should seriously consider relinquishing some jail services to reputable NGOs, philanthropic bodies, and organizations operated by ex-servicemen (Sen, 2000). The *Juvenile Justice (Care and Protection of Children) Act*, 2000 envisages operation of juvenile homes, observation homes and other special homes by voluntary organizations. The Punjab state government, however, is not currently considering any proposal for privatizing any aspect of the jail administration, though its rules do provide for privately managed juvenile homes, observation homes and special homes that must conform to prescribed standards.

In 1999, 11 senior prison administrators attended, for the first time, a two week international training course at King's College in England. The training will hopefully spawn some progressive initiatives. Also in 2002, the Department of Prisons drew up a comprehensive program to computerise the prison administration over the next few years. Once introduced, the program is expected to be a boon to not only the police, but also the judiciary and the prison staff.

CONCLUSION

In spite of having one of the world's largest democratic societies, India's current correctional administration is still struggling with both ideological and practical concerns. As such, it appears that the country's correctional operations are faced with an interesting paradox: "newer" correctional concepts (such as rehabilitation and reform, a reduced reliance on incarceration, etc.) have and will likely not become generally accepted by the administration until they have been proven to be scientifically tested and verified methods of crime control; however, until such actual reforms are undertaken, their theoretical value cannot truly be demonstrated and/or determined.

While current rethinking concerning the efficacy of correctional services is deeply influenced by a universal awareness of human rights, and though major structural and operational changes have been recommended over the last 80 years, India's current overall correctional administration still appears to be slow to act. One needs only to look into the plight of *undertrials* languishing in jails, the often degrading treatment suffered by inmates, and the frequently dehumanizing atmosphere provided by prisons to understand why a variety of legal, judicial and administrative reforms are currently underway. The correctional administration seeks to ensure that innovative services representative of India's socio-cultural and economic milieu will be provided to individuals processed through its correctional system, yet it may be realistic to await these innovations with caution.

India's correctional system has evolved in terms of objective and current international standards. Moving from perceivably draconian forms of often brutal punishment based on an age-old retributive dictum to current goals of rehabilitation and reform, corrections in India has advanced according to the dictates and intents of time and administrators. And while much is still left to be desired with respect to poor prison conditions and an apparent overuse of incarceration and under-reliance on non-institutional correctional measures, comparatively speaking India's worldwide ranking in terms of incarceration is extremely low (at 29 prisoners per 100,000 general population): it is ranked 200th of 205 listed countries. (See: "The International Centre for Prison Studies" at http://www.kcl.ac.uk/depsta/rel/icps/home.html.)

Perhaps one can hope that the central government's scheme of prison reforms scheduled for implementation this decade will establish the recommended changes. As noted, research indicates that the construction of new prisons may help resolve some of the overcrowding problems experienced in India; prison renovations may assist in rectifying the poor living conditions faced by India's inmates; and, the construction of better staff quarters may better the suffering morale of India's prison personnel.

It does appear, however, that financial boosts in terms of construction and renovation may only serve to remedy the physical issues confronting Indian corrections, primarily with respect to the use of imprisonment. Until India's correctional system implements many of the theoretical suggestions which have been recommended over time, financial aid might only improve the tangible physical structuring of the system while still neglecting potentially beneficial operating and systemic changes.

India's observance of and compliance with international human rights issues, however, does represent movement in the direction of improving the system as a whole. For example, in the case of Sunil Batra (AIR 1978 SC 1675), the Supreme Court categorically set out that imprisonment does not, *ipso facto*, mean that an individual's human rights are abandoned when he or she is detained, and noted that even dangerous prisoners and prisoners awaiting the death penalty still have basic human rights and liberties that cannot be overlooked. Such rulings have enabled the National Human Rights Commission and the State Human Rights Commissions to intervene in prison matters concerning the interest of prisoners. Moreover, as one of the signatories of the United Nations Standard of Minimum Rules of the Treatment of Prisoners and Related Recommendations (1955), India has closely complied with its rules and provisions. State governments have been instructed to adhere to these rules and the central government too monitors the work of different state governments accordingly.

In summary, during the last century India has constantly monitored, reviewed and recommended changes to its correctional system corresponding with changing times and international standards. Like any consistently evolving system, progress is ongoing and unfortunately often sluggish; however, a better system is emerging through the rectification of recognized shortcomings, consistent improvement and monitoring of international trends.

Acknowledgments: Dr. Tapan Chakraborty is grateful to Shri V.V. Sardana, Addl. Director General of Police (rtd.), for his valuable guidance and suggestions.

Key Terms

Bloodmoney	British period	Borstal schools	
Central jails	District jails	Open jails	Sub jails
Special jails	Exclusion	Expiation	
Lord MacCaulay	Quaranic law	Muslim period	

Discussion/Study Questions

(1) In what ways have the purposes and uses of incarceration varied over India's correctional history?

(2) How do you feel India's problem with prison overcrowding compares to/differs with the overcrowding problem experienced by other countries represented in this anthology? What suggestions might you make to rectify the problem in India; and, would these solutions apply abroad?

(3) In what ways do you feel that the importance of family and education affect the way Indian corrections is managed, and why? Do you agree or disagree with these principles?

(4) In what ways do you feel the described conditions and aesthetic appearance of Indian prisons influences both inmates and prison staff, and why?

(5) How do you feel about Indian correctional policies involving parole, furlough and remissions? What benefits/detriments do you think can/are experienced under such policies?

Helpful Web-links

This site provides statistical references and supporting papers on Indian corrections and India as a whole:
www.indiastat.com.

International Centre for Prison Studies Website, shows international incarceration rates:
http://www.kcl.ac.uk/depsta/rel/icps/home.html.

For further information regarding India's Tihar prisons:
http://tiharprisons.nic.in.

India's national newspaper online, provides interesting articles relating to corrections:
http://www.hinduonnet.com.

General site relating to India, provides statistics relating to law, order, justice and corrections:
http://www.diehardindian.com.

India's Prison Act:
http://www.corpun.com/iaprr1.htm.

Summary of Recommendations of National Commission for Review of the Constitution of India:
(http://lawmin.nic.in/ncrwc/finalreport /v1ch11.htm).

REFERENCES

Agenda Papers for XXVIII All India Police Science Congress (1997). Phillaur: Punjab Police Academy.

Annual Administration Report 1999-2000. Chandigarh: Punjab Home Guards & Directorate of Civil Defence.

Annual Administration Report of the Jail Department, Punjab for the Years 1997-1998, 1998-1999, 1999-2000 and 2000-2001. Patiala: Central Jail Press.

Annual Report 20001-2002. New Delhi: Department of Justice, Ministry of Law, Justice and Company Affairs, Government of India.

Aujla, G.S. (1998). *Police Training: A Profile.* Ludhiana: Mohindra Bros. Printers.

Bharti, D. (2002). *The Constitution and Criminal Justice Administration.* New Delhi: A P H Publishing Corporation.

Chakraborty, N.K. (ed.), (1997). *Administration of Criminal Justice: The Correctional Service and Social Defence* (vol. 5). New Delhi: Deep & Deep Publications.

—— (ed.), (1995). *Probation System in the Administration of Criminal Justice.* New Delhi: Deep & Deep Publications.

Compendium of Recommendations of the Police Commissions of India (1987). New Delhi: National Crime Records Bureau.

Data on Police Organisations in India as on 1.1.1999 (1999). New Delhi: Bureau of Police Research and Development.

Data on Police Organisations in India as on 1.1.2000 (2000). New Delhi: Bureau of Police Research and Development.

Gonsalves, C., M. Sakhrani and A. Fernandes (1996). *Prisoner's Rights.* Bombay: Vidhayak Sansad and Human Rights Law Network.

Jain, J.K. (2002). *Management of District Police: An Analytical Study.* Unpublished Ph.D. thesis. Phillaur: Punjab Police Academy.

Jindal, V.K. (1998). *The Punjab Jail Manual.* Chandigarh: Chawla Publications (P) Ltd.

Legal Affairs Report for the Year 1997 (1997). Chandigarh: Directorate of Prosecution and Litigation, Punjab.

Menon, N.R.M. (2002). *Criminal Justice Series, Vol. 1, West Bengal, 2001.* New Delhi: Allied Publishers Private Limited.

Metcalf, B.D. and T.R. Metcalf (2002). *A Concise History of India.* Cambridge, UK: Cambridge University Press.

Mishra, R.N. (2000). *All India Services Manual* (7th ed.). Allahabad: Hind Publishing House.

Moharib, N. (2003). "Couple Wrongly Incarcerated in India." *The Calgary Sun,* November 27, p.3.

Prison Statistics 1999 & 2000 (2000). New Delhi: National Crime Records Bureau.

Rajan, V.N. (1983). *Whither Criminal Justice Policy?* New Delhi: Sagar Publications.

Report of Punjab Police Commission 1961-1962 (1963). Government of Punjab.

Report of the All India Committee on Jail Reforms 1980-83, (vol. I.). New Dehli: Ministry of Home Affairs, Government of India.

Sardana, V.V., T. Chakraborty and A. Das (2003). *Criminal Justice Series. Punjab.*

—— T. Chakraborty and A. Das (2003). *Criminal Justice Series. Haryana.*

—— T. Chakraborty and A. Das (2003). *Criminal Justice Series. Chandigarh.*

Sen, S. (2000). *Police in Democratic Societies.* New Delhi: Gyan Publishing House.

Singh, M.P. and V.N. Shukla (1998). *Constitution of India* (9th ed.). Lucknow: Eastern Book Company.

Status Paper on Prisons in India (2000). New Delhi: Bureau of Police Research and Development.

Suda, J.P. *Indian Constitutional Development: Constitutional History of India (1773-1947),* (no date). Meerut: K. Nath & Co..

The United Nations and Crime Prevention (1996). New York: United Nations.

Winterdyk, J.A. (ed.), (2002). *Juvenile Justice Systems: International Perspectives* (2nd ed.). Toronto, CAN: Canadian Scholars' Press.

Appendix 5.1: A Place to Call Home, New Delhi's Tihar Jail
(excerpt)

Tihar Jail Has Gone From Being an Unruly Hellhole to a Global Model for Prison Reform

In the crowded western part of New Delhi sits a vast but packed prison surrounded by high yellow walls. Built in 1958 for a few thousand thieves, murderers and other malefactors, Tihar Jail is now home to more than 11,500 prisoners, most of them trapped by a cumbersome judicial process that keeps suspects imprisoned as "under-trials" (pretrial detainees), often for terms much longer than if they had simply been found guilty. While the grounds are quiet and green, the living conditions are hard, with about 100 people sharing quarters intended for 25.

Prison authorities, however, love to show off their teeming institution. That's because reforms set in motion several years ago by crusading police-woman Kiran Bedi have transformed the medieval hellhole into a place, Tihar administrators say wryly, that even criminals have ceased to fear. When Bedi took charge of the prison, it was a breeding ground for corruption and savagery, where new criminals were trained, killers recruited and dope addicts created. Less than a decade later, Tihar, the largest prison in Asia, is being showcased to penal experts around the world as a place where human rights is a prime concern. There is better food, satisfactory hygiene, proper medical attention and effective rehabilitation programs.

In the days before "Madam" Kiran Bedi; a former police officer, arrived in 1993, an understanding between prison staff and criminals provided fertile ground for running gangster operations outside the walls. There were appalling incidents of bullying, both by wardens and prisoners.[5]

Bedi, who was transferred out in 1995, turned Tihar around partly by bringing in volunteers willing to organize prisoners' time. More than 50 groups work in Tihar today, providing legal aid, running literacy and health programs and encouraging inmates to enroll for private degrees through study centers and courses by mail. Meditation courses help cool hot tempers. Celebrity appearances at cultural shows provide positive role models. Convicts even make their own line of potato chips and other munchies, marketed under the brand name TJ's (for Tihar Jail's) Special. And overall amenities are vastly improved.

Indeed, some believe conditions have become too good. While the bulk of Tihar's menial jobs — cooking, cleaning, managing wards — are delegated to convicts, most aren't required to pitch in. Only those prisoners who have faced trial have to work; 85% are still "under-trials" and tend to hang around doing nothing. Some deliberately enter prison by committing small but culpable crimes to avoid gangster enemies or because they can get better food and lodging. The number of inmates rises by about 10% each winter, as some opt for the four blankets handed out in jail over shivering on the pavements.

At Jail No. 1, the Association for Scientific Research on the Addictions runs a novel program to wean inmates off heroin. About 200 new prisoners enter the jail every day, a few dozen of whom, on average, are addicts. Program leader Dr. H.S. Sethi divides them into a "family tree." Groups of four newcomers, known as "younger brothers," are placed in the care of a "big brother," who is meant to ensure that they are not bullied and to help them handle withdrawal. Groups of four big brothers, in turn, are managed by a "family head." Ultimately, every one of the 700 enrolled in the program is assessed and monitored by the "family." It seems to work. In the past seven years, more than 15,000 addicts have joined the program; it recently won praise from the United Nations Drug Control Program, which is using the model to create a global network of youth against drug abuse.

Among Tihar's model prisoners is Leo Sande Gasnier, a Norwegian who was caught smuggling marijuana from India three years ago. Gasnier, now 22, says he spent his adolescence stoned and angry. He was forced to go clean in prison and then discovered meditation. With newfound introspectiveness, Gasnier confessed and accepted his 10-year sentence at Tihar, even though the prosecution lacked evidence. "I was guilty and deserved to be punished," he says.

Of course, many more of Tihar's inmates contend that they don't deserve to be locked up. "Everyone, from peon to P.M., is committing some crime," says Srivastava. "Crime has not ended because we are in jail." But the improved conditions, he believes, help prevent the relatively innocent from adopting lives of crime. "Earlier," he says, "any man who came in here went out a criminal." Jail may not put an end to crime, but Tihar is at least helping prisoners live a life free of misdemeanor.

In 2003 a story appeared in the Canadian press about a young Canadian couple who had been wrongly incarcerated in Tihar prison. The two students, from Calgary, described their 22-day ordeal as "'conditions were horrible, we were treated like animals...and it must have been hell for (my family) not knowing what was happening, unable to talk to me'...the male partner, Troy Niemans 'was covered in mosquito bites, bug spray and peanut butter, which supplemented a daily diet of rice.'" The charges were eventually dropped and the couple returned to Canada in November of 2003 (Moharib, 2003 — excerpt added by the Editor of this text). Such matters not only speak to the importance of cultural perspectives, but also to the importance of how one evaluates cross-cultural differences.

(Author: Meenakshi Ganguly, New Delhi;

Source: http://www.time.com/time/asia/magazine/2000/1211/india.prison.html). (Also see the link to Tihar prison listed under Helpful Web-links.)

Appendix 5.2: Flow Chart of Indian Corrections

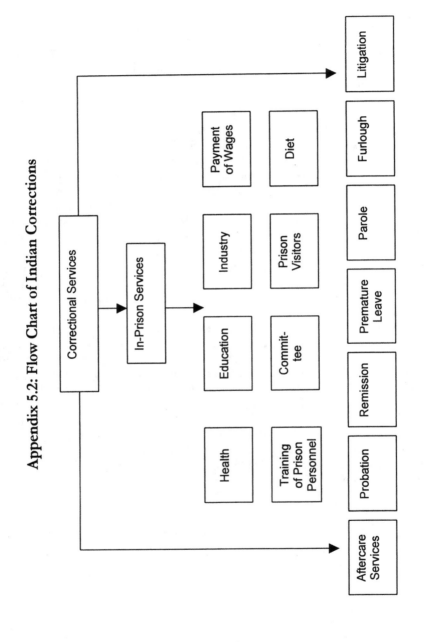

NOTES

1. The *Arthashastra* is an extraordinarily detailed manual on statecraft and the science of living that also contains a relatively detailed account of prison administration based on the Hindu ideology. It was written by one of India's classical and greatest minds, Kautilaya (also known as Chanakya and Vishnugupta) no later than 150 A.D., although the date has not conclusively been established. The treatise is principally instructional in nature for the kings and officers of the state.

2. As imprisonment is the chief correctional method currently employed in India, this chapter's focus shall concentrate on prisons and prison administration.

3. A civil prisoner is one who is not accused of or convicted of a criminal offence, i.e., persons arrested for non-payment of debt.

4. A crèche is a facility and convenience provided to working women with children. Such facilities are appropriately-sized furnished accommodations with toys provided wherein children under the age of six are supervised by trained women while their mothers are at work. Such crèches are to be located, constructed and furnished according to rules outlined by state/UT governments.

5. Bedi published an account of her experiences at Tihar entitled: *It's Always Possible: Transforming One of the Largest Prisons in the World.* (1999). New Dehli: Sterling Pub.

CHAPTER 6.
IRANIAN ADULT CORRECTIONS SYSTEM: CONSTANT EVOLUTION[1]

by

Ali-Hossein Nadjafi
Faculty of Law
Shahid Beheshti University, Tehran

BASIC FACTS ON IRAN

Area: Iran covers 1,648,000 square kilometers and the country is divided into 28 provinces. Located in Western Asia, Iran is surrounded by the Caspian Sea, the Persian Golf, the Oman Sea and the Indian Ocean, and bordered by the countries of Armenia, Azerbaijan and Turkmenistan to the North, Turkey and Iraq to the West and Afghanistan and Pakistan to the East. Therefore, Iran is geographically considered as a crossroad between the East and West. Tehran is the capital city with a population of approximately 6.8 million (1996 census).

Population and Demographics: Iran's official language is Persian (or Farsi) and dialects (58% speak Persian), however provincial languages vary and include Arabic (1%), Luri (1%), Kurdish (9%), and Baluchi (1%). Iran has therefore grown into a multi-cultural and multi-ethnic country. According to 2001 census estimates, the Iranian population was around 66 million, having grown from some 34 million in 1976 (*Iran Statistical Year Book,* 2001). The official religion of Iran is Shi'ite Islam (89%), however Sunni Muslims (10%) as well as other religious minorities such as Armenian Orthodox Christians, Jews and Zoroastrians (making up about 1% collectively) also inhabit Iran. The country's literacy rate is 72%.

Climate: Iran has a variable climate. In the northwest, the country experiences cold and snow during the winter months, while summers tend to be dry and hot. In the south, winters are mild and summers are very hot, with temperatures exceeding 38°C in July. In general, Iran has an arid climate with yearly precipitation averages of 25 centimeters or less.

Economy: The oil, gas and petrochemical industries play a vital role in Iran's economy. They account for approximately 80% of the country's annual income. Iran is a founding member of OPEC and other regional inter-governmental organizations such as ECO (Economic Cooperation Organization) and the OIC (Organization of Islamic Conference) (Beigzadeh and Nadjafi, 2001). The second most important and luctrative industry is textiles. The per capita GDP for 2000 was $3,600 US.

Government: The Pahlavi dynasty, which had governed Iran since 1925, was overthrown in 1979 by an upheaval known as the Islamic Revolution. This resulted in the establishment of The Islamic Republic. After a referendum in April of 1979, leadership in the country was assumed by high-ranking Shi'ite clergymen. The Constitution adopted in December of that year entrusted supreme power to a Shi'ite Mujtahed (a high-ranking Shi'ite clergyman called Ayatollah). He, as Leader, assures that the high political and religious directorship of the Islamic nation state is maintained. He takes his religious legitimacy in continuation of the work of the prophet and twelve shia'a Imams to guide the Islamic Community. He is the first political and religious personage in the Constitution of the Islamic Republic (see art. 107 and art. 113). He is the guardian of the Islamic Shia'a Dogma and thus he plays a vital role in today's Iranian political and social life (Schirazi, 1997). The Islamic Republic on the other hand, is based on the classical Three Powers: the judiciary, the legislative and the executive, inspired from the first Iranian Constitution of 1906-1907 (Nadjafi, 1990). Hence, the Islamic Republic is ruled under a semi-**theocratic** system of government. The system is founded upon two sovereignties: A religious/spiritual sovereignty represented by the Leader, and a popular sovereignty, incarnated by the president of the Republic (Hashemi, 2001). Elections are held every four years to elect a new president, while the supreme leader is appointed by the Islamic advisory board, composed of 86 high ranking clergymen (*Mujtahed*), for an unlimited period of time.

"Those who divide themselves into sects do not belong with you. Their judg-ment rests with GOD, then HE will inform them of everything they had done."

~ Koran (6:159)

BRIEF HISTORY

Iran has a long history that dates back to 4000 B.C., marked by vari-ous dynasties (e.g., Medes 2000 B.C., Achaemenid 559-321 B.C., Safavi 1502-1736, and Zend 1750-1794). With the invasion of Persia by Arabs in 641, Islam replaced Zoroastrianism, which was the religion of Per-sians (see *Columbia University Encyclopedia,* 2003). The autocratic Qajar dynasty (1796-1925) occupied a significant transitional place in Iran's recent history. Although not known to be great reformers, during this period Iran was in the process of becoming acquainted with Western culture by embracing a mainly European approach to justice-related matters. In this regard, the Iranian government employed several Euro-pean advisors and experts for its development and reform.

During his assignment from 1848-1851 and prior to his assassination, the reformist Prime Minister, M. Taghikhan Amirkabir, attempted some political, educational and judicial reforms in conjunction with the Euro-peans in order to restore the concept of justice and the human dignity of convicts and prisoners by prohibiting ill treatment and torture.

The concept of justice in Iran has been closely related to metaphysi-cal and religious beliefs, and the king has always been presented as the symbol of divine justice. Therefore, justice was rendered in the name of the king (see Olmstead, 1948). During the Qajar dynasty, there existed dual forms of criminal justice: governmental/royal justice, which was managed by the officials and based on the governmental rules and regu-lations that were not necessarily religious; and, Islamic justice, which was managed by the Mujtaheds under the *Shari'a* (God-given law). Islamic Law *(Fiq)* and Justice consist of two primary schools of thought (see Table 6.1).

Table 6.1: Islamic Law — Two Primary Schools of Thought

I. SUNNI SCHOOL (also known as Khalife's School or Majority School)			
Primary beliefs: Mohammad did not designate himself his successor. A group of his companions designated successor or Khalife: Abubakr, Omar, Osman and Ali. Within Sunnism, there are 4 different legal approaches to interpreting *Shari'a* sources.			
Legal Approach	**Followers Found In:**	**Legal Sources or References:**	**Main Specifications:**
I. Hanafi School	Turkey, India	Qoran, Sunna of Mohammad,* Consensus and analogy	Personal judgment in exceptional cases.
II. Maleki School	North Africa, Sudan	i. Qoran ii. Sunna iii. Consensus (Idjma) iv. Analogy	Customary Law of Medin is very important. Analogy is rarely accepted.
III. Shafi'i School	Hejaz, Palestine	Qoran, Sunna, consensus and analogy	Reduced place for reasoning by analogy. Customary law is important.
IV. Hanbali School	Saudi Arabia	Qoran, Sunna, consensus, analogy	Based in traditionalism, avoids personal judgment except where absolutely necessary.

II. SHIA'A SCHOOL (also known as the School of the Prophet Family or Minority School or Imamit School)

Primary Beliefs:

Mohammad designated his own successor in the name of Ali (his cousin) as the first of 12 Imams (guides). Within *Shia'a* School, there are 4 different legal approaches to interpreting *Shari'a* sources.

The Main Sources of the Shia'a School of Law are:

   i. Qoran

   ii. Sunna

      ▫ Meaning in this school: the behavior and sayings of 14 pure immaculates or Chardah Masoom who are: Prophet, Fattima (the Prophet's daughter) and 12 Imams (the first being Ali, and the last is Mahdi or awaited — expected Imam)

   iii. Consensus

   iv. Reason (analogy is not accepted)

* Tradition (Behavior and Sayings) of Prophet.

From the early 1500s, Shah Esmail, the king (1502-1510) of the Safavi Dynasty, declared Shi'ism as the religion of Persia. Since then Shia'a Islam has been shaping virtually every aspect of Iranian life. Shia'a clergymen have therefore always played an important role in the social, political, educational and judicial arena. Criminal justice (which is one of the main domains where Shia'a Clergymen have always been active) gained prominence during the Qajar dynasty and competed later with royal/official Justice (Floor, 1983). This judicial duality gradually caused a form of competition and eroded the justice environment. Therefore, the manner in which justice was administered was not uniform throughout Iran. This served as the main reason behind the revolutionary movement in early 1900, and later the downfall of the Qajar dynasty.

Indeed, in spite of all reforms by the Qajars — especially by Amirkabir — and in spite of the employment of Western advisors, finally in the late 1800s these different attempts at reforming the monarchical state still could not prevent the beginning of a revolutionary-constitutionalist movement that finally ended in the establishment of a constitutional monarchy in 1906 without overthrowing the reigning dynasty. Thus, by the end of the **Qajar dynasty** reign, Iran adopted its first Fundamental Law (the first part in 1906 and supplementary text in 1907). It was essentially based on the Belgian and Bulgarian constitutional models. In light of these constitutional provisions, the late dynasty tried to divide the king's power into three separate powers: the legislative, executive and the judiciary. In order to establish a modern police force and penitentiary organization, in 1913 the government employed three Swedish advisors named Vestedhal, Bergdal and Erfas. Staying for more than 10 years in Iran, they were the first to formulate regulations regarding prisoners' rights in Iran's correctional system (Danesh, 1974).

Thus, one can say that the first evolution towards a real carceral organization in Iran was based on European standards. However, due to Iran's internal political unrest and resistance to the proposed reforms, as well as problems resulting from the First World War, these endeavors did not have any practical or functional effect on the political, legislative and judicial structure. In 1919, with the support of the British Government, a military coup d'état occurred, staged by a former officer in Iran's only military Cossack Brigade — Reza Khan (later known as Reza Shah Pahlavi) — and the Qajar dynasty became fragmented. Six years later, in 1925, Reza Khan ended the reign of the Qajar Dynasty and crowned himself founder of the **Pahlavi dynasty** and reigned as the king of Iran until 1941. In 1941, the U.K. and the former U.S.S.R. invaded Iran and forced Reza Shah to abdicate his position and go into exile. However, the westerners allowed Reza Shah's son, Mohammad Reza Shah Pahlavi, to succeed to the throne in return for allowing the United States to use Iran to bring war supplies to Russia in the war against Germany.

It was during Reza Shah's reign however, that fundamental political, legal, judicial, cultural, and economic reforms were implemented and a new era of justice emerged in Iran. Reza Shah is considered by some to be the founder of the modern Iranian criminal, judicial, and penitentiary systems (Nadjafi, 1990), as well as one who helped with the transformation of the country to a more industrialized and educationally more progressive system. But, Reza Shah's dictatorial style slowly eroded any good will of the people. In 1935 Persia was renamed "Iran" by his initiative.

Reza Shah's Minister of Justice, named Ali-Akbar Davar, used the provisions of France's **Napoleonic Codes** (later renamed the Civil Code) [2] — which had been regarded since the approval of the constitution in 1906-1907 as the model for penal codification — for updating and readopting the Iranian penal and criminal procedure codes. During his reign, Napoleon created a commission to prepare criminal procedure and penal codes.[3] The first one, known as the *"code de l'instruction criminelle"* (code of criminal procedure) was adopted in 1808, and the Penal Code was adopted in France in 1810. The penal code introduced the tripartite division of offences — *"crime, délit and contravention"* (*crime* = felony; *délit* = misdemeanour; and *contravention* = summary-minor offence — the legality of punishment and offenses, the equality of offenders in penal repression, and deprivation of social rights and custodial punishment (Stéfani et al., 1973). These codes were taken as models for the codification of criminal law in Middle-Eastern countries such as Iran at the beginning of the 1900s. In this respect, the Ministry of Justice in Iran was also shaped by French judicial and legal advisors who were employed during the Qajar reign. However, the system was gradually reorganized and judicial tribunals were re-established throughout the country (see Box 6.1).

Box 6.1: The Many Faces of Islamic Law

To understand Islamic law and Islamic justice, which have shaped the Iranian penal system since 1979 — is perhaps more complex than justice in many other jurisdictions. Although the core of Islamic law consists of *hudud* offences (see below) in principle, they are defined in accordance with the Koran. Yet, the Koran's influence is limited to some 30 sections in Islamic law. These laws, however, cannot be altered under any circumstances because they are sacred to Islamic faith. In fact, most of Islamic law is formulated from other sources. These sources include the prophet Muhammad, who conveyed various ideas and behaviours (the practices he endorsed and the precedents he set, known as *Sunna*/Tradition). Another source is the consensus of jurists, whose definition remains somewhat unclear, and therefore their role is perhaps not as evident as might be expected. The final source, and perhaps the most influential, for Sunni Muslims is analogy, which involves solving a litigation for which there is no exclusive solution through a similar case that has already been solved. For Shi'ite Muslims the final source is reasoning, which is augmented with a number of legal principles and legislation.

Since the revolution, Iran has been attempting to develop new Islamic law and an Islamic code of procedure in which the general principles of justice and prevailing common interests are outlined (Tellenbach, 2002). Therefore, Islamic law does not possess a similar definition or approach towards penal law as is experienced in the Western world (Forte, 1999). But, given the recent historical events in Iran, it may take some time before Iran sees any significant reforms in its legal and subsequent correctional policies.

The first completely Iranian penal/criminal code was adopted in January 1925. It was modeled, as mentioned, after the Napoleonic Penal Code (among other examples, it introduced "custody" as the principal punishment for most offences). In accordance with these principles, the first set of carceral regulations (prepared in the early 1900s by the Swedish advisors employed under the Qajar Dynasty) were subsequently re-adopted under Reza Shah's reign in 1928. The first correctional facility, the Central Prison of Qasr, was established in 1929 in Tehran. Accused offenders were separated from convicted offenders, and hygienic and nutritional standards were respected. The regulations were again partially reformed in 1936 (Houman, 1960). The new 1936 regulations stated, for example, according to article 1: "prisons are a place for detaining convicted offenders while remand centers are a place where suspects and accused offenders are kept. These two custodial agencies should be separated from each other." According to article 22: all suspects, accused offenders and convicts between the ages of 15 and 18 should be held in a correctional house (*maison de correction*), and in accordance with article 27 the prosecutor has the right to visit all carceral facilities.

The first Regulation of Juvenile Correction and Rehabilitation Centres was decreed in 1968. These centres are intended for juvenile offenders who are under the age of 18. They are to be treated differently from adults. However, during the late 1990s Human Rights Watch reported that Iran was one of only six countries that still uses the death penalty for juvenile offenders — an unequivocal violation of UN standards.[4] Furthermore, the courts have been accused of imposing the death penalty in proceedings that were neither fair nor public, and consequently did not comply with the minimum guarantees of article 14 of the International Covenant on Civil and Political Rights.

In June of 1975, four years before the fall of Mohammad Reza Shah (the last king of the Pahlavi dynasty), a substantial remodeling of the Iranian Penitentiary Organization, based mainly on the UN Standard Minimum Rules for the Treatment of Prisoners (1955), was undertaken. The Regulation of June 1975 is considered a major turning point in the Iranian Penitentiary Policy in general and especially after the revolution of February 1979. In fact, the new regime (i.e., the Islamic Republic) served as a basic model for the new reforms undertaken after the revolution which were, in part, the result of a backlash against Mohammad Reza Shah's secular actions and brought an end to the Pahlavi dynasty.

CORRECTIONS TODAY

In December of 1979, the advent of the Islamic Republic as the new political regime of Iran inaugurated a new era. According to article 4 of the **Constitution of the Islamic Republic (CIR)** all laws and regulations in Iran were to be rooted in Islamic rules (see Box 6.2 below). The key functions were conferred to Shi'ite clergymen. For instance, the Leader, the Head of the Judiciary, the Attorney General, and the Head of the Supreme Court were to be chosen among Shi'ite high-ranking clergymen, thus ensuring religious influence over legal procedures (Nadjafi, 2002).

According to article 156 of the CIR, the judiciary is the guardian of individual and social rights and in charge of the realization of justice. In this respect, the judiciary, which since the establishment of the Islamic Republic has also been in charge of the organization of prisons, has to take appropriate measures in order to prevent the commission of crime and to rehabilitate offenders under the above religious doctrines. Thus, the main function of custodial agencies in the Islamic era is to prevent recidivism by amending, socializing and rehabilitating prisoners — in accordance with legal justice and religious influences.

Punishment is viewed as a means by which to deter people from committing offenses in the first place "since mere prohibition or command is no guarantee against its commitment" (Shaheed, 1994:74). It is also considered justified since Islam is based on the premise that men act as God's *khalife* (representatives), and to break such a trust is worthy of retribution. However, the new constitution claims to promote the idea of treatment of offenders through the individualization of enforcement of punishments — especially *Ta'Azir* (judge-determined punishment in Islamic law). Because, contrary to the other Islamic penalties, *Ta'Azir* punishments, such as custodial measures, are not necessarily fixed in *Shari'a* (God-given law). Therefore, Iranian legislation authorizes tribunals to apportion and individualise these offences.

In light of these new constitutional provisions, the content of the Iranian penal/criminal code and penal/criminal procedural code were substantially reformed (Nadjafi, 1990). Based on the provisions of *Shari'a*, the quadripartite division of "crimes/punishment" was introduced into the new Iranian Penal Code (art. 12). For example: article 13 addresses *Hudud* offences (plural of Hadd), which consist of offenses and their penalties prefixed in *Shari'a*, such as theft with breaking and entering (burglary) (*sariqa*), unlawful intercourse (*zina*), false accusation of unlawful intercourse (*kadhf*), drinking of wine (*shurb*),[5] and highway robbery (*Qat'al-tariq*). *Hudud* punishments are essentially corporal punishments such as stoning, flogging, and amputation of fingers, a hand and/or foot. Yet, other punishments can include a public reprimand in court, a public proclamation of the offender's guilt, or even a suspended sentence.[6]

For crimes involving homicide and bodily harm (wounding) there is considerable variation in how the law can respond. These responses include retaliation (*Qisas*), which addresses voluntary homicide and injuries (art. 14). Article 15 deals with pecuniary composition/blood money (*Diyat* — plural of *Diya*), which involves punishing those who involuntarily commit homicide and cause bodily injury, and *Ta'Azirat* (plural of *Ta'Azir*) pertains to discretionary punishments (e.g., penitence) which, as it has been said, are not necessarily religious and controlled by Islamic law. The legislator has therefore considerable freedom when it comes to defining and interpreting such offences and their penalties (*Ta'Azir* offences). These offences may involve crimes against another individual, produce social and/or public harm, and generally undermine the new values of society; examples include bribery, corruption, embezzlement, crimes against environment, and fraud. Therefore, *Ta'Azir* offences and punishments are not necessarily fixed in Islamic Law (art. 16) because they would undermine the morale of religious intents. *Ta'Azir* punishments under Iranian Criminal Law include: fines, confiscations, deprivation of social rights, flogging, and deprivation or limitation of one's liberty (incarceration and banishment). It is worth noting again that a judge has no discretionary power over *Hudud*, *Qisas* and *Diya* penalties, whereas they can individualize, as we will see, *Ta'Azir* punishments (e.g., imprisonment). These powers became more prevalent after the revolution.

Therefore, crimes under Islamic law remain somewhat fragmented in their order and in how the criminal justice system can/does respond. Forte (1999:95) provides the following general summary of the Iranian correctional response:[7]

- Where there is an offence against God, a sanction is appropriate.

- Offences solely against man are compensated under civil law.

- Some offences such as homicide and bodily harm are defined as crimes against God and man.

- And, under discretionary administrative regulations (*siyasa*) there has historically developed the concept of offences against the state.[8]

ADMINISTRATIVE PROCESS

After the establishment of the Islamic Republic in 1980 the responsibility for supervising prisons was transferred to the Ministry of Justice and to the Judiciary, the head of which is appointed by the Leader and is independent from the Executive (see Figure 6.1). Nevertheless, Iranian reformist activists and international organisations concerned with human rights accuse the Iranian judiciary of being politicized, partial and not independent and, furthermore, disrespectful of internationally accepted standards of fair trial.

Since the early 1980s the Regulation of the Penitentiary Administration/Organization has been the subject of four subsequent reforms which respectively occurred in 1982, 1989, 1993, and 2001.

The Regulations of 1982 contains 269 sections or articles distributed in four parts: (1) Definitions, (2) General Organization Functions and Duties of the Central Administration of Prisons, (3) Preventive Measures Institutions, and (4) General Regulations. For example, according to article 63, a centre for criminological research and studies should be established in order to uncover the etiology of offending prisoners. According to article 1, a prison is a place where accused offenders and convicts are kept for life or for a determinate period, and article 4 enumerates different carceral institutions where convicts and accused offenders should be placed.

The Regulations of 1989 contain 180 articles divided into 10 chapters: admission and diagnosis, census and inspection, daily programme of prisoners, prisoners' internal and general affairs, prisoner's hygienic and dispensary needs, relations of prisoners with the outside world, the education of prisoners, professional training and employment, relations of the prisoners with the prison officers, and finally regulations on release of the prisoners. Under these Regulations the idea of the establishment of a centre for criminological research and studies was abandoned.

The Regulations of 1993 contain 254 articles distributed in four parts: generalities (definitions and functions and duties), general regulations (admission and diagnosis, classification of prisoners, and internal programs), relation of the prisoners with the outside world and regulations on the release of the prisoners. The 1993 Regulation, in fact, amended and completed deficiencies in previous regulations. Article 3 defines prisons as a place where accused offenders and convicts are kept for either their lifetime or a period of time in order to address their social dysfunctions and to serve out their penalty. It is the first time in Iran that a custodial institution has been used as a clinic/treatment centre for offenders (see Box 6.2).

Box 6.2: The Plight of Iranian Corrections — Justice

As will be illustrated below, in spite of accusations regarding various human rights violations in carceral agencies, Iran has slowly begun to show a willingness to find a balance between international ideas of justice and Islamic interpretations thereof. In recent years, various interest groups such as the Student Movement Coordination Committee have campaigned for democratic reform through the country. Also, with increasing awareness of comparative data and international ideas, penal populism (see Glossary) may play a more active role in the evolution of correctional ideology and policy. For example, in June of 2003, for nearly a week, hundreds of Iranians marched in the streets of Tehran demanding more freedom. Although arrests were made, it is a scene and freedom which were unfamiliar to Iranians until recently. Similarly, the government launched an investigation into the tragic death of the Canadian-Iranian photojournalist Zahra Kazemi, 54, who apparently died after she was branded a spy and allegedly beaten while being detained in July 2003.[9]

Other institutional facilities, in accordance with articles 4-22 of the Regulation 1993 include: industrial, agricultural and service institutions, juvenile offender rehabilitation centers and remand centers, centers for the treatment of drug and alcohol addicts, and centers for mentally disordered prisoners. However, the idea of the establishment of a centre for criminological research and studies was also abandoned under the present Regulation, while the establishment of aftercare centers has been envisaged in 1993 under article 240. This is considered something of a milestone for Iranian corrections. These centers, as we will see, protect and help homeless and jobless prisoners after they have been discharged.

Figure 6.1: Iranian Correctional System

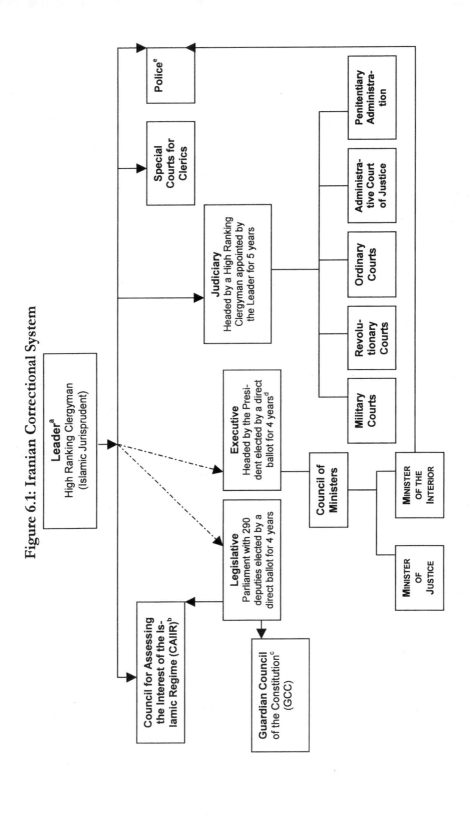

Notes

a. Leader is elected by the Assembly of Leadership Experts (ALE) for an unlimited period. ALE is itself composed of 86 Clerics elected by the people for 5 years (Art. 107 & 108 Const.).

b. CAIIR (or Expediency Council) is composed of 34 members; The chiefs of three Powers, six members of the GCC, the Minister concerned by subject submitted to the CAIIR, other members appointed by the Leader (Art.112).

c. GCC is composed of six Islamic jurists (high ranking clergymen) appointed by the Leader and six civil jurists elected by Parliament among those introduced by the Head of the Judiciary.

d. The Leader should sign the decree formalising the election of the President.

e. The Chief of Police is appointed by the Leader; the exercise of the police duties can be delegated to the Minister of Interior.

The Regulation of the Penitentiary Administration/Organization, which was adopted on 17 July 2001 and is used today, contains 232 sections/articles which are divided into four parts: generalities (definitions, functions and duties of prisons and remand centers), general regulations (admission, diagnosis and classification, internal affairs, daily programs, nutritional programs and hygiene, employment and job-training, educational and cultural activities, public relations, misbehaviors of prisoners and their penalties), relation of prisoners with the outside world (visits, prisoners' correspondence, temporary releases, transfer of prisoners), and preparing prisoners for release. These reforms became necessary in light of the legislative reforms relating to the criminal procedure code and carceral realities in order to improve and update the administrative formalities of admission, placement and treatment of prisoners. The custodial model adopted in 1955, which is in accordance with the UN Rules, can be found to prevail throughout all the reforms. In this regard, the Iranian Penitentiary Organisation established a Research and Training Center. However, in practice, since 1980, the UN Human Rights Commission has often condemned Iran for its human rights violations against prisoners. For example, next to China, Iran has the world's second highest rate of capital punishment. In addition, although having a long history in Islamic law, various human rights groups have accused Iran's correctional practices of violating most international agreements. However, in 2003, Iran began to show a concerted interest in addressing some of the concerns expressed by the UN regarding the punishment and treatment of offenders — in particular political offenders. It would appear that some of these initiatives are somewhat motivated by diplomatic, economic and political interests, as the European Union is attempting to establish renewed business and diplomatic relations with Iran.

Remand Facilities

Articles 3 and 4 of the Regulation of the Penitentiary Administration (2001) separated prisons from Remand Centres. According to article 3, prison is a place where offenders are held in order to serve their sentences and be treated and rehabilitated. The provisions contained within articles 3, 20 and those of some others illustrate that the **clinical model** of incarceration has been reintroduced in this new penitentiary regulation. This means that a clinical, social and psychological survey pertaining to prisoners should be carried out in order to determine the appropriate rehabilitation treatment programs and carceral institutions where they can best be treated.

Not unlike other countries, article 5 contains provisions whereby prisons are classified into categories. They include: closed prisons (walled prisons with internal and external watch towers), semi-open prisons (watched from outside and in which the prisoners are assigned to work in groups manned by a sufficient number of armed guards and after completion of work are returned to the resting places), open prisons (unguarded prisons where the prisoners serve their sentences by working and rendering services), job training centers and work therapy centers (camps/complexes).

For example, according to article 8, semi-open prisons are used to detain:

(1) Offenders who have committed involuntary offences, such as manslaughter due to non-observation of public regulations or due to negligence (article 616 of the Iranian penal code also sentences the offender to pay *Diyé*, which is paid to the parents of the victim); manslaughter resulting from careless driving or from reckless driving or from non-observation of traffic regulations (article 714 of the Iranian penal code also predicates *Diyé* paid to the parents of the victim);

(2) Offenders sentenced with fines who could not afford to pay them and instead serve custodial sentences;

(3) Convicts who could not afford to pay the financial debts or *Diyé*; and,

(4) Offenders sentenced for voluntary offences — such as destruction or setting fire to official documents, destruction of real and personal property belonging to others (article 679 of the IPC), and destruction or setting fire to non-official commercial and non-commercial documents, under the following conditions:

   • offenders sentenced to *Ta'Azir* imprisonment of up to two years;

- offenders sentenced to imprisonment for 2 to 15 years who have already served one-tenth of their sentence in a closed prison; and,

- offenders who have committed more serious crimes and are therefore sentenced to more than 15 years and life imprisonment on the condition of having already served two years in a closed prison.

According to article 10, open prisons incarcerate:

(1) Offenders who have committed involuntary offences (such as offences mentioned in article 8a);

(2) Offenders sentenced with fines who could not afford to pay them but instead serve custodial sentences;

(3) Offenders who could not pay their financial debts or *Diyé*; and,

(4) Offenders sentenced for voluntary offences with the following conditions:

- offenders sentenced to *Ta'Azir* imprisonment terms of up-to two years on the condition that one-fourth of the sentence has already been served either in a closed or in semi-open prison;

- offenders sentenced to imprisonment for more than two to 15 years on the condition that one-fifth of the sentence has already been served either in a closed or in semi-open prison; and,

- offenders sentenced to imprisonment for more than 15 years or a lifetime on the condition that four years have already been served either in a closed or semi-open prison.

Thus, the distribution of prisoners in open, semi-open and closed prisons depends also on the offenders' diagnosed personality traits and their behaviors (as will be explained) in the individualization of the carceral regime.

In accordance with article 14 of the Regulation on the Penitentiary Administration, job training centers and work therapy centers are where drug addicts and drug-related offenders are sent. Drug-related and drug addiction offences represent a serious problem in Iran both socially and economically. According to the official data, in the year 2000 there were more than 2 million drug addicts and 800,000 episodic drug consumers in Iran (Nadjafi, 2001), whereas non-official estimates present a figure of 6 million drug addicts and episodic drug consumers (Rahmdel, 2003). As noted earlier, in accordance with articles 15 and 17 of the regulations, prisoners can also be assigned to industrial, agricultural, and other service institutions operated by the penitentiary organization or independent institutions in order to work and/or to be trained, etc. These services tend to be limited due to financial and economic problems and a lack of requisite space. According to article 19, the Iranian Penitentiary Organization also provides for accused and convicted offenders under the age of 18 to be placed in Juvenile Correction and Rehabilitation Centres where they can be treated, reeducated and rehabilitated in accordance with Islamic, social and educational rules and customs.

As part of the penitentiary's clinical model, the Section of Diagnosis of Unit of Admission and Diagnosis (UAD), in principle, examines each offender who has been sentenced. The objective is to establish a history of the offender's medical, psychological and/or psychiatric condition(s). This is done in order to establish a file regarding the offender's personality or "dossier de personnalité" so that appropriate steps can be taken to assist the offender in his or her rehabilitation. Assessments can take up to two months to complete, and include social, clinical and psychological surveys. However, given the limited resources and spaces within the facilities throughout Iran, few prisoners actually receive such services.

In addition to supposedly providing medical services to prisoners, each prison or industrial facility, agricultural or service institution belonging to the penitentiary organization provides the services of a psychologist, a social worker, and cultural and educational experts. These experts, in accordance with article 42, should meet once a month to summarize their opinions of the behavioral evolution of each prisoner to keep in his or her personality file.

The Council for the Classification of Prisoners (CCP) is in charge of the placement of prisoners into appropriate prisons, or centers, and oversees the employment of prisoners within the various institutions. The CCP also manages prisoners' requests for parole and/or pardons. The Leader grants pardons quite frequently. This is usually and often done during a special religious occasion or during national celebrations (such as during the New Year, Mohammad's birthday, etc.).

The CCP relies on the personality profiles prepared by the UAD to assist in determining the most appropriate response for addressing the offender's situation and needs. This approach is somewhat similar to presentence reports prepared by probation officers in many Western countries. However, in Iran it is the judge who supervises the prison or the director of the carceral institution who interprets the CCP recommendations and ultimately decides whether or not to follow the recommendations or choose an alternative course of action.

The judge who supervises a prison — appointed by the judiciary — or the director of the custodial institution each maintains certain powers relating to prisoners. They include the granting of prisoner-family meetings; the granting of private meetings without the presence of a prison officer; and the granting of 72 hours' release in the case of prisoner illness or passing away of his closed relatives. The granting of encouragement temporal releases — after the convict had served at least two months of his/her punishment — that last at most five days per month renewable one time, is guaranteed by the head of the concerned judiciary province or the judge who supervises the prison. In addition to the judge who supervises the prison, there is also a judge who is in charge of sentence enforcement who is designated according to his jurisdiction. He is appointed by the judiciary and assigns the convicts to their custodial facilities and announces the inmate's release to the director of the prison one week before that release.

The main mission of the UAD and CCP, however, is to offer the most applicable and appropriate treatment to each prisoner according to his or her criminal background, personality and needs. Based on the above-mentioned activities, these two bodies, mainly CCP, individualize the enforcement of custodial punishment in different carceral agencies. The objective is to try and provide a **rehabilitative** approach to addressing the offenders' needs. In order to reintegrate the prisoner safely back into society, the After Care Centre (ACC) — a penitentiary institution which is maintained under the Regulation of 2001 — takes care of homeless and/or jobless ex-prisoners for at least three months after they have been discharged with the help of prisoners' support groups and charity organizations, in order to help them find a job, post-incarceration accommodation, and his or her family/relatives.

PROFILE OF THE CORRECTIONAL POPULATION

"Islam was the first to safeguard personal rights and freedoms for religious minorities. This, it sets an example for contemporary political systems to follow."

~ *Human Rights in Islam*, 1982:11

There are 178 open, semi-closed, and closed prisons, 23 juvenile correction and rehabilitation centers (juvenile correctional institutions), 28 aftercare centers, 18 work therapy centers, and 156 prisoner (and their families) support Associations/Groups in the Iranian Correctional System. With respect to correctional populations, in 1979 there were 13,903 prisoners in all correctional facilities, whereas in 2002 there were more than 160,000 prisoners in Iranian custodial facilities, or approximately 12 times more prisoners than there were over 20 years ago. Among these prisoners, 118,000 are married (see *Resalat News Paper*, 12 June 2002-22/03/1381, S.H., p.14). In fact, according to official data, every 51 seconds one person out of 100,000 Iranians is being sent to prison (*Iranian Prisons at a Glance*, 2000); (also see Table 6.2).

In a forum held on 08 May 2002, the Head of the Judiciary stated that annually, between 700,000 to 800,000 inmates and accused offenders were placed in various Iranian correctional facilities and remain detained for periods of three days up to several months or years. The maximum capacity of Iranian prisons is about 60,000, which means that there are approximately three times more prisoners than the existing custodial spaces provide for. The space allocated to each prisoner is approximately 5 and a half to 6 square meters, whereas according to UN global standards this space should be between 20 to 26 square meters. Therefore, as one can clearly see, the Iranian Penitentiary Organization is confronted with an overcrowded correctional population that increases the risk of promiscuity and homosexual activity, which is treated (according to the Iranian penal code) as a *Hudud* offence. Other problems include compromised health conditions and an environment that tends to promote a criminogenic setting. These issues are apparently due to the increasing number of people being sent to prison — especially those related to drugs, drug addiction and financially-based offences (see Table 6.3). It appears that the judiciary tends to hand down custodial sentences and remand orders (as opposed to non-institutional sentences)

– 219 –

that are difficult to execute in the under-resourced prisons. Yet, in accordance with the Koranic verse "when you judge among the people, judge with justice" [4:58], the judiciary is intended to play a vital role in safeguarding the rights of its citizens.

Given the severe overcrowding problem, there has been a concerted effort to use suspended sentences and parole to alleviate the problem. Provisions for parole and/or suspended sentences are found in article 38 and 25 of the Iranian penal code. For example, according to article 25 the judge can suspend the enforcement of full or part of a *Ta'Azir* sentence for two to five years under the following conditions:

(a) The offender must be free of the following conditions:

- *Hudud* sentences;

- Convictions resulting from the commission of injuries;

- Imprisonment for more than one year for voluntary offences;

- Fine to more than Rls. 2,000,000 (approximately 250 US $);

- Two or more convictions resulting from voluntary offences;

(b) A tribunal, with consideration given to the social background of the convict and the circumstances of the commission of the crime, estimates that the suspension of enforcement of full or part of the punishment is most reasonable.

Article 38 (amended in May 1998) of the Iranian penal code permits parole under the following terms:

If a first-time offender is sentenced to imprisonment and half of the sentence has already been served, the court (which has issued the initial sentence) can grant the parole provided all of the following conditions exist:

Table 6.2: Statistical Information on Prisoners Held from July to December 2002

Item	Subject	Frequency						
		July	August	September	October	November	December
1	Total number of prisoners in the country	168,064	168,356	163,989	156,164	151,062	148,603
2	Percentage of male prisoners	96.42	96.35	96.39	96.32	96.20	96.22
3	Percentage of female prisoners	3.58	3.65	3.61	3.68	3.80	3.78
4	Number of After Care Centres	28	28	28	28	28	28
5	Number of Juvenile Correction and Rehabilitation Centres	21	21	21	21	21	23
6	Number of prisoners in every 100,000 of population	256	257	250	238	230	227
7	Percentage of prisoners under 19 years old (boy and girl)	1.47	1.52	1.71	1.79	1.93	1.97

Source: Iranian Penitentiary Administration (Organization) — 2002.

Table 6.3: Percentage of Prisoners by Offence Type and Offender Occupation

Type of Offense	Percentage
Narcotic drugs *	42.00
Addiction**	10.83
Robbery	10.59
Others	27.70
Occupation	**Percentage**
Laborer	25.94
Unemployed	6.15
Driver	5.66
Tradesman	5.20
Housewife	3.66
Farmer	11.36
Driver of heavy vehicles	2.58
Clerk	1.81
Welder	1.77
Mason	1.58
Student	1.38

Source: *Iranian Prisons at a Glance*, 2000.
*Such as the manufacturing, importation, sale, and possession of narcotic drugs.
**Drug addicts and drug episodic consumers.

(1) The offender has shown good behavior while serving his/her sentence.

(2) From the circumstance and manners of the condemned, it is predicted that after release he/she will not commit any offense (through, for instance, a rapid survey or investigation).

(3) The offender has to compensate the victim as much as the offender can reasonably afford, or has to pay the plaintiff, or has

agreed to pay damages to the victim within a prescribed period of time.

Regarding the punishments of both fine and imprisonment, the offenders pay the fine upon release. Or with the approval of the head of the concerned judiciary province, an arrangement is made for paying the sum of the fine in the future.

It should be noted, however, that the director of the prison and the judge who supervises the prison where the offender is detained or the head of the concerned judiciary province must approve the conditions for payment.

ISSUES CONFRONTING CORRECTIONS IN IRAN TODAY

Although the history of corrections in Iran has undergone many reforms, it has essentially remained **retributive** in its approach by Western standards. This has in large part been due to the influence of Islamic Law and the limited resources and spaces to do otherwise. Furthermore, unlike in many Western countries, penal populism is not readily evident in Iran. Often referred to as the fourth element of the criminal justice system, the public in Iran plays no significant role in forging correctional, or for that matter, criminal justice policy. Consequently, any pressure or influence for reform tends to emanate from the international community (e.g., the UN, Amnesty International, etc.) and Iranian scholars.

Hence, most of the issues facing corrections in Iran today have been identified by foreign entities with which the Iranian government and criminal justice officials do not necessarily always concur. With this in mind, some of the more dominant internal and international concerns and criticisms include:

- Contrary to articles 32 through 38 of the Iranian Constitution, there continue to be reported violations of offenders' rights and treatment.

- Due to a lack of resources and perhaps initiatives by the state, overcrowding and quality of living conditions in most prisons continue to be a problem. For example, several years ago, Mr. Assadollah Lajevardi, the Head of the Prisons Organization, commented that in order "to keep the number of prisoners, we have utilized all the facilities at our disposal. We have even used libraries, mosques, cultural clubs, and...dormitories" as prisons ("Statistics on..." 1997:14). Similarly, reports indicate that HIV and AIDS is a serious concern in Iranian prisons. The high incidence is largely due to the sharing of needles among intravenous drug users within the prisons.

- There need to be clearer distinctions between torture and *Ta'Azir;* some of these punishments are considered by international law to be torture and contrary to the principle of legality of punishments. *Ta'Azir* are discretionary penalties for the Islamic *hakin* (judge); however, in Iranian law these penalties/punishments are fixed by legislation.

There is a great need for financial resources in order to provide the proper care and support of all offenders regardless of age or gender. Until then, it is unrealistic to expect the government to support community-based initiatives for which there are not enough material resources.

CONCLUSION

Although there has been considerable criticism of correctional practices in Iran, since the late 1970s Iran has attempted to address reform issues on four major levels. Throughout each of these reforms, the clinical/rehabilitative model of intervention has remained the underlying constant. However, due to custodial overcrowding and a lack of requisite space, this model, in all respects, cannot be fully applied. Recognizing that the use of custody is neither in keeping with Iran's correctional model nor in keeping with Islamic law, the Head of the Judiciary recently requested that other legal powers be used to help reduce and convert prison sentences to suspend the enforcement of such dispositions in an effort to reduce the overcrowding problem. Article 22 of the Iranian penal code authorizes tribunals in certain circumstances — such as the special background of an accused, a provocative attitude on the part of the victim which results in the commission of an infraction, and efforts of the accused to reduce the consequences of an offence — to reduce and/or convert one *Ta'Azir* or *Bazdarandeh* sentence to another which is more convenient for the accused.

It is perhaps worth briefly mentioning that *Bazdarandeh* punishment is, according article 17 of the penal code, a correction or penalty which the State (legislature) predicates in order to preserve social order and social interests. Punishments included within this category range from a fine to deprivation of social rights. In fact, these are punishments which are not predicated on the *Shari'a* nor are they based on Islamic law. Some of the punishments resemble *Ta'Azir* type sentences and preventive measures. They can be used as complementary punishments to a *Ta'Azir* sentence. However, according to article 728 of the aforesaid code, a judge can also, in view of the features of an offence and offender, proceed to reduce or suspend the sentence and use complementary and convertible punishments (e.g., temporary interruption of the offender's use of public services). Parole is also possible, as are pardons granted by the Leader after a proposal is given by the Head of the Judiciary. All of these provisions, when used appropriately and effectively by tribunals or the Leader, can result in decarceration.

In addition, a commission in the Judiciary is currently preparing a bill on alternatives to custody. Some tribunals for juveniles have already created a judicial practice to employ non-custodial measures such as community service, fines, literacy training, job training, compensation, and restorative measures, towards victims, etc. (see Nadjafi, 2003).

However, in early 2003, French jurist Louis Jouet and his commission colleagues visited prisons in three Iranian cities, where they interviewed prisoners and met with judiciary officials. While they praised their hosts for their cooperation, they observed that the structure and culture of Iran's judiciary and correctional model led to "widespread miscarriages of justice" from an international perspective. For example, they found that very few prisoners were aware of their legal rights and that punishments were not consistent for the same crime ("Iran's Justice System Criticized," 2003). Yet, the fact that observers have been allowed to visit and speak with prisoners represents a significant gesture of openness and a willingness to welcome international support that was previously lacking in Iran.

It could be argued that since the election of President Khatami in 1997 Iran is becoming more sensitive and attentive to its international engagements. Efforts are being made to ensure greater balance between international norms for treatment and the punishment of offenders while still honoring Islamic law and the governing ideology. For instance, the legislature intends to equalize the *Diyé* (pecuniary composition/blood money) between non-Muslims and Muslims (Goldouzian, 2003), and to replace stoning with a conventional penalty, as well as to restore a fair and equitable criminal justice system for juveniles (Nadjafi, 2003).

Finally, when measured against Western ideals, it is somewhat difficult to present an image of correctional practices in Iran that is not critical in its biases. However, any skepticism or critique should take into consideration the social, political, cultural and religious characteristics of Iran. In particular, one needs to be cognizant of the complexity and breadth of the Islamic faith, which has been described by Westerners as ranging from "fundamentalism" to "radicalism" and "traditionalism" — all somewhat pejorative terms.[10] And while it is beyond the scope of this chapter, it is a point worth considering when judging and assessing Iran's, and other Islamic countries in general, correctional practices. Suffice it to say that Islamic law has different concepts of morality and justice from most western ideologies. For example, as was concluded a number of years ago at the 1982 International Commission of Jurists on Human Rights in Islam, Islamic law and correctional practices should not be judged by various political systems or ideologies but by the general principles upon which it is based — the Holy Koran, the *Sunna*, the general consensus, analogy, and personal endeavours (*Human Rights in Islam*, 1982). Nevertheless, in accordance with international guidelines and standards, Iran can benefit from consulting with Iranian scholars, international organizations as well as international support.

> *"For the recompense of evil is evil like unto it; but he who pardons and does well, then his reward is with God; verily, He loves not the unjust."*
> ~ Koran (C 42.40)[11]

Key Terms and Concepts

Clinical model   Constitution of the Islamic Republic

Iranian penal code   Napoleonic Code

Pahlavi dynasty   Qajar dynasty

Regulation of penitentiary administration/organization

Rehabilitative   Shia'a   Shari'a

Discussion/Study Questions

(1) How does the Islamic political regime operate within the modern world?

(2) Given its current practices, what major changes need to be introduced in order to ensure that Iran's correctional system conforms to international standards and guidelines?

(3) How might human rights concerns be integrated with Islamic criminal justice?

(4) How are Iran's prisoners treated in an Islamic legal system? How is this different from or similar to practices in your country?

Helpful Web-links

Descriptive information on Iran:
www.sci.or/ir/.

Information on Iranian Correction Regulations, carceral population, and general statistics:
www.iranprison.org.

The following site includes information on judicial training courses, Iranian laws, Iranian judicial structures and tribunals within Iran:
www.law-training.org.

Iranian Information and Documentation Centre containing Ph.D. and L.L.M. dissertations on different aspects of the Iranian criminal justice system:
www.irandoc.ac.ir.

For an excellent selection on current events about Iran, prison practices, and related matters:
www.netiran.com/laws/html.

REFERENCES

Beigzadeh, E. and A.H. Nadjafi (2001). "Les Problèms de Régionalisation à Géographie Variable (le cas de l'Iran)." *Archives de Politique Criminelle* 23:141-156.

Danesh, T. (1974). *Elements of Penitentiary Science*. Tehran: Daneshe-e-Emrouz Publication (in Persian).

Feiz, R. (2002). "La Notion de Peine chez les Soufis: l 'école d' Ibn Arabi. " *Archives de Politique Criminelle* 23:137.

Floor, W. (1983). *Change and Development in the Judicial System, Qajar Iran*. Edinburgh University Press.

Forte, D.F. (1999). *Studies in Islamic Law*. New York: Austin & Whified.

Goldouzin, I. (2003). "L 'arret Récent de la Cour d'Appel Iranienne Modifiant la Jurisprudence Discriminatoire entre les Musulmans et les non-Musulmans.... à propos de l 'Indemnisation de la Victime dans les Infractions contre l 'Intégrité Corporelle." In: *Revue Pénitentiare et de Droit Pénal* 1 (March):205-208.

Hashemi, S.M. (2001). *Iranian Constitutional Law*. Tehran: Dadgostar Publications (in Persian).

Hemming, J. (2003). Indexed on asia.reuters.com (online), June 18, 2003.

Hosseini, S.M. (1996). "Les Ecoles du Droit Musulman Confrontées à aux Modèles de Politiques Criminelles (Le cas des atteintes à la dignité de la femme)." Thé de Doctorat, Paris I.

Houman, A. (1960). *Prison and Prisoners*. Press of Tehran University, (in Persian).

Human Rights in Islam (1982). International Commission of Jurists, Kuwait University: Kuwait.

Iranian Prisons at a Glance (2000). Online: www.netiran.com/laws/html.

"Iran's Justice System Criticized" (2003). *St. Petersburg Times*, St. Petersburg, Florida, US. (online), Feb. 27.

Iran Statistical Year Book (2001- 2002). Tehran: Statistical Centre of Iran.

Nadjafi, A.-H. (2003). "Les Mineurs Délinquants en Droit Iranien." In: *Revue Pénitentiaire et de Droit Pénal* 1(March): 209-217.

—— (2001). "La Politique Criminelle Iranienne en Matiere de Stupéfiants." In: *Problèmes Actuels de Science Criminelle*, no. XIV.

—— (2001). "The Iranian Penal Policy between the Minister of Justice and the Head of the Judiciary." *European Journal of Crime, Criminal Law and Criminal Justice* 1:299-308.

—— (1990). "La Politique Criminelle Iranienne à L'épreuve des Changements Politiques." Thèse de doctoral d'état, Université de Pau, France.

Olmstead, A.T. (1948). *History of the Ancient Empire*. Chicago, IL University of Chicago Press.

Pansier, F.-J. et al. (2000). *Le Droit Musulman*. Paris: PUF.

Rahmdel, M. (2003). "A Comparative Study on the Iranian, English and Wales Criminal Policy in the Field of Drug Trafficking." Ph.D. dissertation, Faculty of Law and Political Sciences, University of Tehran.

Reichel, P. (2002). *Comparative Criminal Justice Systems: A Topical Approach*. Englewood Cliffs, NJ: Prentice-Hall.

Schirazi, A. (1997). *The Constitution of Iran*. London and New York: I.B. Tauris Publishers.

Shaheed, A.Q. (1994). *Criminal law in Islam* (vol. 1). Karachi, Pakistan: Qureshi Press.

"Statistics on the Prisoners in Iran, by Head of the Prison Organization" (1997). *Iran (Morning Daily)*. June 16, p.14. (Retrieved from: www.netiran.com/laws.html.)

Stéfani, G. et al. (1973). *Droit Pénal Général*. Paris: Dalloz.

Tellenbach, S. (2002). "In Islam, Diversity of Legal Opinion is seen as a Divine Gift." *MaxPlanck Research* (vol. 5:91-93). Freiburg, GER: Max Planck Institute.

NOTES

1. With permission of the author, the editor has included some material that does not necessarily reflect the opinions of the author but which is thought to present an alternative perspective for the reader. Such passages will be denoted by '**' after the first word in the sentence.

2. The Civil Code was retained in its majority after the restoration of the Bourbons in France in 1815. The Civil Code has served as the model for the codes of law of more than 20 nations throughout the world.

3. Under the *ancien regime*, more than 400 codes of laws were in place in various parts of France, with common law predominating in the north and Roman law in the south. The revolution overturned many of these laws. In addition, the revolutionary governments had enacted more than 14,000 pieces of legislation.

4. The other countries include: Nigeria, Pakistan, Saudi Arabia, Yemen and the United States. Note that four of the six countries are of Islamic faith, and that one is better equipped to understand Islamic legal practices if one understands the Islamic faith. As of 2003, only Iran and the United States still regularly executed juvenile offenders, although official data suggest that only 2% of the total persons executed in the United States were under the age of 18 at the time.

5. To help illustrate the complexity of Islamic law, in accordance with the Hanafi school of thought drinking wine is punishable, but not the imbibing of other alcoholic beverages unless drunkenness ensues.

6. There are insufficient reliable data to provide a factual representation of these observations.

7. This passage and reference to the work of Forte has been added by the editor with permission of the author. It does not necessarily reflect the author's views, but is considered to lend another perspective to the chapter.

8. It** is interesting to note that *siyasa* (i.e., discretionary administrative regulations) are designed to help effectuate the *Shari'a*. However, this mechanism has been used to supplant regional control to the hands of the state, risking undermining the intent of *Shari'a* of the secular law (see Forte, 1999).

9. At the time of preparing this chapter, no conclusion to the inquiry had yet been reached.

10. For those interested, there are a host of books that offer varying interpretations on the different Muslim orientations.

11. Ibn Arabi, a known Islamic mystic (1165-1240), comments on this Koranic verse as follows: "To pardon he who has committed a crime prevails over punishing him, because to chastise and punish is a sanction: yet a sanction is not superior to the evil, unless it is applied to protect the public from harm and is carried out in the interest of people" (Feiz, 2002).

CHAPTER 7.
CHANGE IN FUNCTIONS OF JAPANESE CORRECTIONS WITH CRIMINALIZATION

by

Minoru Yokoyama
Faculty of Law, Kokugakuin University
Shibuya-ku, Tokyo

BASIC FACTS ON JAPAN

Area: Japan is 377,880 square kilometers. Japan is composed of five main islands, which from north to south include: Hokkaido, Honshu, Shikoku, Kyushu, and Okinawa. Japan has one time zone.

Population: In 2001, the population was approximately 127,291,000 (population density was 341 per square kilometers), of whom 98.9% were Japanese. Birth rate, death rate and population growth rate per 1,000 amounted to 9.3, 7.7 and 1.6, respectively.

Demographics: Koreans make up 35.6% of the non-Japanese population followed by the Chinese who make up 21.4%. In 2000, 65.2% of the population lived in urban settings. Tokyo is not only the largest city, but is the nation's capital (population 12.1 million). Young persons are required to complete nine years of compulsory education in Japanese. In 2001, the rate of Penal Code offences per 100,000 population amounted to 2,814, of which 65.4% was composed of theft.

Climate: Although mostly temperate, the climate varies from north to south. For Tokyo the average monthly temperature is 5.8°C in January and 27.1°C in August. Heavy snowfall is common along the Japanese Sea in the winter.

Economy: Since World War II Japan has evolved from an agricultural nation to an industrialized and manufacturing one. More recently, an increasing number of people have become employed in the supply and service industry. In 2000, 29.4% and 27.4% of the workforce were employed in the construction/manufacturing sectors, and the service industry respectively, while only 4.5% remained in some agricultural setting. The unemployment rate rose from 2.1 in 1990 to 5.0 in 2001.

Government: Japan is a parliamentary democracy and its legal framework is based on civil law and is prosecution-oriented. The sovereign power rests with the people, who elect both members of the House of Representatives (Diet) and the House of Councilors. The members of the Diet designate a prime minister, who organizes a cabinet. The judiciary is independent. Between 1955 and 1993, the Liberal Democratic Party (LDP) ruled the government. In 1993 a political scandal brought down the LDP. Since then a coalition cabinet has been in power. The autonomy of local governments remains limited.

★　　　　★　　　　★

"It is hoped that Japan will evidence a greater capacity to adapt the 'deeply-rooted prejudices and practice' of its antiquated, feudalistic penal system to bring it into compliance with Japan's obligations under the ICCPR and other international human rights laws."

~ quote from the Human Rights Network,
April 23, 2003

JAPAN'S CORRECTIONAL HISTORY

According to ancient Chinese literature, the Japanese state first existed in 57 A.D. Starting in the middle of the 4th century, emperors began ruling Japan. Between 710 A.D. and 1867, Japan can be politically and culturally characterized as having undergone four major periods: Nara (710-793 A.D.), Heian (794-1191), Kamakura (1192-1333), and the

Edo period (1603-1867). And as will be illustrated, each period has had a variable impact on correctional practice and policy in Japan.

This chapter will focus on how correctional operations have been affected by its traditional practices and by practices introduced by Western countries after the beginning of modernization in 1868. Then, the chief problems and issues facing Japanese corrections will be examined.

Japanese Corrections Prior to the 1868 Meiji Restoration

During the period from 810 to 1156, Japan suspended the execution of the death penalty, apparently due to the influence of Buddhism.[1] After displacement of aristocrats from political power by warriors a Shogun established his own government in Kamakura City in 1192. Warriors were obliged to be loyal to the Shogun and traitors were severely punished.

During the 15th century (the Muromachi period), the Shogunate government began to lose political control. During this period there were many wars throughout the country, and the death penalty was widely used. Methods of punishment varied from boiling criminals in a cauldron, sawing off limbs, placing the offender on a crucifix, to burning offenders at the stake. Decapitation was also used as a method of punishment, after which the offender's head would be publicly displayed — as a form of deterrence.

At the beginning of the 17th century, the Tokugawa Shogunate government was established in Edo (old Tokyo). Under the feudal system Japan's people enjoyed a peaceful period until 1867. Although severe punishment was used for deterring people from crime, the severity of the punishment became more moderate with time.

During this feudal period, punishment served the following functions: eliminating criminals by the death penalty, separating them from the community by banishment, depriving them of honor and property,[2] degrading them through public floggings, and stigmatizing them through the use of tattoos.[3] *Retribution* was the primary focus of correctional practices. However, toward the end of the 18th century, the Shogunate government began experimenting with efforts to *rehabilitate* some vagabonds (i.e., street people) and criminals through the use of a **work house** (see Box 7.1).

Box 7.1: Work House in Edo

In the late 1700s, there were many vagabonds around Edo who had been sentenced to banishment, or had escaped from their native village by reason of poverty. In response to this growing problem, in 1790 the Shogunate government built a work house to accommodate the vagabonds. The work houses received both innocent vagabonds and some vagabonds convicted of minor offences who had been punished by beating or tattoos. In 1793, the average daily population of inmates in the work house was approximately 130 (Ishii, 1964). As the work house was deemed effective for the purpose of rehabilitation (see Glossary), the government decided, in 1820, to expand the use of work houses to also accommodate some offenders. Only offenders considered to be at low risk of reoffending were accepted into the work house. After working in the work house for about five years, inmates were then considered eligible for release. The work house functioned like modern prisons and could be described as embracing the *rehabilitation model*. In 1845, the daily population of work houses increased to an average of approximately 508 inmates.

The work houses were similar in design to tenement houses. Inmates were assigned to rooms according to their occupation (e.g., as rice cleaners, carpenters, plasterers, etc.). Females, the ill and the elderly, were separated from the rest of the inmate population.

If inmates worked diligently, they were released under the guarantee of their protector. If upon release the former inmate did not have a protector, the government sometimes gave him a stall or a small parcel of land in order to engage in productive work. The most diligent were appointed to a caseworker in charge of taking care of inmates scheduled for release from the work house, and were permitted to operate their own businesses in a town. As the Shogunate government encouraged feudal lords, a similar work house was established in several places by the end of the Edo period.

Japanese Corrections under an Imperial Regime after the 1868 Meiji Restoration

Since 701, a penal system modeled after the Chinese system has been used, although warriors established their own system.[4] Soon after the Meiji Restoration, leaders of the national government under the Meiji

Emperor (1852-1912) tried to introduce aspects of a Western criminal justice system, because they wanted to revise the unequal treaty by which the United States, Holland, Russia, England, and France had been given wide extraterritorial rights since 1858. In 1870, the government appointed Shigeya Ohara (1836-1902) as the chief of Criminal Facilities in the Bureau of the Judicial Ministry (Yokoyama, 1982). As he had had an unpleasant experience while being detained in jail, he took great interest in the reform of criminal facilities. He was dispatched to Hong Kong and Singapore and inspected their Western-style prisons. Afterwards he wrote a report which the government used to construct Western style prisons and introduce Western rules of treatment for offenders being detained in prisons. Inspired by the efforts of Dr. Boissonade, from Paris, in 1880 Japan enacted a penal code similar to the French Penal Code (see section below on "The Historical Emergence...").

At the end of 1876, the total number of prisoners, most of whom were confined in prisons administrated by the local municipalities, amounted to 23,268 (Criminal Affairs Association, 1974). In 1877, a major civil war erupted on Kyushu Island, after which some 1,200 defeated traitors were punished. To cope with the increasing number of inmates and to prepare for the enforcement of the above-mentioned new Penal Code in 1882, several large-sized prisons were built. For example, in 1879 Kosuge Prison in Tokyo and Miyagi Prison in Sendai were built. A few years later the government constructed prisons at Sorachi, Kabato and Kushiro on Hokkaido Island. In 1883, Miike Prison was opened on Kyushu Island. By 1885, the prison population had swelled to 78,687, many of whom were gamblers. This is one of three origins of the **Boryokudan,** meaning "the group of violent gangsters" known as *Yakuza* [5] (see Box 7.2).

At the beginning of Meiji Period, Hokaido Island was sparsely populated and undeveloped. Prisoners were treated like slaves to build new roads, railways, and water canals. As the prisoners were not well treated, many died during the harsh cold winters. In essence, the prisons functioned as a supply center for slave labor.

Correctional reform, as we know it today, began during the early 1900s. For example, in 1907 a new Penal Code was enacted after the example of the German Penal Code. This code was influenced by the idea of the new Positivist School, which placed emphasis on the criminal policy of the national government. By 1922, the Ministry had established seven *juvenile prisons* in an effort to prevent the negative influence of older prisoners on younger prisoners. In addition to the juvenile prisons, there were 56 prisons and 53 branch prisons[6] throughout the country which, in principle, operated in accordance with the rehabilitation model.

In 1908, the **Prison Law** was enacted and remains in force today. Its orientation emphasizes the characteristics of the *rehabilitation model.* This orientation is further reflected in the 1933 Ordinance for Prisoner's Progressive Treatment (Yokoyama, 1994). The ordinance established a progressive system with four grades (ch. III). Under this system all those who are newly admitted to prisons are placed into the fourth grade. If an inmate works diligently and does not cause any undue disturbances, his/her grade is progressed step-by-step up to the first grade. As they are promoted to higher grades, they are permitted more privileges such as opportunities to write a letter and to meet with family members, and are offered the possibility of release on parole before the expiration of their term of imprisonment. As the progressive grade system was carried out, the total number of prisoners released on parole increased from 2,346 in 1932 to 6,428 in 1938. The rate of those released on parole among all released prisoners rose from 7.7% to 18.5% during the same period (Shikita and Tsuchiya, 1990). Revocation of parole (art. 29 [1] of the Penal Code) is similar to that of most other countries.

Japanese Corrections between 1937 and 1945: The War Years

By the end of 1938, there were 51 prisons, 105 branch prisons, 2 **detention houses** and 1,244 police jails. Nine prisons and one branch prison were assigned to juveniles. Two prisons and five branch prisons were designated for female offenders, and another three branch prisons were used to house elderly inmates. In 1938, 46,686 criminals were held in prisons in all of Japan, a majority (58.9%) of whom had committed theft. With the establishment of the military regime, prisoners were kept busy producing necessities for the war effort (e.g., from making clothing articles to assisting in the construction of military machines). This quickly came to a halt after Japan surrendered in 1945. Prisons entered a period of economic hardship, which also affected prison conditions.

Table 7.1: Average Daily Populations in Penal Facilities, 1950-2000[a]

YEAR	1950	1960	1970	1980	1990	2000
Convicted prisoners	85,254	63,329	40,917	42,142	41,141	47,684
Suspects and accused	17,258	11,923	8,010	8,285	6,952	10,637
Detainees in workhouses	582	471	189	134	99	366
Detainees for death penalty	76	53	73	24	43	53
Others	34	67	20	11	8	7
Total	103,204	75,843	49,209	50,596	48,243	58,747

Sources: Correction Bureau, Ministry of Justice, *Correctional Facilities in Japan*, 1982, p.18. Ministry of Justice, *Annual Report of Statistics on Correction for 1990 and 2000*.

a. In Japan, all penal facilities report the total number of their inmates to the Ministry of Justice every day. Therefore, the Ministry of Justice can calculate the average daily population in penal facilities.

Japanese Corrections Post-World War II: The Transition Years

Immediately after World War II, the inmate population in all penal facilities swelled to over 100,000 (see Table 7.1). However, during two decades of economic recovery and growth the inmate population began to decline. This drop coincided with the decline in the number of serious offences as well as some practical changes in the criminal justice system. For example, more cases were being diverted under public prosecutors' power to screen cases and judges began to administer more suspended sentences (Johnson, 1996).

The 1950s: A Period of Hardship

As noted earlier, immediately after World War II Japan experienced a severe economic downturn. Overcrowding became a serious issue, along with a general deterioration in prison conditions and services. Between 1946 and 1947, some 1,400 inmates died as a result of food shortages and unavailability of proper medical care. During the same period, some 1,600 inmates escaped from custody as a result of compromised security (Ono, 1993). These general conditions lasted until the early 1950s. In 1950 the prison population was 80,589, of whom 59.7% were thieves (see Table 7.2).

Table 7.2: Number of Prisoners at the End of Year, by Crime Categories

YEAR	1938	1950	1960	1970	1980	1990	2000
Theft	27,483	48,142	30,414	14,941	13,035	11,245	13,307
Other property offences[a]	*	9,242	6,375	2,986	2,810	2,321	3,095
Heinous offences of violence[b]	5,833	15,309	12,260	8,674	6,824	6,376	7,874
Other offences of violence[c]	*	3,296	5,407	3,791	4,228	3,751	3,701
Sex offences[d]	713	517	2,665	3,546	1,917	1,384	1,955
Professional negligence causing death or bodily injury	*	*	*	2,020	1,072	892	695
Other penal code offences	11,859	2,060	1,991	1,898	1,908	1,566	2,310
Narcotics control law **	*	*	995	72	83	120	209
Stimulant drug control law	*	*	170	130	7,370	9,826	13,831
Road traffic law	*	*	*	455	909	627	695
Offences of other special laws	798	2,023	823	1,211	1,679	1,784	2,142
TOTAL	46,686	80,589	61,100	39,724	41,835	39,892	49,814

Sources: Ministry of Justice, *Annual Report of Statistics on Correction for 1938, 1950, 1960, 1970, 1980, 1990 and 2000.*
*No tabulation in original data.
**Narcotic and Psycho Substances Control Law since 1990.

Note:

    a. Other Property Offences = Fraud, Breach of Trust, Embezzlement and Stolen Property.

    b. Heinous Offences of Violence = Murder and Robbery.

    c. Other Offences of Violence = Extortion, Bodily Injury and Assault.

    d. Sex Offences = Rape and Indecency.

Table 7.3: Prisoners at the End of Year by their Age Groups

	1938		1950		1960		1970		1980		1990		2000	
14 to under 18	804	(1.7)	466	(0.6)	54	(0.0)	4	(0.0)	0	(-)	1	(0.0)	0	(-0)
18 to under 20	1,881	(4.0)	5,164	(6.4)	895	(1.5)	259	(0.7)	55	(0.1)	31	(0.1)	0	(-)
20 to under 23	4,174	(8.9)	16,501	(20.4)	8,081	(13.2)	5,300	(13.3)	1,656	(4.0)	1,527	(3.8)	1,424	(2.9)
23 to under 26			15,281	(19.0)	11,942	(19.5)	6,399	(16.1)	2,989	(7.1)	3,077	(7.7)	3,293	(6.6)
26 to under 30			13,397	(16.6)	13,434	(22.0)	7,746	(19.5)	5,834	(13.9)	4,204	(10.5)	6,123	(12.3)
30 to under 40	*39,677	(85.1)	16,944	(21.0)	17,015	(27.8)	12,523	(31.5)	17,166	(41.2)	9,983	(25.3)	13,871	(27.9)
40 to under 50			8,671	(10.0)	6,334	(10.4)	5,287	(13.3)	10,115	(24.2)	12,613	(31.7)	10,559	(21.2)
50 to under 60			3,219	(4.0)	2,5467	(4.2)	1,670	(4.2)	3,148	(7.5)	6,466	(16.2)	9,880	(19.8)
60 to under 70			824	(1.0)	706	(1.2)	472	(1.2)	740	(1.7)	1,716	(4.3)	3,872	(7.8)
70 and older	153	(0.3)	122	(0.2)	92	(0.2)	64	(0.2)	132	(0.3)	274	(0.7)	769	(1.5)
Total	46,686	(100)	80,589	(100)	61,100	(100)	39,724	(100)	41,835	(100)	39,892	(100)	49,814	(100)

*Data between ages 23 and under 70.

Sources: Ministry of Justice, *Annual Report of Statistics on Correction* for 1938, 1950, 1960, 1970, 1980, 1990 and 2000.

Another consequence of the war was the large number of orphans and unemployed youth. Many of the youth turned to criminal activity, and at the end of 1950 those under the age of 26 constituted 46.4% of the prison population (see Table 7.3). The treatment of young inmates therefore became an important priority at that time (see Yokoyama, 2002).

In 1948, a new Juvenile Law was enacted in which the maximum age of juvenile offenders was lifted from less than 18 to less than 20. But because of limited resources the application of the new law to juvenile delinquents of 18 and 19 years of age did not come into effect until 1951 (Yokoyama, 2000a). This is reflected in the fact that in 1950 those between the ages of 18 and 19 made up 6.4% of the adult prison population.

The 1960s: Emerging Problems of Violent Offenders and Drug Abusers

The 1960s were marked by the public's attention to violent crimes (see Yokoyama, 1999a). Of particular concern was the increase in crime among young persons who were part of the "baby boon" immediately after the war (Yokoyama, 2002).

From 1950 to 1960, the number of inmates sentenced for minor violent crimes increased, as contrasted with the decline in those for heinous offences[7] (see Table 7.2). The percentage of the former among all prisoners rose from 4.1% in 1950 to 8.8% in 1960. In addition, more *Boryokudan* members were confined in prisons, as their crimes attracted considerable attention from law enforcement officials (see Box 7.2). Consequently, various efforts to treat violent offenders took priority among correctional administrators.

The other major problem in the 1960s was the increase in the number of drug offenders. The total number of suspects received by the Public Prosecutors' Office for an offence under Narcotic Control Law, particularly an offence concerning heroin, reached a high of 3,093 in 1962, after increasing from about 2,000 in 1958. Although perhaps not considered as extensive a problem as in other countries, Japanese corrections began to feel it necessary to deal with drug offenders.

Box 7.2: The Treatment of *Boryokudan* Members[8]

Since the end of the World War II, *Boryokudan* members have attracted the attention of penologists because they are disproportionately represented among the prison population (Johnson, 1997). The police took aggressive steps to curb the problem when, in 1964, they attempted to apprehend the top members of the *Boryokudan* (Yokoyama, 1999a). Under this strategy many *Boryokudan* members were caught and imprisoned, however efforts to reeducate them while in prison proved unsuccessful. After their release many *Boryokudan* members returned to their criminal groups and were often treated with celebrity-like status.

In 1981, activities by the *Boryokudan* attracted renewed attention after the death of the Godfather of the Yamaguchi-gumi (the largest *Boryokudan* group). Yamaguchi-gumi split into two rival groups and intense fighting resulted (Yokoyama, 2000b). The fighting reached a peak in 1985, when there were a reported 293 cases of fighting between the *Boryokudan* factions — an increase from only 56 such incidents in 1981.

By the late 1980s, the *Boryokudan* had become actively involved in dealing stimulant drugs. In addition, the *Boryokudan* expanded their illegal activities into extortion of ordinary citizens. In response to their growing menace the government, in 1991, enacted the Law to Cope with *Boryokudan* in an effort to combat the problem. Under this law some programs for rehabilitation are offered to the *Boryokudan* members. For example, while in prisons they are talked to regarding severing their relationships with the *Boryokudan*. If they decide to sever their ties, they are encouraged to write a letter to their boss. After receiving a reply from a boss, they are placed on parole supported by a volunteer parole officer.

The 1970s: Problems with Traffic Offenders and Sex Offenders

The economic recovery of Japan in the '50s and '60s was accompanied by an official decline in property crimes such as theft and fraud. In addition, the number of cases investigated for extortion, injury, murder and robbery also declined significantly from 1950 to 1970. However, there was a sharp increase in traffic-related accidents and offences. To address the latter increase, the criminalization of some traffic offences was carried out (Yokoyama, 1990a). For example, judges began to impose punishment on a charge of professional negligence causing death or injury on all drivers of motorcycles whose actions caused the death or bodily injury of another through careless driving.[9] As the number of such offenders increased, prisons had to develop specific treatment programs for them (see Box 7.3).

Another category of offenders that required a different level of attention from corrections were those who were convicted of sex-related offences. Between 1950 and 1970 the percentage of sex offenders among all prisoners rose from 0.6% in 1950 to 8.9% in 1970.

The period between 1950 and 1970 was marked by social change, a dramatic economic change, and a growing cultural diversity with an increased Western influence. Throughout these decades correctional practices had remained relatively unchanged from earlier times. Yet, there were several notable initiatives that focused on rehabilitation efforts. These were promoted by the issuance of the new Prisoner's Classification Rule in 1971.

Box 7.3. Rehabilitation for Traffic Offenders

In 1961, some of the traffic offenders without forced labor sentenced for professional negligence causing death or bodily injury[10] were assembled in Toyohashi Prison, a minimum security facility which specialized in special treatment programs (Yokoyama, 1990b). By the 1970s, three prisons for traffic offenders with minimum security provided inmates with such programs as vocational training, work release, educational activities, recreation, traffic safety education, group-work activities and introspection therapy.

Since the 1980s, judges have more frequently imposed imprisonment with forced labor on such traffic offenders as drunken drivers and drivers who had their licenses revoked. Today, they are also treated in traffic prisons under the programs for rehabilitation.

The 1980s and 1990s: Growing Problems with Foreign Offenders, the Aged and Female Offenders

From 1970 to 2000, the rate of prisoners between the ages of 20 and 30 underwent a dramatic drop, while that of prisoners 50 years of age and older increased sharply. Nowadays the treatment of elderly inmates has become an important focus for prison administrators.

Also, in the 1980s many foreigners rushed to Japan to take advantage of the country's economic success. However, when the economic bubble burst in 1990 there was a sharp increase in illegal activities by foreigners (Yokoyama, 1999b). With the increase in the number of foreign prisoners came a need to address their different needs and address such basic issues as the language barrier. Many foreign offenders were classified as F-class (see Figure 7.2), which meant foreign prisoners needed different treatment from Japanese ones because they were not accustomed to the Japanese lifestyle.

In principle, foreign prisoners, regardless of whether they are classified as F-class or not, are treated in the same way as Japanese. They work together with Japanese prisoners at the prison factory for eight hours per day under the supervision of a correction officer and are obligated to communicate in Japanese. With the increase of Asian prisoners, since 1996 they have been provided with the same foods as Japanese prisoners, although some are offered some special foods because of their religion. Since the beginning of the new millennium, the treatment of the old and foreign inmates remains important in prisons.

In Japan there are five female prisons and one facility for female inmates attached to a prison for males. The rate of females among all prisoners rose from 3.1% in 1980 to 5.0% in 2000. Recently, we also witness overcrowding in female prisons. Female prisoners are classified as W-class for special treatment. They are offered some vocational training programs.[11]

In the late 1990s, Japan experienced an increase in the inmate population. The average daily population in all penal facilities had reached 58,747 persons in 2000 (i.e., 4.6 per 10,000 inhabitants) from 48,243 in 1990. This increase is mainly attributable to the fact that judges began to respond to the conservative and punitive attitudes of the public. That is, judges began administering more severe sentences to offenders.[12]

The Historical Emergence of Japanese Correctional Policies

It was after the Meiji Restoration in 1868 that Western influences were introduced into Japan's legal system. In 1873 **Gustave Boissonade** (1825-1910), an associate professor of the University of Paris, was invited to help with the transition of Japan's legal system. He succeeded in helping to enact the Penal Code and the Code of Criminal Instruction (*Chizai Ho*), which was based on the *inquisitorial* method used in France and many other European countries at the time. The short-lived French model of the Penal Code was replaced by a new Penal Code in 1907.[13] This code was based on the *positivist model* (see Glossary) advocated by Germany, which Japan was consulting with at the time.

Then, after the defeat of Japan in World War II (1945) the Emperor's regime collapsed. Japan was stripped of its empire, and the criminal justice system was democratized under the direction of the Allied Powers. Following the enactment of a new Constitution in 1946,[14] and the revisions of the Penal Code in 1947, a new Code of Criminal Procedures was enacted in 1948. The code was modeled after the American system, which guaranteed *due process*, while Japan's fundamental correctional framework under the 1908 Prison Law remained under the models found in most of Western Europe.

Although a classification (see Glossary) system existed prior to World War II, in 1948 the Ministry of Justice adopted a new classification system based on the American model by issuing the Prisoners' Classification Examination Guideline. Since then, the Ministry has endeavored to establish an efficient treatment system by using both the progressive grading system and classification system.

In 1957, the first classification centre was established at Nakano Prison, where newly confined prisoners were assessed as to their character and observations of their behavior were carefully noted during the first two months of incarceration. In 1966, the Rule to Enforce Prison Law was revised to guarantee the rights of prisoners and to improve the standard of prison life from the viewpoint of the rehabilitation model. Then, in 1971 a new Prisoners' Classification Rule was issued by which the current system of both classification for accommodation and treatment was introduced.

JAPAN'S ADMINISTRATIVE PROCESS IN CORRECTIONS

The Prison Law (Art. 1) identifies four kinds of penal facilities. They include: (1) prisons in which inmates are obligated to work, (2) prisons for those without forced labor, (3) houses of penal detention for prisoners held for under 30 days, and, (4) detention houses to detain suspects and accused persons.[15] The Correction Bureau of the Ministry of Justice, with eight Regional Correction Headquarters, controls all correctional facilities. At the end of 2001, there were 56 prisons, 5 branch prisons, 8 juvenile prisons, 7 detention houses and 110 branch detention houses.

The position of a director-general of the Correction Bureau is always occupied by a public prosecutor, while a top position for correction officers is a director of the Tokyo Regional Correction Headquarters. The elite officers working at the Correction Bureau plan the policies related to corrections, communicate the budget to the Ministry of Finance and allot it to correctional facilities. Those at the Regional Correction Headquarters do supervisory jobs for all facilities in their region. The high-ranking officers and younger elites who pass the promotion examination for high-ranking ones change their administrative positions every two years. Through this personnel management system the Bureau of Correction controls correctional facilities all over the country (see Figures 7.1a and 1b).

Detention Houses

After World War II, both scholars and lawyers alike demanded the abolition of jails as a substitute to a detention house. Detention houses (i.e., similar to remand centers) are used to confine suspects and accused persons until the court makes its ruling regarding final sentencing. Although detention houses are not high-security facilities, there have rarely been any escapes.

The total number of suspects and accused confined to these facilities declined between 1950 and 1990. Then with the slight increase in crime in the 1990s, the use of detention houses began to increase once again. However, unlike the case in many other nations, these facilities did not experience any problems with overcrowding.

Figure 7.1a: Organizational Chart of the Correctional Administration in Japan

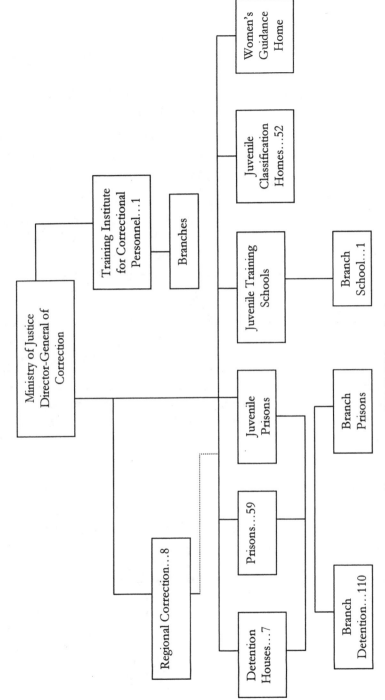

Source: Adapted from http://www.moj.go.jp/ENGLISH/organ.html.

Figure 7.1b: Flow of Treatment of Adult Offenders under the Penal Code

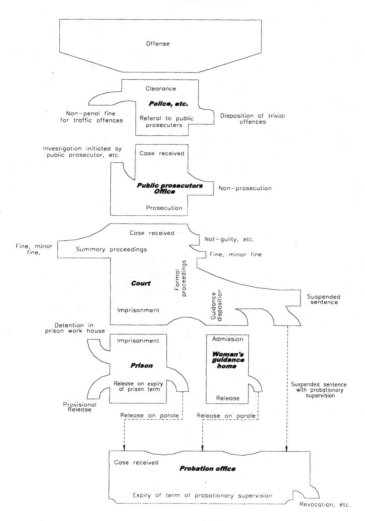

Source: Japan Ministry of Justice, Research and Training Institute (2001). *White Paper on Crime in 2001.*

Prisons

After World War II, Japan fell into economic chaos. As the number of individuals imprisoned increased, the country experienced an overcrowding problem in prisons. However, by the 1960s, as the economy began to recover, serious crimes gradually declined, and the overcrowding problem abated somewhat. The total number of prisoners remained constant at around 40,000 until the late 1990s. Then the country experienced a slight crime increase as a result of economic depression. This was accompanied by an increase in prison disturbances and the inmate population grew. Japan began to experience some problems with overcrowding. As recently as 2001, prisons were at 109.7% of their capacity. Subsequently, the Ministry of Justice acquired an increase in its budget for the fiscal year 2004 so that a new prison could be built for about 1,000 prisoners with less advanced criminal inclinations.

Work Houses

Under Article 18 of the Penal Code, if offenders who were ordered to pay a fine were unable to pay it, they could be placed into a work house to work it off. Given the economic growth in the country, the actual number of detainees in work houses decreased until the economic bubble burst in 1990.

In the 1990s, Japan underwent an economic recession and under a conservative political and social atmosphere judges began to impose heavier fines for a range of offences, especially traffic offences. This resulted in an increase in the number of offenders being detained because they were unable to pay their fines. The number of those detained due to an inability to pay a fine increased from 99 in 1990 to 366 in 2000.

Japan and the Death Penalty

In accordance with Article 11 of the Penal Code, the death sentence must be executed by hanging in the prison. Under Article 475 of the Criminal Procedure Code, the Minister of Justice must issue an order to execute the death penalty within six months after the day when the death sentence is finalized. However, the death penalty shall not be carried out until all chances for a retrial and an *amnesty* are lost. In practice, it usually takes a long time to carry out the execution (see Box 7.4).[16]

Box 7.4: Death Penalty Detainees and Their Rights in Japan

In Japan, death penalty detainees are expected to repent themselves of their crime(s) in order to overcome fear and agony while awaiting their execution. For this purpose, special officers treat each detainee individually, and a chaplain or another volunteer gives counseling on a voluntary basis. Death row inmates are allowed to communicate only with their family members, although they can be permitted to communicate with someone else in a special case under Article 45 and Article 46 of Prison Law. Furthermore, they are not informed of their execution until the very day the execution date is to be carried out. After the execution, only the family is told it has already been carried out.

The process of carrying out the death penalty remains secretive, which has been internationally criticized (Amnesty International, 2001; see second listing in Web-links). For example, in March 2001, Mr. Jansson, who is a chairperson of the Human Rights Committee of the Council of Europe, visited Japan in order to study the death penalty system. His requests were denied by the authorities.

Although Japan does not execute as many people annually as they once did, it is reported that fewer than 10 are put to death each year. Since 1993, when five resolutions on abolition of the death penalty at the UN Human Rights Committee were tabled, Japan has refused to support the resolution. In fact, organizations such as Amnesty International charge that with respect to the death penalty Japan is moving in the opposite direction of most countries. Japan's refusal to ratify these agreements is based on its insistence that public opinion is not supportive of abolition of the death penalty (Dando, 1997). However, public opinion polls have been criticized because they do not include questions allowing the respondent to oppose the abolishment of death penalty (see "Hidden Death Penalty," 2003). As recently as 1998, the International Covenant on Civil and Political Rights recommended that Japan abolish the death penalty. These requests have not only been rejected by the government but it actively cooperates with other countries (especially the United States) that still retain the death penalty, to resist pressure to abolish the sentence.

In the late 1990s, judges were inclined to use the death penalty more frequently in consideration of the *retributive* sentiments of victims and their families. As a result, the total number of detainees for the death penalty increased to 53 in 2000 from 24 in 1980 (Table 7.1).

CORRECTIONS IN JAPAN TODAY

In Japan prosecutors play a key role in the criminal justice process.[17] They are essentially responsible for deciding whether prosecution is warranted for criminological or social reasons. In principle, this process can minimize the risk of negatively stigmatizing individuals and help facilitate their rehabilitation and reintegration back into society (Castberg, 1999). The prosecution is also instrumental in recommending to the court the appropriate sentence. After the finalization of a guilty sentence, prosecutors take the initiative in executing it. Assuming that an offender is found guilty of a criminal offence, the following details the procedural elements of Japan's current correctional system.

Classification Centres

As of 2003, seven prisons and one juvenile prison now have facilities that serve as classification centres. These institutions receive persons between the ages of 16 to 28 who have no prior record of imprisonment and whose sentence exceeds one year. A classification in these centres takes about two months, during which times the offender is assessed in terms of his or her needs before being send to a particular institution. Once assigned, they usually undergo another one week evaluation by the institute, the main purpose of which is to ensure appropriate allocation to prison labor. In this manner, the system attempts to match the offender with an institution and its programs.

Initial Treatment

Japanese corrections attempts to match prison facilities with offenders' needs through the classification system. For about two weeks they receive the initial programs, while staying in a single cell. They are given a number and informed as to the prison rules and how to behave as a member of an inmate group.

Institutional Life

All prisons in Japan provide essential needs for inmates such as food, clothing, and basic hygiene requirements. As the correctional philosophy is based on *social conformity* and *reeducation*, prisoners are only given limited opportunities to use and/or obtain personal items. However, if an inmate exhibits consistent improvement, he or she is allowed some increased freedoms and liberties under the progressive grading system.

When prisoners suffer from an illness, they receive the medical service in their prison. However, in a serious case they are hospitalized under the supervision of three security officers. In addition, seriously physically or mentally handicapped inmates are treated in four medical prisons.

In Japan prisoners lead a highly regimented life which begins at 6:40 a.m. until the lights are turned out at 9 p.m.

Academic Education

Previously, a significant number of inmates were poorly educated because they tended to come from impoverished families. However, as the country's economy improved, the number of inmates with poor educational training has declined. In 2001, prisons throughout the country provided 743 prisoners with basic academic training (Japan Ministry of Justice, 2002).[18] In addition, 4,204 received a senior high-school level of education. Three juvenile prisons in Morioka, Matsumoto and Nara provide youth with correspondence courses that are managed by a prefectural senior high school.

While incarcerated, inmates can take correspondence courses on such subjects as: bookkeeping, calligraphy, penmanship, English, computer programming and/or repairs. In 2001, 3,006 prisoners took one of these types of courses.

Counseling and Guidance

As with the Japanese juvenile justice approach, the adult system relies on many volunteers to assist in providing guidance and social counseling. At the end of 2001, the total number of volunteer counselors appointed by a director of the regional correction headquarters amounted to 1,173. They included specialists in literary art, education, religion, rehabilitation, law, merchandise and social welfare (see Japan Ministry of Justice, 2002).

Before World War II, all inmates were obliged to attend a religious ceremony presided over by a Buddhist priest. As the right to religion was guaranteed under the new Constitution of 1946, prisons are required by law to only allow inmates to listen to preaching by a chaplain on a voluntary basis. At the end of 2001, a total of 1,504 priests of such religious groups as Buddhism, Shinto and Christianity worked as prison chaplains. In 2001, the recorded number of religious encounters with a chaplain amounted to 9,128 in a group setting, and 6,515 on an individual basis (see Japan Ministry of Justice, 2002).

In the late 1990s, the crime victims movement gained strength. Prisons have attempted to offer some educational programs to make inmates repent of their offences. However, they did not succeed in offering these programs without the assistance of volunteers. And early into the new millennium, the idea of *restorative justice* (see Glossary) was introduced. However, prisons do not yet offer any mediation-based programs, although in some juvenile cases this mediation is carried out on an experimental basis.

Life Skills Training

The formal purpose of providing life skills is to help inmates cultivate acceptable behaviors so that they can conduct themselves in an appropriate manner once they reenter the community (see Japan Ministry of Justice, 2002). In order to accomplish this objective, prison rules prescribe, in detail, how an inmate is to behave while in prison. Under the uniform and rigid application of these rules, **the fair and equal treatment of inmates** is achieved.[19]

While the rules are thought to be of educative value, they are also designed to help ensure control over the inmate population. The level of regimentation on the "inside" is not reflective of life on the "outside." For example, those who behave well under the prison rules are not always successful once they are released.

In addition, there is considerable emphasis placed on conformity to the prison rules. Therefore, as has been pointed out by the Human Rights Watch group and the United Nations, inmates' rights to freedom are extremely limited.

Maintaining Prison Conditions

For the past 50-odd years there have not been any (official) riots in any of the Japanese prisons. This would suggest that Japanese prisons are effective in maintaining control over the inmate population. The most commonly acceptable explanation for the "success" seems to be the treatment system by Tanto officers. **Tanto officers** do not carry any weapons, and their responsibility is the care and well-being of their assigned inmates at a prison factory. Previously, Tanto officers were called Oyaji-san (Father), because they behaved like father figures for male inmates. Playing three roles — that is, supervisor, vocational instructor and counselor — Tantos exercised considerable discretion in how they could treat inmates in their charge. They succeeded in establishing good relationships with their charges. This form of treatment is characterized as "**correction through inmates' confidence**" (Yokoyama, 1994).

Since the early 1980s, many of the older Tanto officers have retired. They have been replaced by younger officers, many of whom are university graduates. Inmates refer to them as Sensei (Teacher) rather than as Oyaji-san. As the younger Tanto officers tend to lack the experience of their predecessors, they tend to carry out their duties in a more formal manner and exercise considerably less discretion.[20] Yet, they are encouraged to respect and follow the traditional practices of "correction through inmates' confidence" in order to maintain the reeducative quality.

While in the institution, inmates are not allowed to move about freely. They must be accompanied by a security officer whenever they are moving about. In recent years, given the growing inmate population and limited manpower, modern technologies such as electronic cameras for supervision and machines to identify fingerprints are being used to maintain constant surveillance of inmates. The result has been that in 2001 there were only 18 reported infractions, ranging from escapes, to suicides, to incidents resulting in bodily injury to another inmate. There were no recorded murders, accidental deaths, or prison riots (Japan Ministry of Justice, 2002).

Disciplinary Sanctions

Japan's disciplinary practices are somewhat unique by international standards. Even though its prison law dates back to 1908, prison rules govern every aspect of a detainee's life. Governors of each prison are given wide discretion to implement their own internal rules to regulate the daily operation of their prison. The internal regulations are kept secret. The rationale offered by the Ministry of Justice is that making such information public would compromise the security of the institution (even though there is no evidence to support its statement).

The Ministry of Justice does, however, provide general information regarding how many inmates require disciplinary actions for violating one or more of the prison rules. In 2001, the number of such cases amounted to 34,565 (Japan Ministry of Justice, 2002). Officially, the majority of the cases involve inmate disobedience toward correctional officers, followed by assault against another inmate (15.3%), refusal to work (13.9%), and disputes not involving physical violence (8.4%).[21]

Traditionally, most Japanese are conformists and consequently tend to obey the prison rules. However, given their personal circumstances and conditions within the various institutions, some are known to occasionally resist the rule or the direction of a security officer. Furthermore, as detainees learn more about their human rights, Japan has seen an increase in complaints and protests by prisoners. Amnesty International Japan and the Center for Prisoners' Rights, which was established by Japanese lawyers and scholars of criminal laws in 1995, receive these complaints and protests, and use them to call for reforms to institutional practices so as to protect prisoners' rights and bring Japan's correctional system inline with international standards (see Box 7.5).

Box 7.5: Reaction to a Scandal in Nagoya Prison

Several security officers in Nagoya Prison were arrested for cruel and unusual torture of three inmates, as a result of which two died and one was seriously injured (Yokoyama, 2004). However, the details of these events were kept secret by the authority of Nagoya Prison and the Ministry of Justice even after the first press conference in Nagoya Prison on October 4, 2002.

After receiving the information about the arrest of five security officers on November 8, 2002, on November 20, 2002 Amnesty International issued an appeal that all those responsible for such abuses should be brought to justice. It said, "Japan should ensure that the rights of all prisoners and detainees — as guaranteed in international human rights standards to which Japan is a state party — are protected." In response to this request it appears that Japan should look to reform its existing prison system. Another scandal in Nagoya Prison was exposed in February, 2003. It was not until March 31, 2003, that the Minister of Justice organized the council for prison reform.

Release from Prison

In 2001, some 27,100 inmates were released from Japanese prisons (Japan Ministry of Justice, 2002). Of those released, 43.9% had completed their sentence and 56.1% were released on parole by the permission of a regional parole board.[22] Those earning permission for release on parole receive pre-release education in prisons for two weeks, while others for one week prior to the expiration of their imprisonment term. This education program delivered by the correction officers involves giving inmates essential information on such matters as how to find a job, how to conduct themselves on the "outside," and the conditions of their parole. Volunteers and some officers of other agencies, such as a public employment security office, help with the pre-release education program.

Japan's *community-based correctional* initiatives are carried out by **Hogoshi**, a volunteer probation and parole officer authorized by the Volunteer Probation & Parole Officer Law of 1950. This volunteer officer is placed under the control of the Rehabilitation Bureau of the Ministry of Justice. In 2002, there were some 49,000 Hogoshi volunteers throughout the country (Japan Ministry of Justice, 2002). During the examination on whether a prisoner should be released on parole, a Hogoshi researches the environment in which he/she will return, and reports it to a regional parole board. A Hogoshi supervises a parolee to offer some advice for rehabilitation. He/she sometimes uses the resources in the community to aid in the parolee's rehabilitation.

In addition, 164 associations offer aid such as accommodation and counseling to offenders who wished to rehabilitate themselves after they had been diverted from the criminal justice system or after they had been released from a prison.

PROFILE OF THE CORRECTIONAL POPULATION

In Japan there are two kinds of classification categories; one for accommodation and another for treatment (Figure 7.2). Fundamentally, prisoners are accommodated separately according to their criminal inclinations to prevent negative influences. Therefore, the distinction between A-Class and B-Class is fundamental, which overlaps other categories. For example, YA-Class and YB-Class mean the difference between adults under 26 years of age with less advanced criminal inclinations and those with stronger inclinations, respectively.

By the end of 2000 there were 49,814 prisoners, of which classifications B, A, Y, L, W and F amounted to 50.0%, 20.6%, 6.7%, 6.5%, 4.7% and 3.5%, respectively (Japan Ministry of Justice, 2001:81). On the other hand, of the 38,585 prisoners in 1995, the corresponding rates were 53.8%, 17.8%, 8.3%, 7.8%, 4.1% and 1.5% (Japan Ministry of Justice, 1996:148). Hence, from 1995 to 2000 there were increases in first-time offenders, female prisoners and foreigners.

Figure 7.2: Classification Categories

Classification for Accommodation:

Class A: less advanced criminal inclinations

Class B: more advanced criminal inclinations

Class F: foreigners

Class I: those sentenced to imprisonment without forced labor

Class J: juveniles

Class L: those sentenced to terms of eight years or more

Class M: mentally defective (including three sub-categories)

Class P: those in ill health or physically handicapped

Class W: women

Class Y: adults under twenty-six years of age

Classification for Treatment:

Class E: need for academic education

Class G: need for guidance in daily life

Class O: suitable for open treatment

Class N: suitable for maintenance work for a prison

Class S: need for special protection and care

Class T: need for therapeutic treatment

Class V: need for vocational training

ISSUES CONFRONTING JAPANESE CORRECTIONS TODAY

Until recently, Japan has had a comparatively low rate of imprisonment, which has been attributed to the wide-ranging diversion from the criminal justice system. In Japan, the police and the public prosecutor have wide power to divert criminal cases, although they are obligated to refer all juvenile cases to the family court. For example, the police can dispose of a minor offence, such as a petty theft or an offence under the Minor Offence Law, without referral to the public prosecutor. The public prosecutor also has wide power to divert cases. In 2001, the total number of all suspects disposed of by the public prosecutor amounted to 2,219,810, of which 39.9% and 40.2% were released by suspended prosecution and prosecuted in the summary procedure, respectively (Japan Ministry of Justice, 2002). In addition, judges are inclined to use the sentence of imprisonment only in serious cases or cases of recidivism. In 2001, the total number of all defendants finalized at the court amounted to 967,136, of whom 91.4% were fined. A total of 75,528 defendants were sentenced to imprisonment with forced labor, of whom 61.6% received the suspension of their sentence.

For offenders sent to prison, correction officers endeavor to treat them equally and fairly according to the rehabilitation model. They have established the treatment through inmates' confidence. However, this treatment has been criticized because it is usually carried out by limiting inmates' rights to freedom. Both Human Rights Watch and Amnesty International have cited Japan for international law violations. For example, in a follow-up to its 1997 report, in 2002 Amnesty International identified many of the same issues as in the first report. Prisoners continue to "suffer from systematic cruel, inhumane or degrading treatment" for the most minor of rule infractions ("Abusive Punishment in Japanese Prisons," 2003). The report offers four major areas that require immediate attention:

(1) Removing the secrecy that surrounds prisons in Japan by allowing unfettered access to centres of detention by independent organizations.

(2) Abolishing "minor solitary confinement" in its current form.

(3) Enacting and enforcing clear legislation that details the precise circumstances under which instruments of restraint and "protection cells" may be used in prisons

(4) Abolishing the use of leather handcuffs, body belts and metal handcuffs as a punishment.

With the increasingly conservative attitude towards corrections, both publicly and politically, there has been a move towards increased criminalization that has been accompanied by problems of overcrowding in prisons. To cope with this phenomenon, the Ministry of Justice acquired a budget to expand buildings and equipment in prisons. However, as inmates have to live in the smaller space, their stress seems to be enhanced. In addition, as the number of correctional officers does not increase, their job burden becomes heavier. In such a stressful climate scandals occurred in Nagoya Prison (see Box 7.5 above).

While some have been quick to criticize Japan's correctional policies and practices, in recent years there has been a concerted effort to acknowledge the rights of crime victims as well as explore alternatives to conventional incarceration. As a result of such efforts/initiatives, some laws such as the Code of Criminal Procedure were revised in 2000 to widen victims' rights. In response to this phenomenon correctional facilities have begun to offer some educational programs more actively to assist inmates to acknowledge and take responsibility for their offence(s). However, considerable work still needs to be done in these areas to ensure that they are effective in their objectives.

Future Directions in Japanese Corrections

After the media exposed the scandals in Nagoya Prison, the Ministry of Justice established the council for prison reform. The council has been charged with exploring how it can introduce reforms to fit international standards. Among those reforms that require immediate attention include:

- Ratifying the Convention against Torture and Other Cruel, Inhuman or Degrading Treatment or Punishment and the Optional Protocol to the International Covenant on Civil and Political Rights.

- Ensuring that prisoners have access to adequate, independent and confidential complaints mechanisms. Prisoners must never be punished for making a complaint about their treatment.

- Enacting and enforcing clear legislation which details the precise circumstances under which instruments of restraint and "protection cells" may be used in prisons.

- Conducting a thorough and systematic review of the use and abuse of "protection cells" in prisons and preventing the punitive use of "protection cells," leather handcuffs, body belts, metal handcuffs and *mataware pants*.

- Conducting full, impartial and independent investigations into all deaths in custody and all cases of alleged ill treatment in prisons. If it is established that allegations are well-founded, the perpetrator should be brought to justice and victims should be afforded redress and compensation.

- Removing the secrecy that surrounds prisons in Japan and reinforcing their accountability by allowing unrestricted access to centres of detention by independent national and international bodies, including non-governmental organizations.

- Publishing all prison rules and amending those which do not conform with international human rights standards. Prison officials must be prevented from meting out severe punishments for minor infractions of prison rules ("Abusive Punishment in Japanese Prisons," 2003).

However, these reforms do not appear readily forthcoming because most members of the council seem to prefer the traditional policy of maintaining security and order in prisons, which leaders of the Ministry of Justice, that is, elite prosecutors, emphasize. Yet recently, accountability of public officers has been given increased attention in the aftermath of various publicly disclosed events. Therefore, it is anticipated that domestic and international attention will pressure the council to propose certain reforms.

CONCLUSION

Japan has a rich correctional history and remains, unlike in many other countries, a highly centralized system. It has drawn considerable attention from foreign scholars over the years because of its comparatively low crime rates. These scholars have examined Japan's criminal justice system to see if there are elements of its system that can be applied to their respective systems. In order to do so, one must remain sensitive to both structural and cultural differences. For example, Japan is still a relatively homogeneous society in which tradition and heritage carry considerable importance. And while it is beyond the scope of this chapter to speculate on whether other countries might benefit from examining aspects of Japan's correctional system, this chapter has attempted to provide an overview of Japan's system which will hopefully allow the readers to form their own informed opinions.

Japan's highly centralized approach has ensured that correctional administration and treatment of prisoners is very consistent throughout the country. This is a reflection of Japan's desire to maintain a sense of social harmony and reverence for the law, and for citizens to be treated equally and fairly rather than freely. While such an approach minimizes inconsistencies in programming and treatment of offenders, any problems related to corrections tend to exist throughout the entire country.

Although the prison regime is very strict, by most standards prisons offer a wide range of programming for the rehabilitation of inmates. Conformity is in fact a major part of Japan's culture, and following clear norms and expectations does not pose a major problem for most inmates.

Japanese correctional officers endeavor to treat prisoners equally and fairly in a uniform way. They do not give out any special privileges, even to such inmates as a boss of the *Boryokudan* and a former leader in the political and economic world.[23] Therefore, inmates are rarely afraid of being attacked by another inmate. This advantage is also appreciated by foreign inmates, who work together with Japanese inmates under the supervision of a Tanto officer in daytime. However, they are more sensitive to the extreme limitation of their rights to freedom.

Japanese lawyers and scholars of criminal laws who respect inmates' rights to freedom first of all, have appealed against the invasion of these rights in prisons. In response to their appeal, international bodies have also criticized Japan for various human right violations in prisons. But without prejudice one must view Japan's correctional practices within a societal and cultural context. Ironically, perhaps, even though prisoners have fewer rights to freedom than their counterparts in most other countries, inmates experience few of the problems witnessed in many other prisons around the world (e.g., very few riots, virtually no violence among inmates, and being in good health).

The Ministry of Justice and the prison authorities in Japan are under pressure by domestic and international organizations to promote increased human rights to freedom. By attempting to embrace a more open approach to correctional practices, Japan will be expected to meet the international standards, while maintaining its good heritages in correctional practices.

Key Terms and Concepts

Boryokudan

"Correction through Inmates' Confidence"

Detention Houses

Hogoshi

Gustave Boissonade

Meiji Restoration (1868)

Prison Law

Tanto officers

Work Houses

Discussion/Study Questions

(1) How has the history of Japan impacted correctional practices today? To what extent might Western ideas have helped or hindered correctional ideology in Japan?

(2) The Japanese correctional system is a rather closed system. What problems does this pose for prisoners?

(3) What merit or demerit does prison staff practice what is called "correction through inmates' confidence" have?

(4) Although Japanese prisons have been accused of various human rights violations of inmate's rights, how might Japanese cultural values reflect it?

(5) Volunteers are commonly used in a variety of areas for rehabilitation of inmates and ex-inmates. What are the possible pros and cons of such an approach?

Helpful Web-links

A document discussing the abuse of punishment in Japanese prisons:
http://www.web.amnesty.org/aidoc/aidoc_pdf.nsf/index/ASA22004199 8ENGLISH/$File/ASA2200498.pdf.

Amnesty International:
http://web.amnesty.org/library/Index/ENGASA220052001?open&of= ENG-JPN.

Japan Today news link that has numerous stories on current correctional situations in Japan:
http://www.japantoday.com/e/?content=news&cat=2&page=2.

The Japanese Ministry of Justice (English version):
http://www.moj.go.jp/ENGLISH/index.html.

Organization chart of the Ministry of Justice:
http://www.moj.go.jp/ENGLISH/organ.html.

A link to the Corrections Bureau within the Ministry of Justice:
http://www.moj.go.jp/ENGLISH/CB/cb-01.html.

A link to the Rehabilitation Bureau within the Ministry of Justice:
http://www.moj.go.jp/ENGLISH/RB/rb-01.html.

A comprehensive link with additional information on Japan's criminal justice system and the country's history:
http://www.1upinfo.com/country-guide-study/japan/japan297.html.

REFERENCES

"Abusive Punishments in Japanese Prisons" (2003). Retrieved online at: http://www.llcc.cc.il.us/gtruitt/SCJ290spring2002/Prisons_in_Japan_A mnesty_International.html (Sept. 24, 2003).

Castberg, A.D. (1990). *Japanese Criminal Justice*. New York: Praeger.

CPR News Letters No. 34 (2003). (In Japanese.) Tokyo.

Criminal Affairs Association (1974). *Book on Modern History of Correction in Japan*, vol. 1. (Reissued version of book originally published in 1943, written in Japanese.) Tokyo, Japan: Correctional Association.

Dando, S. (1997). *Theory on Abolition of Death Penalty* (5th ed.). (In Japanese.) Tokyo, Japan: Yuhikaku.

"Hidden Death Penalty in Japan" (2003). (Online — retrieved August 05: http://www.jca.apc.org/stop-shikei/epamph/dpinjapan_e.html.)

"Inhumane Behaviour" (2002). Retrieved online (Aug. 5, 2003): http://www.guardian.co.uk/japan/story/0,7369,841141,00.html (Nov. 15, 2002).

Ishii, R. (1964). *Penalty in Edo*. (In Japanese.) Tokyo, Japan: Chuo-koron-sha.

Japan Ministry of Justice, Research and Training Institute (2002). *White Paper on Crime in 2002*. Tokyo.

—— (2001). *White Paper on Crime in 2001*. Tokyo.

—— (1996). *White Paper on Crime in 1996*. Tokyo.

Johnson, E.H. (1997). *Criminalization and Prisoners — Six Contrary Cohorts*. Carbondale and Edwardsville, IL: Southern Illinois University Press.

—— (1996). *Japanese Corrections — Managing Convicted Offenders in an Orderly Society*. Carbondale and Edwardsville, IL: Southern Illinois University Press.

Ono, Y. (1993). "Trace of Development of Japanese Correction." (In Japanese.) In: T. Morishita, T. Sato, Y. Ono, K. Miyamoto and M. Kamoshita (eds.), *Development of Japanese Correction*. Tokyo, Japan: Ichiryu-sha.

Sameshima, S. (1991). "Random Private Thoughts on Correction." (In Japanese.) *Keisei* 102(8):100-106.

Shikita, M. and T. Tsuchiya (eds.), (1990). *Crime and Criminal Policy in Japan from 1926 to 1988*. Tokyo, Japan: Japan Criminal Policy Society.

Yamamoto, J. (2003). *Record on Life Inside Prison Window*. (In Japanese.) Tokyo: Poplar-sha.

Yokoyama, M. (2004). "Analysis of Prison Scandals in Japan." *Kokugakuin Journal of Law and Politics* 41(4):1-35.

—— (2002). "Juvenile Justice and Juvenile Crime: An Overview of Japan." In: J. Winterdyk (ed.), *Juvenile Justice Systems — International Perspectives* (2nd ed.). Toronto, CAN: Canadian Scholars' Press, Inc.

—— (2000a). "Development of Educative Treatment in Juvenile Training Schools in Japan." *Caribbean Journal of Criminology and Social Psychology* 5(1&2):237-259.

—— (2000b). "Change in Japanese Organized Crime and Enforcement of the Law to Cop with Boryokudan in 1992." *Kokugakuin Journal of Law and Politics* 38(3):1-33.

—— (1999a). "Trends of Organized Crime by *Boryokudan* in Japan." In: S. Einstein and M. Amir (eds.), *Organized Crime: Uncertainties and Dilemmas.* Chicago, IL: Office of International Criminal Justice, University of Illinois at Chicago.

—— (1999b). "Analysis of the Crimes by Foreigners in Japan." *International Journal of Comparative and Applied Criminal Justice* 23(2):181-213.

—— (1994). "Treatment of Prisoners under Rehabilitation Model in Japan." *Kokugakuin Journal of Law and Politics* 32(2):1-24.

—— (1990a). "Criminalization Against Traffic Offenders in Japan." *International Journal of Comparative and Applied Criminal Justice* 14(1):65-71.

—— (1990b). "Treatment of Traffic Offenders in Prisons with Criminalization Against Them in Japan." *Kokugakuin Journal of Law and Politics* 27(4):28-43.

—— (1985). "Criminal Policy against Thieves in Japan." *Kangweon Law Review* 1:191-217.

—— (1982). "How Have Prisons Been Used in Japan." Paper presented at the World Congress of the International Sociological Association in Mexico City on August 18.

NOTES

1. Although Japanese believed in Shinto, a native polytheistic religion, they accepted Buddhism imported from China and Korea around the 6th century A.D.

2. *Seppuku (harakiri)*, a kind of suicide, was an honorable punishment which was only imposed on a warrior.

3. In 1720, tattooing was introduced to stigmatize criminals in the place of cutting their nose and ears. At that time tattoos were popular. Therefore, for the purpose of stigmatizing, a forearm of criminals was curved in two lines by a needle with black ink. As this tattooing was extremely painful, it was a form of corporal punishment.

4. The system, based on a Chinese model, included five types of punishment: flogging with a whip, beating by a rod, confinement, banishment and the death penalty.

5. Today it is estimated that the membership of *Boryokudan* numbers some 84,400 (*White Paper on Police*, 2002:194). By the way, the National Police Agency publishes the White Paper on Police every year to inform people of the crime situation and the police activities. It also publishes the English summary version of the White Paper. In this chapter the author uses the Japanese version.

6. According to the Ministry of Justice's definition, a branch prison is a small-sized prison, for the operation of which a warden of a main prison is responsible.

7. The Ministry of Justice defines the category of "heinous offences" as both murder and robbery.

8. The term *Boryokudan* is used by the National Police Agency to define and describe a group of violent offenders. The term replaced the label of "*Yakuza*," which has been used by gang members in order to portray their good image as those who share the *Ninkyo-do*, that is, a kind of chivalrous spirit (Yokoyama, 1999a:136).

9. Previously, ordinary drivers were charged with simple negligence causing death or injury, for which the maximum penalty is lighter than that for professional negligence.

10. They are mainly prisoners who are classified as I-class (see Figure 7.2). With criminalization against traffic offenders, the rate of I-class prisoners declined from 1,224 in 1972 to 149 in 2000.

11. In Tochigi Female Prison, several inmates, composed mainly of murderers, received training to get a license to become a hair dresser.

12. The average imprisonment term of the newly confined prisoners increased from 22.7 months in 1992 to 27.0 in 2001.

13. The new code was shorter and provided greater judicial discretion in sentencing. However, under the Code of Criminal Procedure of 1948 the principles of due process and "*nullum crimen, nulla poena sine lege*" (no crime, no penalty without law) are guaranteed in substance as well as in practice.

14. Although human rights were prescribed in the old Constitution of 1889, they were guaranteed only within the limits of loyal subjects to an emperor. The "new" Constitution declares the people's sovereignty, and guarantees the fundamental rights in chapter 3 entitled "Rights and Duties of the People."

15. As the substitute detention house, police jails are widely used for detaining suspects in order to interrogate them for up to 23 days. Lawyers and scholars of

criminal laws advocate the abolition of this substitute detention house because it is a hotbed to compel suspects to confess falsely.

16. Detainees for the death penalty have very few chances for a retrial, for which the requirement is narrowly defined under Article 435 of the Code of Criminal Procedure. Since 1975, any *amnesty* has not been given to them from the perspective of maintenance of the public order, which public prosecutors emphasized. However, most of them apply continuously for a retrial or an amnesty. In addition, the Minister of Justice hesitates to issue an order on execution. Therefore, it takes a long time to carry out the execution of a death penalty.

17. Most public prosecutors are affiliated with the Public Prosecutors' Office. In addition, some able prosecutors work in the Ministry of Justice, in which they monopolize all important positions, such as a director-general of the Correction Bureau and that of the Rehabilitation Bureau. Through personnel management and budgets they control correction officers all over the country. They are inclined to look down on specialists in correction. It is a great defect in the Japanese correction system.

18. The Research and Training Institute of the Ministry of Justice publishes a *White Paper on Crime* every year to inform people of the crime situation and the activities such as correction and rehabilitation under the control of the Ministry of Justice. It also publishes the English version one or two years later than the Japanese version. In this chapter the author uses the Japanese version.

19. Surely, inmates form their informal groups, in which a boss controls. In Japanese prisons, correction officers endeavor to maintain security and order without using the influence of such a boss inmate.

20. S. Sameshima, a former warden of a prison, insisted that "correction through inmates' confidence" should be changed into "correction by whole prison organization," that is, the uniform correction by all officers in a body under the law (1991:100).

21. For an overview of some of the key prison regulations, see "Abusive Punishments in Japanese Prisons" (2003).

22. Under Article 28 of the Penal Code, parole eligibility requires that at least one-third of the offender's sentence has been served, or 10 years served if the offender was sentenced to life. Parole decisions are also based on a clear demonstration of reformation by the inmate. Such lenient eligibility was prescribed under the influence of the Positivist School around 1907.

23. Jyoji Yamamoto, a former member of the House of Representatives, was sentenced to imprisonment for one year and a half on a charge of fraud, because he

had appropriated money paid for his formal secretary from the government for the employment of private secretaries. After release on parole, he published a book on his life in Kurobane Prison (which is for prisoners over 26 years old with the less advanced criminal inclinations), by which we know that he was treated in the prison without being given any privilege as a former influential politician (Yamamoto, 2003).

CHAPTER 8.
NAMIBIAN ADULT CORRECTIONS FROM THE PAST INTO THE PRESENT: A DIFFICULT TRANSITION

by

Stefan Schulz
Department of Legal Studies, Polytechnic of Namibia, Windhoek

and

John W. Nyoka
Ministry of Prisons and Correctional Services, Windhoek

BASIC FACTS ON NAMIBIA

Area: Namibia is a vast country of 823,145 square kilometres. It is the twelfth largest country in sub-Sahara Africa, lying on the South West Coast of Africa. It shares its main borders with Angola, Botswana and South Africa. In the far northeast is the Caprivi Strip, an elongated pan-handle consisting of tropical swamplands and bordered by four countries — Angola, Botswana, Zambia and Zimbabwe.

Population: According to the 2001 Population and Housing Census, Namibia had a population of 1.825 million and an annual population growth of approximately 2.6%. The average population density of the territory is approximately 2.5 people per square kilometre. Although Namibia is one of the most sparsely populated regions in sub-Saharan

Africa it has a rich variety of peoples in culture, language and racial origin. While English is the official language in Namibia, many languages are spoken in the country. They can be divided into three categories: the Bantu languages spoken by the Owambos, Hereros, Kavangos, Caprivians and Tswanas; the Khoi-san languages spoken by the San and Nama/Damara; and the Indo-Germanic languages of Afrikaans, English and German. The Owambos are the biggest ethnical group in Namibia. Numbering approximately 900,000 in 2001, they represent about 50% of Namibia's population. Windhoek is the nation's capital.

Climate: Namibia has a dry climate typical of a semi-desert country where droughts are a regular occurrence. Days are mostly warm to very hot, while nights are generally cool. Average day temperatures in the summer vary from 20° to 34° centigrade and average night temperatures in the winter from 0° to 10° centigrade. Rain in Namibia usually falls in summer, with a short rainy season in November and the main rainy season from February to March. Average rainfall figures vary from less than 50 millimetres along the coast to 350 millimetres in the central and 700 in the far northeastern regions. However, because of the high variability of rainfall, especially in the arid regions, the "annual" rainfall does not necessarily give a true picture.

Economy: The pillars of Namibia's economy are mining, fishing, tourism and agriculture, among which tourism is the fastest growing industry. The largest single contributor to Namibia's Gross Domestic Product is general government, and the largest provider of employment is agriculture.

Government: Namibia is a unitary state, which is now divided into 13 administrative regions. Namibia is ruled by a multiparty parliament and has a democratic constitution. The constitution provides for the division of power between the executive, the legislature and the judiciary.

"The mood and temper of the public with regard to the treatment of crime and criminals is one of the most unfailing tests of the civilization of any country."
~ Sir Winston Churchill

GENERAL HISTORY OF NAMIBIAN CORRECTIONS

The unique history of Namibia has a direct relationship to its present correctional system. Namibia is a newly independent state. The territory was proclaimed a German protectorate by Bismarck in 1884. The conquest of German South West Africa by South African troops during World War I resulted in its subsequent administration by South Africa under a 1920 League of Nations Mandate. In December 1946, the United Nations, the successor organization of the League of Nations, rejected South African plans to make Namibia part of South Africa. However, South Africa went on with what was — in practice — an annexation of Namibia. In 1949, South Africa stopped reporting to the UN on how it was administering the country.

On October 27 1966, the General Assembly of the United Nations decided to end the South African mandate over Namibia, but the South African government refused to carry out this and other decisions of the United Nations. It was in the same year that the protracted war for national liberation between the occupying South African forces and the Namibian liberation movement SWAPO (South West African People's Organisation) started (Referat fuer Information und Oeffentlichkeitsarbeit der SWAPO von Namibia, 1979). In 1989, the implementation of United Nations Resolution 435 for free and fair elections resulted in SWAPO coming to power. On March 21, 1990, after 106 years of foreign rule, Namibia achieved independence, installing Dr. Sam Nujoma as its first President.

Namibia's social, cultural and political reality today is largely influenced by the destructive and devastating effects of colonialism and political *apartheid*. It is true that Namibia was not directly affected by the slave trade and early colonialism like many other African nations. But since Germany had declared the territory a protectorate in 1884, land theft and colonial oppression encroached on the indigenous economic and cultural environment with almost the same effects over time. The system of forced labour, introduced in 1907 by the German colonial administration (Nachtweih, 1976), carried on and further developed by the South African administration, led steadily to a destruction of the social and cultural fabric.[1]

The drain of the forced labour caused ongoing friction with the indigenous economic structures. Social disintegration has not stopped with independence, but rather taken an expeditious course since then (Schulz, 1997). This has become particularly visible in the black community, where prior to independence almost any social development had been inhibited by the apartheid regime. While independence has brought a new freedom of choice and opportunity to Namibia, the society continues to struggle with these changes. The prison system — like other institutions of governance — was also affected by the legacy of colonialism and apartheid.

Since 1990, Namibia's Constitution has been based on the principles of a representative democracy reinforced by fundamental rights and freedoms. Namibia has adopted the 1957 United Nations Standard Minimum Rules for the Treatment of Prisoners, and, in principle, the 1990 United Nations Standard Minimum Rules for *Non-Custodial Measures* (Tokyo Rules). Namibia is also a signatory of the several UN human rights instruments, including the International Covenant of Civil and Political Rights. Each of these human rights instruments set limits on what the state can legally or legitimately do to people in conflict with the law. They are meant to promote the rule of law regarding decisions made about offenders and to combat arbitrariness involved in such decisions. As will be shown in the following section, upon gaining independence, the above norms became a veritable challenge, which Namibia was to accept.

Although the Namibian Constitution (NC) of 1990 sets out the minimum fundamental conditions that have to be adhered to by all bodies of government, including the Namibian Prisons Service (NPS), Namibia inherited not only the correctional "hardware," (i.e., the existing infrastructure of prisons), but also the South African Prisons Act 8 of 1959 and the regulations made there under. The *Prisons Act* formed part of the apartheid legislation but remained in existence afterward and continued to be applied after independence by virtue of Article 140 (1) of the NC, which states:

> Subject to the provisions of this Constitution, all laws which were in force immediately before Independence shall remain in force until repealed or amended by an Act of Parliament or until they are declared unconstitutional by a competent Court.

Under the authority of the Executive Powers (Prisons) Transfer Proclamation of 1977, the administration of the Prisons Act vested power (authority) in the Administrator General for the Territory of South West Africa, who delegated his powers to the Commissioner of Prisons. Historically, and until the above proclamation came into force,[2] the Commissioner of Prisons had few administrative powers because he received his directives for daily activities from the Ministry of Justice in Pretoria (South Africa). The Republic of South Africa Prison Reformatory Department was administered under Act 46 of 1920 (with subsequent amendments) until the Prisons Act 8 of 1959 came into force. Amendments made to the legislation, and in particular to the novel Prisons Act 8 of 1959, suggest that the manner in which South African and South West African Prisons were operated was instrumental in the implementation and enforcement of the apartheid policy (see Box 8.1). Training of prison staff, for instance, was conducted in three different centres in South Africa on the basis of race. While whites were trained to become managers, coloureds were trained to play an intermediary role of support staff in offices and blacks were trained to do custodial work. Prisons were also categorized along racial lines.

Over and above the implications of racial discrimination, the organization and operation of the prisons of the apartheid era are best understood in the context of the retributive theory of punishment.

Both the pre-independence and the current Namibian criminal justice system, conform most closely to a combination of the *justice model* and the *crime control* model (see Glossary and Figure 8.1). (For the Namibian juvenile justice system, see: Schulz, 2002a.) Their general features include "due process," crime control and retribution, and are firmly based on the notion of retributive justice. They reflect a moralizing though individualistic world-view, where for the purposes of coercion and conformity the deviant is perceived as an independent author of his/her action(s). If a rule has been contravened, the balance of the scale of justice has been disturbed and can be restored only if the offender is punished. Hence, "the extent of the punishment must ... be proportionate to the extent of the harm done or the violation of the law" (Snyman, 1995). The foundation of the criminal law was (and still is) simple. It is based on a number of unsophisticated assumptions as to the cause-and-effect relationship between punishment or the absence of punishment and the commission of crimes; in particular, the former regime largely denied the role of socio-economic and other factors in the context of criminality. Courts were expected to and did impose prison sentences involving hard labour and offenders were sent to endure this labour, preferably in prisons located in isolated places; e.g., the "Robben Island" concept of isolation, and the "lime and quarry" type of work was a manifestation of this approach.[3]

Box 8.1: Race and Political Power in Pre-Independence Namibia

During the era of political apartheid, people were defined along "racial" lines. The system distinguished between three categories: *black, colored,* and *white.* The highest status was given to whites, who also held (exclusively) all political power (Nachtweih, 1976). The system was obviously devoid of any logic other than the logic of maintaining a power base for the European colonizers and their descendents. Basically, and this is only a simplification of a more sophisticated typology, a *white* person was defined as a person whose progenitors were direct descendents of colonizers with no ancestral link to any descendent of one of the native tribes of the occupied territory. The reverse definition applied to people presumed to be *black.* Eventually, people were defined as *coloured* provided their ancestral lines combined both *black* and *white* ancestors. Non-white people, in a sense, belonged to a serving caste, living and working for the benefit of whites. What appears today as a form of slavery was at the time of apartheid skillfully couched in ideological terms, which served as a justification of the political status quo. Thus it should not come as a surprise if members of the group formerly understood as *white* nowadays feel unfairly maligned when the former dispensation is compared with slavery.

For their part, prison personnel were expected to ensure that the sentences of hard labour imposed by the courts were put into effect, even through the use of force. Thus, it should not come as a surprise that prisons also involved a statutory requirement that in order to be employed in prisons one had to be physically tough and of imposing stature. Height and chest requirements for recruitment into prisons in South Africa and South West Africa were (for men) approximately 167 centimeters, and a normal, unexpanded chest of 91 centimeters (Bukurura and Nyoka, 2000). Whereas the correctional philosophy based on punishment and deterrence can still be found elsewhere (e.g., in some

Western countries), in South Africa and South West Africa this was part and parcel of the machinery of the colonial administration, that did very little, if anything at all, to protect, preserve and safeguard the rights of the colonized majority.

The evolution of Namibia's correctional system has been marked by the advent of the Independence Constitution and a series of judicial interventions. One of the milestones of change has certainly been the abolition of capital punishment. Article 6 of the Namibian Constitution reads: "No law may prescribe death as a competent sentence." Another change took place in 1995, when President Sam Nujoma created a full-fledged Ministry of Prisons and Correctional Services. As a result of the independence Constitution, sentences of prisoners on death row were commuted instead to long prison sentences. With independence, after decades of foreign oppression when Namibians were deprived of their basic fundamental rights and freedoms, political ideas changed from suppression and brutality towards the citizenry to democratisation. So did the penal policy, which also had to be transformed from retribution to the rehabilitation of inmates. In fact, a paradigm-shift was prescribed. The new ministry took forward the process of repealing and replacing the Prisons Act 1959 in order to harmonize prison operations with constitutional requirements. However, many of the structures and personnel responsible for the implementation of the paradigm-shift remained the same, and the dominant thinking of the apartheid regime was internalised by those who were associated with it, including prison officers.

Constitutional Transformation

The constitution as a whole, and its "Bill of Rights" (Chapter 3, Namibian Constitution) in particular, laid down new requirements of governance, necessitated entirely new working practices for prison personnel and brought about new demands from inmates. In accordance with Article 5 of the Namibian Constitution (NC), the rights of prisoners as well as the rights of members of the Prison Service now had to be respected and protected.

The Namibian Constitution does not provide for a constitutional court, like the South African Constitutional Court (SACC). However, by virtue of Article 79 (2) and 80 (2) of the NC, the Supreme Court and the High Court are competent courts to declare any legislation invalid to the extent that it is inconsistent with the Constitution. The advent of the new concept of constitutional supremacy also meant a departure from the narrow procedural review function of the courts. Mahomed AJA[4] — as he then was — seized the first opportunity to state this in the case S v. Acheson (1991 2 SA 805 NmHC 813 A - D):

> The spirit and tenor of the constitution…constitute part of the constitutional culture, which should influence my discretion. No judicial officer should ignore that culture, where it is relevant, in the interpretation and application of the law or in the exercise of a discretion.

Because it had never been part of the old regime to protect, preserve and safeguard the rights of inmates, not many officials within the service knew how this was supposed to be done or why (see Bukurura and Nyoka, 2002). In accordance with the judicial guarantees provided in Article 18 of the NC, inmates who perceived that their fundamental rights and freedoms were infringed could send their grievances to court, and there are several cases in which prison authorities were cited as respondents.

Prison Authorities Taken to Court

Among the first constitutional litigations following Namibia's independence, were those involving the prison administration. Only the two most important cases will be dealt with here.

- Ex parte Attorney General: In re Corporal Punishment by Organs of the State (1991 NR 178 SC)

In the exercise of powers granted to him by the Constitution, the Attorney General asked the Supreme Court to determine whether the imposition and infliction of corporal punishment by the authority of a body of the state was a violation of Article 8 of the Constitution. Among the many pieces of legislation in question were the Prisons Act 8 of 1959 and regulation 100 of the Prison Regulations. Both the Prisons Act and related regulations were part of the apartheid legislation, which remained in existence and continued to be applied after independence under the authority of Article 140 (1) of the NC (supra). Although the Constitution does not contain an explicit prohibition of corporal punishment, on the whole the Supreme Court declared that the imposition of corporal punishment was in violation of Article 8 (2) (b) and there-fore unconstitutional. The decision was in line with the trend at the in-ternational level, but it was also a direct application of the principles of constitutional interpretation as set out in S v Acheson (supra).

- In re Thomas Namunjepo and Commanding Officer, Windhoek Prison (2000 (6) BCLR 671 (NmS)

Thomas Namunjepo was an inmate in Windhoek Central Prison. With four other inmates he applied to the High Court requesting several orders including the following:

> That a declaration be made, that the prison conduct or practice of placing prisoners in irons, mechanical restraints or chains is un-constitutional.

These applications arose out of events that will not be discussed here, except to state that they were brought at a time when the Prisons Act 8 of 1959 was still in force. Against the High Court judgement, which could not find an infringement of constitutional rights, the appli-cants appealed to the Supreme Court. The Supreme Court, which is the highest judicial tribunal in the country, declared that "the placing of a prisoner in leg-irons or chains is an impermissible invasion of article 8 (1) and contrary to article 8 (2) of the Constitution as it at least consti-tutes degrading treatment." In the case of Thomas Namunjepo (see Box 8.2), the Supreme Court declared the use of leg-irons as an invasion of prisoners' rights, but did not go further to examine whether the new Section 90 of the Prisons Act 17 of 1998 is in compliance with the Con-stitution.[5] Section 90 of the Prisons Act 17 of 1998 provides that:

> Where the officer in charge considers it necessary (a) to secure or restrain a prisoner who has — (i) displayed or threatened vio-lence; (ii) been recaptured after escape from custody; or (iii) been recommended on medical grounds for confinement in a separate cell for such period, but not exceeding 30 days, as he or she may deem necessary; or (b) for the safe custody of a prisoner that such a prisoner be confined by means of a mechanical restraint, he or she may cause that prisoner to be so restrained in the prescribed manner, and for such period as he or she may deem necessary in the circumstances.

Box 8.2: Removing the Irons: In re Thomas Namundjepo and Commanding Officer, Windhoek Prison

The Namibian High Court held that in light of the Constitution, decisions of the High Court and the Supreme Court (including Ex Parte Attorney General referred to in the full text), and those of other countries including England, India, South Africa and the European Court as well as the Standard Minimum Rules for the Treatment of Prisoners adopted by the United Nations Congress in 1955, "contemporary society...will not regard the use by prison officials of handcuffs, irons or chains within the confines of the provisions of the **Prison Act**, as treatment which is shocking or staringly inappropriate." The Namibian Supreme Court, on appeal, examined the same material, compared other practices that had been found to violate article 8 of the Constitution and arrived at its conclusion that "the placing of a prisoner in leg iron or chains is an impermissible invasion of article 8 (1) and contrary to article 8 (2) (b) of the Constitution..." Apart from its normative effects, the Namunjepo judgment had at least one further important implication for the day-by-day administration of prisons. It left many prison officers scared, confused and even unaware of how to perform part of their duties. It caused anxiety and confusion among prison officers.

This phenomenon is best understood in the context of two fundamentally conflicting objectives of the prison service, namely keeping inmates in safe custody, and protecting and safeguarding the dignity of all in volatile prison circumstances. In view of the Supreme Court decision referred to above, the question most prison officers ask is, what do they have to do in order to prevent inmates from escaping or attempting to escape, to protect other inmates and staff from violent inmates and/or restrain inmates who have shown a propensity to use violence against other inmates or staff?

There are two aspects to be considered. First, the message derived from the Supreme Court judgment is that *mechanical restraints* shall not form part of the ordinary measures utilized for the preservation of safety and security in prisons. Second, if it appears that infrastructure and staffing of the prison system necessitates the frequent use of mechanical restraints of inmates, it is a constitutional liability of government to ameliorate the situation expeditiously. As the case may be, this could have a considerable impact on budget allocations.

The Supreme Court decision should be seen as reinforcing an emerging human rights culture in Namibia, and thus also in the light of the democratisation process which is permeating the Namibian society since its independence. However, in the absence of any guidelines on how prison officers may go about dealing with the volatile situations envisaged by Section 90, it left the prison administration confused, and most prison officers are unsure and at times even unaware of what is expected from them under the circumstances (see Box 8.2).

CORRECTIONS IN NAMIBIA TODAY

In 1997, at the time when the Prisons Act 1959 was still in force, the Ministry of Prisons and Correctional Services issued a mission statement in which an attempt to strike a balance between necessarily antagonistic objectives of the NPS was made. According to this statement it is the mission of the Ministry:

> ...to keep in safe custody people committed to prison by a court of law and to rehabilitate them. In doing so, the Ministry will operate within national and international law and codes of conduct. Inmates will be cared for in a compassionate and humane manner respecting the dignity of individuals, with emphasis on rehabilitation.

The statement was meant to sensitize prison staff to the requirements brought about by the Constitution and the new working practices that emanated from it without compromising peace and security in prisons. However, the Prisons Act 1959 had remained in place without any amendment until the new Prisons Act 17 of 1998 was finally enacted in June. Prison staff who were used to both the old law and dispensation, by and large continued to think and act as they did before, although they were aware that Namibia had attained independence. The symbolic meaning of conventional structures of the old paradigm informed too strongly the perception of single actors in the system and the internalized dominant thinking of the past did not change significantly even after the political and legislative changes were introduced (see, for example, Box 8.2).

Corrections as a Legal and a Criminal Justice Subsystem

As is the case with most countries represented in this anthology, the major elements of the Namibian criminal justice system consist of law enforcement, prosecution, courts and corrections. As a subsystem of the criminal justice system, corrections fulfills the basic mandate of processing those persons "who have been screened through one or more of the system's other components" (Ekstedt and Griffiths, 1984:9). As in most other countries, in Namibia the operations of the criminal justice system are a by-product of the social values in society, the various statuses found in corrections (e.g. inmates, guards, etc.), and the norms specific to or of concern within corrections (see Figure 8.1). In comparison with the other components of the criminal justice system, corrections receives limited attention. Eventually, the law gives corrections its specific meaning, it defines the programs and agencies that have legal authority over the custody or supervision of convicted offenders. In Namibia, the current mandate of correctional services is informed mainly by the Namibian Constitution, the Prisons Act 17 of 1998, and relevant case law. Members of the prison establishment do not have control over decisions and are mere recipients and implementers of orders made by others. From a more general perspective, Namibian corrections tends to be subject to the effects of social, economic, and political events and pressures (see the Introduction to this text). It is therefore prudent to briefly (infra) examine elements of prosecution and the courts in Namibia.

The majority of (legal) professionals still adhere to an orthodox deterrent approach to criminality: i.e., the cause of crime is seen to be rooted in the individual not in the social structure or social inequality. Therefore the incessant call for "law and order," the demand for police, more punishment, and more prisons continues. Prevailing policies and practices of retribution and deterrence, as well as prominent voices who suggest that criminal justice institutions should be given more powers to combat crime at the expense of and to the exclusion of existing constitutional safeguards (Bukurura, 2002), which seems to bolster prosecutors' and magistrates' attitudes that each and every offender should be put behind bars.

Figure 8.1: Namibian Criminal Justice Model

Justice + Crime Control Model

General Features:
- Due process
- Discretion
- Educational concerns
- Determinate (minimum) sentences

Key Personnel:
- Lawyers/criminal justice actors

Key Agency:
- Law

Tasks:
- Incarceration/punishment

Understanding of client behavior:
- Individual responsibility/accountability

Purpose of intervention:
- Sanction behavior/protection of society and retribution/deterrence

Objectives:
- Respect individual rights/order maintenance

Organizational Structure of the NPS

Namibia is a unitary state, and the responsibility for the administration of custodial sentences lies with central government. Chapter 15 of the Constitution provides for the establishment of the Prison Service. In accordance with article 122 of the Constitution, the Commissioner of Prisons is appointed by the President upon a recommendation made by the Security Commission. Whereas the head of the executive administration of prisons is appointed under the direct authority of the Constitution (which also delineates in broad terms the responsibilities of the

Commissioner), further structure and staffing of the Prison Service is regulated by the legislature. The current organizational structure of NPS is not directly prescribed by the Prisons Act 17 of 1998. Although the Prisons Act provides for the appointment of senior and junior correctional personnel, the precise structure of NPS is left to the discretion of the Commissioner of Prisons.

The Namibian Prison Service Structure allows for the functioning of two levels of Management, the Headquarters and Prison levels (see Figure 8.2). The NPS is a comparatively small service, even by Namibian standards. Prison Headquarters, branching into the three tiers illustrated by Figure 8.2, is responsible for *inter alia*: initiating the management and operational policies for consideration by the Minister; overseeing policy implementation, review and evaluation; and initiating the clear strategic direction of the Namibian Prison Service's operations. The most important functions regarding the transition of the service and the implementation of modern approaches to corrections are vested in the Directorate "Functional Services." In so doing, the directorate assists the Minister in setting priorities in a meaningful and informed way; in the development of standard operation procedures, manuals and guidelines for the organization and monitoring of the organizational performance. In a nutshell, the Head Office is responsible for overall planning, policy development and administration. The Prison level has the responsibility of executing national policies, procedures and programs as set and directed by National Headquarters.

Figure 8.2: The Organizational Structure of the NPS: Executive Level

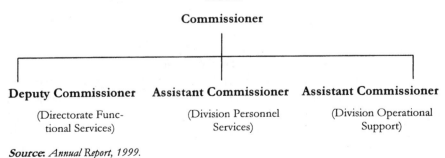

Commissioner

Deputy Commissioner
(Directorate Functional Services)

Assistant Commissioner
(Division Personnel Services)

Assistant Commissioner
(Division Operational Support)

Source: *Annual Report, 1999.*

Policy Document and Mission Statement of the Namibian Prison Service

The current mission statement, adopted in 2000, is an integral part of the Namibian Prisons Policy Document. It reads:

> The Namibian Prison service as an integrated part of the justice system contributes to the protection of society by providing reasonable, safe, secure and humane custody of offenders in accordance with universally acceptable standards, while assisting them in their rehabilitation, reformation and social reintegration as acceptable law abiding citizens.

The Policy Document furthermore, is composed of *Core Values and Guiding Principles, Priorities for the Future*, and *Joint Objectives*.

Whereas the mission statement articulates the broad vision of the Namibian Prisons Service, the Core Values outline the basic and enduring ideals embodied in the Service. Priorities for the future are the key objectives established against the most current shortcomings and deficits in the Service. The Joint Objectives, finally, are the specific goals identified by the Prison Service as essential to achieving the articulated mission.

The (Core) Values and Guiding Principles of the NPS:

Value 1   Correction is that component of the criminal justice system, which has the greatest impact on the freedoms, liberties and rights of individuals.

Value 2   Fundamental to an effective corrections and justice system is a firm commitment to the belief that offenders are responsible for their own behaviour and have the potential to live as law-abiding citizens.

Value 3   The majority of offenders can be dealt with effectively in the community by means of **non-custodial correctional programs;** imprisonment should be used with restraint.

Value 4	In the interest of the public protection, decisions about offenders must be based on informed risk assessment and risk management.
Value 5	Effective corrections are dependent on working in close cooperation with criminal justice partners and the community in order to contribute to a more just, humane and safe society.
Value 6	Carefully recruited, properly trained and well-informed Service members are essential to an effective correctional system.
Value 7	The public has a right to know the activities taking place in corrections and should be given the opportunity to participate in the criminal justice system.
Value 8	The effectiveness of corrections depends on the degree to which correctional systems are capable of responding to change and shaping the future.

Although it is beyond the remit of this contribution to attend in detail to "Priorities for the Future" and "Joint Objectives," we will take a brief look at the priorities and future directions of the NPS.

The NPS has identified two priorities. The first is to recruit and train an adequate number of members, second, to strengthen its commitment to safely reintegrating a larger number of offenders as law-abiding citizens. Without adequate staffing in terms of numbers but also expertise, it will be difficult to realize the mission statement. This has been understood by the NPS, which holds that: "(O)nce recruited, it is the intention of the Service to invest heavily in core front-line correctional studies in specialized areas as well as devotion to subjects concentrating on the rule of law, the Mission and reintegration philosophy, management and human relations. Members must be trained to assist in the rehabilitation of offenders...." As will be shown below (see section on "Future Directions"), these priorities form the basis of current projects directed toward the future of the NPS.

Prison Facilities

By virtue of section 13 of the Prisons Act 1998, the Minister may establish prisons throughout Namibia "for the reception, detention, confinement, rehabilitation, training or discipline of persons liable to imprisonment or detention in custody." Although Namibia is geographically extensive, it has a comparatively small population, which is spread throughout the country. In the absence of a well functioning system of public transport, many family members are prevented from visiting their incarcerated kin, or may only visit them irregularly, with potentially detrimental effects on the prospects of further social re-integration.

As of 2003, there are 13 prisons of which four are classified as Maximum Security establishments, two Open Prison Farms, six District Prisons and one Juvenile Centre (Schulz, 2002). This classification is based on the length of the sentences prisoners are serving. These 13 prisons vary in age, design, and official holding capacities, and most of them were designed and used as instruments of punishment (e.g., the strength of the walls, the bars on the windows, the doors of the accommodation units, the specifications of perimeter walls and fences, and the watchtowers still bear witness thereof). This type of architectural set-up was based on the oldest and most popular belief that crime can be deterred if the punishment is sufficiently severe, with harsh prison conditions. The prisons are located in nine of Namibia's 13 regions. The physical infrastructure of Namibian prisons dates partly back to the beginning of the 20th century (e.g., Swakomund Prison was built in 1909). However, the physical infrastructure of Oluno Prison was built starting in 1992, and the prison went into operation on 4 April 1996. The construction of Prison Farm Scott, which has yet to be completed, started in February 1998. Since 1998, it has operated as a semi-open low-security facility where inmates also perform agricultural work for food production. The Divundu Open Prison Farm is another agricultural operation where huge irrigation schemes are utilized to produce large amounts of food, intended to make the Prison Service more self-sustaining. Windhoek Central Prison, although not the largest prison (see Table 8.1 for more details), has the highest occupancy rate in the country. For example, in early 2002 the prison housed approximately 1,400 inmates, roughly 500 inmates more than Hardap Prison, Namibia's largest prison.

In fact, Namibian prisons have been constantly overcrowded since independence was gained.

Whereas overcrowding is a general problem, the problem is particularly pressing at Windhoek Central Prison. And while some steps have been taken to address the problem, the percentage of overcrowding is still about 55% over capacity. Problems associated with the overcrowding problem include inadequate living space, poor ventilation, possibilities for the outbreak of epidemics and so forth. Although it has been said that overcrowding in prisons renders treatment programs for inmates and any subsequent chance of rehabilitation meaningless (Bukurura and Nyoka, 2002), one must keep in mind that "overcrowding" is a definitional concept, which applies to a set (numeric) standard. However, this is not to deny that Namibian prisons are overcrowded. In fact, over all, the average number of inmates per cell is high, with a maximum number of inmates per cell averaging between 12 (Oluno) and 30 (Windhoek and Farm Scott). Depending on the prison, daytime activities are sometimes carried on outside, providing inmates with little privacy and increasing their risk of being victimized through the imposing nature of prison sub-cultures. As result of this relatively unstructured setting, inmates' basic rights and freedoms as promoted under various UN agreements are seriously compromised.

As important as privacy is for the well being of a person, single cells are currently not considered a priority for developing countries like Namibia. This is not only because it is beyond the scope of any reasonable budget consideration, but also because cultural ramifications are widely understood in a communal rather than individual context.

PROFILE OF THE CORRECTIONAL POPULATION

Statistical data on the aggregate prison population do not extend back before the date of independence, and reliable figures are available only as far back as 1992 (Table 8.2).[6] What can be inferred from the data shown in Table 8.2 is a steady increase of the adult correctional population since 1992, which levels off in the year 2001. The gradient of this increase is an issue of concern. Although crime rates depend on a variety of factors, which cannot necessarily be equated with an actual increase in the incidence of crime, police crime statistics and conviction rates can be taken as a rough indicator of its occurrence. Thus, it appears that

Table 8.1: Namibian Prison Capacities and Total Number of Inmates Admitted[7]

Prison	Capacity	Annual Admission/Number of Inmates					
		1996	1997	1998	1999	2000	2001
Windhoek	912	2717	2056	1626	1644	1594	1406
Hardap	941	257	324	228	193	216	214
Oluno	557	964	1229	1272	1198	1277	1105
Walvis Bay	266	867	548	403	619	488	467
Omaruru	53	1041	859	713	846	692	649
Grootfontein	64	1295	808	599	414	64	139
Swakopmund	84	307	299	234	219	195	148
Keetmanshoop	80	876	1067	874	729	854	1185
Luderitz	290	206	172	73	130	138	156
Gobabis	220	331	584	523	231	565	432
Divundu	275	-	-	-	-	-	-
Elizabeth Nepemba (Juvenile Ctr.)	Construction not completed	-	-	-	-	-	-
Farm Scott	Construction not completed	-	-	-	-	-	-
Total admitted		8879	7946	6545	6223	6083	5955
Number of prisoners in custody on 31 December each year		3442	4074	4381	4629	4883	4727

Table 8.2: Namibian Prison Populations: 1992-2001
(based on persons in custody on 31 December)

Year	1992	1993	1994	1995	1996	1997	1998	1999	2000	2001
Total	2711	3181	2965	3555	3442	4074	4381	4629	4883	4727
Change in % 2711 = 100%		117	109	131	126	150	161	171	180	178
Holding capacity (total)	-	-	-	3514	3822	3822	3822	3822	3822	3822
Male	2665	3133	2906	3488	3372	3986	4296	4509	4779	4640
Female	46	48	59	67	70	88	85	120	104	87

Namibia indeed experienced an increase in crime. Between the years of 2000 and 2002 the number of cases reported to the Namibian Police increased from 44,240 to 46,262 (including traffic offences), or by 4.3%. Yet the increase in the prison population cannot be solely attributed to the development in the incidence of crime. Beyond the incidence of increasing crime rates, Namibia is more concerned with the anomic effects suffered by its society due to the transition from an authoritarian regime to a democratic government. As noted above, Namibian citizens have struggled with a sudden granting of seemingly unlimited freedom, an ever-increasing complexity of life and with social communities/units becoming more and more unstable at the same time.

The imprisonment rate in Namibia is approximately 264 per 100,000 population. This is considerably lower than that of the United States (700+), but is still considerably higher than the average number found in most European countries (approximately 100 per 100,000) (see Figure 1 in the editor's Introduction chapter).

Composition of the Adult Correctional Population

Most of Namibian prisoners are males. The proportion of female inmates in relation to male inmates is small, and in absolute numbers insignificant. Both genders are incarcerated in the same prison facilities, although in different units. For example, female inmates represented only 2.1% (N=104) of the total prison population in 2000, and only 1.8% (N=87) in 2001.

The female-male inmate ratio has remained relatively stable since independence even though there has been a very slight increase in the number of females being incarcerated. As shown in Figure 8.3, the inmate population for Namibia is rather young. The fact that the majority of inmates are between the ages of 18-35 years of age not only mirrors offending characteristics (see Gottfredson and Hirschi, 1990, 124ff.), but also reflects the fact that Namibia is a young nation. According to the Namibia Intercensal Demographic Survey (National Planning Commission, 2001), in 1996 approximately 74.5% of the female population, and 75.8% of the male population were 34 years of age or younger.

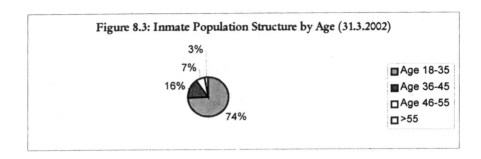

Figure 8.3: Inmate Population Structure by Age (31.3.2002)

Prison Life and Daily Experiences

In accordance with the NPS, for eight hours a day prisoners are supposed to engage in some kind of work. However, due to a lack of facilities that can offer employment to prisoners there are a large number of prisoners who are not working. However, despite the number of prisoners in enforced idleness, the situation has very much improved in comparison with the inherited situation at the dawn of independence. The only prison offering work skills at that time was Windhoek Central Prison, where there was a workshop that provided manual labor for approximately 100 of the 900-odd prisoners. In addition to this well-established workshop, other small workshops have now opened at Divundu and Oluno Prisons. Prisoners involved in these activities, which involve such activities as woodworking, mechanics, etc., are remunerated in a form of gratuity.

There are also other initiatives offered as intervention programs to inmates. In the absence of risk assessment tools, which are currently being developed, treatment programs have been based on productive manual work. This kind of training is intended to instill a work ethic and to impart social skills intended to help the inmates better deal with the mediating causes of their offending behaviour. In addition, there are also unstructured programs for literacy education, both on secondary and tertiary levels. Other programs include individual counselling sessions, social group work, alcohol/drug programs, life skills, pre-release programs, anger control, and so forth. In spite of the range of programs available, only approximately 35% of the inmates are actively involved in any form of programming. Nevertheless, the NPS is attempting to expand its services to include more inmates.

It is anticipated that the recent introduction of Community Service should help reduce the prison population, sentencing in turn will enable the Prisons Service to more effectively manage these programs, and possibly to involve a larger percentage of inmates in these interventions. Currently, there is a National Steering Committee on Community Service headed by the High Court Judge Justice S. Mainga. The service oversees the introduction of Community Service throughout the country. The Steering Committee is made up of members from the criminal justice system, community leaders, NGOs and religious leaders.

Drugs, Violence and Subcultures

Unlike in many other correctional institutions around the world, the smuggling and consumption of illicit, psychedelic drugs has not become a very serious problem in Namibian prison institutions. However, inmates have been more involved in consuming fermented fruit drinks, or fermented *mahangu* drinks, known as *tombo*.[8] In 1997 and 1998, the drug problem coupled with fermented drinks resulted in several riots, jailbreaks and a near collapse of discipline and order in several prisons, especially at Windhoek. This resulted in a joint operation of the Police and Prison Services to quell this situation and the subsequent intensification of security measures, which led to the introduction of an Integrated Security System that includes monitoring by closed circuit television (CCTV).

Gangs are prevalent in Namibian prisons, in particular in Windhoek Central Prison. One of these is known as "Gang 26," which is apparently affiliated with a gang of the same name active in the South African prison system. This gang is known for its involvement in riots, upheavals and other untoward incidences. Another gang, known as "Gang 28," is a facilitator for (homosexual) sex. While perhaps not as pervasive as in other countries, these issues present real challenges for the NPS. Since inmates depend on the prison administration for their protection against human rights violations by fellow inmates, this poses a threat to the credibility of the NPS, which under the circumstances could become vicariously liable for infringements on and the violation of human rights by fellow inmates. Under the Namibian Constitution, according to Article 5, Fundamental Rights and Freedoms also apply horizontally, i.e. directly between citizens.[9] Inmates, who are usually placed under the custody of the NPS against their will, have a claim against the NPS for protection against unlawful behaviour by third parties. The NPS forms part of the executive branch of government, and has the duty to uphold the entitlements enshrined in Chapter 3 of the Namibian Constitution. In a situation of chronic understaffing, it does not require much foresight to understand that the NPS is not able to live up to its obligations.

HIV/AIDS and TB

The Namibian Prison Service Health Care Section is one of the busiest and most important components of adult corrections. Yet, this area too is seriously understaffed. There is only one medical officer catering to the entire prison population, which in 2002 was just over 5,000 inmates. This anomaly has been noted by different authorities (Jackson, 2002) who have visited the Namibian Prison Service (these include the Special Rapporteur of the African Commission on Human and People's Rights on Prisons Conditions of Detention in Africa Dr. Vera Chirwa, the International Committee of the Red Cross, and Namibia's Parliamentary Standing Committee on Security). The NPS has already made recommendations to the government to create more medical personnel posts. While morally commendable, the position is not overly attractive (financially and/or socially), which tends to limit the number of suitable applicants.

In prisons, hypertension is the most common health problem, followed by problems with the respiratory organs (pneumonia, bronchitis), which are usually more common during the winter months. Others include gastro-intestinal, muscle and skin diseases. Special attention is given to inmates who are HIV-positive or who have full blown AIDS. HIV/AIDS, over the years, has become the main cause of prisoner mortality. Medical testing of prisoners is not mandatory, but those who are sick can request, and will receive, proper medical attention. Medical staff are provided educational material as part of their employment orientation to assist incoming inmates by being able to inform them as to how AIDS is transmitted and what precautions can be taken to minimize the risk of transmission. Those patients who are bed-ridden and in the terminal stages may be released on medical grounds to finish their last days with their families on a homecare basis. For the last three years, the number of HIV/AIDS patients has been escalating, which has resulted in an increase in prison death rates as Table 8.3 shows.

Table 8.3: HIV/AIDS Prevalence in Namibian Prisons: 1999-2001

Number of HIV/AIDS Patients	1st January	31st December	Death	Released
1999	195	311	11	17
2000	311	383	12	12
2001	383	523	31	6

ISSUES CONFRONTING CORRECTIONS TODAY

As reflected in its mission statement, the NPS strives to attain a quality of correctional service that is reflective of the declarative clauses outlined not only in the Constitution but also by international standards. In addition, Namibia is an active member of the Conference of East, Southern and Central African Heads of Correctional Services (CESCA), and hosted the biennial CESCA-conference in Windhoek in 2001. Yet, as reflected throughout this chapter, the NPS has its share of challenges. But, these challenges are not unique to corrections alone. There are two main challenges that confound the Namibian criminal justice system. They include a limited financial infrastructure and a system that is more commonly characterized as being reactive than proactive in its approach to handling crime and criminality in the country.

Financial Constraints

The budget of the Ministry of Prison and Correctional Services has historically been small compared with the annual budgets of other ministries. The NPS budget increased from N$122 million in 2002/3 to

N$142.5 million in 2003/4 — an increase from 1.14% to 1.16% of the total annual national budget (approximately N$12.25 billion). The increase for the current year 2003/4 is about 16%, against an inflation rate of approximately 12% in 2002/3 (NEPRU, 2003). Although frugal in comparison with South Africa in terms of expenditure per prisoner for basic needs (South Africa R40.05, Namibia N$23.81),[10] the expenditure on prisoners' basic needs accounts for 35% of the total annual NPS budget.

Based on the 2002 figures, the aggregate expenditure on basic needs for prisoners amounts to N$43 million. Taking into consideration the cost for personnel, it is evident that limited funds are available for capital projects, training and rehabilitation. Unless this changes, correctional programs and resources will likely continue to be compromised.

Re-active versus Proactive Criminal Policy

The Namibian criminal justice system as a whole, not unlike the systems in many other countries, may be distinguished by its reactive approach towards crime and criminality. However, Namibian professionals working in the system may even have a reinforcing effect because the usually unquestioned, and at times mindless and stereotyped adherence to the set standards of the common law emphasizes the societal status quo. It is doubtful whether any other society matches the Namibian inertia in this respect. In a critical light it appears that the principle of precedent (the doctrine of *stare decisis*), holds sway over the deciding of cases. Interestingly, and ironically so, this approach is part of the legacy left behind by the so-called former "colonial masters." It is, however, an irony that common law systems — in the U.K. and even in South Africa — have developed their law into a tool for social engineering without having lost the challenge to preserve normative stability. By contrast, Namibia seems at times to be enamoured in this arcanum of the law. An example of this attitude can be found in the current debate over whether to increase the minimum age of criminal liability from 7 to 10 years. The proposal to adjust the current age to an age limit more in line with the perception of the international community encountered stern criticism from the office of the Prosecutor General, where senior prosecutors argue that the proposed change would probably allow a number of criminals to go free in the future (Schulz and Hamutenya, 2003).

It would, however, be unfair to stigmatize the NPS as voluntarily reactive. Whereas it is true that the above mentioned installation of an integrated Security System with CCTV-surveillance only followed a series of incidents posing a threat to discipline and order, the delay was a result of pressing financial constraints. As will be shown below, the NPS has also taken proactive steps through its active involvement in the promotion of community service as a non-custodial alternative to imprisonment. Apart from the challenges facing Namibian corrections in its role as part of the criminal justice system, the NPS too has its own unique challenges. The following represent some of the more pressing issues for the NPS.

Overcrowding

Overcrowding of Namibian Prisons cannot be attributed to an increase of criminality alone but to a series of interrelated factors. They include, among others: better access to justice, a greater severity on the part of judges with respect to longer sentences, and a proliferation of short sentences for petty crimes. There have been marked decreases in prisoner admissions each year and yet the prison population continues to increase. The longer sentences imposed upon prisoners seem to compound the overcrowding problem. For example, between 1996 and 2001 the number of total committals for those years was as follows:[11]

Year	1996	1997	1998	1999	2000	2001
Admissions	7150	7460	6261	5712	5432	5117

In spite of the declining numbers of admissions, it can be seen in Table 8.2 that the inmate population continues to increase. Yet, in comparison with other African countries, like Tanzania, where the percentage of overcrowding has been reported at 95%, Namibia's 28% overcrowding rate appears comparatively low. However, this is only part of the picture. Whereas in Namibia police cells are known to hold many prisoners who are awaiting trial (Bukururua and Nyoka, 2002), in most other countries these individuals would find themselves in prison. When at some time in the future suspects will be kept in prisons instead of police cells, the problem of overcrowding will enter another dimension altogether. The problem of overcrowding has been a subject of discussion for some time. The NPS has implemented a number of strategies to address this inmate congestion by opening new institutions such as Oluno and Divundu. This is in addition to upgrading and renovating prisons such as Luderitz, Gobabis, and Hardap. Among the many causes of overcrowding that were highlighted by the Law Reform Commission of Tanzania (Bukurura, 2003), there is one reason which appears to be applicable to Namibia: there is an overreliance on custodial sentences by officials in the criminal justice system, and the use of non-custodial sentences is apparently rare and/or infrequent. The law is not short of provisions for alternative, non-custodial sentences. The relevant part of Section 297 of the **Criminal Procedure Act** 51 of 1977 reads:

(1) Where a court convicts a person of any offence, other than an offence in respect of which any law prescribes a minimum punishment, the court may in its discretion postpone for a period not exceeding five years the passing of a sentence and release the person concerned —

    (i) on one or more conditions, whether as to —

        (aa) compensation;

        (bb) the rendering to the person aggrieved of some specific benefit or service in lieu of compensation for damage or pecuniary loss;

        (cc) the rendering of some service for the benefit of the community;

        (dd) submission to instruction or treatment;

        (ee) submission to the supervision or control (including control over the earnings or other income of the person concerned) of a probation officer as defined in the Children's Act 33 of 1960;

        (ff) the compulsory attendance or residence at some specified center for a specified purpose;

        (gg) good conduct; and,

        (hh) any other matter.

There is however, a marked discrepancy between the legislative provisions for alternative sentences and actual use of these measures during sentencing in Namibia. Notwithstanding these legal provisions on the statute books, these sanctions are rarely utilized.

In this situation, the focus of the NPS has nevertheless been shifted to the application of non-custodial options in the form of community service. The analysis of constraints and limitations likely to be encountered in the introduction of such services in Namibia resulted in the recognition of a number of constraints, which should be overcome before the successful implementation of community service as seen in other countries can be emulated. The NPS realizes that first and foremost some established views and perceptions about crime and the severity of punishment would have to be "enlightened" in the public eye, prior to community service being accepted as a legitimate correctional measure. For example, victims of crime, communities and some members of law enforcement agencies feel that community service "rewards" crime and criminals, and they therefore think that community service is a soft approach to crime. Whereas these considerations concern the preparedness of society for community service, the NPS came to the conclusion that even under the most favorable conditions of societal receptiveness, technical aspects warrant heightened attention, too.

The NPS acknowledged that the adequacy of resources is an important factor, in that human and financial resources must be carefully planned and made available prior to the implementation of community service as a correctional technique. This was thought to be impossible without an efficient legislative framework setting out the priorities for planning, organization and coordination of community service activities, the supervision of community service orders, the selection and training of supervisors, and the monitoring of the criteria for selecting the beneficiaries of community service orders. A Draft Bill to this effect has been prepared, discussed and the public has been sensitized on the positive side of Community Service (Ramphaga, 2002, p.13). These Community Service Orders will be applicable to prisoners who are to serve short sentences resulting from petty offences; currently prisoners serving short-term sentences form about 44% of the prison population.

Quality Service – Qualified Personnel

In an effort to develop a correctional system capable of delivering treatment programs to inmates for their social reintegration and to address the need for capacity building, in 1999 a needs analysis for the Namibian Prison Service was conducted to identify the areas of training most in need of improvement. The results enabled the department to decide on local and external courses that were offered by Technikon Pretoria from Republic of South Africa and from the local training institutions within the country. The same year a special program of training members of the Prisons Service on Human Rights was conducted sponsored by the UN office based in South Africa. The training included instructors who were responsible for training other members of the service. The NPS has realized that operating in a political and social vacuum is impossible (see Box 8.3).

Box 8.3: International Cooperation

In pursuit of the best correctional practices, the Namibian Prison Service (NPS) has signed a Memorandum of Understanding with two Canadian Institutions — namely the Correctional Service of Canada (CSC) and with the Canadian Institute for Peace, Justice and Security (University of Regina). The two Canadian institutions are working in partnership with NPS in developing programs of cooperation. The CSC and the NPS are currently working on a pilot project involving an Offender Management System, an automated data and record keeping system, which is derived from specially designed technology for Correctional Service. A set of tailor-made technologies has been designed to determine criminogenic factors for risk assessment of inmates and assessment of needs for the intervention through treatment programs in the rehabilitation and reintegration processes. The Canadian Institute for Peace, Justice and Security is intending to conduct a project on Training in Social Justice in Corrections. This will include short and long courses in assessment of offenders, social work, psychology, treatment of offenders, and community supervision. Other International Organizations in which NPS is involved include the Paris based Penal Reform International (PRI), and the International Corrections and Prisons Association (ICPA).

Against the background of globalization and in the quest for "best practices," Namibia has sought to establish strong relationships with foreign correctional services, and in particular with Correctional Services Canada (CSC). One of the prime objectives of the NPS is to overcome traditional methods of prison management by shifting to the effective *case management* model (see Glossary), which the CSC has been helping to introduce by conducting training sessions and offering seminars to Namibians on an ongoing basis.

Future Directions

Since gaining independence in 1990, Namibia has made progress in its correctional development. The NPS has gradually moved away from its reliance on retribution and deterrence as the primary guiding principles of punishment. However, due to ongoing budgetary constraints some progressive projects have not yet been implemented. Nevertheless, it seems highly probable that since embarking on the introduction of community service as an alternative to imprisonment and with international support, the face of corrections in Namibia will become more representative of the international correctional experience. For example, through French cooperation the Namibian Government has embarked on a three-year pilot project to effectively implement community service throughout the country. In addition, the shift from traditional methods of administration and handling of correctional facilities towards more effective case management approach being supported by CSC is commendable. Therefore the future of corrections is Namibia would appear to hold considerable promise for its citizens.

CONCLUSION

Until attaining its independence in 1990, the history of corrections in Namibia was repressive and often brutal in nature. Since 1990 the NPS has managed to change the direction of Namibian corrections, partly due to its own initiative and partly with the guidance of Parliament and the courts. However, there is still a great deal of room for improvement in all areas of correctional practices and administration. For example, the issue of overcrowding remains a serious concern, as is making intervention and treatment programs more readily available to inmates. Initiatives such as community service are seen as promising alternatives for the NPS. The use of community service sentences is assumed to have a greater chance of reducing prison congestion as well as improving prison conditions. However, the success of community service in Namibia has still to be awaited, since (i.e., as of May 2003) the *Community Service Bill* has not yet passed in Parliament. Furthermore, its success will very much depend on the public opinion of the community where the offence has occurred.

In Namibia the time has come to recognize that prisons are not the appropriate place to send each and every convict. Only those who continuously pose a threat to society deserve to be jailed. The rest should be treated differently. This is not yet a reality in Namibia as some 44% of offenders are serving short sentences resulting from petty offences by offenders who do not pose a serious threat to society. Rather, they are often poor people who have committed offences at the lower end of the criminal scale. The current thinking is to move away from retribution and revenge towards a restorative model of criminal justice and the rehabilitation of inmates. This development of thinking parallels the movement within another sector of the Namibian criminal justice system, namely the Namibian juvenile justice system. The handling of young offenders is currently in a difficult transition from the retributive punitive approach of the adult criminal justice system, towards a system of restorative justice (Schulz, 2002; Schulz and Hamutenya, 2003). Restorative justice and the rehabilitation of offenders are compatible with and requested by the development and consolidation of the culture of democracy and human rights. The NPS's endeavor to meet international standards and its own Constitution is a reflection of its ambitious vision of joining Africa's leaders in the provision of correctional services.

Key Terms and Concepts

Apartheid

Case management

Community Service Bill

Constitutional Transformation

Criminal Procedure Act

Non-custodial measures

Mechanical Restraints

Overcrowding

Prison Act

Discussion/Study Questions

(1) In this chapter you see that the Namibian Prison Service changed from a suppressive and brutal authoritarian regime has towards an accountable system for the reformation of inmates. What are the most important explanations for this change?

(2) Overcrowding is a pressing problem in Namibian prisons. What do you think are the reasons for this phenomenon in Namibia?

(3) What do you think of the introduction of community service as an alternative to imprisonment in Namibia? Do you think that it will have an effect on the prison population?

(4) The Namibian Prison Service is experiencing a scarcity of resources. What do you think may be the impact of the case management system, which is in the offing through the cooperation with Correctional Service Canada, on the quality of treatment in Namibian prisons?

(5) Public opinion and stakeholders in politics are reluctant to provide more funds for corrections, fully aware of the fact that the quality and success of corrections depend largely on the availability of service and treatment offers. What may be the reasons for this reluctance? Do you think these reasons are justified?

(6) What role can/might the international community play in helping Namibia to attain its correctional objectives?

Helpful Web-links

Human Rights Watch website on overcrowding in South African Prisons:
http://www.hrw.org/prisons/africa.html.

The United Nations Minimum Standard Rules for the Treatment of Prisoners and Offenders:
http://www.hri.ca/uninfo/treaties/34.shtml.

The National Planning Commission website on the 2001 National Population and Housing Census:
http://www.npc.gov.na/census.

The Namibian Economic Policy Research Unit:
http://www.nepru.org.na.

Polytechnic of Namibia, Department of Legal Studies website:
http://www.polytechnic.edu.na/Legal/publications.html.

REFERENCES

Bukurura, S.H. (2003). "Prison Overcrowding in Namibia: The Problem and Suggested Solutions." *Acta Criminologica* 16(1):82–92.

—— (2002). "Criminal Justice and the Namibian Constitution: Experiences and Predicaments of the Past Ten Years." In: M.O. Hinz, S.K. Amoo and D. van Wyk (eds.), *10 years of Namibian Nationhood – The Constitution at Work.* South Africa: University of South Africa.

—— and J.W. Nyoka (2002). "Namibian Prison Service and the Constitution: Lessons and Experiences, 1990–2000." In: M.O. Hinz, S.K. Amoo and D. van Wyk (eds.), *10 years of Namibian Nationhood – The Constitution at Work.* South Africa: University of South Africa.

Ekstedt, J. and C.T. Griffith (1984). *Corrections in Canada: Policy and Practice.* Toronto, CAN: Butterworths.

Gottfredson, M.R. and T. Hirschi (1990). *A General Theory of Crime.* Stanford, CA: Stanford University Press.

Jackson, H. (2002). *AIDS Africa.* Zimbabwe: SafAIDS.

Nachtweih, W. (1976). *Von der antikolonialen Revolte zum nationalen Befreiungskampf. Geschichte der ehemaligen deutschen Kolonie Suedwestafrika.* Mannheim, Germany: Verlag Sendler.

Namibia Ministry of Prisons and Correctional Services (2000). *Annual Report for the Year 1999.* Windhoek.

Namibian Economic Policy Research Unit (NEPRU). *The Namibian Economy,* No. 50/March 2003.

Ramphaga, L. (2002). "New Prison Bill on the Way." Windhoek: *New Era* (newspaper).

Referat fuer Information und Oeffentlichkeitsarbeit der SWAPO von Namibia (Bureau for Information and Public Relations), (1979). *Entstehung einer Nation. Der Befreiungskampf fuer Namibia.* London, UK: Zed Press.

Schulz, S. (2002a). "Juvenile Justice in Namibia: A System in Transition." In: J.A. Winterdyk (ed.), *Juvenile Justice System: International Perspectives* (2nd ed.). Toronto, CAN: Canadian Scholars' Press Inc.

—— (2002b). "Legal Interpretation and the Namibian Constitution (A Paradigm Shift: Through Reason towards Justice)." In: M.O. Hinz, S.K. Amoo and D. van Wyk (eds.), *10 years of Namibian Nationhood – The Constitution at Work.* South Africa: University of South Africa.

—— (1997). "Offenses Against/Infringement on Sexual Self-Determination by Persons in Positions of Authority or Power (sexual exploitation)." (Unpublished) study commissioned by Ministry of Justice. Windhoek: Ministry of Justice.

—— and M. Hamutenya (2003). "Juvenile Justice in Namibia: Law Reform towards Reconciliation and Restorative Justice." (http://www. polytechnic.edu.na/Legal/publications.html.) Windhoek: Polytechnic of Namibia.

Snyman, C.R. (1995). *Criminal Law* (3rd ed.). South Africa: Butterworths.

Winterdyk, J. (ed.), (2001). *Corrections in Canada.* Toronto, CAN: Pearson.

NOTES

1. All Africans were forced to enter into "service and labour contracts" with white employers if they were to enter the so-called "*Polizeizone*," which the German colonial administration established in a wide circle around the capital Windhoek.

2. Executive Powers (Prisons) Transfer Proclamation 1977, No A.G. 6/77 of 31 October 1977.

3. Robben Island has become the synonym for the off-shore prison on the small island located in Table Bay (South Africa) with the same name. During apartheid political detainees were kept in this prison. The most famous prisoner was Nelson Mandela who after a decades-long struggle for democracy became the first *black* President of the Republic of South Africa. In South African and Namibian (at the time South-West-Africa) prisons prisoners were subjected to hard labour, which is known under another word, i.e., "lime and quarry" work.

4. At the time of the decision Mahomed, a South African citizen, was Acting Judge of Appeal. He became the first Namibian Chief Justice, i.e., the highest judicial officer, a position which he held concurrently with the position of Chief Justice of South Africa until 1998, when his Namibian term came to an end.

5. See GN 206 of 15 August 1998 (Government Gazette, 1927).

6. This can be attributed to the fact that upon Independence, the representatives of the old dispensation, i.e. the Commissioner of Prisons and his Deputy, as well as several other senior officers, ran away taking with them and/or destroying a considerable amount of important records and documents. What had been left behind was not properly handed over because there was no smooth transition.

7. All data for this chapter were obtained through the Office of the Commissioner of Prisons and are based on unpublished material.

8. Pearl millet and sorghum, commonly named *Mahangu* in Namibia, is one of the most important human staple cereals grown in the world today after wheat, rice, maize, and barley.

9. In this the operation of the Namibian Constitution differs from other constitutions, for instance the German Constitution (*Grundgesetz*), and German constitutional theory. There the individual may invoke Fundamental Rights and Freedoms directly only in relation to the state/public authority, whereas in respect of citizens *inter se* the fundamental Rights and Freedoms apply indirectly through the application and constitutional interpretation of general clauses forming part of the sub-constitutional law.

10. The *Namibian Dollar* (N$) is on a par with the *South African Ran* (R), which is at the same time also legal tender in Namibia. The exchange rate of either currency in relation to the U.S. dollar was on May 9, 2003 about N$/R 7.2 for US$ 1.

11. Admissions listed here include convicted criminals only. They do not include those awaiting trial or remand prisoners. This is in contrast to Table 8.1, which included everybody who was in the prison at that time.

CHAPTER 9.
THE ROMANIAN CORRECTIONAL SYSTEM: A CHALLENGE TO REFORM

by

Dr. Mircea Criste
Ambassador in the Romanian Foreign Office

BASIC FACTS ON ROMANIA

Area: Though often placed in the southeastern part of Europe (especially from a politically-strategic point of view), geographically Romania lies in the center of the old continent, at an equal distance between the Atlantic Ocean and the Urals. It is bordered by Hungary on the west, Serbia and Montenegro on the southwest, Bulgaria on the south, the Republic of Moldova on the northeast and east, Ukraine on the north and east. To the southeast the country has a 193.5 kilometer coastline onto the Black Sea. The country covers a geographic area of 238,391 square kilometers (92,043 square miles).

Population: Romania has 22,459,000 inhabitants (94.2 persons/square kilometer) with a gender make-up of 49% men and 51% women. The rural population accounts for 47.3%, while 52.7% of the population live in urban areas. The birth rate is 10.5% and the death rate is 13.0%. The capital is Bucharest, the so-called "Little Paris" of southeast Europe (population 2,016,000), with other major cities including: Iasi (350,000), Timisoara (328,000) and Constanta (327,000).

Demographics: Romania, because of its rich history, is composed of many nationalities, including: Romanians (89.5%), Hungarians (7.1%), Roma (1.7%), and other ethnic groups such as Germans,[1] Serbs, Croatians, Slovaks, Czechs, Ukrainians, and Bulgarians, etc. (together totaling 1.4%). The diversity of the ethnic groups also determines a diversity of religions, such as: Orthodox (86.8%), Roman-Catholic (5%), Reformed (3.5%), Greek-Catholic (1%), Unitarian (0.3%), Evangelical (0.2%), and other religions like Presbyterians, Baptists, Adventists, Muslims, etc. (totaling 4%). Romanian, the official language, is the mother tongue of 90% of the country's population. The literacy rate is 95.3%. Schooling is free and compulsory for children aged between 6 and 16 in the state schools. There are general secondary schools, grammar schools, professional schools or vocational institutes where suitably qualified pupils can progress to upper secondary education. Higher education in Romania is organized in two types: short-term university education (three-year programs organized in university colleges), and long-term university education (four to six years, provided in universities, academies, conservatories). The rate of criminality is of 1,390 offences per 100,000 inhabitants.

Climate: The climate is temperate continental, with Mediterranean influences in the southwest. The lowest temperature ever registered was −38.5°C and the highest was +44.5°C (the mean temperature is 11°C in the south and 8°C in the north of the country). Romania's physical profile varies: mountains cover 31% of the territory, hills cover 33% of the land, while plains, meadows and the Danube Delta cover Romania's remaining area.

Economy: After the collapse of the Soviet Bloc in 1989-91, Romania was left with an obsolete industrial base and a pattern of industrial capacity wholly unsuited to its needs. Since 1997, the country has embarked on expanding its economic base from being primarily agricultural to diversifying into such areas as petroleum, timber, natural gas, coal, iron ore, salt, and generating hydropower so that today only 23% of the economy is based on agriculture and 51% on industry. The GPD estimated for 2000 was of ROL 796,533.7 billion, increasing, in real terms, by 1.6% over 1999. Yet, Romania's unemployment rate was around 11% and 21.5% of the population was living below the poverty line. The national currency is the Romanian "leu" (ROL), with an exchange rate of 33,916 "lei" (ROL) for 1 dollar (USD) as of November 2003.

Government: The country is divided into 41 counties, including the Municipality of Bucharest. It had a monarchy until the end of 1947. Thereafter, Romania became a communist republic for a period of 43 years. During its last years, the communist dictatorship headed by Nicolae Ceausescu and his *Securitate* police state had become far more oppressive in violating human rights, having a bloodstained end as a result of the revolution set about on December 16, 1989, at Timisoara. In early 1990, with the creation of a new constitution, a new semi-presidential republic replaced the old regime. The president is elected through a universal vote for a four-year period. The parliament consists of 140 senators and 345 deputies, who make up the two houses of the Parliament. The government, led by a prime minister, receives his investiture vote from the Parliament. The political system is a multi-party one, the Social Democratic Party, the Great Romania Party, the Democratic Party, the National Liberal Party, the Democratic Union of Hungarians and the Romanian Humanist Party being at present represented in Parliament. Romania's justice system has a single jurisdictional order which has three levels of judgment, the highest level being the Supreme Court of Justice. The constitutional jurisdiction is represented by a single body known as the Constitutional Court — based on the European model. The Public Ministry, which includes all the prosecutors, is in charge of the penal pursuit.

"The criminal justice system in any country is a key indicator of its level of democracy and of the degree to which human rights are respected."
~ R. Walmsley (1996)

BRIEF HISTORY

The first evidence of the human presence on the territory of today's Romania dates back to the Paleolithic period (2 million years B.C.), but a relatively stable population could be found only in the Neolithic (6000-5000 B.C.). After 150 years as a Roman province (*Dacia*), and the division into three distinct provinces (Transylvania, Moldavia, and Valachia) during the Middle Ages, Romania emerged as a state from the Union of Moldavia and Valachia in 1859.[2]

Through the Great Union on December 1, 1918, Transylvania, the third historical province, joined the other two. Until then each of the three provinces that are now part of Romania had its own correctional system. In Transylvania of the 18th and 19th centuries, under the Hapsburg monarchy's rule, the prison regime was characterized by the terror applied to the detainees. One of the heaviest punishments, applied mainly to those charged of political offences, was beating in detention in handcuffs and chains. The prisons were built according to the Maria Theresa model — that is, in the shape of the letter "M." In Valachia and Moldavia, prisons were improvised in monasteries (especially for nobles), in the cellars of the reign vineyards (royal courts) or in salt mines. Although monasteries were still being used during the first half of the 19th century, prison administrators gradually began to pay better attention to the handling and treatment of prisoners. The joining of Valachia and Moldavia meant the union of their respective penitentiary systems as well, so that as of February, 1874 Romania had a *Law of Prisons*. This law promoted new principles, such as the inmates' separation from each other only at night, also stipulating the establishment of a women's prison and of special correctional houses for children.

After the First World War, the *Law for Penitentiaries and Preventive Institutions* in 1929 not only brought about new reforms but was also the impetus for the establishment of 76 correctional facilities. The law was based upon modern principles of correctional research, attempting to rehabilitate the inmates rather than exclude them from society. Among the measures taken under the new law was the separation of convicts by gender, age, recidivism and levels of indiscipline. The new legislation was also responsible for creation of a mixed and progressive system of penalties, the improvement of educational work for inmates and a comprehensive system of fines and rewards. The same principles were adopted in Prague one year later by the Congress of the International Penal and Penitentiary Commission.

The establishment of the communist regime after World War II led to deep changes within Romanian society.[3] Perhaps, the most dramatic change to correctional practices in Romania after the communist takeover was the introduction of labor camps in 1952, which were veritable death camps. In these, thousands of political prisoners were sentenced to forced labor and harsh living conditions which often resulted in the death of inmates.

According to the thesis — not having any support in reality — that as soon as the new society is built up, the people would improve their behavior and the number of offenders would decrease, the communist state cancelled out and even destroyed some prisons. While in 1969 there were 45 penitentiaries and 25 detention wards, by 1977 27 penitentiaries and 25 detention wards had been closed (see Table 9.1). The downside of this reaction was that the existing prisons quickly became overcrowded.[4] The solution — a temporary one — was the periodic issuance of some pardoning decrees. And, as we will see later, this problem still persists today — an unfortunate legacy of the communist regime in Romania.

Table 9.1: Detention Establishments as of January, 1ˢᵗ 2003

34 penitentiaries, of which:

- 9 maximum security prisons, also with closed and half-open wards (Aiud, Arad, Bucharest-Jilava, Bucharest-Rahova, Craiova, Gherla, Iasi, Margineni, Poarta Alba)

- 22 closed regime penitentiaries, also with half-open wards

- a penitentiary with half-open regime: Pelendava

- a penitentiary for women: Tirgor

- a penitentiary for juvenile and young offenders: Craiova

- three re-education centres for minor juvenile offenders: Gaesti, Tichilesti, Targu Ocna

- six penitentiary-hospitals: Bucharest-Jilava, Bucuresti-Rahova, Colibasi, Dej, Poarta Alba, Targu Ocna.

Other units of the system:

- the Military School of Prison Administration in Tirgu Ocna

- the Unit for Supplies, Husbandry and Repairs in Bucharest

- the Subunit for the transformed prisoners' supervision and escort

Source: www.anp.ro.

The *Law of Penalty Execution* of 1969 (issued during the communist period) is still used today to define the organization and function of penitentiaries. An enthusiastic team from the General Directorate of Penitentiaries started working on a draft of a new law regarding penalties and demilitarization in 1997, and is being guided by the latest international standards and settlements in this field. The project was handed in to the Parliament before the November 2000 elections, but it was withdrawn on February 16, 2001, at the new government's request.

THE ROMANIAN PENITENTIARY SYSTEM TODAY

Until 1990, the Romanian penitentiary system was of the Soviet type, strongly militarized and in which the detainees were more like registration numbers than human beings. With the transfer of the penitentiary administration into the Ministry of Justice, a process of rethinking the system following the West European model has begun. (*Making Standards Work*, elaborated by Penal Reform International [PRI] and the Dutch Ministry of Justice, was translated into Romanian and it became a basic work for the penitentiary reform.)

The Revolution of December 1989 had two immediate and noteworthy impacts on the Romanian correctional system. The first was the abolition of the death penalty (*Decree-Law no. 6/January 10th, 1990*),[5] which was replaced with life imprisonment. The second major change involved the shift of the correctional administration, after 43 years, from the Home Affairs Ministry to the Ministry of Justice (*Law no. 21/October 15th, 1990*). These changes marked the beginning of a long and complex process of reforming the penitentiary system and corrections. Other reform measures involved: (1) the internal organization of the system (*demilitarization, staffing and education, international support, transparency*); (2) the penitentiary regime; (3) cultural and educational programs; (4) modernization of the facilities; and (5) data processing technology.

1) Domestic Organization

In the aftermath of the revolution, Romania experienced not only dramatic political changes but also changes to its correctional system (Walmsley, 1996). There has been general movement towards a more open system and one that is more communicative and interactive towards the civilian community, as well as one that operates in a more "democratic" fashion as compared to the military organization of earlier years.[6] Finally, in 1997, the General Directorate began to institute significant reforms by removing many former military staff and replacing them with personnel who were more reflective of those found in most Western countries (see Figure 9.1).

The General Directorate of Penitentiaries, having 266 positions, is led by a general director and by a deputy director, being composed of five special directorates: Penitentiary Regime and Detention Safety Directorate; Education, Studies and Penitentiary Psychology Directorate; Logistics Directorate; Human Resources Directorate; Financial Directorate; and six departments: Public Relations, Medical Department, Penitentiary Control Department, Computer and Data Processing Department, Legal and Psychological Examination Department, Professional Evaluation.

Each unit from the penitentiary system is led by a civilian (director) or a military man (commander), having the same authority over, assisted by two deputies, one being responsible for guard and safeness issues, the other one for logistics issues. The general director has the control power of all the units and for any issue, the whole staff being at his orders.

Since 1990, 80% of the penitentiary staff has been replaced by new personnel, lowering the average age of the staff to 37 years and allowing for new ideas to be more easily embraced. By the middle of 2002, there were 12,075 persons working within the prison system (although 1,118 positions remained vacant), including 1,307 officers (3 generals), 9,761 military foremen and non-commissioned officers and only 1,007 civilian staff members. Nearly 15% of the staff are female (see Figure 9.2).

Security personnel make up 60% of the staff, over 12 times more than those taking care of the reeducational sector (321 persons at the end of 2002), while the medical staff comprises 6-7% of the correctional staff.

Figure 9.1: The Organization Chart of the Romanian Prison Administration

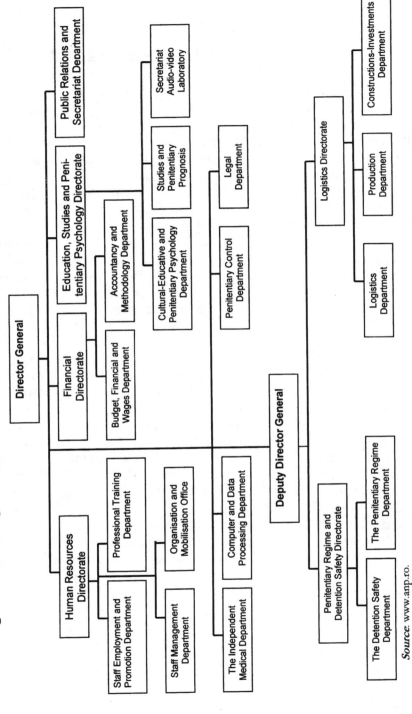

Source: www.anp.ro.

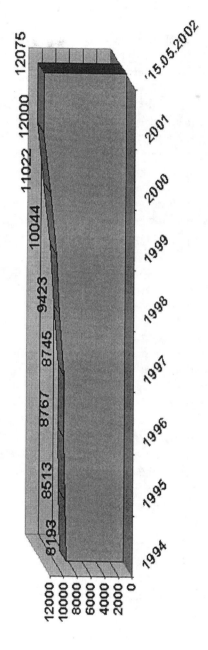

Figure 9.2: Changes in Romanian Penitentiary
Personnel, 1994-2002

Source: www.anp.ro.

In the same period of reference (middle of 2002), there were 52,016 persons being detained in some type of correctional center (over 95% are in penitentiaries and the remainder in re-education centres), with the legal capacity being around 38,000 places. Consequently, there is only one staff member for every eight inmates and there is a noticeable over-crowding problem.[7] The effect of this situation is that prison staff are overworked and any opportunity to provide services beyond basic detention is seriously compromised.[8] The staff members are subjected to conditions of high stress, especially the ones dealing with the security of detention, taking into account that they are responsible for the domestic and the external guard, including the transport and strict surveillance of inmates at their places of work and in the law courts. Correctional staff often work 10 to 14 hours per day.

The budget of the General Directorate is included in the budget of the Ministry of Justice (the sums of money can't be moved from one budget to another one), and it is allocated to the units by the General Director, depending on their necessities, which are always bigger than the sums allocated to the General Directorate of Penitentiaries (see Table 9.2 for the Romanian penitentiary administration budget). The work performed by the detainees[9] is an extra-budget resource (self-financing) that is also taken into consideration when the budget is made up (13% out of the total, in 2002). In the period from January 1 through June 30, 2003, from the average number of 47,844 persons deprived of liberty, 11,290 carried on labor activities, among whom 6,175 performed remunerated works and 5,115 carried on activities for the use of the detention place. In order to use prison labor, The Autonomous Enterprise "Multi-product" has been created specially to offer to detainees the possibility of work and training, with units inside five penitentiaries that are supervised by the Ministry of Justice.

Demilitarization

It is obvious that such a work regime could have been imposed only upon a military staff, a fact that could explain the delay and the difficulties that the demilitarization process of the Romanian penitentiary system are faced with.

Table 9.2: The Budget for Year 2002 (proposed and approved)

Financing source
-expenses-
GDP proposals for 2002
(rectificative budget)
amounts in Romanian *lei*
Approved budget
2002
Covering degree
-%-

Incomes from self-financing
proposed · 240,000,000
approved · 240,000,000
100.0

Allocations from the budget
proposed · 3,042,068,898
approved · 2,442,068,898
80.2

TOTAL, of which:
proposed · 3,282,068,898
approved · 2,682,068,898
81.7

staff expenses
proposed · 1,209,000,000
approved · 1,209,000,000
100.0

material expenses
proposed · 1,673,068,898
approved · 1,073,068,898
64.1

transfers
proposed · 214,132,237
approved · 199,132,237
92.9

capital expenses
proposed · 400,000,000
approved · 400,000,000
100.0%

Source: www.anp.ro.

Box 9.1: The Riot in Romanian Penitentiaries in February, 1997

"The February prison revolts reflected the complexity of the penitentiary situation in Romania.

On 16 February, inmates of the Bucharest penitentiary started a protest, claiming that the prison authorities had failed to inform them about the new system of release on parole decided by parliament in November 1996, extending the compulsory prison period before allowing prisoners to become eligible for parole. The protests extended to other prisons and further problems were taken up, including overlong trials, overcrowding and the bad quality of food. Some detainees went on hunger strike. The revolts were widely covered by the media.

On 23 February, the General Directorate of Penitentiaries decided to employ force to quash the protests in Bucharest: 500 prison officials stormed the penitentiary, using rubber batons and tear gas.

The APADOR-CH (The Association for the Protection of Human Rights in Romania-Helsinki Committee) representatives were given permission to visit the Bucharest prison on 27 February [...] It stated that the intervention of the Bucharest penitentiary staff to settle the conflict was clearly justified, but that there were serious indications that the prison staff had used excessive force to calm down the revolt. It recommended that the Ministry of Justice and the Military Prosecutor's Office start investigations into the methods used during this intervention.

Later in 1997, APADOR-CH received new information that there had been large-scale retaliation against prisoners who had participated in the revolt. The prison administration had allowed some 70-100 inmates to be severely beaten with wooden clubs and other objects by approximately 70 masked individuals. The prisoners were also made to pick up pieces of glass, cobblestones, etc., from the ground in order to humiliate them. Then they were transported to cells other than their own. Few of them were taken to surgery to receive medical care and even fewer to the penitentiary hospital, located next to the penitentiary. Similar incidents took place also in the succeeding days. Some detainees lodged complaints with the Military Prosecutor's Office, denouncing the inhuman and degrading treatment to which they had been subjected.

According to the investigations carried out by a commission of the Senate, the inmates of the Bucharest penitentiary 'had not been subjected to inhuman or degrading treatment'" (IHF Annual Report 1998 – Romania).

From this point of view, the most courageous decision (because it was taken only three months after a powerful riot in several Romanian penitentiaries — see Box 9.1 on the riot of February, 1997) was the one initiated by Valeriu Stoica, Minister of Justice at that time, and by the Secretary of State who coordinated the General Directorate of Penitentiaries, Dorin Clocotici. In May 1997, a judge was appointed as General Director for the penitentiary administration. He became the first civilian (i.e., non-military) director to serve in this capacity since World War II. The initiative appears to have had the desired effect: the subsequent General Directors were all civilians (another judge and two prosecutors), leading to the extension of such appointments to nine other penitentiaries and two centers designated for juvenile re-education.

Since the Revolution, it has been the mandate of the Ministry of Justice to demilitarize the correctional system and to bring its standards of operation in line with those established by the Council of Europe as well as in keeping with various UN standards and conventions. The demilitarization process means: to increase the number of staff positions by 8,000 jobs; to provide supplementary funds estimated at ROL 2,338 billion; to institute a new educational penitentiary system; and, the takeover of external area security and of inmate transfer by the Home Ministry.

Staffing and Education

The educational system for correctional officers is different from the education of non-commissioned officers. Correctional officers have to be either graduates of the Police Academy (Department of Penitentiaries) or be selected from among university graduates who have served time in the military and demonstrate the knowledge to work within a prison setting, while the non-commissioned officers have to attend the National School for Prison Administration. After 1997, the school was moved to Targu Ocna (from Bucharest — the Jilava Penitentiary, a very crowded space with limited resources), which also serves as a center for juvenile reeducation.

International Support

It is worth noting that many of the initiatives undertaken after the Revolution could not have taken place as efficiently and quickly without the support (in a practical and financial context) and cooperation of prison administrators from key partner countries, who offered their expertise in related penitentiary matters (such as England and Wales, France, Hungary, the Netherlands and Spain — see Box 9.2). The end result has enabled Romania to move forward with its reforms.

Box 9.2: Romanian Corrections and International Relations

"Beginning with September 2001 the General Directorate of Penitentiaries has started a Twinning Convention with the General Directorate of Prison Institutions from Spain.

In accordance with the twinning convention, one pre-accession adviser, Mrs. Carmen Martinez Aznar, came to Bucharest and worked 12 months at the General Directorate of Penitentiaries in order to evaluate the Romanian Prison System and to draw up a reform strategy for the penitentiary system in Romania.

Having as purpose the European integration, contacts have been made with the majority of penitentiary systems. Bilateral co-operation agreements have been signed with the Hungarian penitentiary administration (1998) and the penitentiary administration of The Republic of Moldavia (2000). They target the information exchange, documentation visits, seminars and symposia, penitentiary twinning. Also, we have a joint project with the Swiss government for consultancy in view of adjusting the initial training requirements for the personnel of the penitentiary administration at European standards.

At present, 12 detention establishments in Romania are twinned with similar institutions from abroad, as follows:
- Aiud-Szekszard (Hungary)
- Bacau-Over Amstel (Netherlands)
- Bucuresti-Harlem (Netherlands)
- Craiova-Toorenburgh (Netherlands)
- Colibasi-De Standsporten (Netherlands)
- Focsani-Oosterhoek (Netherlands)
- Rahova-Almere Binnen (Netherlands)
- Oradea-Almelo (Netherlands)
- Timisoara-Coldlingley (England)
- Târgu Mures-Kecskemet (Hungary)
- Târgsor-Hectehngowaard (Netherlands)
- Satu Mare-Zupthen (Netherlands)."

Source: www.anp.ro.

Transparency

The new Romanian penitentiary administration has initiated efforts to inform and garner the acceptance of the public by adopting a policy of *transparency* in which it no longer engages in secretive practices. For example, several recent publications have noted Romania's willingness to allow outside observers (including UN observers) to examine the correctional reforms taking place within the country.

Based upon reports received from various human rights organizations, the penitentiary administration has taken the proper measures in order to cease the ascertained deficiencies. Furthermore, through a monitoring program, initiated in 1997 by the General Directorate, each penitentiary now includes a committee of people who have demonstrated a sound understanding and appreciation for the reforms. The task of this committee is to support the reeducational activities within the institution as well as to ensure that inmate needs are being effectively and properly met. There are now 28 non-governmental organizations that have become involved in addressing the needs of prisons. This involves more than 4,000 individuals — again, reflecting a desire not only by the state but by the Romanian populace to support the reform initiatives.

Such an organization is GRADO (The Romanian Group for the Defence of Human Rights), which was involved in the formulation of the Probation Law and training of probation officers. The organization has become an active partner for the Ministry of Justice. In a six-year period, GRADO undertook work in 10 prisons and in two reeducational centers for juveniles, in five stages: preparation for release, post-release assistance, legal aid, education through theatre (in collaboration with UNITER — Theatre Union of Romania and Geese Theatre Co. USA) and proposals for amending the legislation.

The media, who have in the past had limited access to the correctional arena, have been allotted considerable access to observe and comment on the reforms that have either been initiated and/or proposed. For example, in 2001, the media had been granted in excess of 1,000 visits to various correctional facilities and permitted to engage in over 190 interviews with convicted persons. This represents a dramatic change in openness from what was experienced under the prior regime.

Finally, regarding the transparency of Romania's correctional system, it should be noted that since 1997 the Romanian penal administration has had a permanent site on the internet (www.anp.ro), as a result of the work of a team from the Computer and Data Processing Department. On this site one can obtain information on such matters as the history of Romanian penitentiaries, the persons held in custody in penitentiary institutions, detention establishments, activities developed for the prisoners, the correctional budget, statistics and graphics, press releases and the annual reports of activity.

2) The Penitentiary Regime

When the inmate is first assigned to a particular penitentiary, according to the *Law of Penalty Execution* (art. 3), the nature of his or her offence is taken into consideration, as are the length of the punishment, his or her recidivism rate and his or her behavior. With respect to women and juveniles, a special penitentiary exists for each of them, but even when they are distributed to other penitentiaries, they are held in separate sections.

A record is drawn on each prisoner, containing the warrant on the basis of which the imprisonment is made, the individual's identity card and personal data, the record of his or her penal antecedents, his or her fingerprints, a photograph and other data which contributes to the establishment of individually adequate treatment (type of correctional regime, reeducational programmes, etc.). In this confidential record, which accompanies the inmate to each place of detention, all the subsequent references regarding the inmate are noted, such as data about the work he or she has carried out, disciplinary measures or rewards granted.

Consequent to being found guilty and sent to prison, the offenders begin their sentence by spending 21 days in quarantine. During this period they are examined for basic health conditions and assessed as to their ability to perform certain work-related tasks, as one of the main responsibilities of inmates is to perform useful work. On average, inmates are expected to work between 8 and 12 hours daily.[10]

Performing work is just one of the inmates' obligations. Others include:

- Allowing searches whenever they are requested. The inmates may not own things that could be used as weapons, items that could be the subject of an unlawful trade with other inmates or objects that could facilitate communication with persons outside the place of detention;

- Observing hygienic rules, reporting to the medical staff about contagious diseases that they might suffer from or might have suffered from, and undergoing required medical treatment;

- Exhibiting decent behavior towards other persons;

- Not being involved in disciplinary infractions;

- Not gathering in groups after the sleeping time; and,

- Not gambling.

If the rules of domestic order and discipline are not obeyed, the following punishments may apply: reprimand; withdrawal of the right to receive visits or parcels; simple or severe isolation (with the doctor's authorization);[11] and serving a part of the sentence (3-12 months) within a restrictive regime, which is decided by the General Director at the prison ruler's proposal.[12]

Changes were introduced after 1997 in an effort to reduce the potential risk for abuse. Thus, the decision is taken based on a review of the record and it belongs to a board, the inmate having the right to contest it in the presence of the director/commander of the penitentiary and afterwards in the presence of the delegated prosecutor. The use of chains for immobilization has also been forbidden.

In general, prisoners also have a number of rights, such as:

- *The right to food.* The prison administration provides thrice a day a warm dish, the inmate having *the right to receive parcels* with food (e.g., cigarettes, books, medications, clothes, etc.). The amount and frequency for this privilege depends on the inmate's legal condition, length of sentence, and age. Inmates may also buy food with their own money in some units where supply places have been set-up. The lack of enough spaces makes it impossible in almost all places of detention to set up dining halls, therefore meals are typically served in the detention rooms.

- *The right to medical attendance.* Medical care is provided at regular intervals. In the year 2000, one of three inmates was hospitalized in a penitentiary hospital, while 1 out of 53 was taken to a hospital belonging to the Ministry of Health and Family network. There are 6,647 patients with chronic diseases in the penitentiaries. The death rate is 25 and 1 suicide per 10,000 inmates.

- *The right to equipment.* The inmates' clothing, according to season, is provided by the penitentiary administration. The inmates may also use their own shoes and underwear, those who are under remand and the women from the Penitentiary of Targsor may wear their own clothes, while those surrendered to court no longer have to wear the striped penitentiary uniform. The General Directorate is planning on introducing new uniforms, which shall not have a degrading character.

- *The right to rest.* According to the regulations in force, an individual bed must be provided to each inmate, but because of overcrowding this right cannot be granted to everyone. The inmates have the right to sleep seven hours (eight for juveniles) per night, and those who are not taken out to work have the right of walking in special arranged places within the penitentiary yard from 30 minutes to 1 hour per day (1-2 hours for juveniles).

- *The right to communication.* The inmate may be visited, may receive and send mail and may hand in applications and complaints to institutions or bodies. The limits of this right are determined by the inmate's legal situation, the length of his or her punishment, age, penitentiary regime, etc. During visits to the inmate the discussions are not listened to; the guards' duty is solely to ensure that there are no disturbances. The mail, especially petitions, is unlimited and it is censored only in special cases stipulated by the Constitution. Penitentiaries have been endowed with an increased number of telephone sets that are at the inmates' disposal, with the director's approval.

The present regulation doesn't allow for much differentiation or classification of the inmates on several detention regimes. Considering that social rehabilitation activity cannot have any efficiency by applying the same penitentiary regime to all inmates, in 1998 the General Directorate established five types of regimes for inmates: a regime for the inmates on remand; a regime of maximum security; a closed regime; a half-open regime; and, an open regime.

Classification into one of these types of regimes is undertaken by a commission, taking into account the inmate's legal situation, the length of his or her punishment and his or her behavior during incarceration. The five regimes differ in matters of accommodation, guards and supervision, equipment, use for work, and limits of certain rights.

Maximum security is used for those convicted to life imprisonment, those sentenced to long-term sentences under a restrictive regime and, generally speaking, to those who are classified as dangerous inmates. They are supervised by more guards, searched whenever they enter and leave the rooms, exercise under strict supervision, work only inside the penitentiary, and participate in educational activity usually, individually. On the contrary, in open regimes, the emphasis is on inmates' consent and responsibility, while their accommodation is set up in common open rooms. During work they are under the supervision of a few unarmed guardians, they have more freedom of movement in their free time, and they are beneficiaries of a larger number of visits, parcels, phone talks, and permissions, etc.

By the middle of 2002, in the units subordinated to the Romanian Prison Administration were 51,528 persons, held in facilities with a legal capacity of around 38,000 places (6 m^3 per inmate). (See Table 9.3 for the situation on the 1st of June 2002 regarding the offences committed.)

Out of the total, 46,030 were men and 2,051 women; 1,396 were juvenile offenders and 4,138 people were aged 18 to 21. From the point of view of their legal status, the situation was as follows: 4,436 inmates were on remand, 6,073 were being tried in court and 37,467 were convicted persons.

Of those convicted in 2002, approximately 20% had previously served time in prison, some 41% were recidivists, and the balance (approximately 38%) were non-recidivists (i.e., first-time offenders).

Table 9.3: Offences Committed by the Persons Held in Penitentiaries and Re-education Centres on the 1st of June 2002

Nature of offence	Total	%
A. Offences against the state	1	-
B. Offences against a person, including:	12,772	24.80
murder	7,935	15.40
rape	2,543	4.94
injuries leading to death	375	0.73
injuries, bodily damage and serious bodily damage	8,177	1.59
other offences against a person	1,102	2.14
C. Offences against patrimony, including:	33,824	68.64
theft	23,478	45.56
robbery	8,282	16.07
fraud	1,672	3.24
other offences against patrimony	392	0.75
D. Offences against public property, including:	166	0.32
theft	18	0.03
defalcation	111	0.22
other offences against public property	37	0.07
E. Offences against authority, including:	338	0.66
outrage	332	0.65
other offences against authority	6	0.01
F. Offences which disturb some activities of public interest, including:	456	0.88
traffic of influence	120	0.23
bribing and bribery taking	71	0.14
escape	30	0.06
breach of the arms and ammunition regime	55	0.11
destruction and false indication	60	0.12
other offences	120	0.22
G. Economic forgery offences, including:	274	0.53
money counterfeiting	119	0.23
forgery of identity	45	0.09
other forgery offences	110	0.21

Nature of offence	Total	%
H. Offences which infringe on certain relationships		
regarding social life, including:	1,272	2.47
abandon of family	328	0.64
drug trafficking	505	0.98
procuring	193	0.37
outrage against good morals	135	0.26
other offences	111	0.22
I. Offences against the defence capacity, including:	23	0.04
desertion	18	0.03
other offences	5	0.01
J. Decrees and special laws	1,284	2.49
K. Contraventions	1,118	2.17
GENERAL TOTAL	51,528	100.00

Source: www.anp.ro.

Based on interviews with various correctional experts, Walmsley (1996) identified three main factors that could account for the high level of imprisonment. They include:

- legislative requirements which state that recidivists must receive longer terms of imprisonment than others;

- long sentences; and

- the limited availability of alternatives to imprisonment.

Amnesties are usually declared after there has been a significant political change within a country. Such was the case with many of the former Eastern-bloc countries prior to the time of their gaining of independence from the former Soviet Union (see Walmsley, 1996).

Beginning in the 1970s, the Council of State announced an amnesty program approximately every other year. Generally, prisoners serving less than three years or with less than three years remaining on longer sentences were freed, and the sentences of prisoners serving more than three years were reduced. The government reportedly released 90% of those in prison or awaiting trial through an amnesty announced in

January 1988. Amnesties may have been intended to alleviate chronic labor shortages or to clear prisons crowded through strict law enforcement. After the 1988 amnesty, the Minister of Justice reported that there were 7,500 citizens in prison. There had been 75,000 inmates prior to the amnesty (http://www.1upinfo.com/country-guide-study /romania/romania231.html).

Although it has a small number of staff, the Romanian penitentiary system is not confronted with particularly large problems caused by the inmates. For example, in 2002 records indicate that there were only six escapes.

3) Cultural and Educational Programs

The greatest achievement of the Romanian penitentiary system after 1990 was the importance regained by the educative and cultural activities, employed as the main focus of the inmates' reintegration. All of this has been undertaken under conditions as already stated, wherein the number of staff is insufficient and the formal administration has not evolved significantly. A cultural-educative department within the General Directorate coordinates the educative and sports programs; it estimates the qualification possibilities, manages the inmates' counseling activities and cooperates with the social reintegration organizations.

As soon as a person is imprisoned, a "risk assessment" of the inmate is undertaken and a Portrayal Record is drawn out. According to the level of the inmate's education, his level of culture, abilities and options, and his disposition, he is registered into the program, which aims for the maximum improvement of his behavior.

One of the important activities carried out is that of education, sometimes even of teaching to read and write, through the organization of lectures with a qualified staff. This activity is being developed with the Ministry of Education's support; the diplomas handed over to inmates do not contain any reference to the fact that they were acquired in a penitentiary. Prisoners fulfilling the prerequisites, being able to pay the fees and having the approval of the General Directorate are even allowed to sign up for university.

The education programming implies free access to mass media and to a number of books. In each place of detention there is a library, set up through the contribution of the penitentiary administration, donations of and cooperation with the libraries of the local communities. Collectively, there are over 107,000 books available to offenders.

The inmates, in addition to the fact that they may watch TV and listen to the radio, are also allowed to organize their own cultural activities, having access to radio stations and to the TV studios set up in some penitentiaries.

Professional training is just as important for the inmates, playing a significant role for their social reintegration. The prison administration, with the support of the Ministry of Labor and Social Solidarity, promotes courses of training and retraining, focusing on professions that are solicited on the labor market. These courses take place either in the workshops functioning in the prisons or close to them, or even outside them, in the industrial units that organize such activities.

In the penitentiary clubs, the prisoners may practice their artistic skills, the exhibitions of painting and sculpture being highly appreciated. Religious activities take place in each prison, with an Orthodox priest permanently employed, while the access of representatives of other officially recognized religions is also unlimited. The inmates may also practice different sports, individual or in a team, depending on their age and state of health.

4) Modernization of the Present Establishments

The penitentiaries are set up through an Order of the Ministry of Justice, a director (civilian) or a commander (military) is appointed to lead them, and they are subordinated to the General Directorate of Penitentiaries as a part of the Ministry of Justice.

The last 12 years have witnessed the establishment of new penitentiaries in areas where they did not exist before or where the previous ones exceeded the accommodation capacity (such as Giurgiu, Bucharest-Rahova or Arad), the setting up and repopulation of penitentiaries that were closed before 1990 (Bistrita, Ploiesti, the juvenile reeducation centers from Tichilesti and Craiova), the extension and the building of new sections in already existing penitentiaries (Bistrita, Bucuresti-Jilava, Colibasi, Craiova, Galati, Targu-Jiu, Timisoara, Tulcea), the repair and restoration of unused sections (Iasi, Timisoara) and the taking over of some buildings from the National Defence Ministry or from the Health Ministry in order to transform them into places of detention. Due primarily to fiscal restraints, the inmates themselves have done much of the building, restoration and repair works. At the same time, works of modernization and extension of the water supply capacities, sewage systems, and thermal power have been completed, in order to provide normal hygienic conditions in prisons.

Currently, the system includes six penitentiary-hospitals, three juvenile reeducation centers (Gaesti, Tichilesti, Targu-Ocna), one penitentiary for underaged offenders (Craiova), one penitentiary for women (Targsor), one penitentiary with a half-open regime (Pelendava), 24 penitentiaries with a closed regime (some of them having sections with a half-open regime) and nine maximum security prisons (which include sections with a closed or a half-open regime as well). Although there is a concern for the well-balanced distribution of the detention establishments in the whole country, there are 10 counties left still with no penitentiaries.

Special attention has been given to the increase of the capacity of accommodation of penitentiary hospitals and the improvement of their conditions, in order to treat as many cases as possible inside the system. In March 2003, a new penitentiary hospital was inaugurated at Bucharest-Rahova, having a 100 bed capacity and an endowment worthy of every hospital of the Ministry of Health. The results of these actions can be seen, on the one hand, in the increased number of persons who are under medical care in the penitentiary network (e.g., the number of persons sent for hospital care increased from 12,209 in 2000 to 19,162 in 2002), and on the other hand in the decrease of the number of sentence-serving interruptions due to medical reasons (from 428 in 2000, and 257 in 2001, to 104 cases in 2002).

The accommodation capacity of the Romanian penitentiary system on 1st of June 2003 was 37,995 places. Because of overcrowding, each penitentiary has beds exceeding the legal capacity, sometimes with 3- or even 4-level bunks. Even so, for about 6,000 prisoners individual beds can't be provided. The percentage of the occupied places, in comparison to their legal capacity, totals 138% (146% in penitentiaries, 68% in the penitentiary hospitals and 44% in the reeducation centers).

5) The Data Processing Technology of the Penitentiary System

In 1997, the Computer and Data Processing Department was created, subordinated directly to the General Director and it has been developed during the following years. The work of this department involves: analysis and drawing up of applications; programming and programmer testing; network designing; modernization of the hardware; complex graphic and video presentations; Web sites; the organization of training courses for the prisons' staff; and management of documents.

The main achievement of this department is represented by the database containing the inmates' files, which allows quick access to information about a certain inmate and which can be examined by all units of the system and by the Appeal Court from Bucharest. The Ministry of Home Affairs and the Population Evidence Service are to be included in this network.

Other applications developed by this department involve the collection of information about the type of work inmates do, the transfer of inmates, monthly statistics, management of the General Directorate's documents, staff lists management and salary rights.

ADMINISTRATIVE PROCESS AND PROFILE OF THE CORRECTIONAL POPULATION

Romania's **Penal Code**, adopted in 1968, defines punishment as a measure of compulsion and a way to provide offenders with reeducation programs (art. 52).

The penalties are divided into three categories: *main ones* (i.e., life incarceration, imprisonment from 15 days to 30 years, and fines from ROL 100,000, to ROL 500,000[13]), *complementary* ones (the prohibition of some rights for a period of 1 to 10 years and military degradation), and *accessory* ones (the prohibition of certain rights stipulated by law).

Since 1990, the Penal Code has been modified several times and there is a tendency toward being more punitive, the reason being that the risk of severe penalties is supposed to serve as an effective deterrent to lower the level of criminal activity.[14]

Table 9.4 shows a difference between 1999, 2002 and the middle of 2003 in terms of the number of persons serving sentences of different lengths.

Table 9.4: Length of Sentence for 1999, 2002 and the Middle of 2003[15]

Length of Sentence	1999	2002	middle of 2003
up to 1 year	3,097 persons	1,933 persons	1,625 persons
1-2 years	5,120 persons	4,545 persons	3,656 persons
2-5 years	18,694 persons	17,518 persons	17,335 persons
5-10 years	6,664 persons	8,640 persons	8,736 persons
10-15 years	2,160 persons	2,244 persons	2,417 persons
15-20 years	2,570 persons	2,625 persons	2,548 persons
over 20 years	442 persons	695 persons	747 persons
life detention	74 persons	99 persons	103 persons

Source: www.anp.ro.

In accordance with article 59-60 of the Penal Code, **parole** is readily used within the Romanian correctional regime. Approximately 70% of all those released from correctional facilities each year are granted parole. Parole is available to inmates who demonstrate improved behavior (e.g., those who are well-disciplined, hardworking, etc. while serving their sentence) and have served a legally prescribed minimum period of their sentence. In addition, other factors are taken into consideration, such as the risk of perceived recidivism. The final parole decision is up to a judge after a recommendation from a commission which consists of a prosecutor (chairman) and four representatives of the penitentiary (including its director/commander). The proportion of the sentence that must be served before an offender is eligible for parole is between one-fourth and three-fourths of the sentence. The time period is dependent on the length of the penalty, the offenders' age and whether the offence was committed deliberately (e.g., factoring in *mens rea*) or by mistake. Those who are sentenced to life imprisonment may be released on parole after serving a period of 20 years.[16] A sentence is considered served only after the fulfillment of the complete term including the time spent while on parole. If the parolee should reoffend while on parole, the court may revoke its initial decision. Revocation also takes place if the parolee commits an offense against the state, an offense that causes important losses to the national economy or a deliberate crime, such as causing the death of a person.

Since the late 1990s, *alternative punishments* have gained a greater importance. The alternative punishments are not something totally new in Romania. However, in recent years they have received increasing support from various legislators and by a number of judges.

Under the current penal code, an alternative measure is the **conditional suspension** of the penalty's execution (art. 81 Penal Code). After a specified period called a *probation term* (punishment + two years of probation or one year in the case of a fine), the sentence is considered served. A conditional suspension can only be used if the applied penalty does not exceed a three-year term of imprisonment or a fine, the criminal has not been sentenced to more than six months' imprisonment and the purpose of the penalty can be achieved without its execution. Exempted are first-degree crimes, for which the law provides imprisonment for more than 15 years, as well as serious injury crimes *such as* rape and torture. In case of a conviction for a crime which resulted in bodily or physical harm, the court can order a conditional suspension only if the damages were fully repaired or if they were secured by an insurance company. As with parole, the suspension is revocable should the delinquent reoffend during the probationary term.

The suspension of the penalty under observation, introduced through *Law no 104/1992,* can be requested by the court if the applied penalty is at most four years imprisonment and the criminal has not been previously convicted to imprisonment for more then one year. The behavior of those convicted after the crime's commission is taken into consideration as well. The offender shall also respect certain conditions prescribed by the judge (art. 86/3 penal code). The probationary term is made up of the applied imprisonment penalty, to which a period between two and five years is added. As with the previous alternatives, the conditions of revocation apply to this option as well.

The execution of the penalty at the place of work was introduced in 1973 under section III/2 of the Penal Code, which stipulated that, considering the gravity of the crime, the circumstances under which the crime was perpetrated and the behavior of the convicted, the court can request that the penalty be carried out at the offender's place of work, with the employer's written agreement. The following requirements must also be fulfilled: the applied penalty consists of a maximum of five years of imprisonment and the person was not previously sentenced to an imprisonment of longer than one year. The serving of the sentence at the place of work cannot be ordered in the case of first-degree crimes for which the law provides imprisonment for more than 15 years, as well in the case of serious injury crimes such as rape and torture. The convicted cannot be promoted, he cannot fill top positions, and from his/her total income a percentage will be retained.

The execution of the penalty at the place of work as an alternative punishment corresponds to the communist society that lacks a market economy. In this case, the essence of the punishment has more a material nature (i.e., the loss of some wage advantages and of promotion prospects). The rights of the person who serves such punishment are limited in comparison with the rights of an employee, concerning the wage, the professional career, the fulfilling of some obligations imposed by the judge, etc. This is the reason why it is no longer included in the draft of the new penal code.

ISSUES CONFRONTING CORRECTIONS IN ROMANIA TODAY

The future evolution of Romania's penitentiary system should follow and extend in the direction of measures already taken. This means, first of all, the adoption of new legislation that would allow for the development and modernization of the system, adjusting it to fit in accordance with existing international standards. These include:

- The 1948 Universal Declaration of Human Rights;

- The 1950 Council of Europe's European Convention for the Protection of Human Rights and Fundamental Freedoms;

- The 1966 International Covenant on Civil and Political Rights;

- The general UN standards pertaining to the protection and treatment of those detained or imprisoned; and,

- European and UN Conventions pertaining to the application of torture or other degrading modes of treatment or punishment.

In fact, a project for a new penal code has been concluded, and the new rules contained in it will influence to a great extent the penitentiary system. Initiated by the Ministry of Justice and now under parliamentary consideration, it stipulates a new system of punishments, but without giving the details about their administration, which is left to a future law on the serving the sentences. Thus, given that serious penal offences couldn't be included in the same category with the less serious offences, the project makes a distinction between *crimes* and *misdemeanors*, going back, in this way, to the classification that existed before World War II. It doesn't mean simply a return to a system of 70 years ago, but dropping a Soviet type of penal law, and the adoption of the modern continental law (for example it introduces the penal responsibility of the moral persons).

For serious offences, there are three basic categories of sentencing: life imprisonment, imprisonment from 15 to 25 years, and imprisonment from 10 to 15 years. Misdemeanors offences include a wider range of options. They range from: imprisonment from two to 10 years, imprisonment from one month to two years; a fine in the form of fine days, from five to 360 days (each day being valued between 100,000 ROL and 1,000,000 ROL); and work for the good of the community (i.e., between 15 and 90 days, served within one year).

Each type of punishment is to be served in penitentiaries with a specific destination or in special sections of other penitentiaries. The conditions of a sentence are defined under the new penal code

The work for the good of the community is stipulated as the main punishment for misdemeanors, and it has already been introduced in the Romanian legislation through *Law no 82/1999*, which allows the person punished to confinement in prison to perform, instead of prison, five to 300 hours of work in the public service. Whenever a misdemeanor offender is sentenced to a prison term or given a suspended sentence with supervision, the court shall compel the offender to perform unpaid "work for the good of the community" for a period of up to 90 days, performed within one year. Should the offender refuse to perform the work or if he doesn't carry out his duties, the court shall revoke the measure and replace the work for the good of community with a prison penalty.

The project of the Penal Code also provides for two alternative punishments for those offenders who haven't been previously convicted and/or who have committed a deed of minimum gravity and, after committing it, have repaired the caused damage: the *exemption from penalty* and the *adjournment of the application of the penalty*.

Should the court adjourn the application of the penalty, it sets a date on which it is to be pronounced (within two years from the moment of the trial). The interval between the trial and this date represents the period of probation for the defendant. During this time, the court may require the offender to adhere to conditions of supervision and to work for the good of the community.

So, here we are facing a new institution for the Romanian penitentiary system, **probation** (see Glossary), which is being imposed with some difficulty. The name itself has been contested, as in the Romanian juridical literature it also stands for the evidence system. The expansion of probation in Romania has been the result of a good collaboration with the penitentiary administration of various foreign organizations. England has played a particularly important role in this regard. Through the *Order no. 510 from April 18, 1997*, issued by the Ministry of Justice, Arad penitentiary was authorized to collaborate with English consultants (the *Europe for Europe* organization, Exeter University and Devon Service for Probation), as part of the program *Partnership for Justice*, in order to carry out specific activities of probation, as they are defined in the Recommendation R (92) 16 of the European Council. Later on, this experiment was extended and 11 centers of probation have appeared, with the participation of other non-governmental organizations.

During the period 1997-1998, a team composed of specialists from the Ministry of Justice and the General Directorate of Penitentiaries worked on a project for a law of probation, which was taken over and later integrated in the Penal Code project, under the title *measures for the good of the community*. Even though the new Penal Code was delayed by the government of the time, in the summer of 2000 probation services were formally recognized and promoted through the Government's *Order (no 92 from August 29, 2000)*.

Although the Penal Code does not use the word "probation" per se, it does include provision for the social reintegration and the supervision of certain offenders as an alternative sanction. For a long time there was an oscillation between choosing the French model (which is closer to the Romanian law system) or the English one, rather tending to a pragmatic system, which would include elements from both. The Ministry of

Justice coordinates the probation centers, but in their activity they rely a lot on the support of the nongovernmental organizations.

The activity in the probation field is still at the beginning and it is early to make an estimation. It is focused mainly on working with the minors and young people who reside in the probation center, because of the limited financial resources and of the low number of staff (five to six counselors of probation for each center). The services for social reintegration and for supervision are now a formal part of the correctional process and come under the Directorate of the Ministry of Justice. These services give assistance to certain categories of offenders, supervise the compliance with the obligations imposed by the judge, and, at the request of the courts of law, they provide evaluation reports and collaborate in their activity with non-governmental organizations.

FUTURE DIRECTIONS

'The aspiration of any country to enter the European Union and Euro-Atlantic structures is conditioned by the existence of a credible, stable government and institutions, which should guarantee the functioning of democratic principles and ensure the rule of law.' [17]

As has been noted throughout this chapter, Romania is still emerging from the aftermath of the Revolution in the late 1980s, early 1990s. Although significant strides have been made in bringing the country's correctional system in line with international guidelines, there is still considerable room for improvement. Here are some of the key areas that require immediate attention in order to ensure positive progress:

- The Romanian penitentiary system needs new legislation for the carrying out of penalties and a statute that will allow issues pertaining to the administration of prisons and handling of inmates in a manner that is in keeping with international standards.

- A new criminal law is needed that establishes more appropriate sentencing guidelines, in order to promote the use of alternative sanctions.

- Non-custodial alternatives to imprisonment should be created. This will require a reallocation of resources as well as recruiting and retaining appropriate and sufficient staff.

- And the standards of health and services to those being detained should be improved.

CONCLUSION

As in other countries, the organization of the penitentiaries in Romania has two objectives: to isolate the social ill (the offenders) for the protection of society and to provide the appropriate treatment-intervention that will enable the offender to reintegrate into society. Since the Revolution, considerable progress has been made to honor this commitment, but as has been evidenced throughout the chapter, there is still considerable work to be done to rid the system of its archaic, repressive, and at times still totalitarian regime. Efforts have been made to provide the European and UN standards and rules available for all to see and read. Concerted efforts, within the resources available, have been made to improve the conditions within the prisons and provide alternatives to incarceration. Yet, overcrowding still remains a major issue, and until it can be effectively addressed, it will remain difficult to provide necessary services to those being held in detention or prisons. For example, there still are no provisions to house the most serious and dangerous offenders separate from those who are considered less dangerous.

Yet, Romania is composed of people who are proud of their heritage and want to return to the period before the two great wars when the country "held very considerable international respect and the prison system was in the forefront of those in Europe" (Walmsley, 1996:353).

As noted, the country's correctional system has been undergoing a process of reforms for some 13 years. These reforms have, in large part, been supported by the public. However, the enthusiasm and the professionalism of those who work in this field are still wanting. Yet, it is a problem that can't rest on their shoulders alone. Sustained reform will only come through the collective will of the people, correctional personnel, and the government.

It is obvious that in order to succeed in these objectives one should appeal to a budgetary effort, which, unfortunately, hasn't been a priority until now. In a society which wholly crosses an economical, social and institutional reform, the argument that neglecting the problems of the penitentiary system just feeds on the already existing economical and social problems becomes less important in front of the prior care (having an electoral smack) for the disadvantaged categories of the society (young people, pensioners, unemployed persons, people without any income, etc.).

Key Terms and Concepts

Conditional suspension

New penal legislation

Demilitarization

Parole

European Penitentiary Rules

Probation term

Labor camps

Discussion/Study Questions

(1) How has the correctional and prison system in Romania changed following the political changes after 1989?

(2) To what extent has Romania been able to comply with European and other international standards relating to correctional related issues?

(3) How does the Romanian correctional system compare to your country?

(4) What are the alternative punishments in Romania?

Helpful Web-links

Website that includes a host of useful links about Romania:
www.mae.ro and www.insse.ro.

The General Directorate of Penitentiaries:
www.anp.ro.

The Ministry of Justice:
www.just.ro.

Unofficial translation of the Romanian Penal Code:
www.era.int/domains/ corpus-juris/public/texts/legal text.htm.

REFERENCES

Abraham, P. (2001). *Introducere în Probatiune.* Bucharest: Univers.

Balan, A., E. Stanisor and R. Elas (2002). *Administratiile Penitenciare Europene.* Bucharest: Oscar Print.

—— E. Stanisor and M. Minca (2002). *Penologie.* Bucharest: Oscar Print.

Clocotici, D. (1982). "Aspecte de Principiu Privitoare la Stiinta Penitenciara." *Buletinul Penitenciarelor no. 2.*

Dincu, A. (1993). *Bazele Criminologiei.* Bucharest: Proarcadia.

Florian, Gh. (1998). *Dinamica Penitenciara.* Bucharest: Oscar print.

—— (1996). *Psihologie Penitenciara.* Bucharest: Oscar Print.

"IHF Annual Report, 1998" (1998). (http://www.arts.uwaterloo.ca/MINELRES/count.romania/ihf98rom.htm.)

Oancea, I. (1996). *Drept Executional Penal.* Bucharest: ALL.

Pop, O. (1997). *Socializarea si Implicatiile ei în Aparitia si Formarea Comportamentului Predelicvent si Delicvent.* Timisoara: Andotours.

Pop., T. (1924). *Drept penal comparat. Penologie si Stiinta Penitenciara.* Cluj: Ardealul.

Smit, D. van Z. (2002). *Taking Life Imprisonment Seriously.* The Hague, NETH: Kluwer.

Vlasceau, A. and A. Dorobant (2002). *Romania: Criminal Justice Systems in Europe and North America.* Helsinki, FIN: European Institute for Crime Prevention and Control.

Walmsley, R. (1996). *Prison Systems in Central and Eastern Europe.* Helsinki, FIN: European Institute for Crime Prevention and Control. (Publication series No. 29.)

Zidaru, P. (1997). *Drept Executional Penal.* Bucharest: Mihaela s.r.l.

JOURNALS

Directia Generala a Penitenciarelor. *Anuar statistic.*

Revista administratiei penitenciare.

Revista de stiinta penitenciara.

Buletinul penitenciarelor.

NOTES

1. Among 274,979 Romanian citizens who emigrated between 1990 and 1997, 100,988 were German ethnics (www.mae.ro).

2. The first encounter of *Romania* as the official name for the two unified provinces occurred on the 24th of January 1862.

3. See M. Criste (2002), *Controlul Constitutionalitatii Legilor in Romania.* Bucharest: Lumina Lex, pp.19-26.

4. By the middle of 2002, the prisons held 40.55% more inmates than the legal maximum capacity.

5. The last time this penalty was used was on the 25th of December 1989, the convicted being the dictator Ceausescu and his wife.

6. Almost the whole staff of the penitentiary administration has been a military one, with some exceptions in the sections involving reeducating the inmates; even today, the civilian (non-military) staff account for only 8.34% of the total.

7. In some units there is only one staff member for 17 inmates. The same ratio throughout Europe lies between 1/1 to 1/3 (Croatia — 1/0.6, Slovakia — 1/1.5, Hungary — 1/1, Spain 1/2, Russia 1/4.6). (See Balan, Stanisor and Elas [2002], p.105.)

8. See Walmsley (1996) for a detailed account of this issue.

9. The detainees can work in the interior workshops of the penitentiary, at outside places of work of some private groups (under supervision) or in the factories of the prison industry "Multiproduct" (only a few compared with detainees' number).

10. The work is remunerated, 10% being in the prisoner's due. One-third of their wages is made available to the inmate, while the balance is put into trust until their release.

11. Concerning the regime of serving the disciplinary measures by isolation, there is under consideration a draft of an Order of the Minister of Justice that will establish how to organize the isolation area, the rights of the persons deprived of liberty during the application of the disciplinary measures, and the measures that are taken by the staff of the detention place during that period.

12. Juvenile offenders and pregnant women cannot be placed in isolation or under a restrictive regime. In 2002, juvenile offenders made-up 2.95% of the prison population and female offenders 4.5% of the inmate population.

13. The median wage in July 2003 was ROL 4,863,801.

14. For example, for theft a sentence of up to 15 years can be administered, and in cases of theft of certain goods (e.g., crude oil, computer-related offences) the sentence can be extended to 18 years.

15. The apparent difference in the total number of prisoners for 2002 listed in Table 9.3 (51,528) and in Table 9.4 (38,299) is attributable to two distinctions: first, Table 9.3 includes the total on the first of June, 2002, while Table 9.4 refers to the end of 2002; and second, Table 9.3 also counts 1,118 inmates who were imprisoned for contraventions.

16. For an interesting comparative examination of life imprisonment, see Smit (2002). Smit examines and compares life imprisonment in the United States, England and Wales, and Germany, as well as examines the concept within an international criminal justice context.

17. Closing remarks by V. Stoica (at that time Minister of Justice) at the Global Forum on Fighting Corruption, March 31, 2000 in Bucharest. (See http://usinfo.state.gov/topical/econ/integrity/buchar/ bc3.htm.)

CHAPTER 10.
ADULT CORRECTIONS IN THE
UNITED STATES OF AMERICA

by

Philip L. Reichel
Department of Criminal Justice
University of Northern Colorado

and

Harry R. Dammer
Department of Sociology/Criminal Justice
Scranton University

BASIC FACTS ON THE UNITED STATES

Area: Bordering the North Atlantic Ocean to the east; North Pacific Ocean to the west; Canada to the north, and Mexico to the south, the United States is the world's third largest country by size at 9,158,960 square kilometers.

Population: As of May 2003 there were an estimated 290 million persons living in the United States (U.S. Census Bureau, 2003). The birth rate in 2000 was 14.5/1,000 and the death rate was 8.7. Major cities include Los Angeles, CA (9.5 million), New York, NY (9.3 million), and Chicago, IL (9.2 million).

Demographics: The literacy rate is 97% fueled by a free and open public education system on the primary and secondary levels. According to the 2000 U.S. Census Bureau, 84.1% of all persons living in the country are high school graduates and 25.6% are college graduates. The population as a whole has 12.7 median years of schooling.

Climate: Mostly temperate, but tropical in Hawaii and Florida, arctic in Alaska, and semi-arid in the great plains west of the Mississippi river.

Economy: By most indicators the United States is the largest and most technologically powerful economy in the world with a per capita GNP of $36,000. The market-oriented economy is highly diversified and technologically advanced, with private industry and businesses serving the general population and the government. U.S. businesses are often forefront in the development of various technologies, including computers, medical instruments, aerospace, and military arms. After a period of economic growth in the years 1994-2000, the subsequent two years witnessed an economic downturn with rising unemployment, business failures, and bankruptcies.

Government: The United States was recognized as a new nation following the Treaty of Paris in 1783 after the American Revolution and the breaking with the mother country Britain in 1776. With 50 states and the District of Columbia as the nation's capital, the United States is characterized as a federal republic with a strong democratic tradition. The legal system is based on English common law, with judicial review of legislative acts that are posed by a bicameral Congress consisting of a Senate (100 seats) and the House of Representatives (435 seats) (U.S. Central Intelligence Agency, 2002).

★   ★   ★

'Man's capacity for justice makes democracy possible, but man's inclination to injustice makes democracy necessary.'

~ Reinhold Niebuhr, 1944

BRIEF HISTORY OF AMERICAN CORRECTIONS

Prior to the 1700s correctional practices in the American colonies mirrored those of the Middle Ages, when there was little need for jails or prisons to house offenders for the long term because  offenders were

typically subjected to corporal punishment, capital punishment, or exile. If offenders were incarcerated, they were put in secure buildings like dungeons, to prepare them for the torture that would soon extract a confession, to await their execution or banishment, or even to coerce their payment of debts. There was no consistent or structured correctional system during this time period, although in the period preceding the 1800s, a variety of philosophies and methods began to emerge.

Many facilities have laid claim to being the first prison in the American colonies (Powers, 1985). The **Boston Prison**, which opened in 1635, was probably the first and it served the entire Massachusetts Bay Colony for 18 years. Between 1652 and 1776, 11 other similar facilities opened in the Bay Colony, so that each of the 12 counties in Massachusetts was maintaining its own jail. Also around that time period, correctional institutions opened in the two other colonies. In 1773, an old copper mine with an underground dormitory for prisoners, called Newgate Prison (named after the famous Newgate Prison in London, England) was opened in Simsbury, Connecticut. Soon thereafter, in 1776 the **Walnut Street Jail** in Philadelphia began to house petty offenders and debtors as well as those awaiting trial or sentencing.

These early jails served various functions. Pretrial and presentence detention was the most common of these functions, but the jails also served to house a range of convicted criminals, prisoners of war (e.g., East-Indians, French and eventually British soldiers), political prisoners (e.g., Quakers, Jesuits, and Loyalists) and confined those who had not paid a debt, taxes, fines, or court costs. Because the facilities were run by the local jurisdictions and confined a population of both convicted and unconvicted persons, they were more like today's jails than prisons or penitentiaries.

America's first state prison was established in 1785, when Massachusetts converted an old fortress on **Castle Island** for use as a place of hard labor confinement for convicted criminals from around the state (Hirsch, 1992; Powers, 1985). From 1785 to 1798, Castle Island served as the Massachusetts State Prison. Institutions such as Castle Island, Newgate, and the Walnut Street Jail served as forerunners of the idea that long-term imprisonment and hard labor in a secure facility could be used as punishments for convicted offenders.

The new idea of imprisonment and hard labor as an alternative to corporal and capital punishment was especially evident in the activities of Pennsylvania Quakers. In 1787, the Quakers helped establish the Philadelphia Society for Alleviating the Miseries of Public Prisons. The society was essentially a response to the Pennsylvania penal code of 1786, which abolished capital punishment (except for treason and murder) and substituted punishment with hard labor. In addition to the hard labor and imprisonment, the society also believed in solitude for prisoners. As the 18th century came to a close, the dual themes of labor and solitude were firmly established as key ingredients of the Penitentiary era, which is the first of five eras that help describe the history of American corrections.

The **Penitentiary era**, beginning in the early 19th century, describes a penal regimen that relied on prisoner separation from fellow inmates in the belief that solitude would encourage penitence and prevent cross-contamination of evil ideas. A second theme of that era was that prisoners should be required to work. Such labor, it was supposed, would deter them from future crime and could provide a profit for the institution. The Penitentiary era can best be understood by contrasting two parallel views of operating a prison: the **Pennsylvania system** and the **Auburn system** (see Glossary) — the systems' names come from the first locations of their use.

The Pennsylvania system relied on principles of separation and silence that were first introduced at Philadelphia's Walnut Street Jail in the 1790s. This "separate and silent" system, as the Pennsylvania system is sometimes called, is most closely associated with the Eastern State Penitentiary, which opened in Philadelphia in 1829. Prisoners at Eastern State Penitentiary experienced severe mental strain and suicide attempts were not infrequent, but the limited knowledge about mental health in the early 19th century meant that officials did not attribute those problems to the isolation of the prisoners. Instead of expressing concern about such problems, proponents believed that separation provided a significant advantage by restricting prisoners from training each other in the ways of crime.

The **Auburn prison** opened in 1817 in Auburn, New York. In 1821, Auburn officials initially borrowed the separate and silent strategy from the Walnut Street jail for use at the new prison. But the officials soon found it too difficult to maintain complete separation of prisoners, and also realized that separated prisoners were unable to engage in labor that could offset imprisonment costs. In 1823, Auburn abandoned the separate and silent system and turned instead to a system wherein prisoners were locked in separate cells at night but allowed to work and eat together, in silence, during the day. This "congregate and silent" system came to be called the Auburn system.

Between the 1820s and 1860s policy makers, penologists, and politicians debated the merits of the Pennsylvania and Auburn systems. Each system had its supporters and detractors. Pennsylvania system advocates said that in addition to preventing cross-contamination of prisoners, it allowed easier control of prisoners, gave more consideration to inmates' individual needs, and provided more opportunities for meditation and repentance. Proponents of the Auburn system claimed it was superior because it was less expensive to construct and operate, provided better vocational training, and generated income to defray the cost of imprisonment. The economic arguments were very persuasive to other states, and eventually the Auburn system was adopted for prisons in most of the other American states.

With the advent of the penitentiary, and the Auburn and Pennsylvania systems, the United States was at the forefront in putting into operation the first penal philosophies for the long-term confinement of criminals. But after about 50 years of little more than debate about the merits of the Auburn or the Pennsylvania system, corrections was stagnating in America and some prison reformers began looking for new approaches. The result was the birth of the **Reformatory era** (beginning in the mid-19th century) in American corrections.

Those involved in the Reformatory era began to search for ways to soften the impact of confinement on the long-term prospects of convicts, almost all of whom would eventually be back on the streets. One of the most popular solutions of the era involved offering the offender an opportunity for early release through good behavior and goal achievement during incarceration. The opportunity for early release from confinement required legislation that allowed for indeterminate sentencing, wherein offenders received a minimum and maximum period of punishment. If the offender was released before serving the maximum sentence, the time between release and the maximum sentence could be served in the community — that is, could be served on **parole**.

With New York's adoption of an indeterminate sentence law in 1876, the Reformatory era was inaugurated at the Elmira Reformatory in

Elmira, New York. Zebulon Brockway, Elmira's superintendent, ran a facility that emphasized reforming the inmates, providing extensive vocational training, and offering opportunities for academic education. Since the inmates had indeterminate sentences, they could be paroled from Elmira upon showing good behavior and accomplishing goals established by Brockway. The Reformatory concept, with its necessary ingredients of indeterminate sentencing and parole, spread across the country and began impacting more general views about sentencing and alternatives to prison. The belief that some offenders could avoid incarceration also led to the development of **probation** — a sentence that allows an offender the chance to remain within the community and demonstrate a willingness to abide by its laws (see Box 10.1).

Box 10.1: Probation

Probation began in the United States with the innovative work of **John Augustus** (1784-1859). Believing that imprisonment was not appropriate for all offenders, Augustus began serving as surety for some of the people being brought before the Boston courts in the early 1840s. He, and eventually other volunteers, helped his charges find homes, secure employment or ensure school attendance, and soothe family problems. More often than not, the courts were pleased with the results and in 1878 the Massachusetts legislature provided for paid probation officers to supervise in the community those children and adults who were granted probation by the courts. The idea caught on, and by 1920 every state permitted probation for juveniles and by 1930 the federal government and 36 states had adult probation laws.

The reformatory era dominated community correctional thought from the mid-1800s until the 1930s, when it began to be replaced by a professional orientation adopting the language and techniques of the new "science of the psyche."

Drawing on the then-influential psychological work of Sigmund Freud, penologists began to attribute criminal behavior to defective mental and emotional functioning, and the **Rehabilitation era** (beginning in the early decades of the 20th century), also called the *medical model* of corrections, resulted. The emphasis in corrections shifted away from punishment toward programs designed to offer treatment for the offenders' problems that caused their criminality. The primary technique to be used was interpersonal counseling. The medical model, however, was problematic for two reasons: (1) Not all offenders were mentally ill and not all community corrections workers were skilled as counselors and/or psychotherapists. Many "treated" offenders continued to offend, even after treatment; and (2) Many correctional employees practiced a brand of "treatment" that bore little relationship to the grand ideas of Freud and his followers.

By the 1960s, sociologists began to discuss the way in which access to society gave one a stake in society's rules, and how alienation from social benefits meant one had no reason to obey the rules of the game. In place of simply trying to improve an offender's mental health, penologists advocated increasing the legitimate ties of the offender to mainstream society as a correctional philosophy. The impetus for this change came about when President Lyndon Johnson's 1967 Commission on Law Enforcement and the Administration of Justice considered the ideal corrections system. The commission reported that "crime and delinquency are symptoms of failures and disorganization of the community... The task of corrections, therefore, includes building or rebuilding social ties, obtaining employment and education, securing in the larger senses a place for the offender in the routine functioning of society" (President's Commission on Law Enforcement and Administration of Justice, 1967:7).

The stage was now set for the **Reintegration era** (the mid-20th century) in American corrections. This correctional version of the "Great Society" involved job-training programs for ex-offenders, creation of special employment opportunities, and an emphasis on community-based programs. A wide variety of programs existed, all seemingly based on a view that offenders commit crimes because noncriminal choices eluded them due to lives of poverty and social alienation. The point of these programs was to strengthen the offender's social skills, especially those related to employment, and thereby help offenders find legitimate roles in society. The most important change of the Reintegration era was the primacy of non-prison correctional alternatives for handling offenders. Hence, probation and parole became the chief weapons in the correctional arsenal, and a few correctional leaders began to think of the prison as a failed experiment, and therefore obsolete as a correctional technique.

One major event that aided the move toward reintegration and community corrections was the inmate riot and hostage taking at New York State's Attica Correctional Facility (see Box 10.2). Media coverage of the riot helped critics of imprisonment gain support for prison alternatives and for the idea of reintegrating offenders into the community. The reintegration idea was dominant in corrections for about a decade, until the late 1970s, when a series of scholars began to question the effectiveness of existing rehabilitative programs and there was a resulting movement toward a Retributive era, which continues today.

Box 10.2: The Attica Riot

On September 9, 1971, inmates at New York's Attica Correctional Facility took over cell blocks and killed four fellow prisoners. The inmates had already staged a number of peaceful protests at Attica to encourage an improvement of prison conditions, but peaceful protest had now turned to serious rioting. The state police moved in on September 13, and in the fifteen minutes it took to reclaim the prison, twenty-nine inmates and ten hostages were killed and more than eighty people were wounded. The Attica uprising, which received intensive media coverage and criticism, encouraged the American public and policy makers to consider sweeping changes in corrections policies. Prisoner rights were accorded more serious attention as were sentences that relied less on imprisonment and more on community reintegration (Paulson, 2002; Reichel, 2001).

Two related ideals have oriented American correctional policy during this **Retributive era**: the war on crime and the war on drugs. The **war on crime**, a slogan used by politicians since the late 1960s, employed "get tough" rhetoric and imagery that was far more popular with the general public than "treatment" programs. The war on crime has been the most important development in criminal justice over the last 30 years, and its approach towards crime and criminals proved a political gold mine. Electoral politics provided a platform for the candidates to show they took public fears and the rising crime rate seriously. Attacks upon the leniency of corrections had been heard sporadically for years, of course. But the "war" rhetoric and the public response galvanized a dramatic shift away from the preceding *reintegrative* ideal. The attacks on correctional programming were aided by rising crime rates and a growing sense that correctional programs had failed to rehabilitate offenders — a belief that was supported by Robert Martinson's landmark study in 1974: "What Works? — Questions and Answers about Prison Reform." Martinson reviewed the results of over 250 correctional program evaluations and found no evidence that any approach utilized at the time was "consistently effective" at reducing recidivism (Martinson, 1974).

Box 10.3: Drug Offenders behind Bars

In the early 1980s, American jurisdictions began implementing increasingly harsh sentencing policies for drug offenders. One impact of these policies was a dramatic increase in the number of drug offenders in state and local prisons — skyrocketing by more than 1,000% from 40,000 in 1980 to 453,000 by 1999 (King and Mauer, 2002). The harshness of federal mandatory sentencing laws has resulted in a federal prison population growing at an even more rapid rate than in state prisons. The majority (about 57%) of federal prisoners are incarcerated for drug offenses and the Department of Justice anticipates an increase of 50% in the total federal prison population by 2007 if current trends continue. Drug offenders do not represent as great a percentage in state prisons, where they compose about one-fifth of all prisoners (King and Mauer, 2002; Sentencing Project, 2003).

In addition to the war on crime, the **war on drugs** has surfaced as another policy with the intent of being "tough on crime." The drug war reached its peak in 1988 when then-president George H. Bush created the Office of National Drug Control Policy, and this approach has continued in each succeeding administration with each president urging congress to appropriate billions for an all-out enforcement campaign against drugs (see Box 10.3). The war on drugs has had the effect of packing the nation's prisons with drug law offenders.

AMERICAN CORRECTIONS TODAY

The only certain lesson learned by reviewing penal eras in the United States is that the current retributive era is also likely to pass. More difficult to predict is what type of penal philosophy will take its place. Corrections in contemporary America is influenced by lessons from all of the prior eras, and whatever era comes next — if it is not already here — will undoubtedly have components from each of its antecedents. In addition, if the recent rhetoric of the role of *penal populism* (see Glossary) bears true, then it will dominate the reform landscape (see Roberts et al., 2003).

Current penal sanctions reflect, from the preceding eras, a desire for prisoner labor, an interest in reforming and rehabilitating offenders, an increased desire to reintegrate offenders into the community, and a firm belief that offenders must be held accountable for their actions. To accomplish all these goals, contemporary American corrections relies on a wide variety of penal sanctions that range from fines and community service to the death penalty.[1] For example, on December 31, 2001 there were 6.6 million persons under correctional supervision in the United States.[2] This represented 3.1% of all American adult residents or 1 in every 32 adults — an incarceration rate of just under 500 per 100,000 of the nation's population. Of that total, 70% were being supervised in the community and 30% were confined in jails or prisons (Glaze, 2002). Of those offenders under community supervision, most (84%) were on probation and the remainder on parole.[3] Specifics on the administration of these sanctions and on the people to whom they are applied are presented in the next two sections.

Administrative Process

Local, state, and federal jurisdictions all have responsibility for at least some aspect of the American corrections system (see Box 10.4). When local (city or county) ordinances are violated, the offender will be sentenced by the local court and may be punished with sanctions ranging from fines to incarceration in the local jail. Jails, which are usually operated by city or county officials, hold persons sentenced to periods usually lasting no longer than one year. In addition, jails also hold pretrial detainees, those awaiting transfer to another institution (e.g., a state prison) or jurisdiction, and some of those who are appealing sentences.

Box 10.4: United States Criminal Justice System

> The criminal justice system in the United States is actually 51 separate systems. Each of the 50 states and the federal government determine the statutory and procedural laws upon which their justice system operates. This makes it difficult to present a single flowchart of the United States criminal justice system or even the corrections segment. Fortunately, there are more similarities than differences among the states and the federal system, so generalizations are possible as long as one remembers that the generalization will not hold for all parts of every system. The U.S. Department of Justice provides the most widely used flowchart (see www.usdoj.gov/bjs/ustsys.htm), and interested readers are encouraged to view and or download that chart for visualization of the common steps in the U.S. criminal justice system.

When offenders violate state laws, they are sentenced by state trial courts with general jurisdiction. Upon conviction in these courts, offenders may receive sentences — depending on the crime and the state — ranging from fines to the death penalty. Penalties to be served while at liberty in the community are typically under the supervision of the probation department and might include community service, paying restitution, participating in treatment programs, and meeting other conditions as determined by the court or the probation officer.

Sentences to deprivation of liberty (for a period greater than one year) will generally be served in a state prison or in a community residential facility (i.e., a halfway house) operated by the state or, increasingly often, by a private corporation (see Box 10.5).

States with numerous prisons for men and at least one for women are likely to designate the various institutions according to security levels. Generally, prisons for men are classified as being minimum-, medium- or maximum-security facilities. Because fewer women are in prison, most states have just one institution for women combining all three security levels, although the larger state systems like New York and California have women's institutions of different security levels.

Box 10.5: Private Corrections

In the late 1980s, state legislators began looking for alternatives to public correctional facilities. This was at the beginning of the Retributive era in American corrections, so those legislators were interested in alternative facilities rather than alternative programs. In the spirit of capitalism, private corporations indicated an interest in providing those facilities — in return for reimbursement by the government for the care and supervision of the offenders.

At the end of 2001, there were more than 90,000 state and federal prisoners held in private facilities (Harrison and Beck, 2002). That number represented about 6% of all state prisoners and about 12% of federal prisoners. The popularity of private corrections varies by state. Some states (Alaska, Montana, New Mexico, Oklahoma, and Wyoming) have at least 25% of their prison population housed in private facilities, but other states (as of March 2000 according to Thomas, 2002) have not specifically authorized private contracts (10 states) or have actually prohibited them by statute (Illinois and New York).

Proponents of private corrections argue that private operators can design and construct correctional facilities more quickly and can operate them more cost-effectively. In addition, they assert that contractors are more likely to be innovative, flexible, and able to deal with special-needs prisoners (e.g., protective custody, AIDS patients, etc.). Critics of privatization suggest that the cost benefits are not great, but even if they were that it is improper to delegate to private hands the coercive power and authority of the government. In addition, critics argue that private operators may have financial incentives to cut corners, may not have the ability to coordinate efforts with public agencies, and may jeopardize public and inmate safety through inadequate staff levels or training. Evidence to date does not provide a clear picture as to whether private prisons save money, provide better services, have fewer legal issues, or few inmate problems. However, the evidence also does not negate the value of private prisons. What has been shown is that correctional officers in private facilities earn less pay than their counterparts in public prisons, and according to the 2000 *Corrections Yearbook* (Camp and Camp, 2000), the turnover rate of staff is significantly higher among private institutions.

Persons convicted of violating a federal law are processed by federal courts and sentenced to the Federal Bureau of Prisons (BOP). The BOP was established in 1930 to provide more progressive and humane care for federal inmates, to professionalize the prison service, and to ensure consistent and centralized administration of the federal prison system (U.S. Bureau of Prisons, 2003).

Although it is under a single administration, the federal prison system has considerable diversity in both inmates (see the "Profile" section below) and facilities. Today, more than 140,000 prisoners are in the 102 facilities operated by the BOP (U.S. Bureau of Prisons, 2003). The facilities are spread throughout the country in a range of correctional institutions, detentions centers, medical centers, prison camps, metropolitan correctional centers, and penitentiaries. Each is organized according to five security levels: minimum, low, medium, high, and administrative maximum. Offenders are classified to a security level according to such factors as severity of the offense, length of incarceration, prior offenses, and history of violence.

As noted earlier, the majority of state, local and federal offenders (70%) are being supervised in the community rather than confined to jail or prison. The penal sanctions included in this category called **community corrections** (see Glossary) — also called "community-based corrections" — include as their primary types probation, parole, and intermediate sanctions programs (Clear and Dammer, 2002).

Probation is the most common of all correctional options used in the United States. According to the Bureau of Justice Statistics (BJS), nearly 4 million adult men and women were on probation at the end of 2001. Slightly more than half (53%) had been convicted of felony offences, 45% for misdemeanors, and 1% for other infractions. Twenty-five percent were on probation for a drug law violation and 18% for driving while intoxicated (Glaze, 2002). In the U.S., probation sentences may also require the offender to pay restitution to the victim or provide free services to the community (called community service — see Box 10.6) to compensate for the crime. It is also common for the probationer to be ordered to attend treatment programs to deal with the problems that led to criminal involvement.

As noted earlier, **parole** (a period of conditional supervision in the community following a prison term) is the original early release program, and it is now the form of release used for over a quarter of all offenders leaving prison. Parole release and supervision have always been controversial, but they are especially so today. At the end of 2001, more than 730,000 adults were under federal or state parole supervision (Glaze, 2002). Yet, as extensive as parole is in the United States, critics of parole argue that released offenders represent too great a risk to the community and that they should be kept in prison instead. Others question whether or not parole officers have the ability to effectively supervise the number of offenders to whom they are assigned. For example, 46% of persons discharged from parole supervision in 2001 had successfully met the conditions of their supervision (Glaze, 2002). The remainder being discharged from parole in that year (which was similar to prior years) were returned to prison (40%) because of a rule violation or new offense), because they had absconded (9%) or for some other reason (5%). Since the mid-1970s at least 13 states have abolished or severely limited the use of parole, although some have decided to reinstate it. However, all retain some form of post-release supervision of offenders.

Box 10.6: A Community Service/Restitution Program in New York City

The Center for Alternative Sentencing and Employment Services (CASES) in New York City was established in 1989. Today, with a staff of 180 and an annual budget of $12 million, CASES provides services and supervision for almost 4,500 offenders a year.

The mission of CASES is to increase the understanding and use of community sanctions that are fair, affordable, and consistent with public safety. Since its founding, CASES has worked with the justice system to find sentencing alternatives that respond to justice system needs. By addressing the factors that underlie criminal behavior — such as poor education, lack of community support, inability to get and keep a job, substance abuse and low self-esteem — CASES programs help young and adult offenders reintegrate into society. CASES offers structured alternatives that are more substantial than probation, but less costly and intrusive than jail or prison. CASES and its programs contribute to safer streets and save taxpayer dollars each year. Read more about CASES and community service at www.cases.org.

Intermediate sanctions are a variety of punishments that are more restrictive than traditional probation but less stringent and less costly than incarceration. Some of these sanctions are fairly common in the United States. Fines, restitution, and community service are sentences imposed upon the offender, but they cost far less than incarceration and offer the possibility of helping offenders live as better citizens in the future. Other fairly new sanctions — electronic monitoring, residential drug treatment centers, home confinement and day reporting — reflect the belief that offenders deserve to have restrictions on their freedoms, even if their offenses were not serious enough to merit a prison term. The growth of various intermediate sanctions has been considerable over the last 15 years, and the movement is likely to continue to be a major force in corrections in the years to come.

Profile of the Correctional Population

At the end of 2001, there were nearly 1.2 million prisoners held in state prisons throughout the United States (Harrison and Beck, 2002). That number represented a 0.4% change from 2000 and showed an average annual increase of 3% since 1995. Since 1995, the overall growth of the nation's prison population (both state and federal) has steadily slowed, but most experts agreed it is too early to determine if this indicates a trend that will continue.

Although the prison population growth rate is not as high as it was in the mid-1990s, the combined state prison population has increased more than 20% since then (Harrison and Beck, 2002): it remains among the highest rates and growth rates between 1988-1998 in the world (Walmsley, 2000). The increase in prison population was especially high in North Dakota (up 87%), Idaho (up 81%), and Oregon (up 75%), but seven other states also had increases of at least 50%. The total prison population was highest in Texas (162,070 inmates) and California (159,444), and lowest in North Dakota (1,111) and Wyoming (1,684).

Most of the growth in state inmates between 1990 and 2000 was among violent offenders (53% of the total growth) and drug offenders (20%). Public-order offenders (15%) and property offenders (12%) accounted for the remainder (Harrison and Beck, 2002).

The diversity of demographic characteristics found among the 50 states and the District of Columbia makes it unwise to characterize a typical state inmate. In addition, the Bureau of Justice Statistics (BJS) typically provides race and ethnicity data for the total of both state and federal prisoners, so it is not possible to identify the following as applying to state inmates only. But, with that caution in mind, BJS data (Harrison and Beck, 2002) suggest that most inmates are male (93%) and between 25 and 29 years old. Ethnically and racially, 46% of the inmates are non-Hispanic blacks, 36% are non-Hispanic whites, 16% are Hispanics, and 2% are from other groups.

Whereas the BJS includes both state and federal inmates in many of its reports, the Bureau of Prisons (BOP) provides information specific to the federal system. Therefore, it is possible to be more accurate regarding the characteristics of federal prisoners. As of May 2003 (Bureau of Prisons, 2003) the Federal Bureau of Prisons operated 102 facilities and was responsible for nearly 170,000 inmates. The majority (85%) of those inmates were in BOP facilities, and the remainder were held in privately managed secure facilities or other non-BOP facilities (e.g., home confinement or community corrections centers).

Most of the inmates in BOP facilities were categorized as minimum (20%) or low security (39%). Others were at medium (25%) or high (11%) security or had not yet been assigned. The majority of federal inmates were male (93%), white (56%), non-Hispanic (68%), and U.S. citizens (71%). Black Americans comprised the greatest proportion of nonwhite prisoners (41% of the total), and Asian (1.5%) or Native Americans (1.5%) made up the remainder. Citizens of Mexico accounted for 16% of the federal prison population, and they represented the largest group of non-U.S. citizens in the federal prison system. The greatest percentage of federal inmates were serving a 5 to 10 year sentence (29%), and 3% have a life sentence. As of May 2003, 24 federal inmates were under sentence of death.

ISSUES CONFRONTING AMERICAN CORRECTIONS TODAY

The decentralized system of government that characterizes the United States makes it difficult to identify problems or concerns that are common to 51 state and federal jurisdictions. Variation in politics, economics, and crime rates are simply a few factors that result in different issues depending on whether one is speaking of, for example, corrections in California and Rhode Island, Alaska and Texas, or Pennsylvania and Utah. Not everyone will agree that the four issues addressed here are of importance to their state or even to the federal government. But most would agree that they are issues confronting corrections in many American jurisdictions.

Gender Issues

There are over 800 state correctional institutions across the country. Of them, nearly 90% are designated for men, about 9% for women, and approximately 1% are coed (Reichel, 2001). Prisons for women received considerable attention in 1999 when the United Nations Commission on Human Rights (United Nations, 1999) reported that rape of female inmates by male staff was a fairly rare phenomenon in the prisons visited, but that consensual sex and sex in return for favors (e.g., work opportunities, telephone privileges, or even drugs) was a more frequent occurrence not only in the U.S. but also internationally. Much of the blame for a sexually abusive environment was attributed to having male officers supervise female inmates. The UN's *Standard Minimum Rules for the Treatment of Prisoners* require that only female custodial staff supervise female prisoners, but U.S. facilities routinely assign male correctional officers to women's prisons. The United States Supreme Court has ruled that doing otherwise would violate the Civil Rights Act of 1964, which prohibits gender-based employment discrimination.

Race/Ethnicity Issues

One of America's most significant problems today, both in the larger criminal justice system and in corrections more specifically, has to do with race and ethnicity. The criminal justice system has a significant overrepresentation of African Americans and Hispanics (or Latinos, as some prefer). For example, in 2001 there were 462 non-Hispanic white males imprisoned for every 100,000 non-Hispanic white males in the total population. Compare that with the rate of 3,535 non-Hispanic blacks per 100,000 residents of that group and 1,177 Hispanics per 100,000 Hispanic residents (Harrison and Beck, 2002). Similar disparity is found among women prisoners, where the rate per resident population for each group is 36 per 100,000 non-Hispanic white females compared with 199 per 100,000 non-Hispanic black females and 61 per 100,000 Hispanic females.

Some observers argue that these disparities are due to the fact that the system operates as a giant sieve to differentiate offenders, and more people of color end up under correctional authority because they commit more crimes or at least more serious crimes (Walker et al., 1996). Others claim that the sieve is racist and that people of color are treated more harshly by the system (Human Rights Watch, 1997). Still others argue that the criminal justice system operates within the broader context of our society's racism and merely represents one vehicle for its expression (Mann, 1995).

The "racist sieve" argument has received support from some human rights commentators, who suggest that the racial disproportionality in the American correctional system may be in violation of international agreements (Human Rights Watch, 2004). For example, the United Nations *International Convention on the Elimination of all Forms of Racial Discrimination*, directs signators (the United States being one) to:

> take effective measures to review governmental, national and local policies, and to amend, rescind or nullify any laws and regulations which have the effect of creating or perpetuating racial discrimination wherever it exists (Article 2-1-c).

However, it seems unlikely that the convention will influence congressional decisions regarding federal sentencing policy.

Prison Crowding

Over the past two decades the incarceration rate in the United States more than tripled, from 139 inmates per 100,000 in the overall population in the year 1980 to 476 per 100,000 in the year 2002 (see Web-link for U.S. Bureau of Justice Statistics, 2002). Some have referred to American corrections as *turnstile justice* because of the general perceived failure of correctional programs to prevent recidivism among offenders after release. And even though the growth rate has slowed from 6.7% in the year 1995 to about 2.5% per year since 1995 (Harrison and Beck, 2002), the United States still has the highest incarceration rate in the world of 702 (including jail and prison populations) per 100,000 in the year 2002 (Sentencing Project, 2003). Russia, the world's former incarceration leader, dropped from first place as the result of a prisoner amnesty program approved by the Russian Parliament in 2000. The skyrocketing U.S. prison population has created a correctional crisis of overcrowding. At year end 2001, 22 states and the federal prison system reportedly operated at 100% or more of their highest capacity (see Box 10.7). In many states new prisoners have been crowded into already bulging institutions, some making due in corridors and basements. In many states prisoners are held in county jails until prison space becomes available.

Box 10.7: Figuring Prison Capacity

Determining whether a prison is overcrowded is not as easily accomplished as one might suppose. The amount of space available per inmate would certainly be one way, as would be the type of living arrangement (e.g., single versus double bunks) or the type of housing (e.g. cells, dormitories, or even tents). Prison officials in the United States have identified and use three definitions of prison capacity (Harrison and Beck, 2002): *rated capacity* (the number of inmates a prison can handle according to an expert's judgment), *operational capacity* (the number of inmates effectively accommodated given the facility's staff, programs, and services), and *design capacity* (the number of inmates that planners or architects intended for the facility). Rated capacity usually results in the largest inmate capacity for a prison and design capacity the lowest.

Data compiled by the Bureau of Justice Statistics (Harrison and Beck, 2002) show populations according to as many capacity measures as a state provides (with some states providing only one or two capacity measures). For example, at the end of 2001 New Jersey's prisons were at 137% of design capacity compared with Rhode Island's at 86% of design capacity. Florida's prisons were at 89% of operational capacity but at 121% of design capacity.

Courts have chastised a number of states for maintaining prisons so crowded that they violate the Eighth Amendment's prohibition against cruel and unusual punishment. Courts have imposed population ceilings, specified the number of offenders per cell and the minimum floor space per person, and ordered the removal of prisoners from overcrowded prisons and jails.

Research (Gaes, 1985) indicates that inmates housed in large, open-bay dormitories are more likely to visit clinics due to physical injury, have high blood pressure, and to have higher assault rates than prisoners in other housing arrangements such as single-bunked cells, double-bunked cells, small dormitories, or large partitioned dormitories. In the recent past the solution to prison crowding was prison building. However, as government officials are now discovering, there is not an unlimited budget for corrections and difficult decisions must be made regarding how to spend precious resources.

Death Penalty

The death penalty remains a controversial correctional policy in the United States and internationally. Today, 38 states and the federal government have death penalty laws, with the primary method of execution (37 states and the federal government) being lethal injection (Nebraska requires electrocution). Nineteen states authorize other forms of execution (e.g., electrocution, gas chamber, hanging, firing squad) in addition to lethal injection (Death Penalty Information Center, n.d.). A method other than lethal injection (except in Nebraska) would be used — depending on the state — if lethal injection were to be found unconstitutional, if the prisoner chooses another method, or if the prisoner was sentenced prior to a particular date.

Many in the international community express disgust with the continued use of the death penalty in the United States. Critics note that since the U.S. is a signatory of the Universal Declaration of Human Rights (affirming the right of everyone to life), and has also ratified the International Covenant on Civil and Political Rights (affirming every human being's inherent right to life), its use of the death penalty appears to be in violation of these declarations and covenants. Neither document, however, bans the use of the death penalty. Article 6 of the covenant notes that in countries using capital punishment, the death sentence may only be imposed for the most serious crimes and only pursuant to a final judgment by a competent court. Death sentences in the

United States are imposed for the crimes of first-degree murder with aggravating circumstances and, in a few jurisdictions, for treason or kidnapping.

The United States has not signed the Second Optional Protocol to the International Covenant on Civil and Political Rights, aiming at the abolition of the death penalty (ICCPR-2OP). This agreement (with 49 country as signators in December of 2002) specifies that no party to the agreement will conduct an execution within its jurisdiction. Absent its signature on the agreement, the United States cannot be considered noncompliant. However, there is a section of the ICCPR that the United States would be violating were it not for a "reservation" filed when the United States ratified the agreement.

Article 6 of the ICCPR states that no person will be sentenced to death for a crime committed if the offender was younger than 18 years of age. Some states have executed persons who were under 18 when committing their crime. However, when ratifying the ICCPR, the United States provided the following reservation:

> (T)he United States reserves the right, subject to its Constitutional constraints, to impose capital punishment on any person (other than a pregnant woman) duly convicted under existing or future laws permitting the imposition of capital punishment, including such punishment for crimes committed by persons below eighteen years of age (Human Rights Library, n.d.).

Although there have been various initiatives to abolish capital punishment in various states because of issues relating to its fairness, the majority of states still have the option in place. Bills have been introduced in Congress and state legislatures for a national moratorium on executions, to provide for competent counsel for defendants, and to make it easier for inmates to have DNA evidence tested to challenge their convictions. However, in the face of continued public support, the United States Supreme Court has not found the death penalty to be unconstitutional nor does it seem likely that the United States will sign the ICCPR-2OP in the foreseeable future.

FUTURE DIRECTIONS

"I like the dreams of the future better than the history of the past."
~ Thomas Jefferson

There is much to dream about for American corrections — especially given the difficulties of the past and the present. Can state and federal jurisdictions find more alternatives to imprisonment, dispense justice more equitably, find programs that are more effective, or — better yet — significantly reduce the need for "correction" by reducing the occurrence of crime? Such questions will be answered in that elusive "future," but until then it is possible to identify a few areas where attention will undoubtedly be directed.

Drug Courts

There may be reason to believe the trend of imprisoning drug offenders is waning. Treatment options for drug offenders are being considered more often today than even a few years ago, and nearly 800 drug courts now operate across the country. These courts have more sentencing options available, and some state programs seem to be diverting drug offenders from incarceration. For example, the Arizona Supreme Court concluded in a 1999 study that the state's new diversion policy had resulted in 2,622 drug offenders being diverted from prison at an estimated cost savings of $2.5 million (Sentencing Project, 2003). The economic benefit alone, regardless of any treatment benefit that may eventually be identified, has attracted the attention of legislators in other states.

Human Rights and Terrorism

The war against terrorism declared by President Bush following the terrorist acts on September 11, 2001, may have included actions by United States officials that violate the Convention against Torture (CAT). Initial concerns about U.S. actions were raised in January 2002 when pictures appeared of blindfolded and shackled al-Qaeda suspects being "processed" at the American naval base in Guantanamo Bay, Cuba. More than one year later some 600 suspected Taliban and al-Qaeda fighters were still being held in what human rights groups described as a legal black hole. Because the U.S. classified the prisoners as unlawful combatants they were not provided access to courts, lawyers, or relatives. Visits by the International Committee of the Red Cross and by journalists supported U.S. claims that none of those being held were subjected to torture, but complaints continued regarding the apparent absence of due process procedures.

Additional concerns about U.S. actions were raised at the end of 2002 when media reports described how persons held in the CIA interrogation center at Bagram air base in Afghanistan were being subjected to practices very close to torture (*The Economist*, 2003; Priest and Gellman, 2002). U.S. officials were also believed to have handed over suspects to countries whose intelligence agencies have a reputation for brutality. The CAT specifically prohibits both types of behavior, but senior U.S. officials insisted that America was abiding by international agreements banning torture (Diamond et al., 2003). However, American officials directly involved in interrogating terrorist suspects told reports a different story. They described beatings and the withholding of medical treatment and other techniques such as sleep deprivation and forcing prisoners to hold awkward positions for hours as officials attempted to gain information that might lead to the capture of terrorists or to identify future terrorist plans (Priest and Gellman, 2002).

It is tempting to abandon civilized values and signed agreements in the face of terrorism, arguing, for example, that torture is justified in rare cases. For the foreseeable future it seems that American citizens in general — and corrections practitioners more specifically — must confront issues that many believed had been reconciled many years ago.

Abolishing the Death Penalty?

The number of people facing the death penalty has increased dramatically in the past two decades from just over 500 on death row in 1980 to nearly 3,500 on April 1, 2003 (Death Penalty Information Center, n.d.). Two-thirds of those on death row are in the South, with the greatest number in Texas, Georgia, Alabama, and Florida.

In 2000, Illinois Governor George Ryan declared a moratorium on executions in Illinois because of convincing evidence in cases where criminal procedural laws were abused and in others where DNA tests exonerated some death row inmates. He also appointed a bipartisan commission to examine the administration of the death penalty in Illinois and that commission released its report in April 2002, with 85 reforms recommended for the Illinois criminal justice system. The commission also concluded that there would still be no guarantee, even if all the reforms it recommended were implemented, that innocent people would not be executed. Very few other states (e.g., North Carolina in May 2003) have discussed a moratorium on their use of the death penalty, but there certainly has not been a groundswell of support for such action by legislators in states with the death penalty. In fact, in 1991 76% of the public supported the use of the death penalty. The percentage has since fluctuated from a low of 65% in 2001 back up to 72% in 2002 (*Prosecuting Attorney*, 2003). Again, penal populism may play a significant role in the outcome of how this matter is dealt with by officials.

CONCLUSION

Early correctional practices in the United States during colonial times reflected medieval-like corporal punishments and those borrowed from Britain. During this period there was no consistent nor structured correctional system. After the American Revolution, the *Penitentiary Era* spawned the Pennsylvania and New York (Auburn) models of incarceration. Each had a different view of how to best treat criminal offenders. The *Reform Era*, beginning in the mid-1800s, searched for ways to improve prison conditions and provided ways for offenders to change their ways. Among the most influential policies that developed during this time were probation and parole. The 20th century brought three different eras of offender punishment. Beginning in the 1930s with the birth of the modern psychology, the *Rehabilitation Era* aimed at addressing the problems that caused criminality. In the 1960s, the *Reintegration Era* hoped to enhance offenders' social skills, helping them find legitimate roles in society. During the 1970s, the *War on Crime* and subsequent *War on Drugs* shifted correctional policies towards a retributive philosophy that emphasized "get tough" deterrence-based punishments, fueled in-part, by penal populism. The results of the *Retributive Era* led to an astronomical increase in the number of offenders involved in the correctional system.

Local, state, and federal agencies all share in the administration of corrections in the United States. The correctional system currently includes 6.6 million offenders, the majority of whom are involved in community corrections programs. In the last five years there has been a slight decline in the growth rate of the prison population and an increased interest in the development and use of intermediate sanctions. Intermediate sanctions — a range of punishments more strict than probation but less severe than incarceration — are viewed as a possible solution to the major problems facing American corrections today, particularly prison crowding. Other current problems of significance are the growing number and disparities in treatment of female offenders, over-representation of racial and ethic minority offenders in the correctional system, and the fair and just use of the death penalty.

In addition to finding solutions to these problems, one can predict that the correctional system will soon have to find creative methods to deal with a growing number of offenders with "special problems," including drug offenders, mentally ill offenders, and the large number of older offenders who are serving long sentences in American correctional facilities. As the fight against terrorism wages on, issues related to human rights and the treatment of offenders are also sure to surface.

Beginning with the advent of the penitentiary, followed by developments in offender rehabilitation, community corrections, and prison management, the United States has often been widely innovative in developing correctional methodologies. Many of these methods have been adopted in other countries. Likewise, the United States has borrowed ideas from other countries to try and improve their correctional system. Two examples are the widespread use of day fines and the growth of sentencing practices linked to restorative justice (see Glossary). As we move through this new century we can be hopeful and confident that additional innovation is likely, while sharing with and learning from other countries will be the norm in correctional practice.

Key Terms and Concepts

Auburn system	Big House	Boston Prison
Castle Island	Irish system	John Augustus
Intermediate sanctions	Jails	Penitentiary era
Reformatory era	Walnut Street prison	War on Drugs
War on Crime	Federal Bureau of Prisons	Retribution era
Community Corrections	Pennsylvania System	Rehabilitation era
Reintegration era	Probation	Parole

Discussion/Study Questions

(1) How does the correctional system of the United States differ/compare with that of other countries presented in this anthology?

(2) What are the main reasons why the United States continues to have one of the highest incarceration rates in the world?

(3) How effectively has the United States used alternatives to incapacitation and punishment?

(4) What arguments would you present to support a case that the United States violates international agreements when it continues to authorize the use of the death penalty?

Helpful Web-links

American Correctional Association:
www.aca.org.

Corrections Connection:
www.corrections.com.

Death Penalty Information Center:
www.deathpenaltyinfo.org.

State departments of correction:
www.corrections.com.

Statistics about prisons and jails at:
www.ojp.usdoj.gov/bjs.

U.S. Bureau of Justice Statistics:
www.ojp.usdoj.gov.

U.S. Federal Bureau of Prisons:
www.bop.gov.

REFERENCES

Amnesty International (2004). "The Death Penalty." (Retrieved February 5, 2004 from: http://web.amnesty.org/pages/deathpenalty-index-eng.)

Camp, C.G. and G.M. Camp (eds.), (2000). *Corrections Yearbook*. Middletown, CT: Criminal Justice Institute.

Clear, T.R. and H.R. Dammer (2002). *The Offender in the Community* (2nd ed.). Belmont, CA: Thomson/Wadsworth.

Death Penalty Information Center (n.d.). (Retrieved June 1, 2003, from http://www.deathpenaltyinfo.org.)

Diamond, J., T. Locy and R. Willing (2003). "Interrogation is Tough but Not Torture." *USA Today*, March 6, p.4a.

The Economist (2003)."Ends, Means and Barbarity." January 11, pp.18-20.

Gaes, G.G. (1985). "The Effects of Overcrowding in Prison." In: M. Tonry and N. Morris (eds.), *Crime and Justice: A Review of Research* (vol. 6). Chicago, IL: University of Chicago Press.

Glaze, L.E. (2002). *Probation and Parole in the United States, 2001* (NCJ-195669). Washington, DC: U.S. Bureau of Justice Statistics.

Harrison, P.M. and A.J. Beck (2002). *Prisoners in 2001* (NCJ-195189). Washington, DC: Bureau of Justice Statistics.

Hirsch, A.J. (1992). *The Rise of the Penitentiary: Prisons and Punishments in Early America*. New Haven, CT: Yale University Press.

Human Rights Library (n.d.). *U.S. Reservations, Declarations, and Understandings, International Covenant on Civil and Political Rights, 138 Cong. Rec. S4781-01 (daily ed., April 2, 1992)* [electronic version]. (Retrieved March 1, 2003, from http://www1.umn.edu/humanrts/usdocs/civilres.html.)

Human Rights Watch (2004). "Racism, Racial Discrimination, Xenophobia and Related Intolerance." (Retrieved: February 3, 2004 from: www.hrw.org/campaigns/race/hrw-statement2.htm.)

Human Rights Watch (1997). *Cruel and Usual: Disproportionate Sentences for New York Drug Offenders.* (Vol. 9 No. 2[B].) New York.

King, R.S. and M. Mauer (2002). *Distorted Priorities: Drug Offenders in State Prisons* [electronic version]. (Retrieved May 31, 2003, from http://www.sentencingproject.org/news/distorted_priorities.pdf.)

Mann, C.R. (1995). "The Contributions of Institutionalized Racism to Minority Crime." In: D.F. Hawkins (ed.), *Ethnicity, Race and Crime Perspectives Across Time and Place.* Albany, NY: State University of New York Press.

Martin, J.S. (2002). "Jailed Fathers: Paternal Reactions to Separation from Children." In: R.L. Gido and T. Alleman (eds.), *Turnstile Justice: Issues in American Corrections.* Upper Saddle River, NJ: Prentice Hall.

Martinson, R. (1974). "What Works? — Questions and Answers about Prison Reform." *The Public Interest* 42:22-54.

Paulson, L.D. (2002). "Attica." In: D. Levinson (ed.), *Encyclopedia of Crime and Punishment* (vol. 1). Thousand Oaks, CA: Sage Publications.

Powers, E. (1985). *Supplement to The American Prison: From the Beginning... A Pictorial History.* College Park, MD: American Correctional Association.

President's Commission on Law Enforcement and Administration of Justice. (1967). *The Challenge of Crime in a Free Society.* Washington, DC: U.S. Government Printing Office.

Priest, D. and B. Gellman (2002). "U.S. Decries Abuse but Defends Interrogations." [Washington Post, Dec. 26, electronic version.] (Retrieved June 1, 2003, from: http://www.washingtonpost.com/ac2/wp-dyn/A37943-2002Dec25.)

Prosecuting Attorney (2003). "The Death Penalty." (Retrieved June 18, 2003, from www.clarkprosecutor.org/html/death/opinion.htm.)

Reichel, P.L. (2001). *Corrections: Philosophies, Practices, and Procedures* (2nd ed.). Boston, MA: Allyn and Bacon.

Roberts, J.V., L.J. Stalans, D. Indemaur and M. Hough (2003). *Penal Populism and Public Opinion.* NY: Oxford University Press.

Sentencing Project (2003). *U.S. Prison Population — Trends and Implications* [Electronic version]. (Retrieved May 31, 2003 from: http://www.sentencingproject.org/pdfs/1044.pdf.)

Thomas, C.W. (2002). *State and Federal Laws.* (Dated May 17; retrieved June 1, 2003, from http://web.crim.ufl.edu/pcp/.)

U.S. Bureau of Prisons (BJS, 2003). *Public Information*. (Retrieved June 1, 2003, from http://www.bop.gov/.)

U.S. Census Bureau (2003). *Population Clock*. (Retrieved May 30, 2003, from http://www.census.gov/main/www/cen2000.html.)

U.S. Central Intelligence Agency (2002). *The World Factbook 2002* [electronic version]. (Retrieved June 1, 2003, from http://www.cia.gov/cia/publications/factbook/.)

United Nations (1999). "Violence against Women." [E/CN.4/1999/NGO/71 and E/CN.4/1999/68/Add.2], *Integration of the Human Rights of Women and the Gender Perspective*. Geneva: Commission on Human Rights.

Walker, S., C. Spohn and M. DeLone (1996). *The Color of Justice: Race, Ethnicity and Crime in America* (2nd ed.). Belmont, CA: Wadsworth.

Walmsley, R. (2000). *World Prison Population List*. Research Findings Number 116. London, UK: Home Office.

NOTES

1. The United States is one of 83 countries that retain the death penalty, and one of eight countries since 1990 that have executed an offender for a crime committed when they were under age 18 (Amnesty International, 2004). Other countries executing offenders who were minors at the time of their crime are China, Democratic Republic of Congo, Iran, Nigeria, Pakistan, Saudi Arabia, and Yemen. Of the 38 states that employ the death penalty within the United States, 22 allow execution for crimes by juveniles. However, in January 2004 the U.S. Supreme Court stated it will soon decide whether the Constitution allows for the execution of juvenile offenders, a practice the court allowed more than 15 years ago in the case Sanford v. Kentucky, 492 U.S. 361 (1989). For more information on the use of the death penalty for juveniles, see www.deathpenaltyinfo.org.

2. According to the Bureau of Justice Statistics, this is up from around 5.5 million American adults in 1996. Seven of every ten of these people were on either probation or parole.

3. In 2001 there were nearly 4.7 adult men and women on probation or parole, an increase of approximately 2.5% over 2000.